THE MYTH OF RESCUE

THE MYTH OF RESCUE

Why the democracies could not have saved more Jews
from the Nazis

William D. Rubinstein

London and New York

First published 1997
by Routledge
11 New Fetter Lane, London EC4P 4EE

Simultaneously published in the USA and Canada
by Routledge
29 West 35th Street, New York, NY 10001

Typeset in Perpetua by Keystroke, Jacaranda Lodge, Wolverhampton
Printed and bound in Great Britain by TJ International Ltd

British Library Cataloguing in Publication Data
A catalogue record for this book is available from the British Library

Library of Congress Cataloguing in Publication Data
A catalogue record for this book has been requested

ISBN 0–415–12455–7

In memory of Lucy S. Dawidowicz
(1915–1990)

CONTENTS

MAPS

TABLES

INTRODUCTION

The argument of *The Myth of Rescue* is that no Jew who perished during the Nazi Holocaust could have been saved by any action which the Allies could have taken at the time, given what was actually known about the Holocaust, what was *actually proposed* at the time and what was realistically possible. If there are any exceptions at all to this statement, their numbers may be measured in the dozens or hundreds rather than in some higher figure. *All* of the many studies which criticise the Allies (and the Jewish communities of the democracies) for having failed to rescue Jews during the Holocaust are inaccurate and misleading, their arguments illogical and ahistorical. These are indeed sweeping claims, but I would be genuinely surprised if any reasonable person will not be persuaded by the arguments made in this book, most of which have not been made before. A corollary of the arguments made here, which can never be emphasised too strongly, is that Hitler, the Nazis and their accomplices – and only they – bear full and total responsibility for the Holocaust.

This book argues that the subject of the rescue of Jews by the democracies has been consistently misinterpreted. For that reason, after a discussion of the evolution of the historiography of this subject, Chapter 2 focuses upon the remarkably generous refugee policies of the Western world in the years 1933–40, a subject almost invariably misconstrued and on which virtually no new, general interpretation has been offered. The longest chapter of this work, Chapter 3, looks in some detail at the plans for rescue which were actually offered in the democracies during the war, based upon an examination of what as far as I am aware are *all* of the plans for the rescue of Jews proposed by any person or group in America or Britain. The latter chapters of this book deal with a number of other widely held myths of rescue: the myth that it was possible to bomb Auschwitz, the myth that the American War Refugee Board saved the lives of perhaps 200,000 Jews and the myth that it was possible to negotiate with the Nazis to save Jewish lives. Finally, a number of specific proposals of 'what might have been done' made by historians are noted and critically examined.

It might be worth taking a moment to say something of the evolution of my own views on this subject. Anyone who makes the effort to unearth a book I wrote in 1982 on changes in post-war anti-semitism, *The Left, the Right, and the Jews* (London, 1982), or the introduction to a collection of essays by various historians of Australian Jewish history which I edited in 1986, *Jews in the Sixth Continent* (Sydney, 1986), will find that at that time I fully accepted the view that both the democracies, and the Jewish communities of the democracies, 'did nothing' during the Holocaust, and were highly culpable for this failure. Even at that date, however, the illogicality of blaming historical actors of the 1930s and 1940s for what is well known to us, but was unknown to them, and which they were largely powerless to alter, struck me strongly, and I was quite prepared to change my views.

If I had to denote a crucial turning-point in my thinking, it would be a conversation I had with Walter Jona around 1988. Walter Jona is a prominent member of the Melbourne Jewish community and served in the Victorian State Parliament for many years, rising to become a long-serving Cabinet Minister in the Victorian government. Jona's father and uncle were leading members of the local Jewish community (and prominent Zionists) during the 1930s, his father serving as the first president of the earliest representative body of the Jewish community in Melbourne, the Victorian Jewish Advisory Board. I explained to Jona the views of Australian Jewish historians which had emerged during the recent past concerning Australia and the Holocaust, and especially the notions that the highly assimilated Australian Jewish community of the day turned its back on the refugees, and that Australia's record in admitting Jewish refugees was terrible. Jona had evidently not heard these theories before; he looked extremely bewildered and puzzled, and after a few moments' silence said to me, 'No, that's completely wrong. I remember that when I was a teenager my father and I worked night and day on behalf of the refugees.' This chance conversation led, perhaps curiously, to my examining my own views on rescue during the Holocaust; eventually, I reached the conclusion that my own previous views were also completely wrong, and in a sense this book grew out of that conversation with a veteran of the refugee period.

For the most part this book was researched from Deakin University in Geelong, Australia, where I was Professor of Social and Economic History. Several of the chapters were written there as well, the rest shortly after I took up my present post at the University of Wales–Aberystwyth. It is self-evident that no book can be written and researched on America and Britain during the war from Australia without special assistance, and I must record my deep gratitude to three sources in particular. The inter-library loan service at Deakin University is outstanding, and I had no difficulty in obtaining hundreds of pages of articles in the most obscure contemporary sources. The three-volume *Bibliography on*

Holocaust Literature compiled by the late Herschel Edelheit and his son Dr Abraham J. Edelheit (Boulder, Col., 1986–92) proved utterly invaluable. My book could not have been written without it. The same must be said of the thirteen-volume collection of original documents, *America and the Holocaust*, (New York, 1990), edited by Professor David S. Wyman. Although I profoundly disagree with Professor Wyman's interpretation of these events, every scholar is in debt to him for making so much original source material readily available. Of the many correspondents and others who have assisted my research, four should be thanked in particular: Dr Gerald Fleming for his learned and perceptive evaluation of Hitler and the Holocaust; Dr James H. Kitchens III for his extraordinarily deep knowledge of the technical military aspects of bombing Auschwitz; Sir Martin Gilbert for our discussions of this question; and Dr Richard H. Levy of Seattle, who read and commented perceptively on Chapters 4 and 5. I must also (needless to say) thank my wife, Dr Hilary L. Rubinstein, and my typist, Margaret Moulton of Deakin University, who continued her highly professional services long after I emigrated to Wales.

I am also most grateful to the following persons who either supplied me with information, or commented, often at length, on my interpretation: Dr Jacques Adler, Professor Geoffrey Alderman, Dr Mark Baker, Dr Paul R. Bartrop, Professor Yehuda Bauer, Professor Randolph L. Braham, Dr Paul Brown, Professor Richard Breitman, Dr Abraham Edelheit, Professor Henry L. Feingold, Raymond Kalman, Dr Rachael Kohn, Dr Tony Kushner, Isi Leibler, Professor Deborah E. Lipstadt, Pam Maclean, Barbara Rogers, Dr Frank Vadja, William vanden Heuvel (Roosevelt Institute), Professor David S. Wyman and Dr Efraim Zuroff. It will be obvious from this list that many (but by no means all) will disagree with my book; nevertheless, I am most grateful to each of them. I must also thank a number of institutions and libraries for their help, especially the School of Australian and International Studies at Deakin University and the Deakin University Library, the Parkes Collection at Southampton University, the University of Liverpool Library, the Archives of the United States Department of Immigration, the YIVO Library in New York, the Cleveland (Ohio) Jewish Community Center and the F.D. Roosevelt Library in Hyde Park, New York. I presented seminar papers on 'the myth of rescue' to sessions of the conferences of the Australian Association for Jewish Studies and the Australasian Modern British History Association, to the School of Australian and International Studies seminar at Deakin University, to the Oxford Centre for Jewish and Hebrew Studies and to several Jewish groups in Melbourne. I am genuinely grateful, too, for the comments and suggestions I received at the time.

I am not sure whether the late Lucy S. Dawidowicz would have liked my book or not; clearly, however, she would have agreed with much of it. I met Lucy Dawidowicz only once, on a memorable occasion in New York in 1980. But even on so short an acquaintance, her intelligence, clarity, forthrightness and, most of all, common sense have been a continuing inspiration to me, and I believe it appropriate to dedicate this book to a scholar who combined that common sense with deep learning and perceptive historical judgement, a rare combination indeed.

William D. Rubinstein
University of Wales–Aberystwyth

1

THE HISTORIOGRAPHY
OF RESCUE

There can be few subjects in the whole range of modern history on which contemporary opinion differed so sharply from the views of later historians and authors than the topic of the rescue of Jews by the democracies during the Nazi Holocaust. During the Second World War, Jews (and non-Jewish anti-Nazis) looked upon the celebrated leaders of the great democracies at war with Nazi Germany – Winston Churchill and Franklin D. Roosevelt – as the heads of the armies of liberation which would free the whole world, and the Jewish people in particular, from the Nazi scourge. In December 1944, Joseph Hertz, the British Chief Rabbi, issued a birthday message to Winston Churchill which read:

> But for your wisdom and courage there would have been a Vichy England lying prostrate before an all-powerful Satanism that spelled slavery to the western peoples, death to Israel, and night to the sacred heritage of man. May Heaven grant you many more years of brilliant leadership in the rebuilding of a ruined world.[1]

American Jews constituted 'the most loyal and loving' of Franklin D. Roosevelt's constituencies;[2] to American anti-semites, Roosevelt's policies were so philo-semitic and influenced by 'Jewish power' as to constitute the 'Jew Deal'. A Jewish Republican Congressman of the 1930s, Jonah J. Goldstein, concluded that 'the Jews have three *velten* [worlds]: *die velt* [this world], *yene velt* [the next world], and Roosevelt'.[3] Yet recently much has changed. Commenting upon 'the strange turn in the attitude of American Jews towards Franklin D. Roosevelt in the recent past', the famous historian Arthur M. Schlesinger Jr noted that:

> For a long time [Roosevelt] was a hero. No president had appointed so many Jews to public office. No president had surrounded himself with so many Jewish advisers. No president had condemned anti-Semitism with such eloquence and persistence. Jews were mostly liberals in those faraway days, and a vast majority voted four times for FDR.[4]

This great and profound change in the perception of the Allies and their leaders arose fairly abruptly between the late 1960s and the mid-1980s, wholly as a result of a near-universal perception that the Allies did virtually nothing to rescue Europe's Jews during the Holocaust. By the late 1980s, every examination of the Allied response to the Holocaust was compelled to take into account the belief, by then virtually universal, that the democracies 'did nothing' during Hitler's 'Final Solution', and were – to many – guilty of being virtual accomplices in the Holocaust. The list of alleged Allied failures is long, ranging from closing their doors to Jewish refugee emigration prior to and during the Holocaust, forestalling the creation of a Jewish state in Palestine when this was most necessary as a place of refuge, failing to bomb Auschwitz or any other death camp, failing to engage in negotiations with the Nazis with the aim of bartering for Jewish life and failing, until early 1944, to create any specialised government agency to save Jewish lives, oblivious to the fact that Hitler was engaged in a 'war against the Jews'. The alleged reasons for these failings were also manifold, including strong and pervasive anti-semitism and anti-Zionism among both the American and British opinion-makers and masses, ignorance of Nazi intentions, bureaucratic inertia and an inability to internalise the unbelievable horrors of the Holocaust during the war itself. As well, it is widely suggested that the Jewish communities of the democracies were, by later standards, extraordinarily supine during Jewry's hour of greatest need, deeply divided and afraid to become overly visible or demonstrative during a world war.

These are seemingly powerful arguments, repeatedly reiterated by expert historians and by now entrenched in the popular imagination. Yet all of these arguments in my opinion are wrong and lacking in merit; the rest of this work will show why they are grossly misleading and inaccurate. It is first worth examining how the historiography of rescue emerged, in its contemporary form, and how the Jewish and anti-Nazi view of Churchill and Roosevelt as supreme heroes and liberators changed so radically.

For the first twenty years or so after the end of the Second World War, probably no historical work on the Holocaust criticised the actions of the Allies or suggested that much more could have been done which was not done.[5] All of these early works on the Holocaust, not surprisingly, focused upon the guilt of the Nazis and their allies. Perhaps the first considered work to attack the Allies for their failures in rescuing Jews was a little-noted article by Reuben Ainsztein, a Holocaust survivor who was well known as a historian of Jewish revolt in the ghettos and concentration camps, entitled 'How Many More Could Have Been Saved?' Ainsztein's article, which appeared in the British periodical *Jewish Quarterly* in 1967, contained a surprisingly large component of the critique of Allied policy which has since become standard, years before other historians made the same point. For instance, it offered an accurate examination of when news of the 'Final

Solution' first became known in the West, more than a decade before this question was examined in detail by other historians. Ainsztein's claim (p. 17) that

> the racist and antisemitic elements in the United States, allied with the still powerful isolationist forces, were strong enough even in 1943 to provide President Roosevelt and his State Department with excuses for not doing anything that might be interpreted as making the rescue of Jews one of America's war aims

has been echoed in dozens of subsequent examinations of this question. Yet it must also be said that, remarkably early, Ainsztein managed to make virtually every historical and logical error one could possibly make in examining this question, including the *fons et origio mali*, the conviction that the limited number of refugees accepted by the United States after the war began was due to its restrictive immigration laws, rather than to the fact that Hitler prevented these Jews from emigrating, prior to genocide. Perhaps only the alleged failure to bomb Auschwitz – not mentioned by Ainsztein – is absent from the now-standard bill of indictment.

Ainsztein's unnoticed article appeared shortly before the first books to take the failure of the Allies as their themes: Arthur Morse's *While Six Million Died: A Chronicle of American Apathy* (New York, 1968) and David S. Wyman's *Paper Walls: America and the Refugee Crisis, 1938–1941* (Boston, 1968). The 1970s saw yet more books on this theme, among them the balanced and scholarly monograph by Henry L. Feingold, *The Politics of Rescue: The Roosevelt Administration and the Holocaust, 1938–1945* (New Brunswick, NJ, 1970), a work which is, nonetheless, critical of American policy and already aware of the new, negative interpretation of this topic, and also such works as Saul Friedman's *No Haven For the Oppressed: United States Policy Toward Jewish Refugees, 1938–1945* (Detroit, 1973) and Herbert Druks' *The Failure to Rescue* (New York, 1977), whose titles accurately indicate their perspective.

In the late 1970s and early 1980s there appeared the writings which probably had the most significant impact upon the notion that the Allies failed to rescue Jews during the Holocaust. They were by David S. Wyman, a non-Jewish historian at the University of Massachusetts–Amherst.[6] In 'Why Auschwitz Was Never Bombed', published in the influential and widely read American Jewish monthly *Commentary* in May 1978, Wyman did two significant things: he almost single-handedly originated the notion that the Allies could have easily bombed and destroyed the Auschwitz extermination camp in 1944 but, for a variety of thoroughly inadequate reasons, chose not to do so; and he made the alleged Allied failure to bomb Auschwitz into Indictment Number One in the list of American and British failures during the Holocaust. Dramatic and easy for non-historians to comprehend, the bombing of Auschwitz quickly seized the imagination of Jews and non-Jews alike, just at the time when the Holocaust was becoming accepted by almost everyone of good will as perhaps the lowest point ever touched by the human race, as incomprehensible as it was evil, and at a time when the Holocaust came virtually to dominate contemporary Jewish thought.

Six years later, in 1984, Wyman published his considered work on alleged American failure during the Holocaust, *The Abandonment of the Jews: America and the Holocaust, 1941–1945* (New York, 1984), offering a detailed account of America's manifold failings during the 'Final Solution', superficially as disturbing as it was convincing. The villain of the book was clearly President Franklin D. Roosevelt, and some of its popularity was obviously due to its seemingly persuasive evidence that the former god of American liberalism and of the American Jewish community had – to say the least – feet of clay. Wyman also accepted the notion that Revisionist Zionists, Strictly Orthodox Jews and other 'outsiders' within the American Jewish community offered realistic and radical plans for the rescue of Europe's Jews which were rejected by the conservative and unctuous American Jewish 'Establishment'. He repeated, with more details, his suggestion that Auschwitz could successfully have been bombed by the American military in 1944, and offered a seemingly considered and detailed list of points of 'what might have been done'. His book – taken in conjunction with the others which appeared at around the same time – has been tremendously influential, greatly shaping our interpretation of Allied action and inaction during the Holocaust.

On every significant point he makes, it is my considered opinion that Wyman is not merely wrong, but egregiously and ahistorically inaccurate: in a sense, this book is a response to Wyman's work, although it also covers areas such as Britain's role in rescue, not discussed in *The Abandonment of the Jews*. Wyman's book strikes me as wrong-headed in three separate ways, apart from any matter of specific detail. First, the evidence Wyman amasses, when interpreted correctly, in virtually every case goes to show the precise opposite of the interpretation he places upon it. The reason for this consistent inaccuracy is that the situation facing European Jewry after the war began is virtually the opposite of that which underlies his interpretation: the Jews of Nazi-occupied Europe were prisoners, not refugees – the prisoners of a psychopath who was going to kill all of them if he could. Second, many of Wyman's suggestions as to what might have been done to rescue Jews were simply not proposed by anyone at the time. In this work, we will consider in detail the ways to rescue Jews that were actually proposed in the democracies, and it will become consistently plain that these proposals were futile and useless. Third, Wyman seems in the final analysis to understand this perfectly well. He therefore argues that even schemes whose success was unlikely 'should have been tried . . . If that had been done, even if few or no lives had been saved, the moral obligation would have been fulfilled', mindless of the fact that no government, in wartime, will direct scarce and valuable resources from successfully pursuing a war of liberation into projects whose success was dubious. He is also heedless of the fact that most of his proposals which 'should have been tried' were not proposed at the time.[7]

Wyman's work, together with the previous body of scholarship in this field and the increasing visibility of this question, themselves generated further books and articles with remarkably similar themes and premises: Monty N. Penkower's *The Jews Were Expendable: Free World Diplomacy and the Holocaust* (Chicago, 1983), and his 'In Dramatic Dissent: The Bergson Boys' (*American Jewish History*, 69, 1981); Haskel Lookstein's, *Were We Our Brothers' Keepers? The Public Response of American Jews to the Holocaust, 1938–1944* (New York, 1985); and Aaron Berman's *Nazism, the Jews and American Zionism, 1933–1948* (Detroit, 1990), as well as a spate of similar works on Britain and the Commonwealth.

The notion that American Jewry 'did nothing' during the Holocaust, acquiescing in the mass murder of their kinsmen in Europe, became something of an obsession among many American Jews at this time. American Jews contrasted the ever-vigorous, ever-vigilant and often highly successful activities in Washington, DC of the legendary post-war 'Jewish lobby' over such issues as American support for the State of Israel, with the complete lack of success of American Jewry in deterring the Nazi Holocaust, and – with the evidence apparently provided by such works as those by Wyman – drew the understandable but completely erroneous conclusion that it was the American Jewish community and the Roosevelt administration which had failed European Jewry in their hour of greatest need, rather than the more accurate inference that stopping Hitler's genocide was impossible without destroying Nazi Germany. There were curious manifestations of this conviction, such as the so-called 'Goldberg Report' of 1984, an attempt by a commission of American Jewish politicians and academics, headed by former Supreme Court Justice Arthur Goldberg, to address the question of 'why were so many American Jews passive or relatively unconcerned about the plight of European Jews?' (thus prejudging the very question the commission was presumably supposed to examine), which arrived at the conclusion that, in effect, if American Jewry had acted in the 1940s as its progeny acted in the 1980s, more Jews could have been saved – a dubious finding on several grounds.[8] The 'Goldberg Report' includes statements endorsing its findings by several Jewish politicians of the day, including New York City Comptroller Harrison J. Goldin and Brooklyn District Attorney Elizabeth Holtzman, surely the first occasion since the death of Stalin when a controversial historical interpretation was deemed to be true because some political office-holders said it was true.[9] A number of renowned historians of the Holocaust such as Yehuda Bauer and Lucy S. Dawidowicz pointedly declined to join the 'Goldberg Commission'; both Bauer and Dawidowicz wrote scathingly of this commission and its findings.[10]

The thesis that America and American Jewry 'did nothing' during the Holocaust has since been further expounded in a variety of other media forums, including a 1994 American Public Broadcasting System documentary, *America and the Holocaust: Deceit and Deception*, and a 'public trial' held in Jerusalem in 1990: 'Why Auschwitz Was Not Bombed.' Many Holocaust museums, including the US Holocaust Memorial Museum in Washington, DC, contain exhibits or publications on this subject. Most recent histories and general accounts of the Holocaust now contain a chapter on the passivity and indifference (if not far worse) of the 'bystanders' who knew what was going on but chose to 'do nothing'. To cite one very typical example, the excellent work by Michael R. Marrus on the historical questions raised by the Holocaust and discussed by historians, *The Holocaust in History*, contains a section on the 'Bystanders' (pp. 157–83) which, while clearly noting that 'to many it will . . . seem that these exercises are profoundly unhistorical', nevertheless concludes that 'clearly more could have been done – by Jews as well as by non-Jews'.[11]

As well, beyond Wyman and his school there has emerged since the 1980s a semi-scholarly, semi-popular group of writings which accuse America and the Western Allies of complicity in carrying out the Holocaust, assigning them a share in the guilt which seems to exceed that of the Nazis themselves. It often seems that some of these authors would frankly have been happier if the bullet-proof glass cage in Jerusalem in 1961 had not held Adolf Eichmann, but Winston Churchill or (if he were still alive) Franklin D. Roosevelt. In 1989 William Perl, an Austrian refugee who holds a doctorate in law from the University of Vienna, published *The Holocaust Conspiracy: An International Policy of Genocide* (Shapolsky Publishers, New York, 1989), whose aim, according to the book's dust-jacket, is to show

> that it was *not* apathetic inaction of the world's powers which made the Holocaust . . . so tragically effective . . . [but] *deliberate action* on the part of many nations [i.e., the Western Allies] that kept millions of those destined for murder, prisoners in a hostile Europe. Those deliberate actions are conclusively shown to result from conspiracies within individual governments as well as between governments.

The tenor of this work may be gauged by the author's reference (p. 80) to Anthony Eden as 'a Jew-hater' – this of a man who, next to Churchill, was the foremost opponent of Appeasement during the 1930s; the man who officially announced on behalf of the British Government in the House of Commons that the Holocaust was taking place; in 1956 a military ally of Israel.

Two years before, in 1987, Shapolsky Publishers had also produced Rafael Medoff's *The Deafening Silence: American Jewish Leaders and the Holocaust*. This is, in some respects, a valuable and well-researched work, but one whose basic thesis is quite untenable: that American Jewry's mainstream leaders deliberately failed to assist European Jewry during the Holocaust (often, according to Medoff, lobbying *against* changes which might have aided Europe's Jews), because of their 'immigrant psychology' and their fear of 'lifting the lid off a simmering American anti-Jewish backlash'.[12] Not surprisingly, Medoff's heroes are Peter Bergson and his Zionist Revisionist group. (Bergson and his group had no practical plans of any kind to rescue Europe's Jews, as will become clear in Chapter 3 of this work.) What is the bottom line of Medoff's work? What should American Jewry have done? Needless to say, Medoff is here at his absolute weakest, and his answer to this most fundamental of questions is ludicrously inadequate. Medoff compares American Jewry's allegedly inadequate political response with that of American blacks during the war in 1943–4, whose pressures on Roosevelt led to an Executive Order banning discrimination in government defence industries, and with Polish-American lobbying groups which 'skilfully' influenced Roosevelt's 'policy toward Poland at the same time'.[13] Ignoring the fact that Jim Crow continued in America for another twenty years, and that Poland fell into the hands of the Communists (because, it is often suggested, of Roosevelt's inept performance at Yalta), Medoff never addresses the question of what American Jewry should have lobbied Roosevelt to do, or how anything Roosevelt could realistically have done in 1943–4 – apart from win the war more quickly – could have saved Europe's Jews.[14]

Another source of extremist claims about the guilt of the Allies and of the Jewish communities of the democracies is the Strictly Orthodox world in the United States. David Kranzler's *Thy Brother's Blood: The Orthodox Jewish Response During the Holocaust* (published by Mesorah Publications in Brooklyn, New York, in 1987), has as its theme the claim that Orthodox Jews 'demanded action *now*, to correspond virtually minute-by-minute with the deepening mire in Europe'.[15] *Thy Brother's Blood* opens with a lengthy denunciation of Jewish 'secularists', secular Zionists and 'assimilationists', and continues with a long account of the role of Strictly Orthodox leaders (according to the author) in effecting rescue. There is, superficially, a case to be made: Rabbi Michael Dov Ber Weissmandel of Slovakia, praised throughout the book, was probably the first person to call for Allied bombing of the Kosice–Preskov railway line leading to Auschwitz in order to prevent the deportation of Hungarian Jewry, and Strictly Orthodox Jews used mainly unofficial means, especially bribery, to save lives where they could. Their story should, certainly, be told. Still more, however, it should be told accurately, and it was regrettably the case that Strictly Orthodox Jews probably perished in greater numbers during the Holocaust than adherents of any other Jewish ideology. Their leaders could no more protect them from Hitler's genocide than could the Zionists, assimilationists and secularists whom Kranzler denounces. The Strictly Orthodox specialist presses in the United States have produced a steady stream of similar works, whose aim is to show that the Strictly Orthodox effected rescue more vigorously than other Jews, and more successfully.[16] Both claims – alas – are simply untrue.

Many historians have been deeply disturbed by these extreme tendencies, even historians who accept that in some respects the Allied governments did little or nothing. Yehuda Bauer has made the point that:

The wrath and frustration of the Jewish people finally turned against itself. Ever since the Holocaust, an increasing number of books and articles have accused the Jewish wartime leadership of failing to rescue, of negotiating with the enemy, of pandering to hostile 'Allies.' The Nazis murdered the Jews – everyone knows that. The Allies did little to help. But who was *really* responsible? In accordance with 'good' Jewish tradition, many Jewish historians, writers, and journalists blamed Chaim Weizmann, Stephen Wise, David Ben-Gurion, Nahum Goldmann, Yitzhak Grünbaum, Moshe Shertok, and all the rest of the Jews who tried to rescue their fellows. They were responsible because they had failed. This suicidal tendency in historiography is typical of a frustrated public refusing to recognize its essential helplessness in the face of overwhelming force. This tendency is especially pronounced because the situation has changed since the war with the establishment of the State of Israel; now, paradoxically, a much smaller number of Jews wield more, though still not very impressive, power, just like so many other small nations or peoples. Why did Joel Brand fail? We can almost hear the argument that the Israeli Air Force should have dropped him behind German lines. Anachronistic solutions are offered to the problem of rescuing millions of people being murdered by an implacable enemy.[17]

Because of the untenability of the charges levelled against the Allies, and notwithstanding either the ubiquity of the notion that the Allies 'did nothing' or the growth of an extremist fringe which virtually lumps together the Allies and the Jewish communities of the democracies with the Nazis, it is probably also fair to say that, during the past fifteen years or so, something of a reaction to the extreme views of Allied guilt, voiced by Wyman and others, has taken place. Some of this research has built upon an older tradition, dating from the 1970s, of scholarship which emphasised the positive aspects of Allied efforts on behalf of Europe's Jews. This reaction has been limited among academics and scholars to a number of particular facets of the Allied response, and exclusively to the American rather than the British reaction to the Holocaust.

Four areas might be noted where recent historians have offered a more favourable view of the Allied response. The alleged supineness and inaction of the American Jewish community has been much more realistically contextualised by historians like Yehuda Bauer and Henry L. Feingold, who argue that the constraints of the American political system during the 1930s and 1940s, prior to the legitimacy of ethnic groups lobbying on their own behalf, severely limited the response of both the Roosevelt administration and the Jewish community, making impossible the kind of bold action which American Jewry would surely have undertaken a generation later. This view is especially associated with Professor Feingold, probably the most eminent historian of the recent American Jewish community, in works like *The Politics of Rescue: The Roosevelt Administration and the Holocaust, 1938–1945* (New Brunswick, NJ, 1970), his contribution to a magisterial five-volume history of American Jewry, *A Time For Searching: Entering the Mainstream, 1920–1945* (Baltimore, 1992), and especially in a recent book of his essays, *Bearing Witness: How America and Its Jews Responded to the Holocaust* (Syracuse, NY, 1995). It will be seen from the relevant chapters in the present book that Feingold's viewpoint, although much more reasonable than those who claim that American Jewry 'did nothing' is, in my opinion, also inaccurate, and it differs essentially from the argument of this work.[18] American Jewry produced committee after committee and plan after plan to rescue the Jews of Nazi-occupied Europe; they had a surprising degree of immediate access to the President and to congressmen and government officials. What they lacked, alas, was a plan which could actually rescue the Jews of Nazi-occupied Europe, the millions who were prisoners of a murderous lunatic and who were unreachable by any means. Professor Yehuda Bauer's *American Jewry and the Holocaust* (Detroit, 1981), a detailed account of the activities of the American Jewish Joint Distribution Committee (a leading relief body, founded in 1914, which had long been involved in efforts to ameliorate the conditions of oppressed Jewry) during the Holocaust, emphasised its many-faceted efforts on behalf of European Jewry, stymied not by any lack of will but by the relentless nature of Nazi genocide. Bauer's positive view of American rescue efforts has carried over to other writings on this subject, for instance his *A History of the Holocaust* (New York, 1982).

The second area where the notion of American indifference has been usefully challenged is in the debate about the failure to bomb Auschwitz. The alleged failure by the Allies to destroy that extermination camp in 1944, despite the fact that (it is often suggested) this was both logistically possible and widely urged, is perhaps the best-known single component of David Wyman's critique of American policy during the war, and is likely to be known – and accepted – by lay persons with little or no specialist knowledge of this field. Yet, despite the ubiquity with which this criticism is voiced, recent analysis by expert military historians, vastly better informed about the technical aspects of this question than Professor Wyman, have emphasised the near-impossibility of a successful American bombing raid on Auschwitz in 1944. This expert revisionist opinion has been put most cogently by Dr James H. Kitchens III, an Archivist of the United States Air Force Historical Research Centre, in a 1994 article in *The Journal of Military History* and in articles by him and by Dr Richard H. Levy, a nuclear engineer who has closely researched this topic, in *FDR and the Holocaust* (Newton, ed.). There can simply be no doubt that the criticisms raised by Kitchens, Levy and others have undermined the case made by Wyman that the bombing of Auschwitz was a realistic possibility in 1944; there are also a host of other reasons, which I examine in Chapter 4, why recent criticism of the Allied 'failure' to bomb Auschwitz is profoundly unrealistic and ahistorical.

Yet – as with so much about this topic – acceptance of the more favourable view is a painfully slow uphill struggle, even among historians who do not engage in a general indictment of the Allies. For instance, Professor Feingold, in his 1995 book of essays *Bearing Witness*, reprinted his 1979 article 'Who Shall Bear Guilt for the Holocaust?' which contains the statement, unaltered since its original appearance, that 'An article in *Commentary* by Professor David Wyman and another by Roger M. Williams in *Commonweal* demonstrate beyond doubt that, by the spring of 1944, the bombing of Auschwitz was feasible'.[19] (In light of the research by Kitchens and others, this statement is simply untrue, especially if made in the bald form of Feingold's wording.) That the Allies could have bombed Auschwitz if they wished, and that this action could have certainly saved the lives of thousands of Jews, has by now been disseminated in every conceivable medium – books and articles, television documentaries, museum exhibits, academic and non-academic lectures – and it will probably take decades before this piece of folk disinformation loses its popular hold.

Some recent research has also looked more positively at American refugee policy before the war, a subject which had hitherto received comparatively little revisionist attention. The most useful corrective work here has been Richard Breitman and Alan Kraut's *American Refugee Policy and European Jewry, 1933–1945* (Bloomington, Ind., 1987), a very detailed examination of the actual operation of America's policies towards German Jewish refugees, especially prior to the war. Yet it seems indisputable that the pre-war phase of this question has not received the searching, critical examination which it obviously needs; for this reason, *The Myth of Rescue* opens with an account of international refugee policy towards Germany's Jews during the 1930s which will show that, far from being restrictive and harsh, it was one of the more liberal, generous and, most of all, successful attempts to rescue oppressed refugees in modern history.

The fourth area of critical scholarly attention has been an analysis of the various attempts at 'ransoming' Jews (the so-called 'blood-for-trucks' deal, proposed by Eichmann in 1944, being the best-known) apparently advanced by senior Nazis, especially Heinrich Himmler, in the closing phases of the war, although possibly suggested as well on a smaller scale before that, for instance in Slovakia in 1942–4. Historians have been sharply divided between those who view 'ransom' as a genuine lost opportunity and those who believe that these proposals were thoroughly disingenuous. Recently, Yehuda Bauer's *Jews For Sale?: Nazi–Jewish Negotiations, 1933–1945* has examined these proposals in detail. While Professor

Bauer apparently believes that the Nazis were in part sincere in their offers, he is forced to admit that such proposals could not have succeeded; nevertheless, many Jews (and non-Jews) deserve credit for attempting to 'ransom' Jews and succeeding on a limited scale.[20] In this work, I offer an original but fundamental reason for believing that no significant attempts at 'ransom' could possibly have succeeded.

All these revisionist views, it should be carefully noted, are partial and specific: historians have argued that one or another aspect of rescue was impossible (or very difficult), in contrast to Wyman and others who argue that America did little or nothing, too little and too late. Even someone like Professor Feingold has claimed that 'tens of thousands' of Jews who perished in the Holocaust could have been saved by more direct Allied action (Wyman puts the figure at 200,000 or more).[21] So far as I am aware, no historian has argued — as I do here — that American efforts at rescue during the Holocaust were *ipso facto* impossible, given the Nazi policy of genocide and what was actually proposed at the time. Perhaps the two historians who most closely approach the interpretation offered in this book are Frank W. Brecher and Lucy S. Dawidowicz. Brecher's article 'David Wyman and the Historiography of America's Response to the Holocaust: Counter-Considerations' is an important critique of Wyman's views, emphasising the lack of 'factual evidence' and the 'dubious validity' for many of his attacks on American Jewry, in some key respects paralleling the points made in this book.[22] Nevertheless, it is far narrower, failing to discuss (for instance) the question of bombing Auschwitz or British rescue efforts, and apparently accepting that 'the difficult problem of finding . . . suitable places of refuge' for the Jews of Hungary and elsewhere was an important factor in the failure of the Allies to rescue Jews, rather than a *non sequitur*.[23]

The historian whose viewpoint perhaps came closest to that advanced here was the late Lucy S. Dawidowicz, whose essays on the possibility of rescue by America during the Holocaust (collected in her posthumous anthology *What Is The Use of Jewish History?*) are models of sanity and clarity. Unlike most American historians of the Holocaust, Dawidowicz had actually lived among eastern European Jewry, spending a year at the famous YIVO Institute in Vilna as a young woman in 1938–9 just as Hitler was about to strike; her 1989 account of these experiences, *From that Time and Place*, is as valuable as it is moving. For Dawidowicz, the Second World War was literally Hitler's 'war against the Jews', its traditional territorial and strategic dimensions secondary to the *Führer*'s central aim to rid Europe of Jewry. The Nazis bore complete responsibility for planning and executing the Holocaust; Hitler was bent on exterminating European Jewry and could not be moved from his goal by any means; the only role of America (and the other Western Allies) in the Holocaust was to liberate Europe from the Nazi scourge.[24]

These conclusions seem self-evident and unarguable; as with so many unarguable truths, however, many intelligent people refuse to believe them. It was Lucy Dawidowicz's gift to see the facts of the matter clearly. Nevertheless, in this work I would go much further even than she did: I disagree with her on many secondary points and also about the possible role of a Jewish state, if it had existed during the war, in saving European Jews.

The evolution of recent British historiography on the question of rescue during the Holocaust has exhibited all the worst features of American writing on this subject, with little in the way of a dissenting view. The British pattern of negative commentary was set in 1979 by Bernard Wasserstein, in his *Britain and the Jews of Europe* (Oxford, 1979), the first work to use newly declassified Foreign Office and other government documents. Wasserstein found what he took to be a persistent pattern of British government reluctance – often obstruction – to allow more German Jewish refugees to flee to British territory, especially, of course, Palestine. Most of his evidence – necessarily – related to the first two years of the war, before the Nazi policy of genocide had begun (or was known in the West); from that time it was virtually impossible to flee, and the British always accepted fleeing Jewish refugees, offering them safety in a territory outside the reach of the Nazi death machine, if not in Palestine. Many of Wasserstein's examples date from the period 1940–1, when Britain rightly feared that a Nazi invasion was imminent, and normal British standards of liberalism and tolerance – for instance, towards interned refugees – temporarily disappeared. By focusing on this period (in particular) Wasserstein enhanced the sense that Britain's refugee policy was hallmarked by rigid obstructionism, if not anti-semitism, diminishing its generous record in the settlement of refugees before the war (especially after *Kristallnacht*) and the extraordinary degree of sensitivity towards Jewish suffering shown by Britain's elites during the war. As in so many other accounts of rescue during the Holocaust, Wasserstein assumes that many more Jews could have been rescued and that the failure to rescue was caused by high entry barriers put up by Britain and the democracies, rather than by insurmountable exit barriers erected, after mid-1940, by Nazi Germany.

Wasserstein's book predated the growth of a powerful school in recent Anglo-Jewish historiography which views Britain as an illiberal society, Anglo-Jewish history as marked by high levels of intolerance and anti-semitism and the typical response of the British Jewish community as one of supine acquiescence in its subordinate role. This school of younger Anglo-Jewish historians thus differed almost totally from the prevalent opinion of the previous generation, for whom Britain was a liberal society *par excellence* and the course of Anglo-Jewish history an archetypal example of Whig progress towards universal toleration.[25] To this school, the attitude of both British society as a whole and the Anglo-Jewish community during the Holocaust is ripe for reevaluation. The younger school has been unsparingly critical of both, perhaps more critical than critics of American policy during the Holocaust. Possibly the most extreme work on this subject is Richard Bolchover's *British Jewry and the Holocaust* (Cambridge, 1993), which contrasts 'the politics of fear' of the Jewish mainstream, the 'assimilationists' of the Board of Deputies of British Jews and the mainstream Zionist movement with 'the exceptions' – defined by Bolchover as 'socialists, Strictly Orthodox Jews, academics, and Revisionist Zionists', whose active and positive plans to rescue European Jewry were thwarted by the Jewish mainstream.[26] (The parallels of this to much recent American writing on the American Jewish community during the Holocaust is, of course, clear.) Strangely, however, Bolchover neglects to state what these plans for rescue by the 'exceptions' actually comprised.[27] In Chapter 3 we will explore their plans in some detail, reaching the inescapable conclusion that the plans were totally without merit and incapable of rescuing anyone; we shall also find that their plans were virtually identical with those offered by the Anglo-Jewish mainstream.

Bolchover's view of the reaction of both Britain and of Anglo-Jewry to the Holocaust is closely reflected in such works as Geoffrey Alderman's *Modern British Jewry* (Oxford, 1992), and, less directly, in the various writings on this topic by Tony Kushner, such as *The Holocaust and the Liberal Imagination* (Oxford, 1994). Alderman's work, though deeply learned and often incisive, may be read as an extended attack upon the Board of Deputies of British Jews and the United Synagogue, the two pillars of the Anglo-Jewish mainstream. According to Alderman 'on the most delicate [sic] question of possible attempts by the allies to halt the planned destruction of European Jewry, British Jewry was decidedly ambivalent', claiming that 'by 1944 Auschwitz and other death camps were within easy range of allied bomber aircraft . . . [yet] no pressure of any significance was ever exerted upon the British government on this question'.[28] This statement, typical of Alderman's discussion, is deeply misleading, as will be seen in Chapter 4.[29] Kushner's essays, though more balanced and nuanced, compare Britain adversely with America, praising the creation of the American War Refugee Board in contrast with British inaction.[30] Britain's tradition of 'liberalism' made it unable to comprehend the necessity to create bodies to respond to the 'particularistic' needs of oppressed Jewry.[31]

There has been very little in the way of an opposing opinion, especially in the recent past. In the first years after the war, a number of books appeared, such as Norman Bentwich's *The Rescue and Achievement of Refugee Scholars* (The Hague, 1953) and his *They Found Refuge* (London, 1956), dealing sympathetically with British efforts at admitting German Jewish refugees during the 1930s. The essential scholarly work on this question, A.J. Sherman's *Island Refuge: Britain and Refugees From the Third Reich* (Berkeley, 1973), presents a largely favourable view of this subject, while many other accounts of German Jewish migration to Britain are probably more favourable than their American equivalents.[32] For the war itself, Martin Gilbert's well-known *Auschwitz and the Allies* (London, 1981), often seen as highly critical of the Allies' failure to bomb Auschwitz (and regularly cited by historians for that purpose) is actually a sympathetic and well-balanced explanation of the reasons why the Allies 'did nothing', as befits Churchill's official biographer. New evidence (presented in Chapter 4 of this work), available since Gilbert wrote, makes clear the insurmountable technical difficulties inherent in any plan to bomb Auschwitz, even in 1944. Gilbert's book has probably been as central to the debate on this question in Britain as have Wyman's writings in America, albeit in a way which has misconstrued the author's aim. My recent book, *A History of the Jews in The English-Speaking World: Great Britain* (London, 1996) contains a chapter entitled 'Anglo-Jewry and the Holocaust' which augments the arguments made in the present work.[33]

Elsewhere in the English-speaking democracies the picture is mixed. Scholarship on Canada – most notably Irving Abella and Harold Troper's *None is Too Many* (Toronto, 1982) is unrelievedly negative. In Australia, however, a lively debate has emerged about the generosity of Australian refugee policy.[34] (Obviously, neither country could possibly have had the slightest direct effect upon Nazi policy as such.) Recent Israeli scholarship available in English has been marked by an unusual degree of intelligence, especially two fine works, Dalia Ofer's *Escaping the Holocaust: Illegal Immigration to the Land of Israel, 1939–1944* (Oxford, 1990) and Dina Porat's *The Blue and Yellow Stars of David* (London, 1992). Both works show that, beyond doubt, the failure of the *Yishuv* to 'do more' was chiefly if not entirely due to the impossibility of rescuing Jews from Nazi-occupied Europe, and not to any lack of intention.

The Myth of Rescue differs from all previous works on this subject in that it rejects as impossible any further rescue efforts on behalf of Europe's Jews entailing more than the most minor and insignificant numbers. The reasons why this is so have never been made clearly (or, indeed, at all) by previous historians, while the arguments used by historians to indict the Allied governments, or the Jewish communities of the democracies, are – invariably – specious, ahistorical and egregious. There is, in other words, no case to answer.

2

THE MYTH OF CLOSED DOORS, 1933-9

The standard historiographical view of the attitude of the 'bystander' countries towards Jews persecuted by the Nazi regime in the years between 1933 and 1939 is clear-cut: they erected high walls and barriers to refugee migration, resulting in tens of thousands of Jews being trapped in the Nazi Reich after the Second World War broke out in September 1939. Most of those trapped in the Reich – together with millions of others – perished in the Nazi death machine instituted during the war. The 'bystander' countries, including in particular the United States and Britain, thus bear no small measure of indirect guilt for the deaths of Germany's Jews and, indeed, of so many others. Even minimal generosity demonstrated towards the Jews fleeing Nazi persecution would have saved tens of thousands, perhaps hundreds of thousands, of lives.

Virtually every account of the stance of the democracies during those dark years emphasises the inadequacy of their record, the high walls they erected and the anti-semitism and xenophobia underlying these attitudes. Thus Michael Berenbaum's *The World Must Know*, the history of the Holocaust published by the United States Holocaust Memorial Museum in Washington, DC, states:

> There was no place to go. Jewish emigration to Palestine was severely limited by the British. Neutral Switzerland was afraid of being overrun by Jews. The United States raised a formidable series of paper walls to keep Jews out . . . [A]fter the outbreak of war in Europe in 1939, German Jews were barred as potential spies.
>
> The United States, a nation of immigrants, was reluctant to become a haven for Jewish refugees. Reflexive nationalism went hand in hand with widespread antisemitism. . . . That these were victims of Nazi persecution fleeing for their lives did not seem a sufficient reason to let in more than a trickle of refugees.[1]

Nearly every statement made in Berenbaum's work on the attitude of the democracies towards the admission of Jewish refugees from Nazi Germany is incorrect, as we shall see.

Michael R. Marrus' *The Holocaust in History* is a widely known and valuable general assessment of historical opinion about the vexed historiographical questions of the Holocaust: did Hitler have a master plan? Was the Holocaust unique? Did the Jews go to their deaths like sheep? Usually excellent, and written by an internationally known historian, its section on the attitude of the democracies (and, more generally, its material on the question of rescue) is, regrettably, fully reflective of mainstream opinion. According to Professor Marrus:

> Misperceptions of the massacre in Europe were accompanied by an almost universal unwillingness to receive Jewish refugees [and] sluggishness in responding to Jewish appeals for help . . . Numerous works document the closing of doors in the 1930s, in one Western country after another. The refugees, of course, sought entry at the worst possible moment: world depression brought restrictionist sentiment everywhere.

> Restriction . . . marked British policy in Palestine . . . Restriction, intensified everywhere with the outbreak of war.[2]

Literally dozens of other studies of the attitude of the democracies towards Jews fleeing Nazi Germany during the years from 1933-9 repeat these and very similar claims. There cannot be the slightest doubt that a consensus exists among virtually all historians of this subject that particularly high barriers existed to Jewish refugee emigration, resulting in the needless deaths of tens of thousands of German and other Reich Jews once the mass murder of European Jewry got under way in 1941-2. So universal is this consensus that challenging it would appear to be the historiographical equivalent of demonstrating that the sun revolves around the earth.

There is, however, one principal error in the proposition that high barriers to the emigration of German and Reich Jews existed during the years 1933-9, resulting in the subsequent deaths of many thousands: it is almost the precise opposite of the truth. *Fully 72 per cent* of German Jewry escaped from Nazi Germany before emigration became impossible, including *83 per cent of German Jewish children and youth.* Given the general restrictions on *all* refugee migration (including non-Jewish refugees) which prevailed during the inter-war period throughout the world, the emigration of most German Jews not only did not represent failure on the part of the democracies, but constituted one of the most successful and far-reaching programmes of rescue of a beleaguered and persecuted people ever seen up to that time. Far from the doors of immigration being shut just before the gates went up forever with the outbreak of the war in 1939, more Reich Jews found safety abroad in the last year preceding the outbreak of the war than at any time before. What trapped the estimated 140,000 Jews still remaining in the pre-1933 boundaries of Germany, as well as those in Austria and Czechoslovakia in the

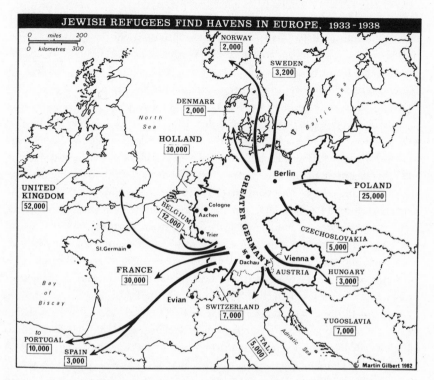

JEWISH REFUGEES FIND HAVENS IN EUROPE, 1933-1938

Map 1 Jewish refugees find havens, 1933–8. Note that these figures include only German Jewish refugees until the end of 1938, and that the figures sometimes disagree with those in the text. (From M. Gilbert, *Atlas of the Holocaust*, 1993. Reproduced by permission of Routledge.)

enlarged Reich, was the outbreak of the war itself: but for the rather unexpected start of hostilities in September 1939, it seems very likely that virtually every single Jew in the Nazi Reich would have emigrated to safety within, say, another three years. But it is imperative that the Jews of the Nazi Reich must, at all times, be distinguished from the 7.5 million Jews of continental Europe who came under Nazi rule between the outbreak of the war and V-E Day. The Jews of continental Europe, apart from Germany, were not refugees, either before or after 1939, were not subject to Nazi rule prior to the coming of the war, or imagined that they would ever be, let alone that they would be murdered in history's greatest genocide.

The story of the rescue of Europe's Jews during the years from 1933–9 thus *exclusively concerns* Germany's Jews and those in Austria and Czechoslovakia who were absorbed into the German Reich in 1938–9. The Jews of Poland, the Soviet Union, Hungary, France, the Netherlands and other parts of Europe, however diabolical their fate after September 1939, form absolutely no part of the international effort to rescue Germany's Jews before the outbreak of conflict, since they were not under German rule. The 3.5 million Jews of the Soviet Union – a number which increased to perhaps 5.5 million following the absorption of eastern Poland, the Baltic States and Moldavia into the USSR in 1939–40 – were beyond reach by any means in the world, being trapped behind Stalin's already impenetrable Iron Curtain. During these years, the height of Stalin's Purges, any expression by Soviet Jewry of a desire to emigrate to the capitalist West or to the Zionist *Yishuv* was tantamount to writing a suicide note.

'Rescue' during the period 1933–9 thus concerned, exclusively, the Jews of Nazi Germany and the areas annexed to it by Hitler, especially Austria and Czechoslovakia. In 1933 the number of Jews in Germany is usually estimated at 499,682 (according to German census data) or about 525,000, including the Jews of the Saar, annexed to Germany in 1935. In 1942, when emigration from the Reich was absolutely forbidden and the deportation of Germany's Jews to the death camps began, the number of Jews remaining in Germany had declined to only 139,000.[3] Most of this decline was the result of emigration abroad; a smaller share – not indicated separately in the statistics from which this data derives – was the result of a natural excess of deaths over births and of suicides, as well as of counting Jews murdered by the Nazis during *Kristallnacht* or in concentration camps prior to the deportations.[4] By May 1939, the total number of Jews within the pre-1939 boundaries of Germany had declined to 213,390. This fell to 185,000 only four months later, at the outbreak of the war in September 1939, to 164,000 by October 1941 and to 139,000 in 1942.[5] Rates of emigration among the younger age-cohorts of the population were even higher, although here it must be remembered that recent German Jewish age-cohorts, even before the Nazis came to power, demonstrated very low birth rates, especially compared with those before 1914; see Table 1.[6]

Impressive as these figures for the rescue of German Jewry clearly are, they are underestimates of the actual extent of refugee emigration preceding the start of the deportations. For another 46,531 German and Austrian immigrants entered the United States in the years 1940–4 inclusive, many of whom were certainly Jews included in the September 1939 figures, while nearly 10,000 German Jewish

Table 1 Jewish population of Germany 1933–9, by age

Age	June 1933	September 1939	Decrease	% decrease
60+	81,400	59,700	21,700	27
40–59	157,400	76,600	80,800	51
25–39	119,700	24,100	95,600	80
16–24	58,600	9,700	48,900	83
0–15	82,700	15,000	67,700	82
Totals	499,800	185,100	314,700	63

immigrants entered Palestine in the years 1939–41.[7] Thus, *at most* only 24,700 Jewish children and youth (and almost certainly fewer) remained within the pre-1933 boundaries of Germany at the outbreak of the war in September 1939. *All of the others had been rescued*, a total of at least 116,600, and perhaps significantly more. Concerning the demographic fate of pre-1933 German Jewry, two other factors have to be kept in mind: many, tragically, emigrated to countries which were subsequently occupied by Nazi Germany, and some would then have been deported to extermination camps in Poland. Strauss sets their number at '30,000'. Some of the estimated 23,000 German Jews present in France in 1938–9, for example, were among the 76–83,000 French Jews who were deported during the Holocaust. On the other hand, about 20–25,000 Jews actually survived the war in Germany itself, chiefly Jews living in mixed marriages with children – an estimated 20,000 persons – who continued to be protected until the end.[8]

The chronology of the emigration of German Jewry also presents many features of interest. Strikingly and indubitably, emigration rose dramatically after *Kristallnacht* in November 1938, a fact which seems *ipso facto* inconsistent with the proposition that doors to Jewish emigration were closing. By years, the approximate number of Jewish emigrants from Germany (pre-1933 boundaries) was as follows:[9]

1933	37,000
1934	23,000
1935	21,000
1936	25,000
1937	23,000
1938	40,000
1939	78,000
1940	15,000
1941	8,000
1942	8,500
Total	278,500

Perhaps the most interesting question which might be asked of this data is why so few Jews emigrated prior to *Kristallnacht*. Only 129,000 Jews – barely one-quarter of Germany's 1933 Jewish population – left Germany during the first five years of the Nazi regime, 1933–7 inclusive. The normal answer, given in most accounts critical of the democracies, is that the doors were firmly shut in their face. The alleged situation in the United States has been summarised by Michael Berenbaum:

> To obtain a visa [to the United States], a would-be immigrant had to fill out myriad forms and submit them to American consular officials in

Europe, whose job was to issue visas sparingly. There were financial tests to weed out refugees who were likely to become a public charge. One of the requirements was a certificate of good conduct attesting to the exemplary character of the immigrant. This was supposed to be obtained from one's local police authority, in this case the Gestapo . . . That these were victims of Nazi persecution fleeing for their lives did not seem a sufficient reason to let in more than a trickle of refugees. Only in 1938 and 1939 in the years between 1933 and 1945 was the quota for Germany and Austria filled.[10]

Writing of the 1930s in Britain, Professor Geoffrey Alderman has stated:

The underlying principle which informed the attitude of Britain's National Government towards Jewish immigration in the 1930s was that Jews, by their presence and by their behaviour, created anti-Semitism. The least possible number would be allowed to enter Britain, and most of these . . . would acquire no right of permanent residence.[11]

To be sure, barriers to the entry of refugee Jews to most countries did exist (as they did during the 1930s, to the migration of most peoples to most countries) but, as the data plainly shows, these barriers came down once it became apparent, following *Kristallnacht*, that Hitler intended to expel virtually all Jews from Germany and brutalise unmercifully virtually all who remained. But the existence of these barriers is, in my view, quite unsatisfactory as an explanation of why so many Jews failed to emigrate until the last minute. Perhaps the most important single reason for the failure to emigrate is that most German Jews assumed that Nazi anti-semitism would (to employ a phrase I have myself heard repeatedly in interviewing German Jewish *émigrés*), 'blow over' once the Nazi government became institutionalised. Many – perhaps most – German Jews who were not directly affected by the initial Nazi measures ridding the civil service and universities of Jews believed that the violence, terrorism and harassment aimed at Jews by the Gestapo and other violent components of the regime would ameliorate with time.

This sentiment is evident from virtually any extensive oral interviews with groups of German Jewish *émigrés* in any of the Western democracies. In Australia, where approximately 10,000 German and other Reich Jews settled – almost all after *Kristallnacht* – extensive oral interviews have been conducted with surviving refugees, and many memoirs of Jewish *émigrés* have appeared. These Jews were, sociologically, identical to those who settled in America, Britain, Canada and else-where (although fewer 'eminent' Jews settled in Australia than in either Britain or America) and their oral testimonies are unlikely to be familiar to historians in the Northern Hemisphere. In their testimonies, one finds, time and again, remarks such as those in the following five extracts:

I wasn't afraid. No, I wasn't afraid at the time [1937]. It was just something we couldn't believe was happening, nor that it would last. When I mentioned going to Palestine to my father, he said 'Oh, come on, it's not going to last'. Of course by the time he wanted to get out there was no way he could. I managed to leave because of my connection with Habonim [a Zionist youth group].[12]

Meanwhile my father had died in 1934 while they were on a trip to Palestine to visit my brother and sister. My mother returned to Germany, but to the city, not the country. By then I realised that it was too dangerous to stay. My husband was not convinced and I had to fight with him to leave. He thought Hitler was just a passing phenomenon and, in time, everything would be wonderful again. I had the feeling it would just not go away. Then came *Kristallnacht* and that persuaded him.[13]

[In 1936] while I was still in Cottbus [a town in Germany] a friend of mine who also studied at the college had heard that the Australian government had decided to issue a very limited number, I think fifty, of entry permits for German Jewish refugees who were 'technical craftsmen'. This friend saw the situation much clearer than I did and was very keen to get a chance to emigrate. So when it was announced that the Australian government had appointed an emissary from Woburn House, the Jewish welfare agency in London, to go to Berlin to interview candidates and pick the best, he wanted to visit Berlin to see him. My friend tried to persuade me to come along and apply also for a permit, but I was at that time determined to stay in Germany, and anyway, who would want to go to Australia which was 'full of blackfellows and kangaroos', that is about the sum total of what we knew of the country. Finally, I agreed, more as a joke, to come along for the ride and the inevitable happened: I was accepted and he was rejected. I must have 'interviewed well'; it certainly could not have been my technical proficiency which gained me this success. Incidentally, my friend later managed to emigrate to Shanghai, converted to Buddhism and became a monk in a monastery in Sri Lanka. For some years he used to send me literature to Australia which tried to link up Buddhism to the latest findings of quantum mechanics and Heisenberg's uncertainty principle before we lost touch. The Australian immigration permit was granted the following year, 1937, but I still did not want to leave the 'Fatherland'. I remained for over twelve months in Germany with the permit in my pocket, being declared a lunatic by all and sundry. I also negotiated for a job in Tilburg in Holland which I very much preferred to Australia, it being so conveniently close to Germany so that one could promptly come back when all this craziness would be over. 'None are so blind as those who do not want to see', to coin a phrase!

Finally when I had to leave Germany . . . the permit had expired and I had to apply for an extension. Had I succeeded in getting that job in Tilburg I most likely would not have been able to write this story, of course, as most Dutch Jews ended up in Auschwitz.[14]

My husband was very well established in business in Halle an der Saale. He had a lot of tenants whom he always looked after very carefully. He was a charitable man. So when Hitler came to power in 1933 people said to him 'Mr. Lifschütz, nothing will happen to you. Don't leave.' A lot of people had already left. All around people were saying, 'Hitler won't last' . . . A woman sometimes has a sixth feeling. I had read all the *Stürmer* magazines and so on because I wanted to be in the picture about what was happening. So I said to my husband, 'You know, I think we will have to leave'. He said, 'No, you won't have a six-room apartment and two servants if we do that'. But I said, 'O.K., then I'll have a one-room flat with you: but I want to be safe'. He wouldn't believe me. He was terribly afraid to emigrate.[15]

We should all have left in 1933 or 1934 or 1935, but we never believed that the Germans were capable of doing the things they did later. Though practically every German had a copy of *Mein Kampf*, few ever read it. I could have gone to Turkey. The Turkish consul's daughter had studied with me and we were close friends, and I had the opportunity to go to Ankara as a tutor or lecturer, but I could not accept it; I could not leave my mother behind.[16]

Interviews carried out with German Jewish migrants elsewhere reveal much the same picture. Jewish refugees in Britain not only assumed that their situation would, sooner or later, stabilise, but they consistently misinterpreted the 'lulls' in the ever more extreme nature of Nazi anti-semitism – such as occurred around the time of the 1936 Olympics, for instance – as evidence that their assumptions were correct. As Marion Berghahn has summarised the situation in her study of 180 German Jewish refugees who migrated to Britain:

The picture which the developments in the 1930s presented to the Jews was confused and confusing not only because the impact of antisemitism varied considerably . . . [A]nti-Jewish regulations were not implemented systematically, but often in contradictory ways: periods of violence and draconian measures were followed by periods of relative calm which gave rise to fresh hopes 'that the madness would stop'.[17]

As indicated in this quotation, one significant reason for the reluctance of so many German Jews to emigrate until the last possible moment was that, to a surprising degree, Nazi anti-semitic restrictions fell upon different groups within German

Jewry quite differentially. Initially, Nazi policy directly affected only civil servants, university professors and political dissidents (including non-Jews) who fell foul of the regime.[18] Several categories of Jews were initially exempted from the worst enactments of the new regime, while the Nazis continued to allow 2 per cent of university entrants to be Jews until after *Kristallnacht*. While the Nazis organised a one-day boycott of Jewish businesses on 1 April 1933 (they were forced to limit an indefinite boycott owing to pressure from President von Hindenburg), Jewish businesses as such were not yet touched by the new regime. Indeed, the fact that the Nazi regime had much success in bringing Germany out of the worst of the Depression led to one of the most extraordinary facts of the whole Nazi era, something which will seem utterly incredible to most people: while in 1933 some 37,000 Jews fled from Germany, in 1934 as many as 16,000 returned to Nazi Germany from abroad.[19] (Most historians who have discussed this phenomenon have also pointed to destitution in other parts of Europe to which they fled, especially France, as an important motivating factor.)

Obviously, Nazi rule in Germany was at almost all times accompanied by terrorist propaganda and official and unofficial violence against individual Jews and Jewish properties, at all times aimed at utterly marginalising them as a prelude to their total removal from German society. Yet many Jews continued to believe that they would be spared the worst excesses of Nazi rule. Prior to *Kristallnacht* – and even afterwards, until 1942–3, in the case of some 'privileged' groups such as former front-line war veterans – it appeared that some Jews would remain relatively unmolested in Nazi Germany, in the context of a lunatic dictator and a regime which regarded them as totally alien to the new Germany. For those who are unaware of the actual evolution of the Nazi regime, it should also be noted that the synagogues continued unhindered until *Kristallnacht*, the Zionist movement (which aimed at encouraging the emigration of Jews to Palestine) was recognised and encouraged until about that time, and a Jewish theatre and press of sorts continued until the war. The major turning-points determining Jewish emigration from Nazi Germany were the Nazi coming to power in 1933 and the events of 1938 – the *Anschluss* with Austria, the acquisition of the Sudetenland and *Kristallnacht* – followed, in 1939, by the annexation of the rump of Czechoslovakia (Bohemia and Moravia) as a German 'protectorate'.

A host of other reasons, apart from expectations that the 'Hitler madness' would ultimately pass, explain why Germany's Jews failed to emigrate. There were the obvious traumas of settling in a country with a different language, a different culture, a different political, economic and professional system, and an entirely different legal system. *Emigrés* were plundered of virtually all their assets, and not until Jews experienced what they perceived as a personal and immediate threat of terrorism and imprisonment in Germany's pre-war concentration camps such as Buchenwald were they prepared to sacrifice every material thing. Many elderly Jews – the majority who were left behind were elderly – were psychologically unprepared to emigrate.[20] It is sometimes overlooked that emigration to the English-speaking world (or to France) meant settlement in countries which only fifteen years before had been at war with Germany and whose soldiers Germany's Jewish troops had cheerfully shot to kill. Many German Jews would still have recoiled from the thought of living in an 'enemy' country until no other option was possible.

It is also, strikingly, the case that German Jews were initially hostile to mass emigration: the official representative bodies of virtually all components of the Jewish community rejected mass emigration, except as an individual's personal decision. As Lucy S. Dawidowicz has put it:

> Emigration was a traditional Jewish response to persecution, but in 1933 in Germany emigration – or flight – was an individual decision, not communal policy within the Jewish community. Every organised group replied to National Socialism with resounding affirmations of the right of Jews to be German, to live in and love Germany. *Daseinrecht*, the right to maintain a Jewish presence in Germany, was construed as a legal right, a moral necessity, and a religious imperative by all Jewish organisations from Orthodox to Reform, right to left, Zionist and non-Zionist.[21]

Given these facts, it is probably not surprising that most German Jews declined to emigrate until the last possible minute. This factor in the emigration equation, the differential willingness or unwillingness of Germany's Jews to leave and its evolution during the Nazi years, is at least as important, and probably more so, than the barriers to emigration elsewhere which obviously existed. The annual figures for emigration are consistent with the factor of internal German anti-semitism being at least as important as the factor of barriers to settlement elsewhere: they rise (and level off) consistently with heightened Nazi persecution of Jews within Germany, and not with ostensible changes in immigration policy in the outside world. On the contrary, again and again it is clear that – within certain limits – the immigration policies of the democracies liberalised in response to heightened Nazi anti-semitism, especially *Kristallnacht*, and were hallmarked by a clear chronology of evolution in the direction of liberalisation in which barriers to immigration and bottlenecks were diminished or removed each time the Nazis engaged in a quantum leap of heightened persecution.

The process of the emigration of virtually all Jews from the *Reich* was abruptly ended (except in the case of limited emigration to the United States and elsewhere) by the outbreak of war in September 1939, when emigration ceased to those countries which were now at war with Germany. Had hostilities not broken out at this time, however, there is no reason to suppose that the pace of emigration would have lessened: in mid-1939 it was clearly quickening rather than slowing down. Many historians believe that Hitler's aim was for the Second World War to begin in 1942–3, rather than in 1939, the unwontedly vigorous response of Britain and France to Germany's August 1939 ultimatum to Poland coming as something of a surprise. If that is so, if the outbreak of the war had been delayed for several years, it seems reasonable to assume that virtually every Jew in the enlarged Reich would have emigrated, those left behind being limited chiefly to the elderly, those who believed themselves to be 'privileged' and those who would not leave their German 'homeland' under any circumstances whatever. From 1938, the German Jewish community's official organised leadership, the *Reichsvereinigung*, 'aimed for the year 1943' as the date when the German Jewish community would cease to exist through emigration.[22]

That the international reception of Jewish refugees was, by 1938–9, highly advanced and relatively generous is further evidenced by the treatment accorded to the two new large groups of persecuted Reich Jews who fell into Nazi hands at this time: those of Austria and Czechoslovakia. At the time of the *Anschluss*, 12 March 1938, a total of 185,000 Jews lived in Austria, of whom 170,000 lived in Vienna.[23] Within eighteen months 120,000 Austrian Jews had managed to emigrate, together with another 6,000 by the end of 1939.[24] Thus, no less than 68.1 per cent of Austrian Jewry managed to flee within twenty-one months – a figure only marginally lower than among the Jewish community of pre-1933 Germany, despite its five extra years of living under Hitler, despite the 'competition' for places abroad provided by German Jewry, especially after *Kristallnacht* in November 1938 and despite the barriers to refugee migration which did exist. The situation in Czechoslovakia shows the same pattern. About 118,000 Jews lived in the provinces of Bohemia and Moravia, annexed by Germany as a 'protectorate' on 15 March 1939. Full German rule was established on 16 April 1939, while the 'Reich Protector', Konstantin von Neurath, was in place on 21 June 1939 – that is, barely two months before the start of the war. Von Neurath issued a proclamation defining the status of Jews in accordance with the Nazis' German legislation, isolating them from society, and expropriating their property.[25] By the outbreak of the war, however, and despite the fact that they had to take their place in the queue behind the remaining Jews of Germany and Austria, about 26,000 Czech Jews – 22 per cent of the community – managed to emigrate over the five months before the outbreak of the war.

In both cases, and in the German case, it is perfectly clear that what trapped those who were left behind, and sealed their fate, was the coming of the war, which closed virtually all hope of emigration to the British Commonwealth, France, most of western Europe or Palestine. But for its outbreak so suddenly in early September 1939, there is little reason to doubt that the overwhelming majority of the Jews of all three countries would have emigrated, and thousands who perished would have survived. The democracies bear no responsibility whatever for this, only the Nazis. Indeed, if (as many historians critical of Appeasement believe) Britain and France should have gone to war with Germany a year earlier in September 1938 during the Sudeten Crisis, probably more than 150,000 additional Jews, who fled from the Reich in the year remaining until the actual outbreak of the war, would have eventually perished in Nazi death camps.

The year preceding the outbreak of hostilities saw a massive increase in the pace of emigration. On any objective analysis, during this time doors were opening – and opening quickly – not closing. This can best be demonstrated by carefully examining the records of the countries to which Germany's Jews fled, and the reasons why some countries received more than others, bearing in mind the conditions affecting all refugees during these years.

Perhaps the clearest example of increasing liberalisation of harsh restrictions on refugee immigration to accommodate the Jews fleeing the Reich occurred in Britain (and, to a lesser but perceptible extent, throughout the Commonwealth). During the nineteenth century and up to 1905, Britain had, in effect, no immigration laws of any kind, and literally anyone could settle in Britain virtually without restriction. As a result Britain gained a wide reputation as a place to which political refugees, ranging in politics from France's King Louis XVIII to Karl Marx, could flee to escape turmoil and persecution in their homes. The Aliens Act of 1905, designed to stem the flow of foreign immigration, especially Russian Jewish immigration to the East End, specifically recognised the right of political refugees to enter Britain. During and after the First World War, however, Britain enacted a series of measures, especially the Aliens Restriction (Amendment) Act 1919 and the Aliens Order 1920, which, in effect, abolished the legal notion of a refugee altogether.[26] Such individual political refugees as Leon Trotsky were refused admission, Trotsky being barred from entering Britain in 1929, after his expulsion from Russia.[27] More significantly, these Acts, and the bureaucratic apparatus of the Home Office used to enforce them, put a stop to any large-scale (or, indeed, small-scale) refugee settlement after the First World War but *before* Hitler's ascent to power.

Barred from any significant settlement in Britain were such groups as anti-Communist Russians fleeing the Bolshevik Revolution and Armenians fleeing Turkish massacres. Although Britain was headed for all but three years between 1916 and 1939 by Conservative or largely Conservative governments which detested Communism and presumably regarded anti-Bolshevist Russians as martyrs and heroes, not more than 4–5,000 Russian refugees were allowed to settle permanently in Britain after 1917.[28] In 1939, the Russian Orthodox church in London had a membership of only 700 persons.[29] Only 200 Armenian refugees were admitted to Britain after the First World War, following massacres in which perhaps 1 million Armenians were murdered in Turkey, Britain's wartime adversary.[30] Even after 1933, the number of *non-Jewish* refugees admitted by Britain for settlement was derisory in its tiny numbers. 'Negligible' numbers of refugees from the Spanish Civil War were allowed to settle in Britain, although in May 1937 3,800 child refugees evacuated from Bilbao were admitted.[31] By May 1938, however, 'approximately 2,000 of the children had been returned to their parents and repatriation has since continued', as Sir John Hope Simpson wrote in late 1939.[32] 'Only a few individuals' were admitted to Britain as refugees from fascist Italy or from Abyssinia after its invasion by Italy.[33]

This rigorous policy of excluding virtually all immigrants, including refugees, *apart from* Germany's Jews had the support of the whole British mainstream (including the Labour Party), for whom the fact that there were never fewer than 1 million unemployed in Britain during the inter-war years was primary. Hope Simpson has summarised the situation as follows:

> Great Britain's record in the admission of refugees is not distinguished if it be compared with that of France, Czechoslovakia, or the United States of America. The strictly enforced restrictive and selective policy of immigration which she has pursued since the War . . . has kept the number of admissions to figures that have little significance in the total number of post-War refugees.[34]

Hope Simpson did, however, note 'one possible exception to this generalisation', namely 'the admission of refugees from Germany', which he attributed to 'the extraordinary effort and generosity of the Jewish community in Britain in under-taking unconditional responsibility for their support'.[35] The preface to Hope Simpson's definitive account of refugees during the inter-war period (which was published in 1939) is dated October 1938, even before Britain's policies towards Jewish refugees from the Reich were liberalised still further and the bulk of refugees admitted following *Kristallnacht*; if he had summarised Britain's receptivity towards these refugees only a few years later, he would unquestionably have been less circumspect in admitting it to be an exception to the general rule of Britain's 'undistinguished' record on refugees between the wars.

Britain initially admitted relatively few refugees from Nazi Germany, with only 2–3,000 (mainly professionals such as university academics) entering by April 1934.[36] After *Kristallnacht*, however, entry to Britain liberalised considerably and a very significant number entered Britain in the last year or so preceding the war. A.J. Sherman, whose *Island Refuge* remains the standard work, sets the figure at about 50,000; other estimates are higher, Berghahn stating that '80,000 refugees from Germany, Austria, and Czechoslovakia' were 'sheltered' in Britain 'during the war'.[37] By the last months before the outbreak of the war, British consular officials in the Reich were granting emigration visas to Britain *virtually without limit*, a fact which has come to light only recently. As Sherman notes in the introduction to the second (1994) edition of his work:

> British consular officials in Germany and Austria issued without reference to London well over 50,000 visas to refugees who did not ultimately take them up for admission to the United Kingdom . . . They were liberally distributed . . . to refugees awaiting their American and other immigration papers, as a means of protecting Jews and 'non-Aryans' from the brutalities of Gestapo interrogation, or obtaining their release from concentration camps. The generosity of British consular officials [was] known to the Foreign Office but never publicised.[38]

During the 1930s too, both the Anglo-Jewish community and the wider British community were notably generous in funding refugee relief. The Board of Deputies of British Jews, the Jewish community's representative body, gave an undertaking in 1933 that no German Jewish refugee would become a public charge but, instead, their expenses would be paid by the Jewish community.[39] The Earl Baldwin Fund, established in 1937 and headed by former Prime Minister Stanley Baldwin, raised hundreds of thousands of pounds for refugee relief from among the non-Jewish majority. Many thousands of ordinary Britons took Jewish refugee children into their homes, often with profoundly beneficial effects in mutual understanding in the long term. A Methodist grocer in Grantham, Lincolnshire, Alfred Roberts, was one such fairly typical example of a gentile Englishman who hosted a teenage refugee. Nearly sixty years later his daughter recalled that, with the help of the Grantham Rotary Club, a 17-year-old Austrian Jewish girl lived in their house before reemigrating to South America. Her accounts of Jews being made to 'scrub the streets' of Vienna vividly impressed the Grantham family, directly alerting them to the dangers posed by Nazism.[40] The grocer's daughter, Margaret Thatcher, eventually became probably the most philo-semitic of recent prime ministers. It was well known that she regarded Immanuel Jakobovits, the Chief Rabbi, as her favourite clergyman and at one time had five Jews in her Cabinet, including the Chancellor of the Exchequer and the Home Secretary.

The period between 1933 and 1939 also established a remarkably wide-ranging infrastructure to facilitate German and Reich Jewish migration to Britain (and elsewhere). Like all such dedicated groups of 'insiders', it gradually built up a web of goodwill and special knowledge of the government, the bureaucracy concerned with immigration and individual bureaucrats, which systematically increased as these groups became more familiar with and adept at what they were doing, and despite the 'chaos' which had initially surrounded the activities of private organisations dealing with Jewish refugees.[41] Public opinion – as we shall see – was overwhelmingly on the side of the refugees, and overcame the

Table 2 Number of Germans and Austrians given permission to disembark in Britain

Date	Nationality	Numbers landed
1937	Austrian	18,722
	German	80,236
1938	Austrian	14,499
	German	79,652
1 January–31 March 1939	Austrian	426
	German	29,429
1 April–30 June 1939	Austrian	677
	German	61,248

hostility posed by the bureaucracy, anti-semitic extremists and perceptions of anti-refugee feeling among ordinary Britons. In July 1939 – just before the war began – the government finally took over the funding of Jewish refugee settlement in Britain.[42] Two motives appear to have been paramount in this decision: recognition that new homes would have to be found somewhere for the victims of Hitler, and a desire to compensate for the apparent diminution of Jewish settlement in Palestine announced in the notorious May 1939 White Paper. The outbreak of the war put an end to any further Jewish refugee migration to Britain. While British bureaucrats were clearly, in August 1939, despondent about the prospect of the imminent expulsion of all Jews from Bohemia and Moravia, the latest direction taken by Nazi anti-semitism in its conquests, it must be appreciated that the pace of Jewish immigration to Britain continued unabated until the war began.

Seemingly, no precise month-by-month figures of refugee immigration exist, but the numbers of Germans and Austrians (of all religions) given permission to disembark in Britain, are instructive (see Table 2).[43]

Thus, no less than 91,780 Germans and Austrians were given permission to 'land' (i.e. disembark) in Britain in the *first six months* of 1939 (there are no subsequent figures). Precisely 191 Germans and Austrians were 'refused permission to land' upon arriving in Britain.[44]

Sherman's *Island Refuge* is certainly not fulsome in its praise of British policy towards the refugees from Nazism, and charts both the twists and turns in British policy, the erection and maintenance of barriers and whatever anti-semitism there was in government policy with brutal frankness. Yet his final summary of Britain's refugee policy is both accurate and very perceptive:

> When a balance sheet is . . . drawn and Great Britain's refugee policy
> compared with that of other countries it emerges, in the context of the

pre-war period, as comparatively compassionate, even generous. There were no simple answers, no obvious or rapid solutions. But the problem was at least in part comprehended; needs were to some extent met; the drawbridge to safety within British territory was in fact only partly raised. It must not, finally, be overlooked that despite all the evidence of brutal persecution few if any in responsible Government positions could have predicted that would-be migrants left behind in the Greater Reich faced not merely privation, but . . . physical destruction.[45]

When the allegedly high barriers and niggardly attitude of the democracies during the 1933–9 period are examined, the first item offered for consideration, and exhibit number one of the indictment against the democracies, is not uncommonly Palestine. Britain's desire to appease the Arabs, it is regularly maintained, led to a closing of the gates of Palestine, and a reneging on Britain's commitment to establishing a Jewish National Home, at precisely the time when the existence of a Jewish state or homeland, with an open immigration policy for persecuted Jews, could have saved hundreds of thousands if not millions of lives. Of course there is a strong element of truth in these claims, and the demography of annihilation during the Holocaust might well have been very different had an independent state of Israel existed ten or fifteen years earlier.

Nevertheless, a careful examination of the actual course of Jewish immigration to Palestine during the years 1933–9 reveals a very different picture indeed, with the most pertinent facts of *aliyah* during these years viewed in a consistently inaccurate light. The statistics of Jewish immigration to Palestine during this period are shown in Table 3.[46]

The most important conclusion about Jewish migration to Palestine, although evident from these statistics, is not in my view properly appreciated and will probably come as a considerable surprise to many readers, that 75 *per cent* of Jewish immigrants to Palestine in these years did *not* come from Germany. (The plurality, about 40 per cent, came from Poland.) Only 55,000 German Jews migrated to Palestine in this period, barely 11 per cent of Germany's Jewish population in 1933, although – as is well known – under the Haavara Transfer Agreement concluded between the Nazi government and the German Zionist movement in November 1933, emigration of German Jews to Palestine was (in the context of the overall Nazi attitude to Jewish migration) deliberately facilitated, with Jews uniquely allowed to transfer a larger share of their capital to Palestine than elsewhere.[47] While more German Jews migrated to Palestine in the years 1933–6 than to any other country, the numbers are surprisingly small, especially in view of the fact that the immigration of Jews with a capital of one thousand Palestinian pounds was still unrestricted by the British authorities.[48]

The reasons for the reluctance of German Jews to emigrate to Palestine are

Table 3 Immigration to Palestine, 1933–41, by source

Year	Total immigration from all sources	Immigrants from Germany		Immigrants from Austria	Immigrants from Czechoslovakia	Total central European immigrants	
		No.	*Percentage of all immigrants*	*No.*	*No.*	*No.*	*Percentage of all immigrants*
1933	30,300	7,600	25	400	300	8,300	27
1934	42,400	9,800	23	1,000	900	11,700	28
1935	61,900	8,600	14	1,100	1,500	11,200	18
1936	29,700	8,700	29	500	600	9,800	33
1937	10,500	3,700	35	200	200	4,100	39
1938	12,900	4,800	37	2,200	400	7,400	57
1939	16,400	8,500	52	1,700	1,700	11,900	73
1940	4,500	900	20	200	400	1,500	33
1941	3,600	600	17	–	–	600	17
Total	212,200	53,200	25	7,300	6,000	66,500	31
Illegal migrants 1933–41	18,100	1,800	10	2,200	5,000	9,000	50
Grand total	230,300	55,000	24	9,500	11,000	75,500	33

Note: Total immigrants from Germany, other than German (mostly of Polish nationality): 6,000, including 500 immigrants originating from the free city of Danzig.

fairly easy to gauge: the relative historical weakness of the Zionist movement in Germany, especially among assimilated Jews, the backwardness and remoteness of Palestine and the dangers posed to the *Yishuv* by militant Arabs, and the whole bundle of attitudes, centring around the belief that Nazi anti-semitism would 'blow over', which deterred so many from leaving Germany until after November 1938. Additionally, the notion of mass migration of an entire persecuted Jewish population to Palestine, a fundamental component of the ideology of the State of Israel since 1948, was also opposed by the Zionist movement at the time (Vladimir Jabotinsky's Revisionist movement being an important exception). Zionists preferred the migration of healthy, idealistic youth with training in agriculture or manual work who would 'redeem the land' with their own hands. Nevertheless, far more German Jews could, certainly, have migrated to Palestine in this period if they had so wished.

There was a considerable decline in the numbers of German Jews migrating to Palestine in 1936–7, which Nicosia attributes to 'the violence of the Arab revolt' of 1936 and the political uncertainty surrounding the Peel Commission of 1937.[49] As well, there are two other extremely important facts which should be kept in mind when considering the statistics for German Jewish immigration to Palestine. First, the lower limits imposed by Britain after August 1937 were always sub-stantially *higher* than the number of Reich Jews who actually emigrated there. From August 1937, Britain imposed a limit of 12,000 Jewish migrants per year, a figure which remained in force until the 1939 White Paper. It will be seen that about 62 per cent of this figure were refugee Reich Jews, even in 1938.[50] Second, and even more significantly, the proclamation of the notorious 1939 White Paper did *not* result in a decline in Reich Jewish migration to Palestine, which actually reached a record figure (11,900) in 1939. (Nor did it result in a decrease in overall Jewish migration.) As a result of the White Paper, Britain gave primacy to Reich Jewish migration, which, in 1939, comprised 73 per cent of all legal Jewish immigration to Palestine. Indeed *only* in 1938–9 did a majority of Jewish immi-grants to Palestine come from the Reich. It was *aliyah* from Poland and other parts of Europe which was squeezed at this time. We now know, of course, that the inability of Polish and other European Jews to emigrate meant that they would perish in the Holocaust. But it is crucially important to realise that the Nazi policy of genocide was both in the future and unimaginable: Polish and other European Jews were not refugees and not under Nazi rule until the war began. Instead, it was German and other Reich Jews who were threatened at this time, and they comprised the majority who were allowed to settle in Palestine.

The situation with regard to refugee immigration to the United States is probably the most controversial and the best researched. A significant number of studies and monographs have examined America's record towards the refugees from Nazi Germany in this period, almost invariably reaching the conclusion that it was grossly inadequate and unfair, with America's leading bureaucrats of immigration such as Breckenridge Long demonstrating 'thinly-veiled' anti-semitism, and President Franklin D. Roosevelt's role weak and uninspiring.[51]

As is well known, after 1921–4 the immigration policy of the United States was determined strictly by a quota system under which the number allowed to migrate to the United States from any particular country was set at a small percentage of those resident in America, but born in that foreign country, in 1890. The year 1890 was chosen because it was just before the zenith of the influx of eastern and southern Europeans to the United States (chiefly Russian Jews, Italians and Poles) which occurred in the years 1900–14. It plainly represented a deliberate attempt to limit the so-called 'New Immigration', and is often seen as, in part, anti-semitic, a fruit of the post-Russian Revolution, post-First World War 'nativist' backlash of the 1920s. Paradoxically, however, its effect was to advantage immigration from Germany, whose annual quota for admission to the United States was fixed at 25,957. This was the second highest quota figure for any country. It was below Great Britain's 65,721, but was considerably higher than the quotas given to the Irish Free State (17,853), Poland (6,524) or Italy (5,802).[52] Overall, 153,774 immigrants were allowed to migrate to the United States in any one year.[53] In 1930, owing to the economic effects of the Depression, President Herbert Hoover tightened even these provisions still further, making it mandatory that a would-be immigrant not become a public charge.[54] Hoover's rule was, however, liberalised considerably in 1936–8 by Franklin D. Roosevelt when the harsh interpretation of this rule by German consular officials dealing with Jewish refugees was brought to his attention.[55]

There seems little doubt, however, that in the early days of the Nazi period, intending refugee migrants to the United States were met with severe obstacles, as well as an application form of singular length and formidability. America's Congress adamantly refused to increase the refugee immigration quotas, and there seems little doubt that no popular majority existed in the United States for immigration liberalisation during the Depression although, paradoxically, all public opinion surveys revealed (as will be discussed) near-universal detestation of Nazi Germany. On the other hand, the existence of a strict quota also meant that the United States could not fail to admit *some* Jews (and others), regardless of the intention of America's nativists, while political pressure could – and eventually did – ensure that Jews were admitted up to the maximum quota limit.

As with the case of Britain, it is most important to keep in mind that the enactment of the quota system in 1921–4 meant the end of America as an auto-matic place of entry for any refugees (or any other would-be immigrants), not only Jewish refugees or refugees from Germany. The Soviet Union's annual quota of only 2,712 meant that anti-Communist Russians were unable to migrate in any numbers, while the quota for the whole of Asia, 1,649 immigrants *per annum*, excluded all but trivial numbers of Armenians, Kurds, Chinese fleeing Japanese imperialism, and many other groups. Spain's quota was only 252 persons per year, meaning that the tens of thousands of persons fleeing from the Spanish Civil War could find no refuge in the United States; in fact, fewer than one thousand persons were admitted to the United States from Spain in the four years 1936–9, when the Spanish Civil War was raging.[56] In contrast, the numbers of Jewish refugees admitted from Germany and the Reich were vastly larger, and represented a concerted and deliberate effort to allow these refugees into the United States because of the odium attaching to the Nazi regime and its persecution of the Jews. Of course, we now know that those trapped behind in the Reich were likely to have been murdered, and thus that their need was greater than the need of other refugee groups, but their eventual fate was unknown to anyone at the time.

The number of German and other Reich Jews admitted to the United States during this period is not absolutely clear. From 1899 until 1943 – most remarkably – the United States Immigration Department recorded the number of 'Hebrews' entering the United States each year by country of origin, although only global figures are available for the years 1933–8. The definition of 'Hebrew' – at the time, a common synonym, or, rather euphemism, for a Jew – is not crystal-clear, although it was apparently meant in an ethnic rather than a religious sense.[57] This information was collected by the captains of all vessels bringing immigrants to the United States; captains were also required to collect similar information on the ethnic identity of all other immigrants. In most cases the designations of ethnic identity employed by the Immigration Bureau were identical to nationalities (for example Mexican, Portuguese, Rumanian), but a number of group designations were those of an ethnic group rather than a nationality, including Armenians, Croatians and Slovenians, Ruthenians, and Slovaks. Italians were sub-divided into 'Italians (north)' and 'Italians (south)'.

This bizarre requirement to collect information on the number of Jewish immigrants, evidently the product of the age of Social Darwinist nativism, was specifically abolished by Earl G. Harrison, Commissioner of the US Immigration and Naturalisation Service, on 8 November 1943, with Jews henceforth being categorised as belonging to the nationality of their country of origin, for example Russians or Germans, or else, in ambiguous cases, as members of the 'White race'.[58] Because of this requirement to collect information on the number of Jews migrating to the United States, apparently complete information for the years 1933–42 exists, although it is arguable that some Jews (especially those classified as 'non-Aryan Christians', persecuted by the Nazis owing to their Jewish origins) were missed, and these figures should be regarded as minimal ones.

Between 1 July 1933 and 30 June 1942 a total of 161,051 Jews migrated to the United States, comprising 35.5 per cent of all migrants (453,205 in all) settling in America in this ten-year period, that is, more than one-third of all immigrants.[59] By year, the number of Jews was as follows:

1933–4	4,134
1934–5	4,837
1935–6	6,252
1936–7	11,352
1937–8	19,736
1938–9	43,450
1939–40	36,945
1940–1	23,737
1941–2	10,608

In both 1938–9 and 1939–40 Jews comprised more than one-half of *all* immigrants admitted to the United States – respectively 52.4 and 52.2 per cent, and were the largest single group identified by the Immigration Department in every year from 1936–7 until 1941–2. In 1938–9, for instance, nearly nine times as many Jews emigrated to the United States as those designated as 'English', who numbered only 5,076. By any standard, these are impressive figures, given the upward limits on the number of migrants permitted to enter the United States and bearing in mind the fact that Nazi persecution was restricted until 1939 to the Reich alone. They are plainly inconsistent with any charge of pervasive anti-semitism, whatever anti-semitism may have existed in individual cases.

Not all of these Jews were, however, necessarily German Jews, and the totals of German and other Reich Jews were lower than these figures suggest, although how much lower is not entirely clear. As noted, the German quota was set at 25,957, but this was merged, on 28 April 1938, with the Austrian quota of 1,413, making an enlarged quota of 27,370 for the post-*Anschluss* Reich.[60] The number of Jews ('Hebrews') admitted from Germany is not available until the year 1937–8; from then until 1941–2 such data is available, but it may well be a significant understatement, since the available statistics refer to the 'country of last residence' of immigrants, and denote very large numbers of Jewish migrants as having been resident in such places as Canada, Great Britain, 'other European countries and so on, many of whom may well be German Jews.

Information also exists for these years regarding the number of 'Germans' who migrated to the United States, given as a category separate from the number of 'Hebrews'. Again, some of these may well have been 'non-Aryan Christians' or persons of partially Jewish descent. For what they are worth, the available statistics for 'Hebrews' and Germans giving their 'country of last residence' as Germany in these years is shown in Table 4.

In addition, Jews emigrating from Czechoslovakia were as follows: 1938–9, 1,650; 1939–40, 704; 1940–1, 230; 1941–2, 93. This suggests that a total of

Table 4

Year	Jews	Germans
1937–8	11,917	5,059
1938–9	30,096	3,144
1939–40	19,880	1,470
1940–1	3,793	191
1941–2	2,067	73

67,753 Jews and 9,937 other Germans migrated from Germany in this period, although the data here are probably an understatement of the true picture.

Critics of America's immigration policies during this period have often focused upon the fact that Germany's quota was underfilled until 1939. In 1937, for instance, only 11,520 persons migrated to the United States from Germany, only 42 per cent of the possible total of 25,957 set by the 1924 quota.[61] Critics of American policy have often attributed this to the 'paper walls' erected by America's consular bureaucracy in Germany, walls which were removed only at the last possible moment, when a vast tide of desperate refugees resulted, at last, in some humanitarianism being introduced into America's harsh immigration administration. There is, of course, an element of truth in this, and many individual cases of bureaucratic pettifoggery and narrow-mindedness, strongly suggestive of anti-semitism, can doubtless be found. Yet this begs perhaps the central question, a question which all critics of the refugee policies of the democracies during these years should certainly address and answer: how many German Jews had actually applied, at any particular point during the years of Nazi rule, to enter the United States (or any other country), but were denied entry through bureaucratic harshness or anti-semitism? No definitive data is available to answer this question, but such information as does exist strongly suggests that the answer is that, until *Kristallnacht*, many fewer German Jews actually wished to enter the United States than one would assume.

On 17 November 1938 – that is, just after *Kristallnacht* – Frances Perkins, the American Secretary of Labor, stated that the German–Austrian immigrant quota was then filled 'for at least fourteen months'.[62] In other words, at this time perhaps only *32,000* Germans and Austrians (Jews and non-Jews) had actually applied to migrate to the United States.[63] At the time perhaps 250,000 Jews remained in Germany and 125,000 in Austria. During the early period of Nazi rule, the number of German Jews who applied to migrate was, almost certainly, much smaller still, and the fact that the quota figure was not met until amazingly late must be attributed in large part to the unwillingness of Germany's Jews to apply to migrate to the United States until the very last moment. If these figures are accurate, one must of course ask why so few Jews actually applied to migrate to the United States until nearly midnight. The primary reason, it would seem, was the widespread belief that Nazi anti-semitism would sooner or later pass, combined with the host of cultural and economic reasons noted above; additionally, America was frequently seen as a nation of hucksters, gangsters and cowboys which had been especially hard-hit by the Depression and whose national ethos was virtually the exact reverse of that traditionally found in Germany's orderly and civilised society. American Jewry, too, it must be remembered, was dominated by Yiddish-speaking eastern European immigrants and their children, so different from the Jewish community of pre-1933 Germany.

Despite all this, the United States took in very significant numbers of Jewish refugees; their numbers increased markedly from 1938 onwards and then continued after the outbreak of the European war until late 1941, when it, too, ceased. Yehuda Bauer states that 4,150 persons migrated from Germany to the United States from July–December 1941.[64] The United States (as well as Britain and other countries) also admitted large numbers of cultural refugees from Nazism, Jewish and non-Jewish. Many of these were leftists in politics, cultural bohemians or pioneers of fields ranging from psychoanalysis to sociology with which American conservatives and nativists were uncomfortable or towards which they were overtly hostile. Yet thousands of cultural exiles found refuge in the United States, hundreds finding academic positions in America despite the depressed university market of the 1930s and competition from qualified American scholars. Some German Jewish refugee scholars became virtually the only Jewish faculty members at Protestant American colleges where, as Anthony Heilbut has written of the historian Hans Kohn at Smith College in Massachusetts, he became 'the representative of European culture . . . the embodiment of the refugee's plight'.[65] The world-renowned luminaries like Einstein, Schoenberg and the non-Jewish Thomas Mann had little or no trouble emigrating to America, where they came to symbolise both the barbarism of Nazi Germany and the best aspects of American democracy. Nor, should one forget, did barriers exist to exclude radicals and 'trouble-makers' such as Hannah Arendt, Theodore Adorno, Herbert Marcuse or the non-Jewish Bertolt Brecht. America's record in its reception of refugees from Nazi Germany was far from perfect, but, on any objective analysis, in the context of the evils of the Nazi regime as they were known at the time – and not with post-Holocaust eyes – it is far better than its critics maintain.

There were, as well, three or four other significant areas of the settlement of refugees from Nazi Germany before the war. Latin America took a surprising number of refugees, despite its remoteness and the enactment of explicitly or implicitly anti-semitic measures in many countries. Scant information exists, however, as to the precise figure, with estimates ranging from 37,000 to 84,000 for all of South and Central America, with 52,000 as the median estimate.[66] By country, the best estimates of Jewish migration during these years are as follows: Argentina, 20–30,000; Brazil, 12–15,000; Chile, 12,500; Colombia, 5,000 (plus 'non-Aryan Christians'); Cuba, 10–12,000; Ecuador, 3,000; Uruguay, 3,500; Peru, 600–2,000; Paraguay 1,000, with smaller numbers coming to other countries.[67]

In 1938–9 a number of events occurred in Latin America which augured well for Jewish refugees. In Brazil, where a deep cultural and political battle over Jewish immigration was fought out during the 1930s, a distinct liberalisation occurred in 1938–9, due chiefly to American pressure and to the appointment of Oswaldo Aranha as Brazil's Foreign Minister the previous year.[68] While the total of 4,601 Jews entering Brazil in 1939 seems small, this was a higher total than in any previous year since 1929.[69] Of this number 2,899 came from Germany.[70] For Bolivia, where immigration from all sources had been limited to only 250 persons per month, some 7,000 Jews entered in the first three-quarters of 1939.[71] By 1939, according to Eric D. Kohler, Bolivia's Jewish population had grown from 250 in 1933 to 30,000.[72]

Probably the best known of Latin American rescue opportunities just before the war occurred in the Dominican Republic, where that country's dictator, Rafael Trujillo, offered at the Evian Conference of 1938 to admit up to 100,000 German refugees.[73] This offer was, apparently, a perfectly serious one, which was 'unanimously approved' by the Dominican parliament.[74] A Dominican Republic Settlement Association Inc. was established, and acquired 22,230 acres at Sousa, on the Republic's north coast.[75] Owing to delays caused by the outbreak of the war, refugees did not arrive until 1940, and only 705 Jews passed through the settlement.[76] Nevertheless, about 5,000 Dominican visas were actually issued, allowing their holders – in some cases – to emigrate elsewhere.[77] If the Dominican scheme had become operational, it alone would have provided a place of refuge for the great majority of Jews remaining within the pre-1933 boundaries of Germany, as improbable and unsatisfactory as refuge in an impoverished Caribbean island might have seemed to them.

The first places of emigration of German Jews, especially during the early days of the Nazi regime were other continental European countries. They were close to Germany, less expensive to reach, and were often chosen as places of refuge to facilitate return to Nazi Germany once Hitler's anti-semitism and totalitarianism had 'blown over'. When the non-Jewish Marxist Bertolt Brecht went into exile in 1933, he is reported to have told another émigré: 'Don't go far away. In five years we will be back.'[78] In the first years of his exile, 1933–5, he lived in Prague, Vienna and Zurich.[79] This was fairly common, though doubtless Brecht's own case was unusual. While between 72 and 77 per cent of German Jews fled to other European countries in 1933, Hitler's first year of power, this declined to only 15 per cent in 1937–8.[80]

France was, in some respects, an exception to the pattern of the raising of barriers to refugee migration after the First World War which occurred in the English-speaking world. France traditionally welcomed refugees and, as Hope Simpson has observed, 'there has always been a return to liberal thinking' after the two observable outbreaks of inter-war anti-refugee feeling, in 1934–5, and 1937.[81] The Decree Law of 2 May 1938 restated France's humane practice towards refugees; that 'the doors of France still stood wide open to persecuted people asking for asylum' at this date is his verdict.[82] In late 1938 Hope Simpson estimated the total number of refugees in France as 180,000, including anti-Communist Russians, Armenians, Italians and Spaniards, as well as German Jews.[83]

By the third quarter of 1933 France had accepted as many as 50–60,000 Jewish refugees from Germany, of whom over 20,000 quickly moved on to other countries such as Palestine.[84] In 1938 there were apparently about 10–15,000 German Jewish refugees in France, 70–75 per cent in the Paris area.[85] Refugee migration was relatively easy until late 1938, when the French government began to signal that it intended to place barriers in the way of future large-scale immigration.[86] Yet by early 1939 there were 25,000 Reich Jews living in France, including 2,000 from Czechoslovakia.[87] On the eve of the war France probably had about 40,000 refugees from Germany, although some estimates were as high as 60,000.[88]

Significant numbers of German Jews also migrated to other countries. About 15,000 entered Belgium between 1933 and September 1938. There were 25,000 refugee Jews present in Belgium in March 1939, with 400 more entering each week.[89] Approximately 6,500 Jews entered Czechoslovakia between 1933 and 1936. Ten to twelve thousand were present in the Netherlands in February 1939. Rather remarkably, 6,000 refugee Jews were present in Italy in September 1938, when Mussolini's adoption of anti-semitic legislation (for the first time) led to 10,000 Italian Jews fleeing the country by September 1939.[90] Switzerland, known for its harsh restrictions on migrants, nevertheless took in 10,000 German refugees by mid-1938 (with another 3–4,000 from Austria), while 10–12,000 Reich Jews were present there in late 1938 and early 1939.[91]

The third area of refugee migration was the British Commonwealth, apart from Britain itself and the Mandate of Palestine. English-speaking, politically liberal and stable, and economically advanced, such countries as Canada and even remote Australia appeared as relatively attractive places of refuge once (but not necessarily before) it became evident that German Jewry had no future under a Nazi regime. Unfortunately, in most of the independent Dominions, the refugees had to contend with unusually severe nativist pressures, with conservative politicians who viewed most foreigners, and especially European Jews, as Marxists and agitators, and with economic conditions which, during the Depression, deteriorated even more harshly than elsewhere. Most of these Dominions retreated, after the First World War, from the left-liberal progressive ideologies often to be found there in the late Victorian and Edwardian period – for instance in Australia, 'the paradise of the working-man' – to a particularly narrow, introspective conservatism which was fearful of foreigners, modernism and all radical doctrines. Several of the Dominions, notably South Africa and Canada, contained large and important non-Anglo-Saxon groups with traditions of anti-semitism not found in the English-speaking population. On the other hand, in most of the Dominions there was a well-established Jewish community which was almost always perceived in a friendly and benign light. A sharp distinction was characteristically drawn between 'good Jews' – those of long residence and acculturation in that country – and 'bad Jews', those of European, especially German, Polish and Russian, extraction, particularly radicals.[92] In Australia, which exhibited all these features, Sir John Monash, Commander-in-Chief of Australia's armies in France during the First World War, was probably the first Jewish general of modern times. He was universally regarded as Australia's greatest national hero, and his funeral procession in 1931 was a national event '[as] if the King had died'.[93] Australia's Governor-General (head of state) from 1931–5, Sir Isaac Isaacs, was also a Jew. There were, in Australia and elsewhere, plenty of liberal anti-Nazi and philo-semitic opinion-makers who wished to open doors to increased Jewish refugee migration.

The results of these cross-pressures were felt in different ways throughout the Dominions. In South Africa, about 6,000 Jews arrived, almost all before extremist Afrikaaner pressure led to a sharp decline in refugee migration in 1937.[94] Canada, too, was subject to extreme nativist and even anti-semitic pressure, especially from Quebec, and limited the number of Jewish refugees to perhaps 6–8,000.[95] Australia admitted perhaps 9,000, and agreed in 1938 to admit 15,000 over the next three years, the first time Australia had ever admitted a group of refugees as such.[96] The outbreak of the war put a stop to these plans. Smaller numbers were admitted elsewhere – 5,000 to the Irish Free State, 1,000 or so to New Zealand and so on; often, Britain's Dominion Office did everything possible to induce its former colonies to accept greater numbers.[97] All in all, probably 40–45,000 refugee Jews found safety in the British Empire apart from Britain itself and Palestine.

The final place of refuge was Shanghai, which was renowned at the time as being the only place in the world not requiring an entry visa for immigrants. Reich Jews began arriving there soon after *Kristallnacht*, and by August 1939 about 14,000 refugees had arrived there. By December 1941 their number had risen to 17,000, including newer refugees from Poland and elsewhere.[98] Refugees continued to arrive until Japan entered the war in December 1941, by which time Jews were, almost without exception, forbidden to leave Nazi-occupied Europe in any case. A census of 1944 revealed that there were 13,496 Jewish refugees in Shanghai, of whom 8,114 were Germans, 3,942 Austrians, 1,248 Poles and 236 Czechs.[99]

With post-Holocaust hindsight, there is, of course, virtually no country which cannot be criticised for erecting pointlessly high barriers for those faced – it transpired – with certain death. Such a view is profoundly ahistorical, for no one at this time – that is, until the invasion of the Soviet Union in June 1941 – could foresee genocide as the end result of Nazi anti-semitism. Such a view is, as well, misleading on a number of other grounds. First, although virtually every country admitted only limited numbers of Jews and refugees, *collectively* the democracies and other nations and places from Latin America to Shanghai admitted a great many: as noted at the outset, 72 per cent of all Jews within the pre-1933 boundaries of Germany managed to emigrate. Much of the profoundly wrong-headed historical analysis of this question is, in my view, due in fact to viewing the efforts of each country in isolation – when they invariably appear half-hearted and lacklustre – rather than as an international effort in which many nations did their share. Second, the time factor, and the extreme reluctance of German Jews to migrate prior to *Kristallnacht*, have been given insufficient weight in most *post hoc* analyses.

In effect, the democracies had less than a year to evacuate the bulk of Germany's Jews, a number growing rapidly through Germany's conquests of Austria and Czechoslovakia. That they succeeded as well as they did is prima facie evidence of the sympathy which Jewish persecution aroused. As noted, too, for the most part the English-speaking world had pointedly disowned its tradition of liberality towards large-scale refugee migration after the First World War but before the Nazi period, and the large numbers of German and other Reich Jewish refugees who were allowed to settle marked a total reversal of this post-1918 policy; in some cases, for example Australia, it marked the first time a country had admitted refugees as such in its history.

There is another element in the policies of the democracies towards Germany's Jews which is also worthy of some comment. Repeatedly, fears were expressed that an overgenerous response to the plight of those Jews would result in the forced expulsion of other European Jewish populations, especially those of Poland and Rumania. 'What if Poland, Hungary, Rumania also expel their Jewish citizens?' Lord Beaverbrook's *Daily Express* asked in March 1938.[100] These fears are usually dismissed as part and parcel of the 'failure' to rescue, but they are perfectly understandable and eminently reasonable, and should not be disregarded without closer examination. *If* all a country had to do to rid itself of any unwanted portion of its population was to brutalise them, safe in the expectation that the democracies would automatically take them in, then any country with an unscrupulous or ultra-nationalist regime obviously would do so: indeed, it would be foolish for any country with a minority 'problem' to refrain from doing so, especially during a calamitous Depression.

While Jews would certainly have comprised the first wave of those brutalised in eastern Europe, they would not necessarily have been the last: Poland in its 1918–39 boundaries contained 3 million Jews but also 9 million Ukrainians and many others; Rumania held 750,000 Jews, but also several million Hungarians – and so on. If a few pogroms and discriminatory legislation could reopen the doors of Ellis Island, then no ethnic minority in Europe was safe. It is evident that by declining to respond with wholly open doors the democracies deterred the regimes of eastern and central Europe from excessively persecuting their minorities, including especially their Jews, but probably many other groups as well. Indeed, the policies of the democracies possibly had a marginally ameliorative effect upon Nazi anti-semitism before the very end, for – prior to ghettoisation and genocide – the presence of significant numbers of totally impoverished Jews in Germany was a drain upon the Nazi regime's resources. Only when Hitler's maniacal anti-semitism reached its most extreme limits did ideology wholly overrule necessity.

The policies of the democracies in this period were not so different from the policies of the democracies towards the world's refugees today, when (chiefly because of the Holocaust and its lessons) the developed world is much more aware of its responsibilities towards refugees and much more liberal in its refugee policies. With the possible exception of the Federal Republic of Germany since 1949, no country allows any and every refugee to enter without limit: nearly every country imposes numerical quotas and limits upon refugee migration. These limits exist in part to deter the less scrupulous and more impoverished regimes of the world from dumping their unwanted peoples, without limit, on the developed world.

A nation such as Australia (to take one example), whose record on refugees since the 1950s has unquestionably been admirable, normally imposes an annual limit of 10–15,000 refugees permitted to enter. South-east Asian 'boat people' are routinely housed in wretched conditions on Australia's remotest northern coastal areas until their cases are adjudicated, a process which can often take years, and those who cannot prove their refugee status are then sent home forthwith. This policy – which enjoys the support of virtually the whole Australian political spectrum, and was rigidly enforced by the Australian Labor Party during its period of office between 1983–96 – exists quite explicitly to deter more 'boat people' and other 'economic refugees' from arriving. The numerical limits are defined primarily by Australia's economic and social ability to admit these refugees – refugee intake has declined during the recent recession – and without regard to the number of refugees in the world or their plight. Virtually every Western country has a similar arrangement, and internal political pressure on this issue is, certainly, supportive of tightening up immigration restrictions still further rather than liberalising them.

If these immigration restrictions exist and enjoy near-universal support today, why were they immoral and unethical sixty years ago? The one and only reason is that we now know the ultimate fate of those Jews in Nazi-occupied Europe who were unable to reach safety. But – to reiterate – this knowledge was unknown and unknowable to anyone before June 1941 when the mass murders of European Jewry began. Today's refugee policies among the democracies are, in fact, surprisingly similar to those of sixty years ago, however much they possess a more humane face, and simply represent judicious common sense in a radically unequal world. In so far as they prevented radically nationalistic governments from brutalising ethnic minorities with the explicit intention of forcing the democracies to admit those persecuted peoples without limit, they were actually instrumental in diminishing and deterring racial and religious persecution, compelling ultra-nationalistic movements to desist from persecuting minorities beyond endurance. In the Nazi case, they were probably helpful in diminishing the persecution of the Jews until Hitler's monomaniacal anti-semitism went beyond any limits imposed by Western civilisation.

Nothing, of course, can adequately summarise the anguish, despair and panic of Germany's Jews, especially after *Kristallnacht* when most of them literally searched through world maps and atlases to find somewhere that would admit them. As well, there are many legitimate criticisms which might be made regarding the rescue of Jews in the Reich before the outbreak of the war, although these shortcomings – like everything else concerned with this subject – appear much more reprehensible in hindsight than they did at the time. There was never a concerted, coordinated international effort to rescue Germany's Jews. All such schemes foundered on the refusal of the Nazi regime to agree to 'orderly' emigration, on the increase in the number of Jews under Hitler's control after 1938 and on the fact that Nazi policy did not fully exclude Germany's Jews from national life until *Kristallnacht*, less than a year before the war began. The schemes foundered, too, on the inability of the democracies to coordinate efforts, the United States being stymied by its refusal to raise the German quota, and Britain by the Palestinian question. Centrally, however, such schemes as the 'Schacht Plan' for the orderly emigration of most German Jews failed because Hitler continuously radicalised his anti-semitism, especially as war approached.

Within Germany, not all Jews were equal in their access to the means of emigration. By and large, the higher one was on the socio-economic and educational scale, the less trouble one had in emigrating. For example, university professors and ministers of religion (including rabbis) were allowed to migrate to the United States outside the normal quota system.[101] There were certain exceptions to this: physicians often had a difficult time in emigrating because of obstacles placed in their way by local medical associations fearing competition, but even so most German Jewish physicians probably did escape. A total of 3,097 Jewish refugee physicians succeeded in migrating to the United States between 1933 and 1940, where fifteen states (including New York, Illinois and California) allowed non-citizen physicians to practice.[102] Normally, however, high-status professionals and industrialists had little trouble in finding somewhere to go. After the mid-1930s, preference was given by German Jewish bodies, wherever possible, to children and youth, and various *Kindertransporten* were organised, meaning that, as noted, virtually all German Jewish children had emigrated before the walls went up.

Who was left behind? Disproportionately, they were the elderly and women, although just before the war working-age women emigrated in large numbers as domestic servants. One-half of those remaining in the Reich at the outbreak of the war were over 50.[103] Others remained behind because of close ties to elderly relatives who could not leave.[104] Another category probably overrepresented among those left behind were Jews from small towns. Jews from cities of less than 100,000 inhabitants comprised only about 10 per cent of a sample of refugees in Britain, compared with 33 per cent of all Jews in Germany in 1933. Forty-nine per cent came from Berlin, compared with 31 per cent of all Jews in 1933.[105]

An interesting essay by Henry R. Huttenbach has looked in detail on the process of emigration from the German city of Worms. Between 1933 and November 1938 the Jewish population of Worms declined from 1,104 to only 370. Of the 726 Jews who had left the city, 517 had emigrated abroad.[106] A further ninety-two Jews emigrated between *Kristallnacht* and September 1939, the largest number of whom (thirty-two) went to England, and another thirty-three left (sixteen to the United States) between September 1939 and October 1941, when emigration became all but impossible.[107] Through deaths in the community, only 191 Jews remained behind at the time, 17.3 per cent of the total there in 1933.[108] Remarkably, even in March 1940, thirty had no plans to emigrate. Almost all were elderly.[109] The others had arranged to emigrate, chiefly to the United States, but were prevented from doing so by the end of Jewish emigration. Of the 161 remaining behind, five were children, eighty-eight were adult women, fifty-eight adult men. Only thirty were under 40 years of age.[110] Precisely three Jews were alive in Worms on V-E Day; 142 had been killed and sixteen more 'disappeared'.[111] The Jews of Worms who perished were, however, unreachable and beyond rescue by anything the Allies could possibly have done apart from winning the war even sooner. Responsibility for their deaths lies totally and wholly with Adolf Hitler and the Nazi barbarians; given what was known at the time and what could be done, most of Worms' Jews – and others throughout the Reich – managed to emigrate in a rescue operation that was both generous and successful.

A major reason for the relative generosity and success of the democracies in admitting German and other Reich Jews during these years was the genuine loathing and detestation felt by both elites and opinion-leaders in the democracies, and by the average person, for both Nazism and Nazi anti-semitism. It was this loathing, above everything else, which allowed most German Jews to emigrate, despite the unpopularity of foreign immigration during the Depression and in contrast to other refugee groups. As with so many other aspects of this subject, virtually all accounts of the treatment of Germany's Jews by the democracies view this question in a manner which is almost the precise opposite of the truth, focusing on fringe extremists such as Father Charles E. Coughlin in the United States and Sir Oswald Mosley in Britain, and wholly missing the impressive and convincing evidence which exists of the detestation of Nazism and sympathy for the plight of the Jews. From the first day of Nazi power in January 1933, detailed, lurid and revolting accounts of Nazi excesses and brutality were reported on a day-to-day basis throughout the democratic world. These were supplemented by movie newsreels – newsreels of book-burnings, vandalism against Jewish properties, Hitler's maniacal rallies and speeches and of the obviously aggressive military build-up of Germany's armies – which millions of ordinary people in the democracies viewed at the cinema on a weekly basis, perhaps the first time in history that a totalitarian regime could be seen with the immediacy of the movie camera.

It is widely supposed that American public opinion in the late 1930s showed a lack of sympathy for the plight of Germany's Jews, a product of the endemic social and economic anti-semitism which is often said to have pervaded such fields as the admission of Jews to 'elite' universities, restrictions on the sale of upper-class real estate to Jews and their hiring by well-established companies and firms. Whatever the extent of American social and economic anti-semitism during the 1930s, however, there is remarkably little evidence from public opinion survey data of the time to support the view of endemic anti-semitism or pro-Nazism. Very surprisingly, the precise opposite appears to have been the case, and the weight of survey data shows instead a remarkable degree of American hostility to Nazism and the oppression it inflicted. These findings have been almost wholly ignored by historians, perhaps because they sit so uncomfortably with the popular image of America as having 'done nothing' for the refugees, with anti-semitism seen as an important element in this attitude.

From 1935 the George Gallup polling agency conducted many surveys of American public opinion on the major issues of the day. *Without exception* those taken on issues relating to Nazi Germany in the years before the outbreak of the war demonstrate overwhelming – often almost unanimous – hostility by American public opinion to the Hitler regime. The most significant survey question (and the only one to touch directly on American attitudes towards Nazi persecution of the

Jews) was taken on 24–29 November 1938 (two weeks after *Kristallnacht*), and asked: 'Do you approve or disapprove of the Nazi treatment of Jews in Germany?' The results were as follows: Approve, 6 per cent; Disapprove, 94 per cent.[112] During November 1938, the Gallup agency also asked Americans: 'If there were a war between Germany and Russia, which side would you rather see win?' Despite America's pervasive anti-Communism and the adverse publicity generated by Stalin's Purges, the results here were almost equally striking: Russia, 83 per cent; Germany, 17 per cent.[113]

Every question asked by the Gallup agency during this period revealed very similar patterns of public opinion. A month earlier, Americans were asked: 'Chancellor Hitler says that he has no more territorial ambitions in Europe. Do you believe him?' Eight per cent of respondents replied 'yes', 92 per cent 'no'.[114] Also in October 1938, respondents were asked: 'Which European country do you like best?' Great Britain topped the list with 48 per cent of the vote, followed by France, with 12 per cent, and Switzerland with 6 per cent. Germany received only 4 per cent of the vote, and Russia only 2 per cent.[115] In November 1938 Americans were asked: 'Would you join in a movement in this country to stop buying German-made goods?' Apart from the Jewish community and other dedicated anti-Nazis, no one at this time was seriously advocating such a boycott, while most Americans, it is believed, wanted desperately to avoid another European entanglement. But the results were as follows: 61 per cent, 'yes'; 39 per cent, 'no'. Not surprisingly, Jews overwhelmingly supported a boycott, by 96:4 per cent, but Protestants also supported an anti-Nazi boycott by 64:36 per cent, and Catholics by an identical 64:36 per cent.[116]

In August 1939, Gallup asked: 'Do you think Hitler's claims to Danzig are justified?' It found that 13 per cent of Americans believed that they were, while 87 per cent replied 'no' to this question.[117] In early September 1939 the Gallup poll asked respondents 'Which country or countries do you consider responsible for causing the present war?' (hostilities had just broken out). 'Germany' was named by 82 per cent of respondents, compared with 3 per cent naming 'England and France', 3 per cent naming the 'Versailles Treaty' and 1 per cent naming 'Poland'.[118] A month later, the survey asked: 'Which side do you want to see win the war?' Eighty-two per cent named the 'Allies', only 2 per cent 'Germany', with 14 per cent neutral.[119]

In late April and early May 1941 respondents were asked whether they were 'familiar with the views which Charles A. Lindbergh has expressed concerning American foreign policy' and whether or not they agreed with them. By April 1941 Lindbergh, the celebrated aviator, was among the best-known and most vocal supporters of isolationism in the United States. He had lived for some months in Germany in 1938 and had frequently met Nazi leaders (although not Hitler). Lindbergh had spoken at several large America First rallies shortly before this poll was taken, attacking American aid for beleaguered Britain. This time, however, he had not yet made his notorious Des Moines, Iowa speech of 11 September 1941 naming 'the three most important groups who have been pressing the country toward war' as 'the British, the Jewish [*sic*], and the Roosevelt Administration'.[120] Lindbergh's strident isolationism was, however, rejected by a large majority of Americans who had heard of them. Among the 58 per cent of respondents who were 'familiar' with his views, only 24 per cent agreed with them, compared with 63 per cent who disagreed, and 13 per cent of 'no opinion'.[121]

In September 1938 a special survey was conducted among American lawyers, asking them 'Whom would you like to see President Roosevelt nominate to the Supreme Court?' By far the most popular single choice was Felix Frankfurter, named by 27 per cent of those surveyed, followed very distantly by Learned Hand and John W. Davis with 5 per cent each.[122] Harvard's renowned Jewish legal scholar was in fact appointed, serving with great distinction until the 1960s. In January 1939, Gallup specifically asked whether the newly appointed Frankfurter 'will make a good United States Supreme Court Justice?' Eighty-two per cent of respondents replied 'yes' and only 18 per cent 'no'.[123]

It might be imagined from these figures that most respondents adopted a hostile stance towards Nazi Germany and showed sympathy for persecuted Jews for fear of appearing bigoted to the pollsters or through some foretaste of what is now termed 'political correctness'. If true, this would itself be significant, but respondents in the Gallup surveys of this period showed much greater conservatism on a variety of other issues. In January 1937, Gallup asked interviewees: 'Would you vote for a woman for President, if she qualified in every other respect?' Only 34 per cent of respondents answered 'yes', compared with 66 per cent who answered 'no'.[124] In February of the same year, Gallup surveyed attitudes towards the parole system. Asked if the parole system 'helps to restore prisoners to a useful place in society', 46 per cent responded affirmatively, while 54 per cent answered in the negative. Eighty-two per cent of respondents believed that parole boards should be 'more strict', only 3 per cent that they should be less so.[125] Asked in October 1937 for their opinions on a federal anti-lynching law, 53 per cent of respondents approved of such a bill, 47 per cent opposed it.[126]

Many other examples of a considerable degree of American conservatism on social and political issues could be cited. Hostility to Nazi Germany and revulsion at its anti-semitic excesses were thus not necessarily part of a predominant left-liberalism ascendant at the time, but particular exceptions to a much more ambiguous pattern. Both Nazi Germany and Nazi anti-semitism were thus genuinely *un*popular in the United States in the period when Hitler appeared to be moving effortlessly from triumph to triumph.

Gallup made few other queries during the Nazi era of relevance to the Jewish situation, but in 1944 and 1945 he asked two further questions which it is highly relevant to note explicitly. In November 1944 – after the Holocaust had been in the news for two years, but before the concentration camps had been liberated (and photographed) – Gallup asked: 'Do you believe the stories that the Germans have murdered many people in concentration camps?' This survey found that 76 per cent of respondents answered 'yes', 12 per cent 'no', while 12 per cent had 'no opinion'. Interestingly, results were very similar in each region of the United States, with respondents in the South, for instance, demonstrating a 77:9:14 percentage distribution.[127] In early May 1945, just at the time of V-E Day, Gallup asked: 'What do you think of the reports that the Germans killed many people in concentration camps or let them starve to death – are they true or not true?' The results here were as follows:[128]

True	84 %
True, but exaggerated	9 %
Doubtful, hard to believe	1 %
Not true	3 %
Can't decide	3 %

Other surveys of American opinion during the Nazi era pointed to very similar conclusions, with opinion-leaders and public notables likely to be even more strongly anti-Nazi than American public opinion as a whole. In June 1936, the Non-Sectarian Anti-Nazi League to Champion Human Rights, a coordinating body dedicated to mobilising opposition to the Hitler regime, sent a questionnaire to 4,000 notable Americans, asking them whether the American people should 'join in an effort to protest Hitlerism'. If so, should there be a 'general boycott of German goods'? And if not, 'what alternatives do you suggest?'[129] Those surveyed included all state governors, senators and congressmen, university presidents, writers, clergymen, professors, publishers, prominent businessmen and others comprising a cross-section of America's leadership elite and opinion-makers. Seventy-one per cent of responses supported the prosecution of a boycott, with 'only a few' calling for a 'hands-off policy'. Only one response, out of 4,000, 'might have been construed as approving Hitlerism'.[130] To be sure, some opinion-leaders (especially politicians) might well have told an organisation known as the Anti-Nazi League what it wished to hear, but it is difficult to believe that most of these persons were not expressing sincere feelings of disgust. The opinions of the American leadership elite in this matter also mirrored the sentiments of American public opinion as a whole, as measured by Gallup surveys on the issue.

Other polling agencies which surveyed American opinion on these questions reported very similar results. In 1937 and 1938, for instance, the American Institute of Public Opinion (an affiliate of the Gallup organisation) asked: 'Do you think there is likely to be a widespread campaign against Jews in this country?'[131] The results are shown in Table 5.

Table 5

Date	Yes	No	No opinion
April 1938	19 %	81 %	14 %
March 1939	20 %	65 %	15 %
May 1939	19 %	70 %	11 %

Respondents were then asked, 'Would you support such a campaign?' The results are shown in Table 6.

Table 6

Date	Yes	No	No opinion
April 1938	12 %	88 %	7 %
March 1939	12 %	80 %	8 %
May 1939	12 %	78 %	10 %

The March 1939 sample was then asked further 'How strongly do you feel about this?' The results are shown in Table 7.

Table 7

Intensity of feeling	Yes	No
Strongly	6 %	49 %
Mildly	6 %	22 %
No answer	(Less than 0.5%)	9 %
Total	12 %	80 %

From all these studies, it appears clear that hard-core anti-semites in the United States comprised perhaps 5–12 per cent of the population, with 70–90 per cent (or more) of the American people being avowedly opposed to anti-semitism. The significance of the anti-semitic proportion of the American population was probably enhanced by the control exercised in Congress by hard-core nativists, especially southern 'Dixiecrat' anti-semites, and by the publicity generated by anti-semitic propagandists such as Father Coughlin.

The patterns in all these surveys and polls are so striking that they seem un-questionably to point, without any exception, to an astonishing degree of American sensitivity to anti-semitism and hostility to Nazi oppression.[132] They seem sharply, indeed signally, to contradict the widespread image of American indifference to the fate of the Jews or indeed a sneaking admiration for Hitler, even if he 'went too far'. One reason for this image is the well-known, often quoted results of another public opinion survey which provided a sharply deviating response to the central question of refugee migration to the United States at this time.[133]

In July 1938 (several months before *Kristallnacht*) *Fortune* magazine, as part of its quarterly survey of American public opinion, asked: 'What is your attitude toward allowing German, Austrian, and other political refugees to come to the U.S.?'[134] The results were as follows:

We should encourage them to come even if we have to raise our immigration quotas	4.9 %
We should allow them to come but not raise our immigration quotas	18.2 %
With conditions as they are we should try to keep them out	67.4 %
Don't know	9.5 %

Fortune provided few other details about the survey. It did note that, not surprisingly, Jewish respondents included in the survey comprised an 'exception' to the overall pattern, with 'only 18.4 per cent of them . . . for the exclusion of refugees'.[135] *Fortune* also noted that respondents on the 'Pacific Coast' were the 'least exclusionist', but that, even so, fully 60.9 per cent were opposed to refugee immigration. *Fortune*'s surveys were conducted by a group of market researchers including Elmo Roper, and (like the Gallup polls at the same time) differed from today's survey techniques in attempting to poll a quota of respondents by matching their geographical and socio-economic characteristics with national census results. It was not a random sample in the modern sense.[136] Nevertheless, it was surprisingly accurate, predicting in October 1936 that Franklin Roosevelt would be reelected with 61.7 per cent of the vote, compared with his actual total of 60.5 per cent.[137]

It is not necessarily quibbling over semantics to question the precise terminology of the *Fortune* survey, which did not use the word 'Jew' but instead mentioned specifically 'political' rather than 'racial' or 'religious' refugees. Similarly the wording 'German, Austrian, and *other*' refugees was something of a red herring. To many respondents, the term 'political refugees' might well have suggested such groups as left-wing fighters in the Spanish Civil War, Stalin's Marxist opponents in Russia and Communist non-Jewish opponents of Hitler, whose entry to America would have been considered undesirable on purely political grounds, and not the persecuted Jews of the Reich as such. Nevertheless, it must be assumed that the *Fortune* survey of American opinion at this time was reasonably accurate, and that, in the context of the Depression, only a minority of Americans were willing to admit significantly more refugees. This was so regardless of how much the survey research, far more extensive and equally valid, revealed their strong detestation of Nazi anti-semitism and other policies of the Hitler regime. It thus seems clear that no popular base existed for a rise in America's refugee intake at that time (although the situation might well have changed after *Kristallnacht*), a fact of life which politicians were compelled to take into account.

This striking dichotomy in American attitudes certainly did not occur uniquely in relation to Jewish refugees from Nazi Germany. In the 1990s, for instance, strong domestic pressures certainly existed in the United States to cut America's annual immigration quotas significantly, while at the same time it was equally clear that most Americans sincerely deplored the murderous onslaughts which had developed in Bosnia, Rwanda and elsewhere. Many Americans of good will simply did not view the migration to the United States of more than a limited number of the victims of such carnage as a desirable response, or, indeed, appear to have seen a link in their apparently deviant attitudes.

Whatever this cognitive dissonance on refugee immigration, by the end of the inter-war era American public opinion – especially 'elite' opinion, but also mass opinion – had hardened sharply and definitely *against* Nazi anti-semitism. So strong was this sentiment that any *public* expression of anti-semitism by a leading mainstream figure, especially if linked to support for the Nazi regime, became taboo virtually in the same manner as in the post-Holocaust era. (That this occurred at the same time as public sentiment still apparently opposed the admission of more refugees seems puzzling and unsatisfactory, but it is, nevertheless, an accurate facet of American opinion in this period.)

One striking instance of the growing American taboo on overt anti-semitism which occurred during this period was the reaction to Charles Lindbergh's notorious 'Jewish race' speech delivered at Des Moines three months before the attack on Pearl Harbor. Lindbergh, the first man to fly solo across the Atlantic Ocean, was an authentic American folk-hero, a status only augmented by the appalling ordeal he and his wife, Anne Morrow Lindbergh, endured during the celebrated kidnapping and murder of their baby in 1936. Although still only 39 in 1941, he was frequently mentioned as a possible future President, and it should be noted that his father had been a prominent Republican congressman from Minnesota. During the 1930s Lindbergh had become closely involved with the isolationist movement, visiting Nazi Germany in 1938 and opposing American lend-lease assistance to Britain. He was probably, to the general public, the best-known member of the America First Committee, the leading isolationist group in the years prior to Pearl Harbor.[138]

Until September 1941 Lindbergh had never mentioned the Jews in any public speech, although his private diaries in the period 1938–41 contain several anti-semitic attacks on 'the Jewish influence in our press, radio, and motion pictures' and the like. They also attacked Nazi Germany for 'unreasonably' dealing with its 'difficult Jewish problem' during *Kristallnacht*.[139] In the Des Moines speech, which as mentioned named the Jews, the British and the Roosevelt administration as the three most important groups pressing the United States to join the war, Lindbergh stated:

> It is not difficult to understand why Jewish people desire the overthrow of Nazi Germany. The persecution they suffered in Germany would be sufficient to make bitter enemies of any race. No person with a sense of the dignity of mankind can condone the persecution of the Jewish race in Germany. But no person of honesty and vision can look on their pro-war policy here today without seeing the dangers involved in such a policy, both for us and for them.
>
> Instead of agitating for war, the Jewish groups in this country should be opposing it in every possible way, for they will be the first to feel its consequences. Toleration is a virtue which depends upon peace and strength. History shows that it cannot survive war and devastation. A few far-sighted Jewish people realise this, and stand opposed to intervention. But the majority still do not. Their greatest danger to this country lies in their large ownership and influence in our motion pictures, our press, our radio, and our Government.[140]

Lindbergh went on to stress that 'I am not attacking either the Jewish or the British people. Both races I admire.'[141]

Those remarks were made in the last months before America entered the war, just after the SS *Einsatzgruppen* had embarked upon the beginnings of genocide in the Soviet Union, but before this was known in the West. Reaction to the remarks was immediate and furious. It is no exaggeration to say that, although he lived for another thirty-three years, Lindbergh's public career came to an abrupt end the moment he delivered his Des Moines speech. 'Rarely has any public address in American history caused more of an uproar, or brought more criticism on any speaker', Wayne S. Cole has commented.[142] Denunciations came immediately from every quarter, and a torrent of editorial abuse and denunciation was voiced by dozens of newspapers. Conservatives and Republicans were no less eager to dissociate themselves from Lindbergh's anti-semitism than were others. Wendell L. Willkie, the Republican party's presidential candidate in 1940, termed it 'the most un-American talk made in my time by any person of national reputation'. Governor Thomas E. Dewey, the Republican presidential candidate in 1944 and 1948, denounced the remarks as 'an inexcusable abuse of the right of freedom of speech'.[143] Rather unexpected sources were aghast at Lindbergh's words. The lower house of the Texas legislature – not a body one would associate in 1941 with left-liberal philo-semitism – 'adopted a resolution advising Lindbergh he was not welcome on any speaking tour he might plan in that state'.[144]

Lindbergh's three paragraphs of apparent public anti-semitism – combined, of course, with the discrediting of his arch-isolationist views after Pearl Harbor – at a stroke made him into a virtual political pariah, a fringe figure beyond the pale. That this occurred in an America where genteel social and economic anti-semitism was still widespread, and where Congress, reflecting public opinion, refused to increase the refugee quota, is strange, even unaccountable. But it is nevertheless true: most definitely, American opinion, especially 'elite' opinion, was repelled by Nazi anti-semitism and genuinely shocked by any public reflection of it in the United States.

Above and beyond America's opinion-leaders there was Franklin D. Roosevelt, America's President. Roosevelt was universally perceived as the Western world's most vigorous and inspiring champion of democracy and an adamant opponent of Hitler. He was also perceived, just as often, as a champion of the Jews and a defender of the Jewish people against Hitler. The New Deal was widely known to extreme right-wingers as the 'Jew Deal' for the large number of Jewish advisers and office-holders it employed. Certainly no previous presidential administration had made so many prominent Jewish appointments, for instance of Henry Morgenthau Jr to the post of Secretary of the Treasury and Felix M. Frankfurter to the Supreme Court.

America's Jews, most of whom were only thirty years removed from the immigrant ships, supported Roosevelt with an even more intense loyalty, delivering to him perhaps 90 per cent of their ethnic vote. Roosevelt brought about a seemingly permanent realignment of the Jewish vote in American politics, so that to the present day over 80 per cent of American Jews normally vote Democratic, despite a socio-economic profile that should naturally make them strongly Republican.

The most notable fact about this love-affair between Roosevelt and America's Jews is that it failed to affect Roosevelt's popularity by even one iota: hostility to Roosevelt based upon political anti-semitism failed to find a constituency in America. In 1936, for instance, Roosevelt received 60.8 per cent of the popular vote and carried forty-six of the forty-eight states. He was opposed by a Republican, Alfred M. Landon, and also by an extreme right-wing candidate, William Lemke of North Dakota, candidate of the Union Party. Lemke was strongly supported by the populist anti-semitic priest and radio broadcaster Father Coughlin, and the Union Party was widely seen as an extension of Coughlin's organisation, the National Union for Social Justice.[145] Though not anti-semitic as such, the Union Party ran on a platform which attacked 'private bankers' and called for strict isolationism in foreign policy.[146] Despite the turmoil caused by the Depression, that party received only 1.96 per cent of the vote, achieving 5 per cent or more of it only in heavily Catholic Massachusetts and Rhode Island,in Lemke's home state of North Dakota and in adjacent Minnesota.[147] In southern states where the party was on the ballot and might be expected to find a constituency, it received derisory shares of the vote, gaining only 0.2 per cent of all presidential votes cast in Alabama and 0.4 per cent in Texas.

As with Roosevelt and the Democratic party (with the exception of hard-core southern racists) so the mainstream of the Republican party was also strongly anti-Nazi and, if anything, even more sensitive to Jewish issues than was Roosevelt. The three Republican presidential candidates of the Nazi period, Landon, Willkie and Dewey, were at all times strongly supportive of petitions and measures aimed at denouncing Nazism and supporting the beleaguered Jews, as were such right-wingers in the party as Herbert Hoover and Robert Taft. Political anti-semitism simply found no mainstream voice in America of the Nazi period, being confined to fringe extremists such as Coughlin and to some (but by no means all) racist southern Congressmen. The overwhelming majority of American politicians were anxious to oppose Nazism and Nazi anti-semitism. That this was consistent with a refusal to lift refugee immigration quotas may strike us as inexplicable, but the anti-Nazi beliefs of America's political notables were sincere and genuine.

Similarly, the American press was, from the first, almost totally hostile to Nazi Germany, especially when the Nazis did something particularly brutal and barbaric. According to Guy Stern, who has studied the burning of books in Nazi Germany in 1933, Americans 'reacted with remarkable and surprising appropriateness' – surprising to those who wrongly believe that most Americans harboured a sneaking admiration for the Nazis – with protests being held in many American cities and editorial denunciations in many newspapers.[148] Deborah E. Lipstadt's *Beyond Belief: The American Press and the Coming of the Holocaust, 1933–1945*, is like so many other works of its genre fundamentally critical of American attitudes, being predicated upon the premises that Americans were remiss for not foreseeing Nazi genocide long before it occurred and that cogent plans for the rescue of Jews by the democracies existed during the war (although none did). Nevertheless, Lipstadt notes time and again the near-universality of American press hostility to Nazi barbarism – often, it might seem, with thinly disguised disappointment that she could find no more anti-semitism than she did. At the time of *Kristallnacht*, as she accurately notes, 'though the press may have offered differing explanations for the pogrom, there was little doubt about its revulsion at Germany'.[149]

The virtual unanimity of American press aversion to Nazi Germany, especially when Hitler escalated his war against the Jews, was, in fact, central and continuous. The American press held a variety of views about almost every issue of the day – much of it was, of course, strongly pro-Republican and often extremely hostile to Roosevelt and the New Deal – but its revulsion at Nazi anti-semitism was a virtual constant from 1933 until 1945. *A fortiori*, too, the American left and its publications such as the *New Republic* and the *Nation*, so influential among intellectuals, were by definition hostile to Nazism.

The situation in Britain offers an almost precise parallel to that in the United States, again in complete contradiction to the most common view of British society at that time. In contrast to the widely held view that the British 'Establishment' was anti-semitic and demonstrated thinly disguised admiration for Hitler, the precise opposite was the case. As in America, virtually all opinion-leaders, intellectuals and politicians were appalled and repelled by Nazi anti-semitism. Repugnance at Nazi treatment of the Jews was a factor, albeit probably a minor one, in Britain's decision to go to war in September 1939. Similarly, such survey evidence as exists shows clearly that the great majority of the British people were anti-Nazi.

Gallup polling began in Britain in January 1937.[150] Before the war only one Gallup poll ever directly surveyed public opinion on the refugee issue, but many questions sought public opinion on attitudes to Nazi anti-semitism and a forth-coming conflict. Invariably, these showed a surprising degree of popular hostility to Nazi Germany, surprising given the commitment of the National Government to Appeasement until the first half of 1939.

The only Gallup poll to survey British attitudes on refugees was taken in July 1939, shortly before the outbreak of the war.[151] Its results were as follows:

Should refugees be allowed to enter Great Britain?

Yes	70 %
No	26 %
No opinion	4 %

Asked of those who responded in the affirmative: should they be allowed to enter freely or with restrictions designed to safeguard British workers and taxpayers?

Freely	15 %
With restrictions	84 %
No opinion	1 %

There was, thus, overwhelming public support for the entry of refugees to Britain, provided this did not disadvantage Britons, a proposition which would self-evidently be assented to by the great majority.

In March 1938 a question was asked as to whether respondents believed that Anthony Eden, the Foreign Secretary, 'was right in resigning' in protest against the government's Appeasement policies. When asked on 5 March 1938, 'yes' respondents totalled 72 per cent, 'no' respondents 18 per cent and 'don't knows' 10 per cent. A week later (12 March 1938), 'yes' respondents rose to 73 per cent while 'no' respondents declined to 13 per cent.[152] Also in March 1938, respon-dents were asked: 'In the present war in Spain, are your sympathies with the government, with Franco, or with neither?' Pro-government responses totalled 57 per cent, pro-Franco supporters only 7 per cent with 36 per cent favouring 'neither'.[153] In October 1938 a question was asked concerning the proposal to hand back Germany's former colonies (such as Tanganyika, seized in 1918), a proposal suggested by Germany and pro-Appeasers. Only 15 per cent were 'in favour of giving back any former German colonies', with 85 per cent opposed. Those who were opposed were then asked: 'Would you rather fight than hand them back?' Seventy-eight per cent answered 'yes', only 22 per cent 'no'.[154]

In March 1939, a Gallup poll asked: 'Would you like to see Great Britain and Soviet Russia being more friendly to each other?' Eighty-four per cent answered 'yes', despite the odium the Soviet Union widely enjoyed; only 7 per cent 'no'.[155] A month later, another poll asked 'Are you in favour of a military alliance between Great Britain, France, and Russia?' To this, 87 per cent answered 'yes', only 7 per cent 'no'.[156] In September 1939, just after the outbreak of the war, a survey asked, 'Would you approve or disapprove if the British government were to discuss peace proposals with Germany now?' Seventy-seven per cent 'disapproved' of this proposition; only 17 per cent 'approved'.[157]

In March 1940, the Gallup organisation asked: 'If a smaller war cabinet were formed for the more active prosecution of the war, which five leaders would you like to see in it?' Sixteen persons were named by 3 per cent or more of the respondents, among them the Prime Minister, Neville Chamberlain (34 per cent) and First World War leader David Lloyd George (29 per cent). Winston Churchill – who became Prime Minister two months later but was at the time only First Lord of the Admiralty – topped the list, named by 67 per cent of respondents, with Anthony Eden a close second at 65 per cent. In third spot, however, was Britain's Jewish Cabinet minister Leslie Hore-Belisha, named by 46 per cent of respondents, far ahead of Clement Attlee, the leader of the Labour Party (24 per cent), Lord Halifax the Foreign Secretary (34 per cent) and a dozen other leading names.

In July 1940, when a German invasion of Britain appeared to be a virtual certainty, the Churchill government interned all enemy aliens (citizens of Germany and its satellites or Italy) resident in Britain. This was a panic measure, motivated by the necessity to rid Britain of any possible 'fifth column' at a time of utmost danger to her survival. Most of these 'dangerous' enemy aliens were Jews and other anti-fascists who had themselves escaped from the Continent one step ahead of the Gestapo; others were 'ordinary' German and Italian tradesmen and their families, who had been long and peacefully resident in Britain. The policy, though understandable in the context of an imminent invasion, was obviously both illogical and, in a very real sense, un-British. It was reversed within a few years – though not before a good deal of harm had been done – and has been condemned by all recent historians.[158]

Internment of all 'enemy aliens', including Jews and anti-Nazis, was demanded by the British press. Nevertheless, a July 1940 Gallup poll found a considerable degree of popular common sense on this issue. It asked:[159]

Which do you think is the wiser course for the government to follow in dealing with enemy aliens: to intern them all; to intern only those who may be unfriendly and dangerous?

Only unfriendly and dangerous   48 %
All   43 %
Don't know   9 %

In August 1944, just after D-Day (and after news of the extermination of the Jews became generally known), Gallup asked a series of questions centring around German war guilt. These were the closest that the Gallup organisation came to asking Britons directly about the Holocaust; it never polled on this issue. These results showed overwhelming British hostility to Nazism and Nazi leaders.[160] Two of the questions were as follows:

Do you think Hitler, Himmler, Goebbels and the other chief Nazis should be punished or not punished?

Punished   97 %
Not punished   2 %
No opinion   1 %

What should be done with members of the Gestapo, SS, and other German terrorist organisations against whom no specific charges of war crimes can be brought?

Shoot them with or without trial	21 %
Imprison them; solitary confinement	14 %
Put on trial and punished	12 %
Put to forced labour	9 %
Torture them; nothing horrible enough	8 %
Exiled	6 %
Hand them over to the Jews, Poles, or their own people	5 %
Re-educate them	2 %
Let them go; ignore them	1 %
Miscellaneous	12 %
No answer	10 %

The British Institute of Public Opinion, affiliated with the Gallup organisation although not directly a part of it, also conducted one relevant survey in this period. In November 1938 (at the time of *Kristallnacht*) it asked the British public 'Do you think the persecution of Jews in Germany is an obstacle to good understanding between Britain and America?'[161] This survey's responses were as follows:

Yes	73 %
No	15 %
No opinion	12 %

As in America, vivid reportage of Nazi atrocities against the Jews was printed in every British newspaper from the first day of Hitler's ascension to power. Overwhelmingly, this resulted in a fierce reaction of hostility to Nazism and Nazi anti-semitism in Britain, as did direct contact with pro-Hitler Germans. This reaction was especially strong among Britain's intellectuals and writers, including those who had routinely and unthinkingly engaged in writing the parlour, mildly anti-semitic stereotypes so common in English fiction before the 1930s. It extended as well to writers who were, in the past, strongly associated with more overt forms of anti-semitism.

Perhaps the most striking recantation of erstwhile anti-semitism by a noted anti-semitic writer was the following statement by G.K. Chesterton, the famous Catholic apologist, whose Edwardian writings were replete with anti-semitism of a kind. In September 1933 he was reported in the *Jewish Chronicle* (Anglo-Jewry's weekly newspaper) as stating:

> In our early days Hilaire Belloc and myself were accused of being uncompromising anti-semites.
>
> Today, although I still think that there is a Jewish problem, and that what I understand by the expression 'the Jewish Spirit' is a spirit foreign to Western countries, I am appalled by the Hitlerite atrocities in Germany. They have absolutely no reason or logic behind them, and are quite obviously the expedient of a man who, not knowing quite what to do to carry out his wild promises to a sorely tried people, has been driven to seeking a scapegoat, and has found, with relief, the most famous scapegoat in European history – the Jewish people. I am quite ready to believe now that Belloc and myself will die defending the last Jew in Europe. Thus does history play its ironical jokes upon us . . .
>
> By treating harmless and, in scores of cases, valuable and distinguished Jewish citizens of the German Reich as he has, Hitler has forfeited all claims to the label statesman. He had a great chance to do incalculable good; all he has done is the worst possible mischief. The real evils in Germany are still there, more rampant than ever.[162]

Agatha Christie's earlier detective novels contained sinister Jewish characters. These are stock cardboard figures, designed to pull the wool over the reader's eyes by turning their (imagined) prejudices against themselves, for in no Christie novel is there a Jewish villain – instead, the 'least likely person', previously unsuspected, of course, turns out to be the murderer. Nevertheless, in 1933 Christie was radicalised on the subject of Nazi anti-semitism when, in Baghdad with her archaeologist husband Max Mallowan, she met the Director of Antiquities at the local museum, a German and a 'fanatical Nazi' named Dr Julius Jordan.

> At tea one day in his house someone mentioned Jews. Agatha noticed the expression on Dr. Jordan's face changed suddenly in an extraordinary way that I have never noticed on anyone's face before. 'You do not understand!' said the Doctor. 'Our Jews are perhaps different from yours. They are a danger. They should be exterminated. Nothing else will really do but that.'
>
> Agatha stared at him unbelievingly. It was, she wrote later, the first time she had come across any hint of what was soon to happen in Germany.[163]

'From that date offensive references to Jews cease in her novels', wrote one of her biographers, Robert Barnard.[164] The place of the sinister foreigner in her stories was now taken by Greeks, Levantese and other non-Jewish exotics.

By the time of *Kristallnacht*, any writer who failed unequivocally to condemn Nazi anti-semitism risked an automatic barrage of hostility; Nazi anti-semitism was now 'beyond the pale'. An interesting example of this occurred in November 1938 when Enid Bagnold (1889–1981), the author of *National Velvet* and *The Chalk Garden*, returned from a visit to Germany and published her impressions.[165] She was, she later admitted, a complete political *naïve*, and spoke virtually no German. Among her obviously jejune impressions were the claims that 'Hitler had decided that the Jews were to be not more than the touch of yeast in the bread. The proportion of yeast in the continental loaf is too old and too strange a problem for English minds' and 'Are we, then, to condone the persecutions? We shall have to accept them as we have had to accept Abyssinia.'

A storm immediately broke over her head. Jewish mothers wrote, contrasting her book *The Squire* 'with its hymn of praise to motherhood and the giving of life', and Nazi destructiveness. So, too, did Philip Guedalla, the Jewish author, who sent her a sarcastic telegram. Maurice Baring, often depicted as an Edwardian anti-semite, suggested that 'she re-read the story of the Emperor's New Clothes'. Leonard and Virginia Woolf, her neighbours in Sussex, 'henceforth . . . mistrusted her'. Violet Bonham-Carter, a friend of long standing, wrote her a long, hurtful attack, pointing out case after case of brutal Nazi anti-semitism. A Labour MP, Reginald Fletcher, wrote a scathing personal attack in *Time and Tide*, noting that Bagnold was also the wife of Sir Roderick Jones, the head of Reuters, which

> owes much to the ability of those Jews whom the firm employs . . . It is a little incongruous perhaps to owe part of the good things one enjoys

in life to Jews while at the same time accepting persecutions as part of the natural order of things for them. I hope those who gather news for Reuters are more accurate observers than the wife of the head of the firm.

'Of course I was wrong', she later admitted, and, after the war, when she lived in New York and wrote plays for Broadway, she moved in a chiefly Jewish circle of friends. The point here is not that a political *naïve* should be fooled by Hitler or casually accept his persecution of the Jews, but that the reception she received was universally hostile.[166]

The British political elite was neither pro-Nazi nor pro-Mosley. No more than about 6 per cent of Conservative MPs (twenty-eight out of 432) in the parliament elected in 1935 belonged to either the Anglo-German Fellowship, the chief organisation of right-wing supporters of friendship with Germany (not all or even many of whom were anti-semites) or to the extreme right-wing body 'The Link', headed by Sir Barry Domvile, an open anti-semite.[167] They were certainly outnumbered by anti-Appeasement MPs such as Churchill and Eden; indeed, the number of overtly anti-semitic MPs in the Conservative Party at that time could not have exceeded half a dozen and was surpassed by the number of Jewish Conservative MPs in the 1935 Parliament. Revulsion at Sir Oswald Mosley's anti-semitism was probably the central reason why he became a political outcast, although there was near-universal disgust at his violence and thuggery almost from the beginnings of the British Union of Fascists. Crucial to this was Mosley's notorious Olympia rally of 7 June 1934, in which hecklers were beaten up and forcibly ejected by Blackshirt thugs. Stanley Baldwin sent his Parliamentary Private Secretary, Geoffrey Lloyd, MP, to the Olympia rally. Lloyd reported on his feelings in the *Yorkshire Post* (9 June 1934) that:

> I could not help shuddering at the thought of this vile bitterness, copied from foreign lands, being brought into the centre of England. I came to the conclusion that Mosley was a political maniac, and that all decent people must combine to kill his movement.

From the time of the June 1934 Olympia rally, Mosley was banned from appearing on the BBC, Britain's sole broadcasting outlet. Although the BBC is supposed to be quite independent of the government, Mosley's ban was entirely due to official pressure, especially from the Foreign Office.[168] Mosley repeatedly asked for air time to present his views, and he was universally acknowledged to be one of the very best public speakers in the country. The ban on him appearing on the BBC remained in force until 1968. For those who believe that the British 'Establishment' had an ill-concealed admiration for fascism, it is difficult to imagine evidence more disconfirmatory.[169]

Nazi Germany's treatment of the Jews was one reason why a united British nation was taken into the war in 1939 and why, from the first and virtually unanimously, it was considered a just war. At the time of *Kristallnacht* in November 1938, Oliver Harvey, Private Secretary to Lord Halifax, Britain's Foreign Secretary, observed that 'the Jewish pogroms have shaken up world opinion – even the City – as to the character of the criminal regime we are up against in Germany'; the country 'was beginning to stir' with 'uneasiness and dissatisfaction' over the government's Appeasement policies.[170] An oral history of (of all things) Britain's debutantes of the 1939 season, the last before the outbreak of the war, found – surprisingly to those who imagine that this social milieu might be pro-Hitler – that detestation of Nazism and Nazi anti-semitism had become almost ubiquitous by the outbreak of the war. According to one former debutante interviewed in this study, Mollie Acland:

> By then [August 1939] we were totally and absolutely conscious that war was imminent. We just wondered, is it coming tomorrow or the next day? My uncle said, 'The Germans will just wait till the harvest is in and then they'll march on Poland,' and he was absolutely right.
>
> I wasn't a bit frightened – it never *occurred* to us that we could lose. There was a gallant mood among the people then. It wasn't a depressing time at all, and I don't remember even thinking of it as 'a last fling.' *I think we wanted to kill Hitler* . . . I think it was as simple as that. Obviously we didn't know about the full horrors of the Holocaust, but many of us knew Jewish refugee families and we thought that Hitler was a very bad man and ought to be out of the way before he conquered the world. I think we were totally prepared to die for that.[171]

By 1939, these attitudes were extremely common, in America, Britain and elsewhere.[172]

Why are these facts, and this interpretation of the events of 1933–9, encountered so infrequently among historians, and so grudgingly when presented at all? A significant, but less important reason is the pervasive belief, encountered over and over again, that the elites and political leaders of the Western democracies must somehow have been anti-semitic rather than philo-semitic and anti-Nazi. This interpretation is, in my view, simply wrong, and ignores the abundance of evidence that the Western democracies loathed Nazi anti-semitism. A more central reason, however, is that which permeates virtually every recent discussion of this topic, the remarkably difficult effort necessary to view those years with the eyes of the 1930s rather than through post-Holocaust lenses.

A perfect example of the ahistorical treatment of these events, now so common, may be found in many accounts of the ill-fated and tragic voyage of the SS *St Louis*, a luxury liner on the Hamburg–America Line which left Germany for

Cuba in May 1939, carrying 936 passengers, of whom 930 were Jews. Although granted permits to land in Cuba, the Cuban government refused to honour those certificates. The plight of the Jews on the *St Louis* became world-renowned, the subject of innumerable newspaper editorials and the like. Eventually, owing to world-wide pressure, the passengers were admitted to western European democracies, about one-third to Britain and the others to France, the Netherlands and Belgium. One would have thought that, however agonisingly slow refuge was in coming, justice was done by the Western world for these wretched Jews. Not so, says Michael Berenbaum, author of *The World Must Know*, the United States Holocaust Memorial Museum's official account of the Holocaust. After denouncing a 'hand-wringing editorial in the *New York Times*' (which condemned the cruise of the *St Louis* as 'cry[ing] to high heaven of man's inhumanity to man'), Berenbaum states:

> For a while, the sad voyage of the *St Louis* seemed to have a happy ending
> . . . But within months, the Nazis overran Western Europe. Only the 288
> passengers who disembarked in England were safe. Of the rest, only a few
> survived the Holocaust.[173]

In other words, the leaders of France (with a standing army of 1.5 million men), Belgium and the Netherlands (neutral in the First World War) were blindly moronic (if not somehow anti-semitic) for not realising: (1) that Germany would overrun and conquer their countries; (2) that the Nazis would fundamentally reverse their policies from exiling Jews to imprisoning and killing them; (3) that, beginning three years later, the Jews of western Europe would be deported to extermination camps in Poland, something unimaginable by anyone in 1939. The writing of history cannot easily be more illogical or misleading, yet this example is probably no worse than innumerable others which bedevil the subject of rescue.

3

THE MYTH OF PLANS
FOR RESCUE

The outbreak of the Second World War brought about a fundamental change in
the status of Jews in Nazi-occupied Europe and in the direction of Nazi intentions
towards them which culminated in the attempted genocide of Europe's Jews. The
nature of this fundamental shift – from being refugees to being prisoners – is
surprisingly ill-understood, but is absolutely basic to coming to terms with the
fact – the fact which forms the subject of this chapter – that no scheme of rescue
of the Jews could possibly have succeeded. No scheme which could possibly or
realistically have rescued any of the Jews of Nazi-occupied Europe was actually
proposed by anyone or by any group in the democracies during the war. In retrospect and with the knowledge of these events from the vantage point of decades
afterwards, it might just be possible to concoct realistic schemes of rescue. But
the success of such schemes – even with hindsight – was likely to have been far
less extensive than sanguine observers might now suppose, while in any case all
such plans devised by historians after the war are ahistorical and inauthentic.

Before turning to the situation of the Jews in Nazi-occupied Europe and to the
actual plans for rescue proposed during the war, there are two preliminary
matters of relevance to this question which it would be fruitful to discuss: the
evolution of Hitler's treatment of the Jews, and the pre-war circumstances of
the Jews in continental Europe. All historians of the Holocaust are, of course,
aware of the two 'debates' which have grown up over the past decades about
the development of Nazi policy towards the Jews and over the timing of the start
of the policy of genocide. The first is normally labelled as a debate between
the 'intentionalists' and the 'functionalists' – that is, between those who view
the genocide of the Jews as the long-sought goal of Nazi policy and those who
argue that it grew out of the fact that, in 1939–41, vast numbers of Jews fell into
Nazi hands while any realistic policy of their mass deportation, for instance to
Madagascar, was precluded by the closure of the sea routes and other circumstances of the war.[1] The second concerns the date from which the Nazi policy of
extermination began and became unalterable, with several recent works arguing

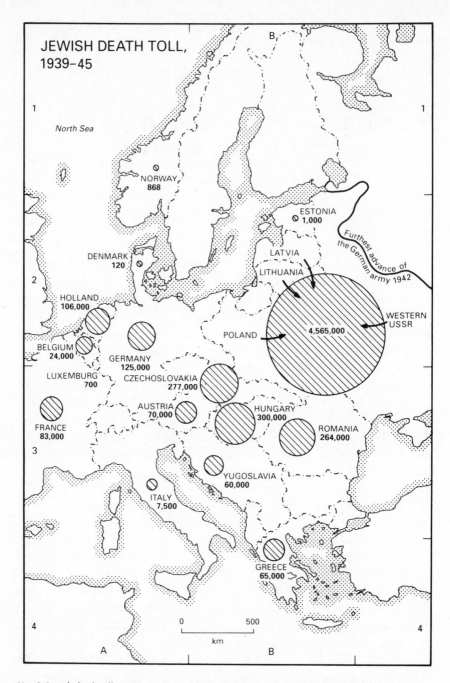

JEWISH DEATH TOLL, 1939–45

North Sea

NORWAY
868

ESTONIA
1,000

DENMARK
120

LATVIA

LITHUANIA

HOLLAND
106,000

POLAND

Furthest advance of the German army 1942

WESTERN
USSR

4,565,000

BELGIUM
24,000

GERMANY
125,000

LUXEMBURG
700

CZECHOSLOVAKIA
277,000

AUSTRIA
70,000

HUNGARY
300,000

ROMANIA
264,000

FRANCE
83,000

YUGOSLAVIA
60,000

ITALY
7,500

GREECE
65,000

0   500
km

A   B

Map 2 Jewish death toll, 1939–45. Note that the figures for deaths in Poland, the Soviet Union, and the Baltic States are combined here, and that all of these figures are subject to margins of error. Note, too, that the Romanian death toll is for Jewish deaths occurring in the pre-1939 boundaries of that country. Most of these deaths occurred in Transylvania, which was part of Hungary when these Jews were transported to their deaths. (From D. Cohn-Sherbok, *Atlas of Jewish History*, 1996. Reproduced by permission of Routledge.)

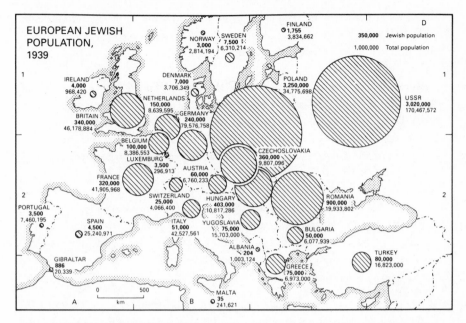

Map 3 European Jewish population, 1939.

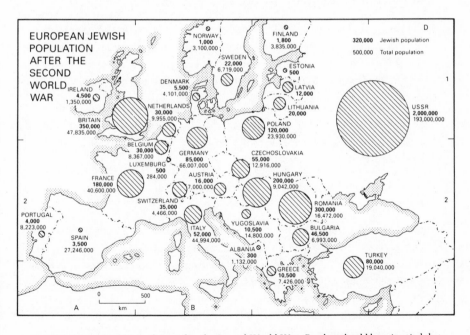

Map 4 European Jewish population after the Second World War. Readers should bear in mind that the figures in both maps are subject to wide margins of error, especially because of boundary changes as in the case of Romania. (From D. Cohn-Sherbok, *Atlas of Jewish History*, 1996. Reproduced by permission of Routledge.)

that this did not occur until some time after the invasion of the Soviet Union in June 1941.[2] In the context of the argument advanced here, there are several relevant points to be made about Hitler's anti-semitism and that of the Nazi movement.

The first and most important point is that Hitler's entire conceptualisation of the world, of world politics and of the movement he headed was biological and Social Darwinistic, entailing at all times the clash of races – biological entities – as the fundamental and underlying basis of all history. Hitler was the most extreme and most thorough-going biological determinist who has ever come to power in modern history; possibly the most extreme biological determinist who has ever lived. The thorough-going ideology of racial superiority and racial conflict as the basis of all history and politics is also more marked in Hitler than in any other leader of the Nazi movement, even than those, like Himmler and Eichmann, who enforced the 'Final Solution'. Hitler's biological determinism is evident on virtually every page of *Mein Kampf* and in virtually every lengthy private conversation of his which is recorded.

> The State represents no end, but a means. It is, to be sure, the premise for the formation of a higher human culture, but not its cause, which lies exclusively in the existence of a race capable of culture.[3]

> The state is a means to an end. Its end lies in the preservation and advancement of a community of physically and psychically homogeneous creatures. This preservation itself comprises first of all existence as a race and thereby permits the free development of all the forces dormant in this race.[4]

> No, there is only one holiest human right, and this right is at the same time the holiest obligation, to wit: to see that the blood is preserved pure and, by preserving the best humanity, to create the possibility of a nobler development of these beings.[5]

> The folkish state . . . must set race in the centre of all life. It must take care to keep it pure.[6]

Quite literally hundreds of other very similar statements on this theme made by Hitler could be cited, at any point in his career. This biological determinism, too, surely distinguished the Nazi movement either from previous instances of German right-authoritarianism, or from other fascist movements of the inter-war period, for whom the 'nation' always embodied other elements besides the biological and racial and always admitted of the possible legitimation and assimilation of racially 'alien' groups over time.[7]

Second, and closely related to this, is the fact that Hitler habitually conceptualised the world in terms of long historical epochs and of lengthy periods of historical evolution: his writings and statements on virtually any political issue are invariably an historical disquisition on that topic. Three very typical examples — and dozens of others could be cited — are these paragraphs (à propos of virtually nothing) from *Mein Kampf* on the Catholic Church and *Hitler's Table Talk* on the Venetian Republic and on the biological basis of world domination.

In this the Catholic Church can be regarded as a model example [of drawing its leaders from the common people]. The celibacy of its priests is a force compelling it to draw the future generation again and again from the masses of the broad people instead of from their own ranks. But it is this very significance of celibacy that is not at all recognised by most people. It is the cause of the incredibly vigorous strength which resides in this age-old institution. For through the fact that this gigantic army of spiritual dignitaries is continuously complemented from the lowest strata of the nations, the Church not only obtains its instinctive bond with the emotional world of the people, but also assures itself a sum of energy and active force which in such a form will forever exist only in the broad masses of the people. From this arises the amazing youthfulness of this gigantic organism, its spiritual suppleness and iron will-power.[8]

Things won't improve in Italy until the Duce has sacrificed the monarchy and taken effective control of an authoritarian State. This form of government can last for centuries. The Republic of Venice lasted for nine hundred and sixty years. It ruled the eastern Mediterranean throughout that period, and that thanks to the authority conferred upon the Doge. Under the monarchic form, that would not have been possible. Venice couldn't have claimed more — but whatever she coveted, and whatever lay within the scope of her ambition, she got. The example of the Hanseatic cities likewise proves the quality of this system. All that *they* lacked was the Imperial power.

The British maintained their position of world domination for three hundred years solely because there was during that period nothing on the Continent comparable in race or intelligence to oppose them. Napoleon himself was no real menace to them, because, in the frenzy of the French Revolution, he had no solid basis on which to found a new order in Europe; and apart from him, there has never been in Europe, since the disintegration of the old German Empire, any State which, in either quantity or quality, could compare with the British.

Thanks to the development of National Socialist Germany, I firmly believe, if only on purely biological grounds, we shall succeed in surpassing the British to such an extent that, with one hundred and fifty to two hundred million Germans, we shall become the undisputed masters of the whole of Europe. A recrudescence of the problem [of] Rome or Carthage in the new guise of Germany or Great Britain is not, in my opinion, possible. For the result of this war will be that, whereas in Britain each additional million of population will be an additional burden on the island itself, the increasing growth of our own races will have open to them horizons of political and ethnological expansion which are limitless.[9]

It will also be seen that – if it makes sense to speak like this of a psychopath – Hitler's remarks, though steeped in fantasy, taken on their own terms are not unintelligent, and are based in a wide-ranging knowledge of history and a real talent at historical analysis at this level of generalisation, albeit an historical imagination entirely untutored and autodidactical. It might be noted that Hitler's habitual preference for historical analysis, especially that entailing a broad sweep of history based on surprisingly wide learning, presents a close parallel to the thinking of many Marxist theorists and writers of that time who also habitually conceptualised the world, almost by definition, in broad historical terms, but in an evolutionary matrix based upon class rather than race. Both extremes of the spectrum, one might point out, are distinguished in this from most democratic politicians, particularly in the English-speaking world, whose knowledge of history was slight and restricted to jejune grade school clichés about national heroes and great events, the exceptions to this pattern, like Winston Churchill, being notable for their rarity.

This particular combination of elements in Hitler's habitual modes of thought, his all-consuming racial world-view and his historical conceptualisation, was both the progenitor and byproduct of an even more striking element in Hitler's outlook: his utter lack of concern for the welfare of an individual person or indeed for a group, provided the biological germ of the superior race was preserved intact or at least capable – after a destructive war, for instance – of racial resurrection. The only exception to this was the handful of leaders with superior 'personalities' who would be placed in positions of authority in the fascist state, based upon the principle of the 'authority of every leader downward and responsibility upward'.[10] The National Socialist state would be sharply bifurcated into this elite and the rest: 'The National Socialist state knows no "classes", but politically speaking only citizens with absolutely equal rights and accordingly equal duties, and, alongside of these, state subjects who in the political sense are absolutely without rights', Hitler wrote with great frankness.[11] He strongly implied, however, that this leadership elite could emerge from any social class; if anything, they were more likely to emerge from the lower than the higher reaches of society. Provided the germ of the 'master race' was preserved from generation to generation, these leaders would automatically reappear within a relatively brief time.

The third central element in Hitler's world-view is, of course, his Manichaean view of 'international Jewry' as a diabolical evil. 'The Jews inhabited Hitler's mind. He believed that they were the source of all evil, misfortune, and tragedy, the single factor that, like some inexorable law of nature, explained the workings of the universe', Lucy S. Dawidowicz has truly written.[12] So much has appeared on Hitler's hatred of the Jews that it may seem pointless to say anything further, but there are a few things perhaps worth stating. Hitler's attitude was irrational in the sense that he was endowing what was really an extremely small group of people – there were only 500,000 Jews in Germany compared with 65 million German 'Aryans', only 280,000 Jews in France out of 40 million Frenchmen, only 3 million Jews in the Soviet Union compared with 170 million others – with powers equal to, if not superior to, the vastly larger 'host' population, even those groups which, in the same breath, Hitler proclaimed to be biologically superior and hence, presumably, able to withstand the defilement of the Jews.

Hitler's hatred of the Jews was irrational, too, in the sense that the Jews manifestly did not possess the qualities he attributed to them: rather than comprising a unified conspirational group, the Jewish people in the first half of the twentieth century were, to an unusual extent, deeply and fundamentally divided into a range of hostile ideological groups. Hitler depicted the Jews as arch-capitalists, but they played virtually no significant role in the development of capitalism in the world's leading economic power, the United States (although American entrepreneurs of German descent, such as the Astors and the Rockefellers, did) and a hardly greater role in Britain. Hitler also depicted the Jews as Marxists, leftists and revolutionaries, but Jews played virtually no significant role in the development of the political left in many countries where they lived – in France and Britain, for example, or in Spain or Italy. One could continue through the entire catalogue of qualities and preferences Hitler attributed to the Jews: on closer examination, these are half-truths or sheer nonsense. The Jews were the central obsession of Hitler's life: he could literally not speak freely and uninterruptedly for more than five minutes without returning to his central fixation.

Hitler was, in other words, plainly deranged on the subject of the Jews: he was, in fact, a monomaniacal psychopath whose eventual aim, whose life's mission, was the goal of killing as many of them as he could. This simple fact – which even now is not fully appreciated by all historians – is highly relevant, in particular, to the question of 'rescue', especially to the possibility of reaching deals with the Nazis for the rescue or 'sale' of Jews during the war. The question of why Hitler was so centrally obsessed by the Jews has, of course, attracted an enormous literature: there is general agreement that a convincing explanation is beyond our grasp.[13] Without Hitler's obsessive and destructive anti-semitism, it is most unlikely that the Holocaust would have occurred.

If Hitler had been assassinated soon after he came to power in 1933, it seems very likely that his successor – probably Goering or Hess – would soon have moderated the destructive, all-consuming and eventually murderously anti-semitic aspects of German National Socialism, in all likelihood turning the movement into one (like Italian fascism) centrally anti-Bolshevist, and while fighting 'subversive' and Marxist Jews, especially those from eastern Europe, willing to tolerate, or even to admit as members, 'patriotic' German Jews. Even if Hitler had been assassinated in, say, 1942, it is at least arguable that his successor at that stage – perhaps Himmler or even Goebbels – would have demonstrated considerably greater flexibility over the genocide of European Jewry or even stopped it entirely, especially if some bargain could be struck with the Allies. It will be argued here that, with Hitler, any such bargain, and any such mitigation of the process of destroying the Jews, was *ipso facto* impossible under any circumstances.

Adolf Hitler, it must be clearly kept in mind at all times, was the absolute dictator of Nazi Germany and its realms: his word was law and any disobedience of the *Führer*'s command meant, potentially, an instantaneous death sentence, even for the most senior of Nazi leaders, let alone for others. One rather striking fact might also be noted here: after the mid-1920s (if not earlier), Hitler had apparently never voluntarily spoken to a Jew; when the Holocaust began in mid-1941, Hitler had had no voluntary contact with any Jewish person for sixteen years or more.[14] Other top Nazis such as Goering and Himmler, in contrast, were compelled to deal directly with Jewish leaders throughout the Nazi period.

Despite Hitler's monomania, it is nonetheless clear that there was, in Karl A. Schleunes' phrase, a 'twisted road to Auschwitz'.[15] That 'twisted road' has unquestionably led to much justified confusion among historians: did Hitler intend, from day one, to kill the Jews, or did the genocide develop from the specific circumstances in which Germany found itself in mid–late 1941?

The best possible answer to this central question, it will be argued here, is that Hitler intended to do the maximum possible harm that he could to the Jews at that point in time, but that the maximum possible harm changed and evolved between 1933 and 1941–2, almost always in the direction of allowing the Nazis to do greater harm to the Jews of Germany, the *Reich* and eventually most of Europe. It would seem to be unarguable that a fundamental shift in Hitler's planning for the Jewish question, in the direction of preparing for genocide, occurred with the preparations for the invasion of the Soviet Union in late 1940 or early 1941. There is no reason to suppose that prior to that time Hitler did not view the resettlement of the Jews in Madagascar as the eventual climax of Nazi policy.[16] In February 1941, however, Hitler told a group of assembled senior Nazis, including Bormann, Keitel, Speer and Major Gerhard Engel (Hitler's Adjutant), that he 'was thinking of many things [concerning the Jews] in a different way, that was not exactly more friendly'.[17] In the absence of further evidence, the causes of this fundamental change in Hitler's policies can only be guessed at, but a number of points seem crucial. Hitler's conquests after March 1939, when the rump of Czechoslovakia was taken over as a German 'Protectorate', culminating in the invasion of the Soviet Union in June 1941 marked an essential – indeed total – break with Nazi policy in the past.

Before 1939, Nazi policy had aimed at creating a totally 'Aryan' German *Reich* within its 'true' ethnic/linguistic boundaries, that is, by absorbing Austria, the Sudetenland, etc. The policy of expelling all Jews was consistent with creating an all-'Aryan' *Reich*. While Hitler – in common with previous generations of German right-wing leaders – had of course looked to *Lebensraum* and expansion into eastern Europe as a component of his policies and world-view, there is a sense in which the expansion of Germany to include tens of millions of Slavic and other non-Germanic peoples represented a direct contradiction to the ideological basis of Nazism, with its obsession with an ethnically pure *Reich*. It could not necessarily be predicted as a likely development of Nazi policy, let alone a certain next step, and the fact that British and French policy-makers and opinion-leaders assumed that the creation of an ethnically pure *Reich* by the absorption of German-speaking territories excluded by Versailles was the principle aim of Nazi foreign policy was a powerful underlying force behind Appeasement: once the reunification of all German-speaking areas within the *Reich* had been completed, it was naturally assumed, Germany would be satisfied and hence peaceful. The conquest of eastern Europe, with its vast population of 'helot' and 'sub-human' peoples, appeared to be a total contradiction of Nazi Germany's 'Aryan' ideology.

However, it is important to understand that once the conquest of eastern Europe had been decided upon by Hitler, the demographic position of the Jews in the Nazi realm was utterly transformed. In 1933 Germany's Jewish population of 500,000 represented only 5 per cent of Europe's total Jewish population of 10 million or so. Even if every Jew in Nazi Germany had emigrated, the demographic position of the Jews in Europe would hardly have been altered at all, and nor would the economic, political and ideological 'dominance' of the Jews as seen in Nazi ideology. But with the conquest of eastern Europe (combined with the victories in western Europe, which brought the Jewries of France, the Nether-lands, Belgium, etc. into the Nazi orbit), all this changed fundamentally: Hitler was now master of virtually all the 9 million Jews of Europe, the 300,000 Jews of Britain comprising the sole remaining Jewish community of significance outside of the Nazi empire.

It is important, however, to understand that the successful invasion of the Soviet Union was a crucially necessary pre-condition for this fundamental change. Under the Nazi–Soviet Pact of August 1939, eastern Poland was absorbed by the Soviet Union, as were the Baltic republics and Moldavia, formerly a part of Rumania. As a result, by mid-1940 the Soviet Union's Jewish population had risen from 3 million to 5 million or more, and any series of conquests by Germany which omitted the subjugation of the Soviet Union would still leave more than one-half of European Jewry untouched – and moreover the 'worst' Jewry of all, the spawning ground of 'Judeo-Bolshevism' itself. *With* the conquest of the Soviet Union, however, the opportunity arose – for the first time – of embarking upon what would indeed be the 'final solution' of the whole Jewish question.[18]

It hardly seems possible that Adolf Hitler could have embarked on the planning for the invasion of the Soviet Union without fully considering how the demography of European Jewry would thereby be altered. In my opinion, it was not the impossibility, after 1940–1, of any alternative scheme for the mass expulsion of Jews from Europe, especially to Madagascar, which altered Hitler's position to that of beginning the process of genocide (as some historians, such as Browning, have argued). Rather, it was Hitler's evident reconsideration of the changed demographic realities of Europe's Jewish population following any invasion of the Soviet Union, with virtually all of Europe's Jews now in Nazi hands. Their sheer numbers probably ruled out their forced exile to a remote place such as Madagascar, but it did not rule out, for instance, their continued existence as slave-labourers in ghettos (such as Polish Jews experienced until early 1942) for an indefinite period. Given Hitler's obsession with the historical, biological and demographic aspects of the 'Jewish question', it seems plausible that he decided upon genocide once he became aware that he could now destroy the Jews of Europe in one fell swoop.

To this must be added some important factors personal to Hitler. He was apparently obsessed with the likelihood of his own early death as well as with the decline of his health and abilities after 50.[19] 'The time is short. I have not long to live' was fairly typical of Hitler's comments.[20] In 1939 Hitler told Baldur von Schirach that 'You see I'm getting old and need glasses. Therefore I prefer to have this war now that I am fifty rather than at sixty.'[21] There was an obvious deterioration in Hitler's mental and physical health in the course of the war, with all his psychotic tendencies progressively heightened as the conflict dragged on. He had also received literally thousands of dosages of quack medicines of every description in the decade after 1935.[22]

As well, Hitler almost certainly regarded the extermination of the Jews as both an act of revenge – revenge for the innumerable 'Aryan' deaths, including those of women and children – in Allied (that is, 'Jewish') air raids, and as a kind of 'justice' done to the Jewish 'instigators' of the war who would, if unpunished, suffer far less than their Aryan 'victims'.[23] British bombing raids on Germany began on 11 May 1940, when Hitler must have first seriously been planning the invasion of Russia. While the tonnage of bombs dropped on Germany was low by subsequent standards, bombardments increased steadily and relentlessly, rising from 1,668 tons in May 1940 to 4,300 tons by the summer of 1941, when the

Einsatzgruppen began their work.[24] When Molotov visited Berlin in October 1940, his state dinner with von Ribbentrop was interrupted by a British air raid, causing Molotov to dispute Germany's prediction of an imminent British collapse: 'If you are so sure that Britain is finished, then why are we in this shelter?'[25]

Recent historians have debated whether the beginnings of genocide stemmed from Hitler's 'euphoria' during his first victorious days in Russia or from his depression and frustration after the victories of the first weeks of the Soviet campaign had been stemmed.[26] In truth Hitler himself apparently gave a perfectly clear account of his motivations which seems to show that *either* success or failure in the war was seen by him as justifying the extermination of the Jews. He apparently told Himmler in the spring of 1943 that

> Revolutionary times are governed by their own laws. Should we win the battle, no one will ask us afterwards how we did it. Should we lose, then we shall at the very least have hit decisively these subversives. Therefore, Himmler, I have after much deliberation decided to blot out once and for all the biological bases of Judaism, so that if the Aryan peoples emerge weakened from this conflict, at least a crippling blow will have been dealt to those other forces.[27]

If accurate, this statement is among the most important and telling ever made by Hitler about the Holocaust: it clearly shows that, to him, the extermination of the Jews was at once based in biology, motivated by demographic considerations, was revenge for the age-old 'crimes' of the Jews against the Aryans and was, most of all, a decision absolute and irreversible.

From early 1942 until literally the day of his suicide, Hitler repeatedly described the war as a life-or-death struggle between the Jewish and Aryan races. On 30 January 1942 Hitler told the Reichstag that 'the war can end in two ways, either by the extermination of the Aryan peoples or by the disappearance of Jewry from Europe'.[28] Hitler's proclamation of 24 February 1942 to celebrate the foundation of the Nazi Party declared that 'the war will not exterminate Aryan humanity but the Jew'.[29] If anything, as the war progressed – and began to go badly for Germany – Hitler became more rigidly and obsessively devoted to killing the Jews of Europe, the only 'victory' he salvaged from the ruin of the war. It is simply inconceivable that Hitler would ever have voluntarily deferred or modified his aim of making Europe *judenrein* for any 'rational' reason whatever.

To be sure, a number of important details of the initiation and execution of the Holocaust remain unclear. Hitler certainly initiated the genocide of the Jews through clear and unequivocal verbal orders to Himmler, probably in the first half of 1941. Nevertheless, we do not know, and are unlikely ever to know, the manner in which Hitler continued to confer with Himmler, and others in Hitler's immediate circle, after the Holocaust began. We do not know, for instance, whether at some stage early in 1944 Hitler told Himmler 'the time has come to exterminate Hungarian Jewry', although it is likely that he did. We do not know whether Hitler took a keen interest in the details of the extermination process, or whether he left its execution entirely to Himmler and the SS once general orders had been given. We do not know whether, for example, Hitler ever directly discussed the genocide of the Jews of Old Rumania and Bulgaria (who survived the war) but decided against proceeding, and if so, why. Remarkably, we do not know whether Hitler ever saw photographs of an extermination camp or heard detailed and frank accounts of the killing process. We do not know whether Hitler played a direct role in the decision, taken at the end of 1941 or early 1942, to use gas in extermination camps to kill Jews in large numbers rather than killing them by shootings conducted in forests and pits at the edge of town. It seems unlikely that any major, fundamental decisions about the Holocaust could possibly have been taken without Hitler's full knowledge and approval, particularly if there were funding and resource implications, but no direct evidence now exists.

All such matters were, apparently, discussed in secret, face-to-face conferences between Hitler, Himmler and perhaps one or two others, of which no transcripts were made or survived. It seems clear, however, that Hitler did not discuss or take any direct part in the extermination process with any but Himmler and the most senior members of the *Führer*'s entourage such as Goebbels, any more than he would have discussed military operations in the field during the war with an ordinary colonel or major rather than with the most senior generals. One very striking piece of evidence for this is that there is no reason to suppose that Adolf Eichmann (who held the rank of lieutenant-colonel in the SS) ever met or spoke to Hitler at any time during his life; Eichmann apparently only met Himmler on three occasions.[30] Quite conceivably, Hitler wished to distance himself as much as possible from direct participation in anything as barbaric as the Holocaust, while – needless to say – being solely responsible for ordering it.

The second significant point which ought to be considered here is that of the perception by Europe's Jews outside Germany of any potential threat to their lives posed by Nazi expansionism. If Germany's Jews were often reluctant to emigrate from Germany until the last minute, imagining that Hitler's anti-semitism would moderate and 'blow over', *a fortiori* one would not expect Europe's Jews outside Germany, with the rarest of exceptions, to perceive themselves, their families and their communities as in mortal peril, a peril which could only be escaped by emigration to a remote and secure place. Indeed, inability to foresee, even in the late 1930s, that millions of Jews were then living out their last years, was a near-universal feature of European Jewish life in that period.

The actual facts of the matter are very much at variance with the impression given in many later depictions of continental European Jewry during the inter-war period, wherein millions of Jews desperately wished to migrate to the *Yishuv* in

Palestine and were prevented from doing so only by sharp British restrictions on their immigration, vexatiously placed in order to appease the Arabs. The reality is quite different: surprisingly few Jews, even those shortly to be placed in the gravest peril, gave any direct evidence of wishing to emigrate, while most, quite explicitly, wished to remain where they were. Self-evidently, if unrestricted immigration to the United States was still possible (as was the case before the early 1920s) or if unrestricted *aliyah* to Jewish Palestine was encouraged (as became a reality in 1948), many more Jews would have emigrated from continental Europe than actually did so before 1939, although this would have been chiefly to ensure a brighter economic future for themselves and their children rather than to escape an impending Holocaust, and would not in all likelihood have been on the scale many now imagine.[31]

Much of the evidence which may be given for this is very striking indeed. Central to the misunderstanding which has occurred about the desire of Europe's Jews to emigrate is a hindsighted exaggeration of the strength of Zionism and the Zionist movement during the inter-war period. Contrary to popular belief, the organised Zionist movement was weak rather than strong: so weak and unpopular as to be virtually a fringe rather than a mainstream movement of the Jewish people. In 1920–1 the number of shekel-holders (financial members of the Zionist movement) totalled only 778,487 out of a world Jewish population of perhaps 15–16 million.[32] Low as it was, this total *declined* consistently during the 1920s, reaching its nadir in 1928–9, when there were only 387,106 shekel-holders in the world. In 1930–1 there were only 425,987 shekel-holders out of a Jewish world population of perhaps 17 million – only *2.5 per cent* of the world's Jews. This number began to revive just before Hitler came to power, and then increased to 978,033 in 1934–5 and to 1,042,054 in 1939.[33] It goes without saying that these totals are underestimates of Zionist strength: many sympathisers with Zionism would have failed to join through poverty, inertia or the failure of Zionist bodies to reach all their potential constituents; all Jews in the Soviet Union would *de jure* and most Jews in the Arab world would *de facto* have been outside the Zionist fund-raising web. Nevertheless, if every possible allowance is made for sources of understatement, it seems clear that not more than 10–15 per cent of the world's Jews (and probably fewer) were active Zionists on the eve of Hitler's seizure of power.[34]

As its *raison d'être*, Zionism posited emigration from the 'zone of anti-semitism' in continental Europe to a Jewish national homeland in Palestine, and it might be supposed that Zionism would have been extremely popular in those countries where anti-semitism was most pervasive and where, one imagines, there was the greatest appreciation of the mortal peril posed by the German maniac. Yet *even in Poland*, Zionism was amazingly weak and was not growing in strength after Hitler's ascent to power: the opposite in fact appears to have been the case. In Polish

Jewry's *kehilla* (Jewish communal) elections of the mid-1920s, all the Zionist parties and factions together received about 31 per cent of the total Jewish vote.[35] In 1936, the Social Democratic Bund won a sweeping victory in Jewish *kehilla* elections in Poland, emerging, in Marcus' words, 'as the strongest Jewish party in Poland' just before the war.[36] The ideology of the Bund centred around the maintenance of an autonomous, secular, socialist Yiddish-based culture among Poland's Jews; its main hallmarks included 'an unyielding hostility to Zionism' and to the Zionist enterprise of Jewish emigration from Poland to Palestine.[37] The Bund wished Polish Jews to fight anti-semitism in Poland by remaining there and cooperating with Polish socialists and workers.

The Zionist goal was also *opposed*, as a matter of principle, by all the other major parties and movements among pre-1939 Polish Jewry – by most Strictly Orthodox Jews on religious grounds, by the Folkists (middle-class non-socialist advocates of an autonomous Yiddish culture) on linguistic and cultural grounds, by Jewish Marxists as 'bourgeois nationalism' and so on. All those groups *as a matter of official policy* wished Poland's Jews to remain in Poland rather than to emigrate, especially to Palestine. There were just 156,142 shekel-holders in Poland (including east and west Galicia) in 1930–1 and 405,756 in 1934–5. In eastern Galicia in 1936, the largest single area of pre-war Zionist strength, shekels were purchased by 22.2 per cent of the Jewish population in 1936.[38]

The one man who is often said to have foreseen the impending catastrophe was Vladimir Jabotinsky, the brilliant, charismatic leader of the Revisionist Zionists (the progenitors of Israel's Likud Party). Jabotinsky's scheme for the 'evacuation' of either 750,000 or 1.5 million Polish Jews from Poland to Palestine *over a ten-year period* was regarded as extraordinarily radical even by most Zionists. With hindsight, we now know that, had the scheme succeeded, their lives might have been saved. Yet at the time Jabotinsky's proposals received amazingly little support *among Polish Jewry* (or, indeed, within the mainstream Zionist movement). In 1934, the year following Hitler's ascent to power, Jabotinsky presented his so-called 'Revisionist Petition' to the Polish government, signed by his followers. This petition (welcomed by Poland's anti-semites) stated that 'the only way of normalising my existence is for me and my family to settle in Palestine . . . I ask the Polish government to intervene with the mandatory power so that the unjust immigration restrictions may be revised'. Jabotinsky's petition was signed by 217,000 persons, no more than about 8 per cent of the total number of Polish Jews, or about 13 per cent of adults.[39] Thus, only five years before the Nazis began the systematic ghettoisation of Polish Jewry prior to genocide, 87 per cent of adult Polish Jews *declined* to sign a petition demanding free and immediate immigration to Palestine!

The number of shekel-holders in Poland actually *declined* in the latter 1930s, from a peak of 405,756 in 1935 to only 275,632 in 1939.[40] As late as *August 1939,* moderate Zionists – let alone non-Zionist Jews – continued to *oppose* mass Jewish emigration to Palestine. Marcus notes that the very last issue of the Polish Zionist newspaper *Heint*, dated 23 August 1939, contained an article in which the President of the Zionist Organisation of central and eastern Poland, Apolinary Hortglas, animadverted on Jabotinsky's plans for mass Jewish evacuation to Palestine, stating 'To other than ideologically motivated emigration to Palestine, we say "no, never".' ('Indeed, "never" it was to be', is Marcus' wry comment).[41]

The continuing weakness of the Zionist movement among the mass of Jews was noted and lamented by Zionism's leaders again and again. In April 1936, for instance, David Ben-Gurion remarked explicitly that 'the Zionist ideal has only gained a footing among a minority of the Jewish people. A decisive majority of Jews still remains outside the Zionist Organisation.'[42] Ben-Gurion attributed the relative failure of Zionism up to that point to 'assimilation', 'communism' and 'ignorant indifference'.[43] 'In Congress Poland . . . the number of shekel-payers only amounts to 10 % of the Jewish population . . . in the United States [to] no more than 3 % of American Jewry', he lamented.[44]

Elsewhere in eastern Europe, where Jewish politics were not pursued with as much zeal as in Poland and where perceptions of official and unofficial anti-semitism were perhaps more muted, Zionist strength was weaker still. In Hungary (Herzl's birthplace) there were precisely 3,500 shekel-holders in 1928–9, 3,450 in 1932–3 and 5,763 in 1934–5, out of a Jewish population of 450,000.[45] In Rumania shekel-holders totalled just 5,340 in 1930–1 and 13,883 in 1934–5, out of 700,000 Rumanian Jews.[46] There is thus no compelling evidence that emigration to Palestine was seen as a desirable option by more than a small minority of eastern European Jews, even after Hitler's monomaniacal anti-semitism was – it seems to us – clear to all.

If Israel had existed as an independent Jewish state in the 1930s, how many additional Jews might have been saved? In all likelihood not as many as one might suppose. Professor Ezra Mendelsohn, whose important essay on inter-war Zionism has been cited, suggests that 'instead of the 140,000 Polish *olim* [migrants to Palestine] during the entire period, there would perhaps have been half a million who went to Palestine'.[47] This estimate – that 15–20 per cent of Polish Jewry might have emigrated to a Jewish state (while 80–85 per cent would *not* have emigrated) seems reasonable. Nevertheless, as much as one might have wished that an independent Jewish state, peopled by unlimited Jewish immigration, had existed in the 1930s as a refuge for the persecuted, two very important *caveats* should be noted. First, no *Zionist* group or leader called for the immediate creation of an independent Jewish state at this time (the goals of the Revisionist movement being the creation of a Jewish majority over perhaps ten years, followed by statehood). Strange as this may now seem, the first time the mainstream Zionist movement actually went on record as favouring an independent 'Jewish Commonwealth' in Palestine as its goal was the Biltmore Declaration of May 1942, after the Holocaust actually began. Second – and this will be discussed again – the Jewish community in Palestine was not necessarily preordained to survive the war. If Rommel had won at El Alamein, the *Yishuv* might well have been conquered by the Nazis, while the existence of an independent Jewish state in Palestine in 1939–42 might, in and of itself, have caused Hitler to have placed its conquest much higher on the list of his military priorities than was the case.

Additionally, there were millions of Jews, shortly to perish in the Holocaust, who had no choice in the matter of emigration. The 3,020,000 Jews of the Soviet Union identified in their country's 1939 census were, of course, forbidden to leave; expression of sympathy for Zionism or any other Jewish cause apart from the narrow range officially approved by Stalin was tantamount to suicide. In 1939 and 1940, the Soviet Union also acquired a further 1,910,000 Jews as a direct result of the Nazi–Soviet Pact, annexing the whole of eastern Poland, the Baltics and Bessarabia, including such renowned Jewish centres as Vilna, Bialystok, Brest-Litovsk and Lodz. Sovietisation, with its absolute denial of Jewish group identity except in the context of Stalinism, was rapid and all-encompassing.[48] Because of the Nazi–Soviet Pact, criticism of Germany or reporting of its anti-semitic enormities was forbidden, and most Jews in areas incorporated into the Soviet Union in 1939–40 were literally unaware of the consequences of a German invasion (which, even before genocide began in mid-1941, meant ghettoisation and the systematic denial of all rights) and were thus unable to flee ahead of the Nazi armies to areas unoccupied by Germany.[49]

In western Europe, democratic and happily outside the 'zone of anti-semitism' – as inter-war eastern Europe has come to be known – few indeed foresaw the dangers just ahead. A typical example here was the Netherlands, and a consideration of the question of emigration as it affected Dutch Jewry is instructive. The Jewish population of the Netherlands stood at about 112,000 in 1930 and at 140,000 by the outbreak of the war, swollen by the influx of German refugees, who of course saw the Netherlands as a place of safety rather than of peril. Dutch Jewry was highly assimilated, well-educated and resident in a country with less of a tradition of anti-semitism than perhaps anywhere else on the Continent, yet 75–80 per cent of Dutch Jewry – a higher percentage than any country in western Europe – were to perish in the Holocaust.

The number of Dutch Jews who foresaw the mortal dangers ahead and attempted to emigrate while they could was small indeed. Between 1933 and 1939 not more than 679 Dutch persons (Jews and non-Jews) migrated in any one year to the United States, although the annual quota of Dutch immigrants allowed to enter the United States was 3,153.[50] In most of these years the total of Dutch immigrants admitted to the United States was microscopic, amounting to just

379 in 1937 and 365 in 1938, for instance.[51] Native-born Dutch Jews emerged disproportionately from an acculturated, well-educated milieu, and would, one supposes, have had relatively less trouble in migrating to the United States than most other European Jews, yet virtually none made strenuous efforts to do so.

In addition to the United States, there were two other places of refuge to which Dutch Jews might have fled prior to the German invasion. The first was Surinam (Dutch Guiana), in South America, virtually on the doorstep of the United States and also relatively convenient for reemigration to other Western Hemisphere countries with significant Jewish populations such as Cuba and Brazil. As well, Surinam had a long-established Jewish community with a number of synagogues. For those blessed with the ability to foresee the future, Surinam would have been an absolutely safe place to which to flee: as a nation in the Western Hemisphere, it was protected by the Monroe Doctrine, and any attempt by Germany to interfere with its inhabitants would have been construed by the United States as an act of war. The second place of potential refuge was the Dutch East Indies (now Indonesia), the Netherlands' largest and most important colony, and one obviously beyond the scope of Hitler's ambitions at their most grandiose. Yet there was no noteworthy Dutch Jewish migration to either of these places, the *Encyclopaedia Judaica* noting only that 'During World War II a few Jewish refugees from the Netherlands and other parts of Europe settled temporarily in Surinam'.[52] Plainly, Dutch Jewry felt itself to be utterly immune to Hitler's plans as they foresaw them to be. They remembered that the Netherlands had been neutral in the First World War and presumed that even Hitler would respect Dutch neutrality in any future war. No Dutch Jew could foresee the forthcoming genocide (or its preceding events such as the fall of France and the invasion of Russia), a failure of precognition they shared with all other European Jews and their leaders.

Both of these considerations – Hitler's all-consuming, biologically-based anti-semitism and the astonishing disinclination of Europe's Jews to flee to safety even as (seen in hindsight) midnight approached – are both extremely important to the argument made here, but are not the central point which must be understood if the alleged failure of the democracies is to be seen in an accurate light. The central point is this: in 1939-40 the Jews of Nazi-occupied Europe *ceased to be refugees but instead became the exact opposite: prisoners* – prisoners of a psychopath whose life's mission consisted in killing every last one of them and who happened to be the absolute dictator of most of Europe.

In international law, a 'refugee' is a person who is compelled to flee from his or her homeland because of 'a well-founded fear of persecution'. This is an obviously accurate description of the position of the Jews in Nazi Germany and elsewhere in the *Reich*, especially after *Kristallnacht*. But it is an entirely inaccurate description of the Jews of Nazi-occupied Europe after the war began, especially after 1940–1, and certainly during the period of the Holocaust itself. The Jews could not flee from German-occupied or controlled Europe *even if they wished to do so*. The fact that the Jews were *forbidden to emigrate* is also of crucial importance in assessing the responsibility of the democracies in allegedly failing to do more to assist the Jews. To many historians, considerable responsibility for the fact that so many Jews perished in the Holocaust rests with the Allies and the high barriers to Jewish refugee immigration they allegedly erected. In reality, this claim is wholly or almost wholly a *non sequitur*, since the Jews could not emigrate from Nazi-occupied Europe. The barriers to Jewish emigration from Nazi-occupied Europe *were deliberately erected by the Nazis themselves*, without reference to and certainly not in response to, the refugee immigration policies of the democracies – which were, in any case, far more liberal than is often imagined.[53] The Nazis, and the Nazis alone, bear total and complete responsibility for erecting these barriers to Jewish *emigration*, obviously in preparation for genocide.

Both contemporaries of the Holocaust in the democracies and, more disturbingly, many later historians, have simply failed to understand this fundamental distinction between refugees and prisoners, or the basic change in the status of Jews in Nazi-occupied Europe which occurred with the outbreak of the war or shortly thereafter. The failure to understand this distinction, it is surely no exaggeration to say, is at the heart of the entire historiography of 'rescue' and of the many conceptual and factual errors and misconceptions evidenced in the historical literature of this topic. This failure to understand the distinction between a 'refugee' and a 'prisoner' was in evidence throughout the war itself, with the Jews trapped in Nazi-occupied Europe being habitually and almost invariably described as 'refugees' (when they were no such thing) and the only governmental body created anywhere in the democracies during the war specifically to deal with the plight of the Jews being named, most misleadingly, the United States 'War Refugee Board'.

The fact that most contemporaries of the Nazi Holocaust, as well as more recent writers and observers, have thought of the Jews of 1939–45 Europe as refugees rather than as prisoners has in itself been a powerful factor in raising the assumption and expectation that it was possible for the democracies to have done something more to rescue those Jews, when in reality they were powerless to do anything at all apart from defeating Hitler. Finally, it has led many to view the period 1933–9 – when most German and other *Reich* Jews, who were then truly refugees, did emigrate and thus managed to survive – as of a continuous piece with the plight of the Jews after 1939 and especially after mid-1941, when emigration became impossible or virtually so. One is reminded of the story of the poor Jew in nineteenth-century Bialystok who suggested that a marriage take place between his son and the daughter of Baron Rothschild. 'And already', he proclaimed, 'we are 50 per cent in agreement!' About rescue, there was 50 per cent agreement: the only relevant party who was proving troublesome, alas, was Adolf Hitler.

Jews were explicitly forbidden to emigrate from Nazi-occupied Europe by stages from 1939 to (at the latest) 1942, although this process varied from country to country. Perhaps the most important and significant decree forbidding Jewish emigration from Nazi-occupied Europe was the 'Regulation for the Ban on Jewish Emigration from the Government-General' of Poland, issued by the Reich Security Main Office on 23 November 1940, shortly after the creation of the Warsaw Ghetto on 2 October 1940. This document is surprisingly little-known, and certainly unappreciated, although it heralded a basic shift in Nazi policy towards the Jews, from officially encouraging their emigration to officially forbidding it. While it cannot directly be coupled with the genocide of the Jews (which began with the invasion of the Soviet Union in June 1941 or shortly thereafter), it was a *sine qua non* for future genocide, certainly for mass murder on the scale which actually occurred.

The language of this 'Regulation' is highly significant, and it ought to be reproduced in full:

REGULATION FOR THE BAN ON JEWISH EMIGRATION FROM THE GOVERNMENT-GENERAL, NOVEMBER 1940

In a Decree of October 25, 1940, the Reich Security Main Office (*Reichssicherheitshauptamt*) has informed me of the following:

'Owing to the fact that the emigration of Jews from the Government-General still further considerably reduced the already shrinking opportunities for emigration for Jews from the *Altreich* [pre-1938 Germany], the *Ostmark* [Austria] and the Protectorate of Bohemia and Moravia, contrary to the wish of the Reich Marshal, I request that no such emigration be considered.

'The continued emigration of Jews from Eastern Europe [to the West] spells a continued spiritual regeneration of world Jewry, as it is mainly the Eastern Jews who supply a large proportion of the rabbis, Talmud teachers, etc., owing to their orthodox-religious beliefs, and they are urgently needed by Jewish organizations active in the United States, according to their own statements. Further, every orthodox Jew from Eastern Europe spells a valuable addition for these Jewish organizations in the United States in their constant efforts for the spiritual renewal of United States Jewry and its unification. It is United States Jewry in particular, which is endeavoring, with the help of newly immigrated Jews, especially from Eastern Europe, to create a new basis from which it intends to force ahead its struggle, particularly against Germany.

'For these reasons it can be assumed that after a certain number of emigration permits have been issued, creating a precedent for Jews from the Government-General, so to speak, a large part of the entry visas [which are] mainly for the United States, will in future only be made available for Jews from Eastern Europe.'

I fully accept the point of view of the Reich Security Main Office and request that you will not pass on to the office here for decision any more applications by Jews to emigrate. Such applications would of course have to be rejected here.

I empower you to reject without further investigation any applications by Jews from the Government-General for permission to emigrate. It is requested that applications to emigrate shall be forwarded here only if they involve Jews holding foreign citizenship. As there is no further question of emigration by Jews from the Government-General as a matter of principle, there is also no need for a Jew to receive a permit to visit the Reich for the purpose of obtaining a visa from a foreign consulate in the German Reich. It is requested that even applications by Jews for the issuing of a permit for the purpose of obtaining a visa from a foreign consulate in the Reich should also be rejected.

(for) Eckhardt[54]

It will be seen that the 'continued emigration' of Jews from Poland was directly linked by the SS to the 'continued spiritual regeneration' of the Jews in the West, especially the United States, particularly by 'orthodox Jews' – a theme seldom encountered in Nazi propaganda. With the most limited of exceptions, chiefly those of 'Jews holding foreign citizenship', virtually all Jewish emigration from the General-Government of Poland was, from that date, forbidden, a *Diktat* which applied to Jews of all conditions and (despite the phrasing of the 'Regulation') all religious and ideological viewpoints.

Since Poland's Jews were, at this point, being herded into ghettos, it might be assumed that a general regulation forbidding emigration would be redundant. In fact, however, Jews could, in the absence of such an edict, theoretically have emigrated – although probably in limited numbers – to the United States (still neutral in the war, and with a now-unfilled Polish immigration quota), to Latin America, to Shanghai, to Rumania and Hungary, even to the Soviet Union (which had shortly before entered into the Nazi–Soviet non-aggression pact) or even to Palestine, where fewer Jews actually migrated in this period than allowed under the ceiling placed by the MacDonald White Paper (although of course Britain, and hence Palestine, was officially at war with Germany). In the *absence* of such a gratuitous Nazi edict forbidding Jewish emigration, it is reasonable to assume that *some* of these Jews trapped in central Poland would have emigrated. The doors, however, were firmly shut: by the Nazis, it must be emphasised.

Similar edicts forbidding emigration followed in all countries under direct Nazi control: after 1940–1 it was in effect impossible for Jews legally to emigrate from Nazi-occupied Europe to places of safety. In May 1941 the emigration of Jews from France and Belgium was forbidden, the reason given by Walter Schellenberg, acting for Reinhard Heydrich, being 'the undoubtedly imminent Final Solution of the Jewish question'.[55] In mid-1941 Heinrich Himmler placed a blanket ban on the legal emigration of Jews throughout newly conquered Nazi territory, with Heydrich stating that 'In place of emigration, a further possible solution has now begun in the shape of the evacuation of the Jews to the east, in accordance with the prior approval of the Führer'.[56] On 23 October 1941 Heinrich Müller, the head of the Gestapo, banned further Jewish emigration from Germany itself. Legal emigration of Jews to the United States and elsewhere had continued until that date, but thereafter only 'extremely limited' numbers of Jews could legally leave, although the position of German Jews remained curiously 'privileged' until 1943 or 1944.[57]

As the distinguished historian Saul Friedlander has noted, 'All emigration of Jews from occupied Europe was forbidden (order of October 23, 1941), and construction work on the Belzec extermination camp in the Government General [of Poland] had begun'.[58] The Nazi order forbidding emigration was transmitted to Germany's embassies in satellite countries such as Rumania and strong pressure was placed upon the anti-semitic regimes there to enforce this policy.[59] In Rumania, for instance, newspapers were forbidden to print travel or shipping notices likely to assist Jews wishing to emigrate.[60] German naval patrols policed the coast of Rumania and Bulgaria to halt fleeing Jews.[61]

Jews in semi-independent states under ultimate Nazi rule remained theoretically free to emigrate for slightly longer: Jews in Vichy France, for instance, could emigrate until 'the summer of 1942' when their further emigration was 'blocked'.[62] Most – perhaps virtually all – of the criticism levelled by subsequent historians at the Allies for failing to rescue more Jews concerns the limbo period between initial Nazi German occupation and the imposition of the full horrors of deportation, for example the schemes to allow several thousand Jewish children to emigrate from Vichy France to Britain and America in 1941–2, a period before knowledge of the scope of the 'Final Solution' had reached the West, and hence before the Western Allies knew what fate lay in store for Jews trapped in Nazi-occupied Europe.

A certain amount of Jewish refugee emigration also took place from Poland and Slovakia to Hungary and Rumania, where, although increasingly vicious anti-semitic legislation was in force, there were no deportations to Auschwitz (in the Hungarian case, of course, these began in March 1944). However, the relatively high figure of 70,000 often given as the number of Jewish refugees allowed to stay in Hungary 'cannot be substantiated,' according to Livia Rothkirchen: the actual figure appears to have been about 25,000.[63] Many, perhaps most of these, subsequently perished after the Nazi occupation of March 1944. Perhaps a further 300–350,000 Polish Jews from areas of their country occupied by Nazi Germany during its invasion in September 1939 managed to flee to the Soviet Union or to areas of eastern Poland annexed by the Soviet Union.[64] Nevertheless, owing to both the Nazi policy of refusing to allow Polish Jews to emigrate and to a hardening of Soviet attitudes towards the free migration of refugees, 'the number of Jewish refugees decreased in the spring of 1940 and ceased almost completely during that summer'.[65] Many thousands of these were subsequently murdered by the *Einsatzgruppen* following the invasion of the Soviet Union in June 1941 or perished over the next few years in Nazi extermination camps, although a large number – perhaps 250,000 – were alive at the end of the war and were allowed to reemigrate.

Because the Jews of Nazi-occupied Europe were prisoners rather than refugees, they were quite literally unreachable by the Allies. (If there were any exceptions at all to this generalisation, they were extremely limited in number.) It is commonly supposed that through 'indifference' to the fate of the Jews on the part of either the Allied governments or on the part of the Jewish communities of the democracies – or because of thinly veiled anti-semitism or anti-Zionism on the part of Allied government leaders, officials and policy-makers – nothing was 'done', or certainly very little, to rescue the doomed Jews of Europe. In my opinion, this supposition is fundamentally misguided and misleading. Nothing was 'done' to rescue the Jews of Europe because no one, anywhere in the democracies, could think of any effective action which would rescue the Jews of Nazi-occupied Europe. *Not one plan or proposal, made anywhere in the democracies by either Jews or non-Jewish champions of the Jews once the mass murder of the Jews of Europe had begun, could have rescued one single Jew who perished in the Nazi Holocaust.* This is a sweeping statement indeed, and one which can be justified only by considering the plans for rescue which were proposed in the democracies for the rescue of Europe's Jews – something which has, strikingly, never been systematically undertaken in any of the hundreds of books on the Holocaust. Once again, if any scheme or plan for rescue proposed at the time might have actually succeeded in rescuing any Jews at all – if there were any exceptions to my sweeping claim – these were extremely limited in number and effect.

The historian must also draw a distinction between proposals for rescue made *at the time* and those devised by historians and armchair strategists many years later. With the benefit of hindsight, it is, I suppose, possible to think of plans for rescue which might have worked. There are two points to be made here. First, such a procedure is profoundly ahistorical: with the gift of historical hindsight, no one is less than omniscient. This gift, an attribute of the Divinity, is not one, alas, which is possessed by mortal human beings, whom the historian must assess on their own terms and in the context of his or her own knowledge and assumptions. Second, *even with hindsight* there appears to have been remarkably little which could actually have been done.

It is also necessary to object to the view that nothing was 'done' because of a failure either to accept or to internalise the magnitude and unprecedented evil of the Holocaust. To be sure, since nothing like the Jewish Holocaust was deliberately attempted in modern history (the mass murders of the Armenians during the First World War being the only arguable precedent), it is not surprising that many fair-minded people were unconvinced of the reality of the Holocaust until the liberation of the camps, the Nuremberg Trials and, above all, the photographs of the corpses and the surviving living skeletons. Many senior Jewish leaders in the democracies later confessed that they did not fully believe the truth of the reports of the Holocaust until after the war. An example here is that of Professor Selig Brodetsky, President of the Board of Deputies of British Jews throughout the 1940s. Brodetsky, who was born in a Ukrainian *shtetl* and barely survived a pogrom, was the first Jew of eastern European background to become leader of Anglo-Jewry, a position normally reserved for scions of Anglo-Jewish 'grandee' families such as the Rothschilds. Brodetsky was also a lifelong Zionist and his election, in 1939, is often seen as the triumph of the Zionist-oriented immigrants over the assimilated Anglo-Jewish 'cousinhood'. Yet in his autobiography Brodetsky pointedly insisted that:

> We still did not realise the terrible extent of the annihilation of the Jewish populations of Europe carried out systematically and in cold blood, till it all came out at the Nuremberg Trials of the chief war criminals, when the war was over.[66]

Nevertheless, the failure fully to understand, or even believe, the reports of the Holocaust as they filtered to the West after mid-1941 (with the first descriptions of the gas chambers reaching the West in mid-1942), is simply a *non sequitur* to the possibilities of rescuing any of the Jews remaining in Nazi-occupied Europe unless it can be shown that viable plans of rescue were proposed at the time (or since then) and ignored by sceptical governments. *No such viable plans for rescue were made by anyone.* Most recent scholarly books on this subject, even those by worthy researchers and historians, simply obfuscate this fact, typically by failing to discuss the actual proposals of the schemes for rescue which were made at the time.

A typical example here is Deborah E. Lipstadt's *Beyond Belief*, published in New York in 1986. A well-researched account of American press reaction to Nazi anti-semitism, its central theme is that the mass murder of the Jews during the war was 'beyond belief', and that 'skepticism always tempered belief'.[67] Professor Lipstadt goes on, however, from this unsurprising fact to castigate the American government (as do so many other historians) for allowing their scepticism to deter schemes for rescue which 'could have saved thousands and even hundreds of thousands'.[68] Her book devotes a chapter to 'Reluctant Rescuers' (pp. 197–217), examining press reports of rallies by 'rescue' organisations and of the Bermuda Conference of April 1943, but nowhere explains what fruitful plans for saving Europe's Jews were proposed and not acted upon, or what these proposals were, assuming – with no evidence at all – that potentially fruitful schemes for rescue actually were made. In fact, no potentially fruitful proposals for rescue were made by anyone, and her argument is a *non sequitur*. The Jews of Nazi-occupied Europe were, to reiterate, prisoners of Hitler, whose rescue was impossible so long as Nazi policy remained committed to genocide.

Writings in the American and British press during the initial period of the war about the fate of the Jews under Hitler's rule were less frequent than before; the Jews were invariably referred to and discussed as 'refugees', and the problem continued to be conceptualised by Americans concerned with the Jews of Europe in this way.[69] *At the same time*, the Western world's press also contained, within months or even weeks, remarkably accurate reports about the herding of Poland's Jews into ghettos and brutal conditions there.[70]

Reports of the mass killings of Jews by the *Einsatzgruppen* in Russia appeared in American newspapers by October–November 1941, shortly after they occurred.[71] The first knowledge in the West of Auschwitz and the other extermination camps has been frequently debated and examined; the telegram sent to Britain and the United States in early August 1942 by Dr Gerhart Riegner, the World Jewish Congress's representative in Geneva, announcing that a plan that 'the total of the Jews living in Germany and German-occupied Europe . . . should be exterminated' had been 'discussed' by Hitler, is often seen as the first authoritative report of the genocide.[72] Riegner's message, it will be clear, was extremely vague; specific news of *Auschwitz* did not reach the West until April 1944, nearly two years later.[73] Riegner's message reached the American State Department on 11 August 1942, but they regarded it as 'unbelievable,' and did not transmit the telegram to Rabbi Stephen S. Wise, President of the American Jewish Congress, who was widely regarded as the primary leader of the American Jewish community at the time. Riegner had specifically asked that his message be relayed to Wise.[74]

Wise did receive Riegner's message from other sources in August; in September reports reached other American groups, such as the Agudath Israel World Organisation in New York.[75] Wise waited for official confirmation of these reports for several months, finally receiving official confirmation from Sumner Wells, American Under-Secretary of State, on 24 November 1942.[76] Wise held a press conference on the same evening, incidentally becoming the first senior Jewish leader in the West forced to confront the most fundamental questions of a response to the terrible news: what could be done? What should be done? Those questions would be posed and reposed – and remain unanswered – until liberation in 1945.

Rabbi Wise's months of delay, and those of the American State Department, have been repeatedly criticised by extreme historians and others who argue that the West's Jewish leadership was indifferent if not complacent in the Holocaust. Such criticism is simply nonsense: neither the West's Jewish leaders in late 1942, nor the American government, had the slightest power to stop Hitler's genocide, and knowledge of the Holocaust in the West did not – and *could not* – have halted or diminished the death toll, given Hitler's psychotic monomania. Yehuda Bauer has criticised one such essay which puts the view that American Jewry and the Allies were indictable in a notably incisive way. Referring to Saul S. Friedman's essay on 'Jewish Powerlessness' in the 'Finger Report', Bauer notes that:

> Friedman, too, is very angry, and he slips occasionally, sometimes very, very badly. Typical is his statement that while Wise procrastinated, between August 28 and November 24, 1942, 'five to ten thousand Jews . . . [were] being evacuated daily from the Warsaw ghetto to Treblinka' . . . [T]he innuendoes and implications of Friedman's statement come very close to a blood libel. He says, in effect, that had Wise not procrastinated in those weeks Warsaw Jewry would not have been murdered . . . One wonders how this preposterous piece of irresponsibility found its way into the [Finger] Report.[77]

Concerning the six months or so following Wise's press conference, a number of facts about the behaviour of the American Jewish community, its leaders and major organisations, seem clear. The first is that, far from being indifferent to the fate of Europe's Jews, American Jewry was centrally obsessed by it, realising full well what Hitler was likely to have in mind. The second point is the total and absolute inability of American Jewry to suggest any cogent or realistic means of rescuing Europe's Jews. The third point is that American Jewry's organisations and leaders settled upon, as a substitute for feasible plans or proposals for rescue, a group of pseudo-proposals, repeated again and again, which were without actual value or merit, in part because they still conceptualised the problem before them as the relief of refugees as it had been before the war, and in part because they were presented with a problem which was inherently without a solution. The fourth point is that it is very difficult to discern any difference in the likely effectiveness of their proposals between the strategy and plans of 'Establishment' organisations and leaders of the American Jewish community, such as Rabbi Stephen Wise, and those of 'fringe' bodies and activists outside the mainstream, such as Rabbi Peter Bergson and the Hebrew Committee of National Liberation, the Yiddish-speaking community, Revisionist Zionists or Strictly Orthodox Jewish groups. Despite frequent attempts made subsequently by these groups or their post-war supporters to contrast their own dynamism and activism with the lethargy and indifference of the American Jewish 'Establishment', no such dichotomy existed, while the proposals for rescue made by American Jewry's fringe groups were just as pointless as those made by the Jewish mainstream.

The final point is that mainstream Jewish opinion in the democracies, especially in the United States, hardened during the war in favour of the Zionist movement and the creation of an independent Jewish state in Palestine, positions not really central before Hitler took power. This transformation came as a result of the Holocaust with its demonstration of Jewish powerlessness in the most extreme form imaginable, but Jewish mainstream opinion now looked as well to the creation of a Jewish state as 'compensation' for the Holocaust, and as an achievable goal, obviously momentous in terms of Jewish history, which might go some way towards redressing the losses in Europe. The centrality of Zionism to Western Jewry after about 1942 was a direct response to its effective powerlessness in the face of Hitler and would probably not have become so had Nazi anti-semitism not existed.

Within days of Rabbi Wise's confirmation of news of the Holocaust, a meeting was arranged between four prominent American Jewish leaders and President Franklin D. Roosevelt. The leaders represented the span of Jewish opinion in the United States, comprising Wise, Henry Monsky of B'nai B'rith, Rabbi Israel Rosenberg, head of the Union of Orthodox Rabbis of the United States, Maurice Wertheim of the American Jewish Committee and Adolph Held of the Jewish Labor Committee.[78] This meeting, held on 8 December 1942, followed a national Day of Mourning for the Jews of Europe initiated by Wise and other American Jewish leaders on 2 December 1942.[79] Wise had no trouble organising this presidential meeting, which followed only six days after writing to Roosevelt requesting it.[80] This group comprised, incidentally, the only Jewish delegation to meet with Roosevelt on any matter during the whole of the war.[81]

Roosevelt was, of course, highly sympathetic and noted that he was 'well acquainted' with 'the horrors' befalling the Jews; he also made one of the very few pertinent comments made on the subject of rescue during the whole of the war, stating that:

> we cannot treat these matters in normal ways. We are dealing with an insane man – Hitler, and the group that surrounds him represent an example of a national psychopathic case. We cannot act toward them by normal means. That is why the problem is very difficult.[82]

He also said that he had interceded to release the Jews in North Africa from Vichyite 'concentration camps' and 'to abolish all the special laws against the Jews', and readily agreed to endorse any statement drawn up by the delegation. 'I leave it entirely to you.'[83]

At Roosevelt's request the delegation made a number of suggestions: the only one which is recorded in Adolph Held's 'Report' on the visit was 'about the possibility of getting some of the neutral representatives in Germany to intercede on behalf of the Jews'. Roosevelt 'took notice' . . . but 'made no direct replies'.[84]

On the same day that the Jewish delegation visited Roosevelt, the three great Allies issued their first official statement on the genocide of the Jews, which 'condemn[ed] in the strongest possible terms this bestial policy of cold-blooded extermination'.[85]

In effect, the leaders of the American Jewish community had no lucid suggestions to make. This was obvious at the moment that news of the mass murders reached America and was just as obvious on the day Hitler killed himself. This failure was most certainly not because of indifference, disunity, fear of latent anti-semitism, hero-worshipping of Roosevelt, a reluctance to enter the political thicket or to rock the boat during wartime, or any of the other explanations which have been offered time and again. If there were indeed any effective and cogent proposals to be made as to how, realistically, Hitler could be stopped from killing Europe's Jews, someone in the American Jewish community would have identified them within a few days, and certainly during the course of the war. No such proposals were ever made.

The Governing Council of the American Jewish Congress (AJC), the premier representative body of the American Jewish community, considered both the Nazi Holocaust and the recently held meeting with Roosevelt only a few days later, on 10 December 1942. Among the thirty-five key Jewish leaders present at this meeting were Louis Lipsky, Jacob Fishman, Marie Syrkin, and (as an invitee) Nahum Goldmann of the World Jewish Congress. The meeting then discussed the concrete proposals 'for further action' which had been made up to that point.

PROPOSED ACTION ON EUROPEAN SITUATION

The meeting then devoted itself to the consideration of possibilities for further action. Mr. Sagal reiterated proposals previously presented, namely:

1) Day of Universal Mourning.
2) Procession of hundreds of thousands of Jewish men, women and children in the streets of New York, and, if possible, in other large cities.
3) Heads of public schools should be approached for permission for Jewish children to participate in the processions and the reason therefor explained to other children.
4) Meetings should be held at all colleges and professors invited to speak and express their horror.
5) If the Jewish processions are held on a weekday, all Jewish stores should be closed. Work should be stopped. The CIO and the AFL should be persuaded to order stoppage of work on that day.
6) Paid advertisements should be placed in all the leading American papers setting forth the demands of the Jewish people, covering not only the present but the future.

7) Appeal to the United Nations to express their horror at the Nazi crimes and issue grave warnings to the German people that those guilty of the crimes will be punished after the war.

8) An effort should be made to secure proclamations from all the Governors of the States and the Mayors, calling upon the population on the day of the processions to participate in the Jewish mourning and protest.

9) Radio commentators should be urged to comment on the massacres.

10) American Women's Organizations should be approached by the Jewish women to join us for humanitarian reasons.

11) The City Council of New York should adopt a solemn protest. Attempts should be made to have other city and state legislatures take similar action.

12) Since Nazi physicians use their medical skill to murder Jews in as large numbers as possible, the medical profession should be called upon to express its horror at this debasement of the physician's function and this violation of the Hippocratic oath.

13) An attempt should be made to reach the millions of German-Americans who cannot be in sympathy with the murder scheme. A protest from them, broadcast through the underground radios to Germany, should be secured.

14) An effort should be made to reach other organizations in the U.S., made up of Czechs, Poles, etc., with a view to getting them to express their sorrow and to call upon the United Nations for action on behalf of the Jewish people.

15) The Churches should be approached. On a given day, every religious head throughout the country should speak out in protest against the massacre of the Jews. In addition, some outstanding Catholic, like Alfred E. Smith, should contact the Pope and have the Pope take action.[86]

These suggestions were discussed by the meeting, with few changes made. A Coordinating Committee was established to deal with rescue, after Dr Nahum Goldmann recommended the establishment of four committees by the AJC 'to arouse the Jewish masses', 'to deal with the clergy [and] the Christian churches', 'to rouse public opinion' and finally 'to bring about action by Washington', without specifying what 'action' they had in mind.

Even a cursory consideration of the points made by the AJC in December 1942 will reveal their complete futility. Of these fifteen proposals, thirteen referred to action within the United States itself, chiefly aimed at arousing American public opinion against the horrors of Nazism. As such, they were irrelevant to assisting the Jews of Europe: Hitler took no heed of German public opinion, let alone American, while in any case America had already given signal evidence of its feelings towards Nazi Germany by declaring war on it. The only two points of substance, numbers (7) and (12), were also both useless. The United Nations, and the leading Allies, repeatedly condemned Nazi atrocities against the Jews and, from 1943 at the latest, were officially committed to post-victory war crimes trials for the top Nazis and those who carried out the killings of Jews and other civilians. The effect of these actions on either the direction or the pace of the Holocaust was, it could be argued, precisely zero, although threats of post-war justice arguably influenced some of the rulers of the Nazi satellites such as Admiral Horthy, so long as this remained possible. Point (12), about Nazi physicians, was similarly useless: Dr Mengele and his ilk paid no heed to the Hippocratic oath.

It will also be seen that some of the points heard most often in post-war discussions of what could have been done were nowhere to be seen, especially the bombing of Auschwitz (the name was, of course, unknown at this time in the West) and the other extermination camps, the interdicting of the train lines and other proposals of this kind. No such proposals were made by anyone before mid-1944 and they would, in any case, have been logistically impossible prior to the beginning of 1944 at the earliest.

Throughout late 1942 and early 1943, the AJC spent most of its time and energy coordinating measures concerned with the Holocaust. A memorandum issued by its Governing Council on 10 December 1942 maintained that 'more dramatic undertakings are necessary *now*', and all the statements of this body and others within the American Jewish community show a profound sense of the necessity of urgency. Most of their proposals at that time, however, centred around arousing American opinion, especially the media and the churches, as well as mobilising Jewish opinion within the United States. The 'Agenda' of the Planning Committee of the AJC, formulated less than a week after the meeting with Roosevelt, did contain a number of new proposals seemingly of more relevance to the situation of the Jews in Europe. Most of this 'Agenda' – probably three-quarters of the points made – concerned the arousal of American public opinion. But several of the points made in this document for the first term should be expressly noted:

AGENDA

PLANNING COMMITTEE ON THE EUROPEAN SITUATION
December 14, 1942

A. <u>AFFIRMATION OF THE OBJECTIVES, NAMELY,</u>
a. Stern warning by the United Nations.

b. Havens for those that can be saved.

c. Establishment of the Commission to investigate the crimes against civilian populations.

d. To make known to the Axis people that all those who are responsible for the crimes will be held to strict accountability . . .

6. REPRISALS

a. Conference with military authorities to discuss the question of feasibility of military reprisals.

b. Conference of influential Americans to which diplomatic representatives of subjugated countries should be invited to launch slogans of reprisal against German civilian population.

c. Establishment of courts of justice to try and condemn to death the guilty . . .

8. HAVENS

a. Havens for children in Switzerland.

b. Proposals for haven in Sweden, etc.

c. Publications.

aa. Proposal that the various documents recounting the outrages be made available in such form to be distributed to the widest public.[87]

The new points made there were a discussion of how actually to issue a warning ('proposals: radio, leaflets') to the peoples of Europe on the treatment of the Jews; a proposal for a 'conference with military authorities to discuss the question of the feasibility of military reprisals' and the matter of 'havens' in Sweden, Switzerland and elsewhere.

Once again, these suggestions reflect a bankruptcy of practical ideas rather than lucid inspiration. Radio broadcasts on the fate of the Jews were repeatedly made throughout Europe; their effect was nil because the peoples of Europe had no say in the matter. 'Military reprisals' against Germany, in the form of thousand-plane raids by night and by day, were mounted continuously by the Western Allies. In 1945 the three great Allies had approximately 37 million men under arms, with the Anglo-American forces having the year before coordinated the greatest invasion in history. Their effects upon the Nazi death machine increased to greater than nil only when the concentration camps were actually liberated. The creation of 'havens' in neutral countries shows the greatest confusion of all, for only refugees can flee to havens of safety; prisoners cannot, and corpses cannot.

A 'Strictly Confidential' typescript memorandum drawn up jointly by the AJC, and the World Jewish Congress (WJC), apparently in mid-January 1943, elaborated on these points. Again, most of the memorandum was concerned with invoking the support of American public opinion, but this document also gave more detail to the 'methods' of 'rescue' advanced before, as well as adding some new points.[88] The sections of this memorandum dealing with the substance of rescue were these:

CURRENT OBJECTIVES

1. Having secured the Declaration by the United Nations, the further objectives are:
a. The establishment immediately by the United Nations of a Commission to assemble the crimes against the Jews and other civilian populations with a view to bringing the guilty to the bar of justice immediately. To this Commission should be attached a Jewish advisory council or a Jewish advisor.
b. To secure a Declaration similar to that of the United Nations from the Latin-American members of the United Nations.
c. To make known to the Axis peoples through a continuous program that all those who are responsible for the crimes will be held to strict accountability in the hope that such a program will serve to deter the criminals and may move the populations to revolt against them.
d. To rescue the many thousands who can be rescued through the creation by the United Nations of havens in neutral and Allied countries.
e. To make possible the feeding of the stricken Jewish populations in order to avert their destruction on the grounds claimed by Hitler, that they deprive the Axis populations of food.

4. Rescue

The work of rescue of those who can still be saved has been one of the leading undertakings of the Congress movement. Involved in this effort are political negotiations of the highest importance, since the first essential is to secure the issuance of exit permits from Germany. These negotiations have now led to an undertaking by an influential Government to secure the issuance of such permission to leave German occupied territories.

The action of the British Government in bringing about the admission of children to Palestine from the Balkan countries followed a request by the representatives of the American Jewish Congress and the World Jewish Congress that such efforts should be undertaken.

Negotiations are continuing to secure the admission of Jews to such neutral countries as Sweden, Turkey, Portugal and Spain and to Allied countries, such as Britain, the possessions of the United States and member countries of the United Nations. Negotiations with respect thereto are being conducted with Washington by the representatives of the American Jewish Congress and in London by representatives of the World Jewish Congress.

6. Feeding

Since Hitler and his cohorts have offered as one of the reasons for the accelerated tempo of the extermination of the Jews the fact that this would eliminate the necessity of feeding the Jewish population, the idea has been revived that an offer should be made to secure some special status for the starving population of Europe, similar to that of the Greeks. This more particularly since the State Department itself vouches for the fact that none of the food intended for the Greek population falls into enemy hands. Negotiations in this respect are being conducted with the International Red Cross in Geneva, with the State Department and with the American Red Cross in Washington.

It will be seen that these proposals amounted to complete fantasy, and were based on an inability to come to terms with the sheer, relentless inhumanity of the Nazi regime as well as the fundamental confusion between refugees and prisoners. In reality, there was no possibility of 'an undertaking by an influential Government to secure the issuance of . . . permission to leave German occupied territories'. A special programme to feed the Jews of Nazi-occupied Europe, seen as a parallel towards efforts to feed the Greeks, was, unfortunately equally impossible. Until 1943 or even 1944, the Germans *did* continue to allow Jewish and non-Jewish relief sources abroad to send food and medical supplies into the Polish ghettos, possibly as a result of pressure by the German Red Cross, certainly in order to camouflage the Nazi programme of genocide.[89] The SS regularly robbed most of these donations, so that only a limited proportion reached the ever-diminishing number of Jews left alive in Poland.[90]

The reason given by the AJC as to why such a programme seemed to be possible, that 'Hitler and his cohorts have offered as one of the reasons for the accelerated tempo of the extermination of the Jews the fact that this would eliminate the necessity of feeding the Jewish population', is sheer nonsense. Hitler offered no public explanations. 'The necessity of feeding' the Jews is not an argument encountered in any Nazi rationale for the Holocaust, which in any case was based on Hitler's seizing the opportunity to remove forever 'the biological bases of Jewry' rather than on any 'rational' considerations. No special Western relief programme of feeding the Jews would have been allowed to succeed. The final point of substance, 'the admission of children to Palestine from the Balkan countries' will be considered below. It must be noted, however, that the two largest Jewries of the Balkan countries, Rumania and Bulgaria, survived the war, while those of Yugoslavia were unreachable because the Nazis had previously occupied the country.

The AJC and other leading Jewish and liberal organisations in America then sponsored a mass rally at New York's Madison Square Garden on Monday 1 March 1943. More than 20,000 persons crowded into the hall, with an estimated 75,000 others turned away for lack of space.[91] It was preceded by a press campaign of full-page newspaper advertisements that read: 'America Must Act Now!' The rally was addressed by a wide range of luminaries, including Chaim Weizmann, Governor Thomas E. Dewey (the Republican presidential nominee in 1944 and 1948), New York's colourful Mayor Fiorello La Guardia, Supreme Court Justice William O. Douglas, William Green, President of the American Federation of Labor, the Presiding Bishop of the Episcopal Church in the United States, and, in absentia, Sir William Beveridge, whose speech was broadcast from London. The rally adopted eleven resolutions, described by one commentator as 'restrained and practical', which summarised how mainstream Jewish and liberal groups and activists in the democracies viewed 'rescue' five months after the genocide of European Jewry was confirmed in the West.[92]

1. Through neutral intermediaries, Germany and the governments of the states it dominates should be asked to release their Jewish victims and permit them to emigrate.

2. The United Nations should designate sanctuaries, in Allied and neutral states, for Jews whose release may be arranged for.

3. American immigration procedures should be revised in order that refugees may find sanctuary here within existing quotas.

4. Great Britain should be asked to receive a reasonable number of new refugees and accommodate them for the duration.

5. The United Nations should urge the Latin American republics to modify their immigration regulations sufficiently to provide refuge for agreed numbers of Nazi victims.

6. England should be asked to open the doors of Palestine for Jewish immigration.

7. The United Nations should provide financial guarantees to neutral states offering refuge to Jews from occupied territory.

8. The United Nations should organize the feeding through neutral agencies of victims forced to remain under Nazi oppression.

9. The United Nations should undertake the financing of the program here outlined.

10. The United Nations are urged to establish an intergovernmental agency to implement the program of rescue here outlined.

11. The United Nations are urged to appoint a commission forthwith to implement their declared intention to bring the Nazi criminals to justice.

The programme for 'rescue' summarised here continued to comprise, with only limited additions, the essence of the American Jewish mainstream's proposals for saving European Jewry throughout the war. No further significant proposals were made by American Jewish mainstream groups for 'rescue' until the earliest proposals for bombing the rail links to Auschwitz were first voiced over a year later. It will be seen that these proposals were – in common with all others made in the democracies during the war – valueless and ineffective. Hitler was as likely (if asked politely) to agree 'to release [his] Jewish victims and permit them to emigrate' as he was to declare *Purim* a legal holiday throughout the whole of the *Reich*. To be sure, some of Hitler's satellites, especially Hungary and Rumania, would have been only too happy to allow their Jews to emigrate: unfortunately, Hitler would not have allowed it and any deal over (of all things) the large-scale emigration of Jews which these countries might have entered into with the West would obviously have quickly come to Hitler's attention and assuredly triggered a quick despatch of the SS to that satellite nation, probably in conjunction with a pro-Nazi *coup d'état* (as occurred in Hungary in 1944 when precisely this appeared to be happening).

The other proposal (point (8) above) directly concerned with the plight of Jews in Nazi-occupied Europe, to feed Jews 'forced to remain under Nazi oppression' is, with hindsight, similarly ludicrous and evidence of how little the West understood the all-consuming nature of the Holocaust, however well and immediately they understood its diabolical end. The remaining points chiefly demanded greater generosity towards Jewish refugees: proposals altogether worthy and meritorious, save for the unfortunate fact that Europe's Jews were not refugees. Perhaps the only proposal of any remotely practical value was the final one, dealing with the trial of Nazi war criminals, although it had, and could have had, no effect whatever upon Hitler's murderous plans.

Almost as soon as the AJC and other mainstream American Jewish bodies began to deal with the plight of European Jewry, voices of dissatisfaction and independent action were raised within the American Jewish community. The best known of these was the group associated with Rabbi Peter Bergson and the Hebrew Committee of National Liberation. Bergson, whose real name was Hillel

Kook, was a nephew of Rabbi Abraham Kook, the famous Ashkenazi Chief Rabbi of Jerusalem, who was instrumental in reconciling the political Zionist movement and a component of Strictly Orthodox Judaism. Other prominent Jewish activists connected with the Bergsonites included Ben Hecht, the playwright and Hollywood scriptwriter, who proved to be the publicity genius of the group, the impresario Billy Rose and Eri Jabotinsky, the son of the Revisionist Zionist leader.[93] Many among the Bergson group were in fact supporters of Vladimir Jabotinsky (who had died in 1940) and his Zionist Revisionist movement,[94] which had long been accustomed to standing outside the mainstream Jewish movement, demanding independent and radical action.

Bergson and his supporters also held a giant rally at Madison Square Garden, on 9 March 1943; it was apparently the intention of this marginal group to hold a mammoth public rally which spurred America's mainstream Jewish organisations to stage a rally of their own.[95] The Bergson group secured the support of dozens of American public notables, few of whom had been approached by the AJC, including former President Herbert Hoover, thirty-four senators and thirty-seven American generals and admirals.[96] The Bergson group's rally centrally featured an elaborately produced stage pageant, 'We Will Never Die!' celebrating the Jewish contribution to Western civilisation, written by Ben Hecht, produced by Billy Rose, and directed by the famous writer Moss Hart. It included music by Kurt Weill and featured Paul Muni and Edward G. Robinson in starring roles.[97] Forty thousand persons attended its two New York performances.[98] 'We Will Never Die!' then went on an America-wide tour, being performed in most of America's largest cities. The Bergson group supplemented these activities with a massive press campaign, certainly dwarfing that of the Jewish mainstream.

It is superficially easy to see why many post-war commentators have praised the vigour and activism of the Bergson group and contrasted it with the seemingly lethargic, overly subtle diplomacy of the AJC. Nevertheless, the actual proposals for rescue put forward by the group had as little to commend them as did the programme of the Jewish mainstream. The heart of the group's agenda consisted of advocating the creation of a Jewish Army, a goal which Revisionist Zionism had sought before the Holocaust began.[99] The Jewish Army was to consist of 'stateless and Palestinian Jews', recruited from the *Yishuv* and from 'stateless Jews living in North Africa.' The group estimated the size of the Jewish Army at 200,000.[100] What would such a force do?

> Suicide squads of the Jewish Army would engage in desperate commando raids deep into the heart of Germany. Jewish pilots would bomb German cities in reprisal. A Jewish Army would imply a call to arms of all stateless Jews living in North Africa so that they may participate in the imminent invasion of the European continent.[101]

It is not surprising that so many of the Bergson group were prominent in Hollywood, given this movement's view of total war – let alone total war as conducted by the Nazis – as similar to a B-grade Hollywood action film; it is equally unsurprising that it had little real following in the serious mainstream. The group's proposals were, of course, totally risible and fatuous. The Allies would never create and fund, nor should they have considered creating, an independent army exercising power without responsibility: the Jewish Army could only have existed, if at all, as a minor adjunct to the Anglo-American forces, its role entirely determined by the Allied High Command.[102] Without proper weaponry, equipment, reserves, air support, reinforcements, lines of retreat and communication, or professional generalship, and fighting alone in totally hostile territory hundreds of miles from the Allied front lines, the Jewish Army would indeed have consisted of 'suicide squads', merely adding pointlessly to the Jewish death toll in Europe.

The figure of 'Palestinian and stateless Jews' likely to be attracted to it also appears hopelessly inflated. The Jewish population of North Africa at this point numbered only about 340,000; it was highly problematical that they could be conscripted, given Vichy's continuing hold. But even if the 500,000 Jews of the *Yishuv* in Palestine were conscripted in the same proportions as was America's population as a whole, this would raise an 'army' of perhaps 50,000 men – less than one-third the size of the United States Coast Guard or of the British Merchant Marine in 1945. Additional manpower was not the Allies' problem: the United States could raise this number twenty times over by reducing very marginally its draft exemptions. The problem was the production of adequate weaponry and equipment, and the fact that the German war machine was still awesomely powerful. The exodus of so many able-bodied Palestinian Jews from the *Yishuv* (many surely sent to their deaths) would have seriously weakened the Jewish community in Palestine, possibly encouraging an Arab revolt or attempted massacre of the remaining Jewish population.

The central objection to the 'Jewish Army' proposal was, however, that it was completely irrelevant to the dilemma actually faced by European Jewry, the fact that they were unreachable and marked for death. No 'Jewish Army' acting alone could save them, and no 'Jewish Army' would persuade Hitler to stop his genocide.[103] It is rather difficult to believe that Bergson's implausible proposal did not have far more to do with creating the nucleus of a Jewish Palestinian force, to be used against the British and the Arabs, than with saving Europe's Jews from the Nazis.

The Bergson group also made several other proposals. One was for the United Nations officially 'to consider the cessation of atrocities against the Jews as an immediate aim of their military and political operations'.[104] This was a worthy objective, although it is difficult to see what positive effect its adoption would have had on Hitler. The group also placed a number of full-page advertisements in newspapers urging the West to take up Rumanian dictator Ion Antonescu's offer of 'selling' 70,000 Rumanian Jews in Transnistria to the West, their advertisement appealing to readers to send money for this purpose to the Bergson Committee.[105]

The Transnistrian proposal for the ransom of Rumanian Jews is often discussed in the literature of rescue as a classical lost opportunity. While it, and other such proposals, will be discussed below, two very basic points must be made here: first, the Transnistrian Jews *survived* the war, with the killings there carried out by Antonescu and his anti-semitic Iron Guard (and *not* by the Germans) ending by 1942. The Transnistrian Jews continued to live in wretched conditions of poverty and disease, but they managed to survive. Second, it was the Germans who firmly and strenuously opposed these proposals, as they did *all* such proposals which were floated by either the satellite governments or the Allies.[106] Bergson, and others who proposed a 'ransom' payment for the Jews of Transnistria, of course had no way of being aware of either the lack of independence of the Nazi satellite states nor, it would seem, Hitler's single-minded obsession with genocide, and Bergson and his supporters obviously deserve credit for attempting to offer practical suggestions. Nevertheless, none of their proposals were feasible and the vigorous and 'independent' Bergson group had no more insight into how to rescue the Jews of Nazi-occupied Europe than did 'Establishment' bodies such as the AJC.

On 15 March 1943, most of America's major Jewish organisations were represented at an emergency meeting held to devise new proposals for rescue.[107] The meeting was spurred by an urgent telegram from Szmul Zygelbojm, the Jewish representative of the Polish government-in-exile in London, begging Western Jewry to take 'extraordinary steps' towards rescue.[108] It established a Joint Emergency Committee for European Affairs, comprising delegates from eight large American Jewish organisations, which held numerous meetings and drew up another series of proposals for rescue.[109] That set of twelve proposals was then submitted to the Bermuda Refugee Conference held by the Allied governments from 19–29 April 1943.

Those proposals were remarkably similar to those suggested the previous year, but are included here for the sake of completeness:[110]

I. The United Nations should approach the German Government and the governments of the states it now partly dominates or controls, through the Vatican or neutral governments like Switzerland, Spain, Sweden, Turkey, Argentine, with a view to securing their agreement to the release of their Jewish victims and to the emigration of Jews to such havens of refuge as may be provided.

II. The United Nations should, without delay, take steps to designate and establish a number of Sanctuaries in Allied and neutral countries to accommodate substantial numbers of Hitler's victims and to serve as havens of refuge for those Jews whose release from captivity may be arranged for, or who may find their way to freedom through efforts of their own.

III. The procedure that now prevails in the administration of the existing immigration law in the United States, which acts as a deterrent and retardation of legal immigration under the established quotas, should be revised and adjusted to war conditions, in order that refugees from Nazi-occupied territories, within such quotas, may find Sanctuary here.

IV. Subject to provisions for its national security, England should be asked to provide for receiving a reasonable number of victims escaping from Nazi-occupied territories and to provide for their accommodation for the duration.

V. The possibilities in several British territories, both in Africa and in the Caribbean, should be explored without delay. Sanctuary has already been afforded to thousands of refugees in these territories and there is room for many more, if not for permanent settlement, at least for the duration.

VI. The United Nations should urge the Republics of Latin America to modify such administrative regulations that now make immigration under the law extremely difficult, and to endeavor to find temporary havens of refuge for a substantial number of refugees.

VII. Overriding pre-war political considerations, England should be persuaded to open the doors of Palestine for Jewish immigration and the offer of hospitality made by the Jewish Community of Palestine should be accepted.

VIII. The United Nations should provide financial guarantees to all such neutral states as have given temporary refuge to Jews coming from Nazi-occupied territories and provide for their feeding and maintenance and eventual evacuation. The neutral states should be guaranteed that the refugees will not become a public charge and that they will be transferred to permanent Sanctuaries as soon as possible.

IX. In order to do away with the lack of identity which many stateless refugees present, and to give them sponsorship and protection, an arrangement similar to that which existed under the League of Nations should be established and the Stateless refugees should be given identification passports analogous to the 'Nansen' passports.

X. In view of the fact that mass starvation is the design of the Nazi regime, the United Nations should take appropriate steps without delay to organize a system for the feeding of the victims of Nazi oppression who are unable to leave the jurisdiction and the control of the Axis.

XI. It is submitted that the United Nations undertake to provide the financial guarantees that may be required for the execution of the program of rescue here outlined.

XII. The United Nations are urged to establish an appropriate inter-governmental agency, to which full authority and power should be given to implement the program of rescue here outlined.

In support of these proposals an *aide memoire* is appended.

In the name of humanity and of the ideals which the Armed Forces of the United Nations have arisen to defend, we respectfully submit this appeal in the hope that effective action will be taken without delay.

As before, it will be seen that these proposals were perfectly useless. Most relate to increasing the number of refugees received in Allied and neutral countries: and these had no relevance to the actual circumstances of Europe's Jews. Probably the only novelty of any kind was the inclusion of approaches to the Vatican in order to facilitate the release of Jews. The Vatican was not mentioned in previous American schemes; its role in the treatment of Jews in Nazi-occupied Europe is, as is well known, highly controversial and much debated.[111] In all likelihood – a likelihood probably amounting to a near-certainty – Hitler would have paid no heed whatever to any pronouncement on the Jews made by the Vatican (which had denounced Nazi anti-semitism before the war began). Theoretically, and in hindsight, the Pope might have excommunicated all Catholic members of the SS (or of the Nazi Party) although the only likely effect of such a pronouncement would have been that the Nazis denounced the Pope as an agent of 'Judeo-Bolshevism' and an imposter. The Vatican had more influence on Catholic satellite states such as Hungary, which it used to good effect whenever it could. Significantly, however, the proposal made by the Joint Emergency Committee merely asked that the Vatican be approached to act as an intermediary to facilitate the release of Jews to neutral countries, and not for something more sweeping.

Another idea for rescue which was proposed at about this time was for the Allies to demand that Jews in Nazi-occupied Europe be treated as prisoners of war, and therefore be entitled to Red Cross assistance and protection. The earliest proposal to treat the Jews as prisoners of war which was officially made by the Jewish community was apparently in the 'Appendix' to the Joint Emergency Committee's proposals for rescue of April 1943. There it was suggested that 'the jurisdiction of the International Red Cross should, therefore, be broadened to render to Jews in ghettos and similar concentration areas the same services as are rendered to prisoners of war'.[112]

The difficulty with this proposal is similar to that which attaches to all the others: Hitler would not have allowed it. For Hitler to have given the Jews of Europe a new, higher status as 'prisoners of war' rather than sub-humans marked for death would have been tantamount to a total alteration of his most fundamental of fundamental policies. The Emergency Committee's assumption that Jews to be given this status were still 'confined in ghettos and penal labor colonies under pain of death' merely shows how imperfect was their knowledge of Hitler's empire of death.[113] In any case, we now know that the role of the International Red Cross in the Holocaust was strangely equivocal and blameworthy.

The Bermuda Refugee Conference, held in April 1943, has universally been seen as a sham and a failure by historians who believe that more should have been 'done'. Professor David Wyman titled the volume of primary sources and documents in his thirteen-volume collection *America and the Holocaust* which deals with Bermuda, *The Mock Rescue Conference*. He notes that 'American Jewish leaders were not deceived by the hoax carried out at Bermuda', and claims that both the American and British delegations 'strained to find reasons why the rescue proposals submitted to the conference were not workable'.[114] Other historians who have been more critical of the claim that more could have been 'done' and less critical of the Allies, have also echoed a measure of this criticism. For instance, Professor Yehuda Bauer, a voice of historical reason and clarity, notes that while 'Jewish organisations in America were, on the whole, fairly well informed about the failures of the Bermuda Conference . . . they did not respond with plans of their own'.[115] This is not accurate: plans were submitted, especially the 'Program For the Rescue of Jews From Nazi Occupied Europe' proposed by the Joint Emergency Committee for European Affairs in March–April 1943. These were not adopted in large part because they were utterly irrelevant to the actual plight of Europe's Jews. There were other reasons, of course, why the Bermuda Conference was a failure, especially the issue of Zionism and Jewish migration to Palestine, which plainly clouded the stance of the British government. Nevertheless, those other reasons were minor ones.[116]

The Bermuda Conference failed because it forced both the Jewish community and the Allied governments directly to confront and answer the question of 'do what?' What could, realistically, be done? Since this question, in April 1943, had no answer, it is not surprising that the Conference was a failure. The impossibility of rescue was clearly noted at the conference by many delegates, especially on the British side. Their remarks were not obfuscation or thinly disguised anti-semitism but the simple truth. Osbert Peake, Under-Secretary at the British Home Office, stated in Parliament on 19 May 1943 that the Jews 'for the present [were] mostly beyond the possibility of rescue . . . We must, I think, recognize that the United Nations can do little or nothing in the immediate present for the vast numbers under Hitler's control', a remark which, however blunt, was self-evidently true.

Sir Herbert Emerson, Director of the Intergovernmental Committee on Refugees, stated in a memorandum prepared for the Conference that

> the remedy that transcends all others is the victory of the United Nations as early as possible. During every day that the war continues, more persons will lose their lives than can be saved by any rescue measure so far suggested.[117]

This was harsh, but entirely valid. Emerson also stated that 'limited numbers' of Jews in Axis satellites could be rescued by negotiation with their governments, a claim which was, if anything, overoptimistic.[118] He was highly sympathetic to assisting the escape of Jews from Nazi-occupied Europe, and claimed that the Allies had put pressure on countries such as Spain and Switzerland to take in anyone who fled.[119]

At the Conference, the leader of the British delegation, Richard Law, MP, Parliamentary Under-Secretary at the Foreign Office, noted that such proposals as making a 'deal with Hitler' and bringing in food supplies to the Jews were 'manifestly impossible', and that only 'limited' measures, such as assisting those in Spain who had managed to flee, were 'profitable'. The leader of the American delegation, Dr Harold Dodds (President of Princeton University) agreed. The chief dissenter was Congressman Sol Bloom of New York, an outspoken champion of the Jews, who believed 'that we should at least negotiate to see what could be done'.[120] Perhaps they should have done this, although Hitler's drive to kill the Jews is very likely to have meant that any such negotiations were absolutely impossible. The Conference then discussed the matter of refugees at great length – that is, Jews who had *already* successfully fled from Nazi rule, chiefly those who had found their way to Spain or French North Africa. Since they were in no danger from the Nazi death machine, it is not surprising that the discussions on their behalf proved to be so much wasted time, and became increasingly conflated and confused with the (quite separate) issue of Jewish migration to Palestine.

Because 'rescue' was normally still conceptualised in terms of assistance to refugees – those who had already emigrated – rather than those who were trapped as prisoners, and since practical help to Hitler's prisoners was, in April 1943, quite beyond the power of the Allies, no one should be surprised that Bermuda proved a failure. The only surprising feature of Bermuda is that any subsequent historian should have imagined anything else, or that the Conference should have been viewed as a malign anti-semitic conspiracy rather than as mission impossible.

The period from May 1943 until the establishment of the War Refugee Board in January 1944 saw the foundation of yet more organisations devoted to rescue.

Chief among them was the American Jewish Conference (a body with close ties to the mainstream American Zionist movement) chaired by Rabbi Wise, Henry Monsky and Dr Israel Goldstein, founded specifically 'to consider and recommend action on . . . the status of Jews in the post-war world . . . [and] with respect to Palestine', an agenda broadened to include 'the problem of the rescue of European Jewry'.[121] (It will be seen that providing for the enhanced status of Jews in the post-war world, especially the question of Palestine, was by 1943–4 regarded as of at least equal importance to America's Jewish leadership as rescuing Europe's Jews.)

Within the Conference, a 'Commission on Rescue', chaired by Rabbi Irving Miller and Herman Shulman, backed by a committee of no fewer than fifty-seven members, met regularly from late October 1943 until mid-1944.[122] In its 'Report', the Commission was careful to note that 'opportunities for rescue work were . . . extremely limited', and in practice restricted to 'five major courses of action':

1. Psychological warfare against the Nazi program, on the one hand, to deter the Nazis by threats of punishment and on the other hand, to encourage people within occupied Europe to shelter Jews and assist them to escape;

2. Cooperation with the underground to assist Jews in ghettos and to smuggle Jews from their places of hiding across borders;

3. Pressure on satellite countries and encouragement to neutral countries to admit and maintain Jews pending their transfer elsewhere;

4. Establishment of new havens of rescue so that refugees might be transferred from the border countries and room made for newcomers; and

5. The transmission of food, medical supplies and clothing to occupied areas.[123]

A number of these points revealed much more sophistication than contained in earlier plans, especially the second. The other suggestions appear as pointless as those made previously, especially points (4) and (5).

In November 1943, the Commission adopted a more detailed programme of thirteen proposals 'as a basis for the Commission's work'; these were later submitted to the War Refugee Board:

A – Psychological

1. The leaders of the United Nations should again address a solemn warning to the Nazi leaders, their satellites and agents, that they will be held responsible for crimes against the Jews and brought to trial at the earliest opportunity.

2. The Commission on War Crimes now sitting in London should begin to function without delay and should start its public activities at an open session at which representatives of the principal powers should make it clear that their jurisdiction extends to all administrative acts, as well as actual atrocities which have been designed to hasten the extermination of the Jews.

3. These declarations and statements should be continuously broadcast to the German and satellite populations and disseminated through leaflets dropped by airplanes.

B – Relief

The deprivation of food and medical supplies constitutes a major factor in the program of extermination. In this respect the Jewish populations are in a far worse situation than the other subject populations; the Jews in Poland, for example, are allotted under the rationing system only about half the amount permitted the Poles; but even this half is rarely available. Supplies sent to the ghettos and concentration camps would save Jews from starvation.

4. Funds should be placed at the disposal of the International Red Cross for the sending of medicines and food packages to those areas in which the International Red Cross can and may operate.

5. Measures should be taken to attain the status of civilian prisoners of war for Jews confined in ghettos and concentration camps so that their friends and relatives may be enabled to send them food and clothing from free countries.

6. Jewish relief organizations should be given the necessary licenses for the transmission of funds to neutral countries bordering on Axis Europe from which supplies may be sent to the ghettos.

C – Rescue and Refuge

7. It is urgent that the United Nations publicly state their readiness to receive refugees who may escape. The United States could itself make an immense contribution by adjusting prevailing procedure in the administration of the existing immigration laws so that present quotas may be used in full. Palestine, which is in close proximity to escape routes, should be declared open to any Jewish refugee. If necessary, every refugee reaching territory of the United Nations could be held in specially prepared camps until his bona fides is [sic] fully established.

8. Neutral governments should be encouraged to receive refugees by the United Nations who should offer food and funds, and who should undertake to facilitate repatriation or resettlement after the war.

9. Machinery should be established in consultation with the military authorities and the underground movements to assist the escape of Jews whose lives are in jeopardy.

10. Pressure should be exercised on satellite countries, particularly in the Balkans, to permit the emigration of their Jewish populations and the transit of Jewish refugees across their territories. In this connection, it is urgent that the Rumanian Government should be pressed to return to Rumania those 75,000 Jews who have been removed to Transnistria, where they are now in danger of extermination by retreating German troops.

11. Measures should be taken by the military authorities to remove Jews from areas of military operation where, in case of reoccupation by the Nazis, they are likely to be destroyed. This applies particularly to such areas as Adriatic islands which have been held for brief intervals by guerrilla troops.

12. Many Jews could be saved by exploring the possibilities of the exchange of Axis nationals and sympathizers now in the territories of the United Nations for Jews under Axis control.

D – Machinery

13. It is clear that if this work is to be conducted effectively, some special agency must be established in consultation with the military authorities and in contact with underground movements. As this agency develops its work, new methods of assistance will appear.

Some of these more detailed proposals also give evidence of a degree of progress. In particular, point (6), suggesting licences for 'the transmission of funds' by Jewish relief organisations, occasionally (though not often) allowed some Jews to be ransomed by independent Jewish bodies, at least in very limited numbers. The proposal here recognised that this procedure seemed promising, although it must be noted that the Commission advocated the 'transmission of funds' purely to purchase 'supplies' to be 'sent to the ghettos', which was of course impossible. Another novel proposal, one strangely enough not officially made by any American rescue body before November 1943, was point (12): the exchange of 'Axis nationals and sympathizers' for Jews. The Commission's claim that 'many Jews could be saved' by such exchanges was, however, surely remarkably optimistic: a very limited programme of such exchanges did rescue a few German Jews, although never Jews in any other part of Europe. (This will be discussed more fully below.)

The remaining proposals, however, appear to be the usual *non sequiturs*, spiced with a good measure of ignorance and wishful thinking. It was true, for example (*pace* the beginning of section B), that 'Jews in Poland' were 'allotted under the rationing system only about half the amount permitted the Poles', but this state of affairs, lamentable as it was, continued only until the deportations to the extermination camps had begun in early 1942; by November 1943 probably fewer than 200,000 Jews remained alive in Poland, compared with 3.3 million in mid-1939. In any case, the statement here that 'supplies sent to the ghettos and concentration camps would save Jews from starvation', while unquestionably true, foundered on the twin rocks that no 'supplies' could be sent to the ghettos and concentration camps and, that moreover, virtually no Polish Jews remained alive. The other points were much of a muchness, running up against the inescapable fact that Hitler wished all the Jews in Europe to be killed and was carrying out his wish in a single-minded way.

One other proposal which was made at this time (but not earlier) was the creation of an *ad hoc* American governmental body specifically to deal with Hitler's Jewish victims. Nearly all of the earlier plans for rescue discussed here advocated the establishment of a *United Nations* body to rescue Europe's Jews. Among the eleven points adopted by the 9 March 1943 Madison Square Garden rally, for instance, was one in which 'the United Nations are urged to establish an intergovernmental agency to implement the program of rescue here outlined'. The establishment of such an international agency was one of the few positive outcomes of the Bermuda Conference. At some stage in 1943 the idea of a specific *American* rescue body, established and funded by Congress, began to gain ground.

Admirers of the Bergson group have claimed that the idea emerged from a suggestion by the Emergency Conference to Save the Jewish People of Europe, a Bergsonite meeting, held in New York in July 1943.[124] This was so, but it must be emphasised that the proposal took shape only during the course of the conference rather than before. A memorandum on the 'Emergency Conference To Save the Jews of Europe: An Outline of Its Program and Purpose', issued just before the Conference began, contains no reference to any such American body, only 'the suggestion of proposing to Governments the creation of a United Nations Agency . . . to save the remaining millions of Jews', similar to what had been proposed by mainstream Jewish groups more than a year before.[125] The other suggestions for discussion in this 'Outline' of the Emergency Conference's programme are the usual ones of 'direct relief in food and clothing for the Jews in Europe' and 'mass exodus of Jews from Europe' and the like, which were so utterly futile and pointless, and had all been made before.

At its conclusion the Emergency Conference produced a two-page summary of its 'Findings and Recommendations', which is reproduced here.[126]

FINDINGS AND RECOMMENDATIONS
of the Emergency Conference to Save the Jewish People
of Europe

As a result of its deliberations, the Emergency Conference has arrived at these three basic conclusions:

1. That saving the Jewish people of Europe constitutes a specific problem which should be dealt with as such, and not as part of the general refugee problem.

2. That most of the four million surviving Jews of Europe can be saved from annihilation prior to the cessation of hostilities, without detriment to the successful prosecution of the war.

3. That a specific governmental agency should be created for that purpose.

I. GOVERNMENTAL AGENCY
The government of the United States is urged to create an official agency specifically charged with the task of saving the Jewish people of Europe.

The other United Nations should be invited to participate in this agency, with a view to its ultimate conversion into a United Nations agency; but, because of the urgency of the problem, action should not be postponed pending the adherence of other nations.

II. TREATMENT OF JEWS IN AXIS COUNTRIES
1. The satellite governments of the Axis should be urged through the intermediary of the International Red Cross, of neutral countries, or of the Vatican, to guarantee treatment of Jews in accordance with the minimum standards guaranteed to other inhabitants. These minimum standards should particularly include freedom from execution without just cause or on a discriminatory basis, freedom from forcible deportation, equal food rations, and equal access to medical and health resources. The carrying out of this undertaking should be supervised by the International Red Cross or by neutral governments mutually agreed upon.

There are good grounds for the belief that the satellite governments of Germany, convinced as they are of the inevitable defeat of the Axis, will agree to this request.

2. If necessary, importation of limited quantities of food and medical

supplies should be permitted into Axis-held territory with a view to providing the Jews the same amount of nourishment as is received by non-Jews. These supplies should be distributed under the supervision of the International Red Cross or of neutral governments, following as far as possible the precedent established in feeding the people of Greece.

III. EMIGRATION OF JEWS FROM AXIS-HELD TERRITORY
All Axis countries should be urged through the intermediary of the International Red Cross, of neutral governments or of the Vatican to permit Jews to leave the territory controlled by the Axis.

IV. REFUGE IN NON-BELLIGERENT TERRITORY
1. The non-belligerent countries in Europe – Sweden, Ireland, Portugal, Spain, Switzerland and Turkey – should be urged to grant temporary asylum to all Jews escaping Axis-controlled territory. The governments of the United Nations should undertake to assist in feeding and clothing these refugees, and should further undertake to make arrangements for their evacuation from the non-belligerent countries of refuge during hostilities, and within a reasonable period after the cessation of hostilities.

2. The governments of the United Nations are urged to operate their foreign exchange controls so as to make possible financial assistance to Jewish refugees in non-belligerent territory.

V. REFUGE IN TERRITORY CONTROLLED BY UNITED NATIONS
1. Every government and authority associated with the United Nations should be urged to grant temporary asylum in territories under its control to all Jews who may escape or have escaped Axis-controlled territories, and whom it may be impracticable to maintain in non-belligerent territory; it being understood that such admission shall not constitute a claim to permanent residence after the end of hostilities.

2. Special attention should be paid to the practicability of the admission of Jewish refugees to Palestine. Indeed, Palestine is close to Axis-controlled territory; it can be reached without diverting shipping space; its Jewish community has repeatedly expressed readiness to welcome an unlimited number of Jewish refugees; and the country has already proven its capacity to absorb Jewish refugees in large numbers. The opening of Palestine to Jewish refugees from Axis-held territories is particularly important since the continued prohibition of their entry into Palestine, internationally designated as the Jewish national home, serves as [a] precedent for other United Nations and neutral countries in similarly barring their entry.

3. All non-belligerent countries should be requested to grant transit

facilities to all Jewish refugees from Axis-controlled territory who might be en route to any territory controlled by the United Nations, whether as refugees, as immigrants, or as repatriates.

VI. TRANSPORTATION

The following facilities, available at present without interference with the war effort of the United Nations, should be made use of in transporting Jewish refugees from Axis-controlled territory to their places of refuge:

1. Road and rail communications operating between Axis-held territory and Turkey and between Turkey and territory controlled by the United Nations.

2. Road and rail communications operating between Spain, Switzerland, Sweden, and Axis-controlled territory.

Note: Experts associated with the Relief and Transportation Panel of the Emergency Conference estimate that available neutral shipping alone can transport 50,000 persons per month from European countries. The number of people which can be transported by rail and road exceeds this figure many times.

3. Neutral shipping at present lying idle in United States ports.

4. Idle tonnage of neutral registry in other ports.

VII. MILITARY AND PUNITIVE MEASURES

1. In line with the announced policy of the United Nations that all atrocities and crimes against humanity committed by the Axis powers be met with just reprisals immediately, and with punishment of the guilty after the war, it should be specifically declared that such reprisals and punishment will also be inflicted for any atrocities and crimes committed by Axis countries against the Jews.

2. This policy should be officially brought to the notice of the Axis governments and – through the use of the radio, leaflets, and other appropriate means – to the knowledge of their populations.

3. More particularly, all Axis governments and authorities should be informed that they will be held strictly accountable for the death through murder, torture, deportation, starvation or denial of medical help of all Jews in territories under their control.

4. The same policy of just reprisals already applied by the United Nations, should be immediately extended to any authenticated case of anti-Jewish atrocities.

5. Special use should be made in such reprisals, and in the most dangerous military operations against the Axis in general, of available Jewish manpower not yet included in the armed forces of the United Nations.

Attention is called in this connection to the fact that there is already in existence a Jewish Palestinian military force consisting of approximately 23,000 persons.

It is also estimated that there are available perhaps 100,000 stateless Jews outside of the United States who have not been used for military service, many of whom have had previous military training.

It is, therefore, recommended that full military use of this source of manpower be made, preferably in Jewish military units.

Note: The experts associated with the Military Affairs panel of the Emergency Conference go on record unanimously to the effect that the recommendations made herein to rescue the Jews of Europe will not cause any adverse military repercussions or in any way impede the war effort of the United Nations. In fact they will greatly help the war effort.

VIII. PUBLIC OPINION

In addition to the above measures urged upon the governments of the United Nations, it is essential that public opinion in America be fully and frankly informed of the facts of the situation:

the extent and horror of the special tragedy endured by the Jewish people of Europe, and by them alone, in being marked by the Nazis for mass slaughter;

the desperate urgency of their need for help;

the common responsibility of the peoples of the United Nations to end this blood-bath; and

the many avenues of rescue actually available which could be put to immediate use by the governments of the United Nations.

IX. ORGANIZATION

The Emergency Conference resolves to transform itself into an Emergency Committee to Save the Jewish People of Europe, to further the policies herein recommended and to continue in function until the emergency is over.

More particularly, the Committee shall submit the above recommendations to the President and other public officials of the United States, shall seek to secure the co-operation of the Congress of the United States, and shall call for the continued support of the American people.

It was the Bergsonite Emergency Conference of mid-1943 which first introduced the proposal of a specific American government agency to deal solely with saving the lives of Europe's Jews onto the agenda of any American rescue organisation. It deserves full credit for this, although it will be argued in Chapter 5 that the War Refugee Board, the government body which emerged in part from this proposal, actually did virtually nothing whatever to save the lives of Europe's Jews, while it must be reiterated that no American group, including the Bergsonites, had proposed such a government agency before this.

A number of other points about the 'Findings and Recommendations' deserve highlighting. As with every other set of 'rescue' proposals, all were useless, offering no solution to the central dilemma that Europe's Jews could not escape and were beyond the influence of the Allies. It is also notable that the proposal for a 'Jewish Army', trumpeted only a year before by the Bergsonites in full-page newspaper advertisements as a virtual panacea for the Holocaust, has here been demoted to sub-point (5) of proposal (7), the estimated number of potential recruits being now drastically reduced. It will also be seen that the proposals of the mainstream and Bergsonite groups were virtually identical, with the Commission's advocacy of licences for 'the transmission of funds' by relief organisations and the Bergsonite proposal for a government body representing the chief difference between the two.[127]

By late 1943, pressure to establish an American government body specifically to deal with the extermination of the Jews was growing: this was chiefly the work of the Bergsonite group. Demand for such a body was an important component of a march in Washington, from the Capitol to the White House, held on 6 October 1943 (the day before the eve of Yom Kippur) by 400 Strictly Orthodox rabbis, organised by the Bergson group.[128] A resolution to establish such an organisation was introduced into Congress, where it had widespread support, including the endorsement of arch-conservatives such as Senator Robert Taft of Ohio. It was also widely commended in American newspaper editorials.[129]

As introduced, however, the resolution urged 'the creation by the President of a commission of diplomatic, economic, and military experts to formulate and effectuate [sic] a plan of immediate action designed to save the surviving Jewish people from extinction at the hands of Nazi Germany' rather than a body, such as the War Refugee Board seemed to be, with wide-ranging powers.[130] The Roosevelt Administration initially proved to be very lukewarm in its support of an American rescue body, which also received only indifferent support from Rabbi Stephen Wise.[131] As is well known, Roosevelt prevaricated until the end of 1943, when Secretary of the Treasury Henry Morgenthau, the highest-ranking Jew in the executive branch of the government, became (for the first time) extremely active in the rescue campaign.[132] A close friend and neighbour of Roosevelt for many years, he had considerable access to the President.

Pressure was also brought to bear on government policy by a group of (non-Jewish) liberals in the Treasury, including John W. Pehle, who became head of the War Refugee Board. This group of Treasury officials was disgusted and alarmed at the tiredness and lack of vigour of the American State Department over the rescue issue, and was in particular concerned with Assistant Secretary of State Breckenridge Long, who was viewed by most Jews and liberals as a tireless defender of the *status quo* and probably an anti-semite. As a result of this pressure the US War Refugee Board was established by President Roosevelt on 22 January 1944.

In February 1944, the newly established War Refugee Board asked twenty-seven Jewish and non-Jewish organisations concerned with rescue and the relief of refugees to make suggestions for specific policies for rescue to be pursued by the Board. This was the most comprehensive attempt by any source during the war to devise policies for rescue. Fourteen Jewish and non-Jewish organisations responded to the Board's request, among them virtually all major American Jewish bodies other than the B'nai B'rith.[133] A total of about 120 separate and specific proposals were made, which the War Refugee Board summarised in a valuable 'Digest of Suggestions Submitted to the War Refugee Board By Various Private Organizations in Response to a Circular Letter'.[134] As such, it represents the 'state of the art' of the rescuing of Jews from the Nazis as seen by America's best-informed and most active rescue organisations two and a half years after the genocide began and a month before the SS herded Hungary's Jews into ghettos prior to the last major act of genocide. Because of its importance, it is reprinted in full as an Appendix to this chapter. (The War Refugee Board is considered in more detail in Chapter 5.)

It is not precisely true to say that these suggestions were totally without merit: the last set of proposals made, advocating the transmission of funds, by implication to bribe Nazi officials where this could be done, might have saved some Jews. The extension of Red Cross facilities to the Jews of Shanghai might have worked and improved their lot, since the Japanese were not genocidal (but, by definition, neither were the Jews of Shanghai in any danger of genocide). Perhaps one or two other suggestions might have made a minor difference.

On the whole, however, and with minor exceptions, this lengthy set of suggestions, encapsulating every idea which had occurred to all the Jewish relief organisations in America since Hitler's plans for genocide had been confirmed twenty-eight months before, was without any practical value whatever. It is difficult to determine the most egregious single proposal included in this 'Digest'. But the suggestion made by the Union of Orthodox Rabbis (often a sophisticated and well-informed source) to 'send mercy ships to ghettos' is as good a candidate as one might find; indeed, that suggestion might serve as an epitome of the whole concept of 'rescue' as it emerged in the democracies during the war. Leaving aside the facts that in February 1944 only two ghettos continued to exist, and the Germans were unlikely to greet 'mercy ships' with white flags, the geographical absurdity of that proposal qualifies it as unintentional black humour of an especially macabre kind.

Virtually all the other suggestions reflect the wholly inaccurate conceptualisation of 'rescue' which marked almost everything said on the subject since 1942, especially the confusion of refugees with prisoners; underlying everything else was the impossibility of the task and the fact that even in 1944 no one could think of a single really fruitful proposal to make. It will also be seen (and it is especially noteworthy) that three months before Hungarian Jewry was sent to Auschwitz no one – not one single relevant body or group in the United States – recommended bombing Auschwitz or any other extermination camp or the rail lines bringing Jews there.

We have now examined all the proposals for 'rescue' made by any Jewish or non-Jewish organisation in the United States prior to the genocide of the Hungarian Jews (when the first proposals to bomb the rail lines to Auschwitz were made). It is assuredly self-evident that, taken *in toto*, a greater confession of bankruptcy, helplessness, inaccuracy and wishful thinking is difficult to imagine: not one group concerned with rescue made a single truly practical suggestion for rescuing anybody in the three years after the genocide of the Jews began (or, indeed, until the war ended, as will become apparent). It should also by now be perfectly evident that the reason that so little was 'done' was that rescue was impossible, and not because of any of the factors ranging from disunity through anti-semitism regularly given by historians.

Several groups in the American Jewish matrix, independent or relatively independent of the mainstream, also put forward their views on rescue. Yiddish-speaking American Jews comprised a community closer than their English-speaking co-religionists than to the Yiddish-speaking eastern European Jews who bore the brunt of the Nazis' extermination policies. Yiddish-speaking American Jews had, as a rule, emigrated more recently, kept up contacts with their kinsmen and compatriots in Poland and elsewhere, and were able to read eastern European newspapers and publications. Yet all the evidence suggests that the Yiddish-speaking community in America was far more pessimistic about the possibilities of rescue than other American Jewish groups. One thorough survey of the attitude of the Yiddish press in America to news of the Holocaust has described the suggestions which emerged in these terms:

> In total, the articles expressed anxiety over the daily murder of thousands and over the intolerable physical conditions of those who continued to suffer in Occupied Europe. But the rescue themes that emerged were sporadic, diversified, and inconsistent. They reflected the writers' frustration and total inability to come up with any sort of workable solution. The articles did, however, describe the situation and give the readers enough evidence and analysis to understand the blow against European Jewry.[135]

In March 1943, the Seventeenth Annual Conference of the Yiddish Scientific Institute (YIVO), recently transferred from Lithuania to New York, circulated a petition addressed to President Roosevelt and signed by 283 'prominent scholars in America', who were 'associated with 88 colleges and universities and 19 research institutes', calling upon the President to act to save the Jews of Europe. What did these scholars suggest?

Mr. President:

We appeal to you to speak and to act.

We appeal to you to find the means to let every German know what is being perpetrated by his rulers and to warn the German people that for generations this guilt will rest upon them unless the hands of the murderers are stayed.

We appeal to you as soon and as effectively as possible to apply hitherto unused methods to save the millions of European Jews doomed to death by the enemy of civilization.[136]

Strictly Orthodox Jews were another group (often divided among themselves) who were marginal to the mainstream of American Jewish life at that time. Since 1945 they have grown significantly in both numbers and centrality and a number of studies of Strictly Orthodox Jewish activities in America during the Holocaust have recently appeared by adherents of the movement.[137] The theme of most of these works is the contrast presented between the activism and unorthodoxy of America's Strictly Orthodox Jews and the torpidity of the Jewish 'Establishment'. The Strictly Orthodox, according to Kranzler,

> demanded action *now*, to correspond virtually minute-by-minute with the deepening mire in Europe. While other activists were content to do little or nothing about rescue, Orthodox activists fought for more visas, for relaxed entry requirements, for illegal food shipments, and increased Allied action and ransom. While others chose to remain passing [*sic*] and obey the laws, the Orthodox created fictitious bank accounts, forged papers, used illegal cash transfers and secret cables, pleaded and wept before high government officials, and risked imprisonment and death to save lives.[138]

There may be a modicum of truth in several of these claims. Some Strictly Orthodox Jews may have been saved from extermination by the bribery of minor Nazi officials in certain untypical situations. Strictly Orthodox rabbis were among the first to call for the creation of what became the War Refugee Board while – a point Kranzler omits – they were also among the very first to call for the bombing of the rail line between Preskov and Kosice, joining Hungary and Auschwitz.

Apart from some limited achievements of this kind, however, the extravagant claims made on behalf of Strict Orthodoxy are misleading. Strictly Orthodox Jews perished in precisely the same way as other Jews in Nazi-occupied Europe: they were not spared and not 'rescued'. Indeed, since most Strictly Orthodox Jews lived in Poland and Lithuania where the casualties were highest, in all likelihood a much higher percentage of Europe's Strictly Orthodox Jews perished than in other sections of the Jewish people.

Of course some Strictly Orthodox Jews managed to escape, such as the students of the Mirer Yeshivah, perhaps as many as 3–5,000, who managed to find their way to Japan, Shanghai and central Asia, but these had *already* fled from eastern Poland to the Soviet Union in 1939–40, following the division of Poland by the Nazi–Soviet pact, and managed to escape from Soviet rather than Nazi hands. Those trapped in *Nazi* territory – the great majority of Strictly Orthodox Jews in Poland and elsewhere – died in the Holocaust. Most claims for 'rescue' made in works representing the Strictly Orthodox viewpoint are of this kind, hallmarked by disingenuousness and equivocation, almost always in the context of extended gratuitous attacks on other streams within Jewry.[139] With the most limited of exceptions, Strictly Orthodox Jews did not rescue anyone from the Nazis, who were engaged in the deliberate destruction of 'the biological basis of Jewry' in Europe.

Central to the claims made by historians who view Strict Orthodoxy as having dealt with the Holocaust in a markedly more successful way than other strands in Jewry is this remarkable statement made by Kranzler in *Thy Brother's Blood* (pp. 57–8):

> In some ways, throughout the entire Holocaust period, the Nazis and others proved themselves no different from other barbarians who have intruded darkly into Jewish history. They were vicious, violent, murderous anti-semites who swore eternal hatred for Jews with greater technical means and efficiency – but were at times ready to offer Jews as human chattels for sale and saw no contradiction in their position. This was especially true of SS Chief Heinrich Himmler.

Unfortunately, this statement is flatly untrue. Even if some Nazis at some times were willing to offer some Jews for ransom – and the number of such *bona fide* offers was microscopically small – there was one supreme but immovable stumbling-block to the 'sale' of Jews on any scale: the permanent, unalterable hostility of Adolf Hitler to anything which would allow any Jews at all to survive in Europe. Hitler's monomaniacal anti-semitism was both the cause and central driving force of the Holocaust, and distinguished it from all previous experiences of anti-semitism without exception.[140]

Individual writers and commentators also put forward purported schemes for rescue. Perhaps here, among individual experts with no communal axes to grind, one might find a useful proposal? Alas, one searches their proposals in vain for evidence of any new practical suggestions. Max Lerner, the famous author and critic, who became very active in Bergson's rescue movement in 1943, produced 'Not Easy – But Possible' for *Answer*, the Bergsonite periodical, in August of that year. Conceding that 'the task is immense. The difficulties are disheartening', and in full knowledge that 'in the case of the Jews' the Nazis 'are determined to destroy the whole people', Lerner suggested that the United Nations 'explore . . . every possible method' of rescue, that the Red Cross give 'protection' to those Jews still alive, and that 'quietly but with a cold determination' the 'German murderers' be told that 'measures of reprisal' will be used against them during and after the war. 'The particular measures to be used are not for me to discuss now . . . [but] while the Nazi leaders are sadists, they will not continue their barbarous murder of Jews if to do so involves paying a drastic price with their own civilian population', Lerner stated confidently, and with complete inaccuracy.[141] Lerner also proposed that the United Nations 'demand publicly of the satellite countries that they release as many as possible of their million and a half Jews', believing the Nazi satellites such as Hungary to have freedom of action to do this. Lerner also demanded 'havens of refuge' in neutral Europe and Palestine, thus making the most fundamental of erroneous assumptions about Europe's surviving Jews.[142]

In December 1943, the World Jewish Congress's American magazine, *Jewish Comment*, asked in an editorial 'What Can We Do?'. The magazine bewailed the fact that 'much that could have been done four years ago or even one year ago cannot be done today'.

> What could we have done at that time? There are many obvious things which the United Nations might have done. They might have relaxed the blockade or tried to arrange through the International Red Cross to provide food to the incarcerated Jews. The simplest and most obvious way would have been to open their doors to the Jews of Europe.[143]

What, then, could be done at the end of 1943? Of this the World Jewish Congress's organ had less to say. Its only concrete suggestion was to allow more Jewish 'refugees' into the United States and Palestine and to put pressure on the Nazis' 'jittery collaborationists' in south-eastern Europe 'as well as the Germans passively opposed to the Nazis' to 'help rescue the Jews'.

> We are convinced that if, backed by these evidences of popular demand, the executive arms of the United States, and the United Nations generally, undertake, as they have already begun to do, to put into effect specific measures designed to deal with the specific problems of the Jews and other

endangered groups in Axis Europe, they will find suitable methods for rescuing them. We cannot, indeed, anticipate all the openings which will reveal themselves to agencies which may be entrusted with such a function . . . But the main lines of a rescue program have long been clear.[144]

Earlier in the same year, the *Nation*, the left-liberal American weekly, carried an article by Philip S. Bernstein, 'The Jews of Europe: Seven Ways To Help Them Now'.[145] What were these seven ways? 'Announce immediately that the Jews, as Jews, will have a hearing in the councils of the United Nations'; 'grant to Palestinian and stateless Jews the right to fight against the Nazis . . . let Jewish regiments be formed'; 'open the doors of Palestine at least to the legal immigration assured by the MacDonald White Paper'; 'frontiers should be open for transit purposes wherever possible; where necessary, they should be forced open. The plight of the 500 Polish Jewish children now in Teheran is a case in point'; '[Allied] governments [should] guarantee to neutral countries the cost of maintaining escaped Jews during the war';[146] 'a safeguarded program of feeding . . . [should] be extended to millions of men, women, and children . . . Jews in America still receive word that packages of food sent to relatives in Poland in some instances reach their destination'; 'Save the children. Let every technical barrier be set aside . . . Even the Nazis are reluctant to shoot children in cold blood.'

There are a number of frequently reiterated criticisms about the organisation and response of American Jewry to the Holocaust which might usefully be reconsidered in light of the points made here. One such constant refrain is that American Jews were 'disunified', and that this, in itself, was arguably a significant element in the failure successfully to rescue Europe's Jews. David S. Wyman has, for instance, devoted a volume of his thirteen-volume collection of primary documents in his series *America and the Holocaust* to *American Jewish Disunity*. Edward Pinsky, in a sensible discussion of this topic, has termed American Jewish disunity 'lamentable':

> While one will never know for certain to what degree American Jewish disunity made a difference in the tragic fate of European Jewry, one might still ask whether a unified Jewish voice would have been more successful in pressing the United States Government to act if Jews had spent less energy and resources in internecine conflict.[147]

The plethora of bodies which were formed to deal with rescue and which were not infrequently at each other's throats, lends a superficial plausibility to disunity as a factor in the failure of American Jewry to succeed at rescuing Europe's Jews.

Logically, however, disunity could have been a relevant factor in the failure to rescue only if unity could have produced a viable plan for rescue, or resulted in pressure being successfully exerted upon the American government which would have produced viable means of rescue. Since no practical plans existed, and nothing the American government might have done, which it did not do, could possibly have saved any Jew who was trapped in Nazi-occupied Europe, American Jewish disunity was as relevant to the fate of Europe's Jews under Hitler as is the fact that the tribes of New Guinea speak 500 different languages. Even if all of America's Jewish leaders and organisations, without exception, had agreed to adopt a unified set of proposals for rescue as suggested at the time and had successfully lobbied the Roosevelt administration for its implementation, it is simply difficult to see how any of them could have worked: nothing proposed by any group or person in America during the war was of any practical value in the actual task of rescuing Europe's Jews. In any case, it is apparent from an examination of the American proposals for rescue actually made during the war that they were virtual carbon copies of one another, each, as it were, making the same mistakes.[148]

A closely related argument, and one which is also encountered frequently, is that the Jewish community's deep respect for President Roosevelt deterred any threat to use the 'Jewish vote' against Roosevelt or the Democratic Party unless Roosevelt proved more forceful at saving Europe's Jews. There are, however, many flaws with this argument. It is very doubtful whether America's Jewish leaders could have successfully moved more than a small fraction of the 'Jewish vote' to the Republican camp even if they had tried: American Jews would have had to be willing, in very large numbers, to vote Republican, a dubious prospect in the early 1940s. Roosevelt would have pointed out, with considerable truth, that he was the Western world's arch-liberal and, with Churchill, its primary opponent of Hitler and Nazism, and that America was waging total war against Nazi Germany and its fascist Allies; the Republican party, in contrast, had a lengthy record of isolationism abroad with 'reactionary' policies at home. He would also surely have noted the fact that he did create the War Refugee Board in January 1944, ten months before the 1944 presidential election, and that it was Congress, not the White House, which legislated for such matters as immigration laws. In any case, and fundamental to everything else, was the fact that no party or leader, and no one in the Jewish community, had any feasible proposal to make which would actually have effected genuine rescue in Europe; this would have become instantly apparent whoever was the American President at the time.

In the absence of influencing the Roosevelt administration to assist genuine rescue endeavours, the lobbying activities of the Jewish community and of others concerned with the plight of Europe's Jews became focused on what might be termed an effort at pseudo-rescue, the admission of more so-called refugees to the United States. In June 1944 (during the presidential election campaign), after conferring with John Pehle, head of the war Refugee Board, and with Henry Morgenthau, Secretary of the Treasury, Roosevelt announced an executive decision to create a so-called 'free port' at Fort Ontario in Oswego, New York, for 1,000 refugees who would be returned to Europe after the war. Most were Jews, but, by deliberate policy, many were non-Jews. These 'free port' refugees were not permitted to leave the camp, and only with difficulty were they finally allowed to remain in America after the war.[149]

If the Oswego refugees had somehow been transported to the United States from Auschwitz, or from concentration camps in rural Hungary, where they were at that time being assembled for shipment to Auschwitz, or from hideouts in cellars and attics in Berlin, the Fort Ontario experiment would indeed have constituted a most striking example of rescue in the true sense. Of course they were not: Jews under Nazi control and domination were beyond the reach of Franklin Roosevelt or anyone else in the West. Instead, these were Jews from southern Italy, Spain and other areas whose governments were either neutral or had been recently conquered by the Western Allies. These Jews, in June 1944, were in just as much danger of being murdered by the Nazis as were Jews living on Central Park West in New York. The Oswego 'free port' no more constitutes a valid example of rescue than any other movement of Jews in the world outside Nazi-occupied Europe. It was self-evidently a deception, an attempt by Roosevelt to appease the 'Jewish vote' during a presidential election campaign. It need not be added that – with very limited but well-known exceptions made by Himmler in the closing phases of the war – Jews were not rescued from Auschwitz or from cellars and attics in Berlin, until allied troops physically liberated these Nazi-held areas. Historians have taken at face value this – and many other – examples of 'pseudo-rescue', of the removal of Jews by the Allies from places where they were no longer in danger from the Nazis to even safer locales.

Another point frequently alleged against America's Jewish community (as well as the Jewish communities of Britain and other Western countries) is that they were deterred from forceful action by fears of arousing anti-semitism. Clearly, the so-called 'Jewish lobby' of the recent past, with its remarkably successful lobbying and coalition-building tactics, especially over support for Israel, did not exist in the same form prior to the end of the 1940s or later. Undeniably, too, far more frank social and economic anti-semitism existed during the war than decades later, although arguably far less than recent historians believe. Nevertheless, no one objectively examining the record of the American (or British) Jewish community during the Holocaust period can fail to be struck by how *little* the fear of anti-semitism affected their responses or their actions, or how similar their attempts at coalition-building and at influencing America's legislators and opinion-makers were to the successful efforts of Jewish groups since the war. That they failed to 'rescue' the millions of European Jews who perished was due solely to the inherent impossibility of their task.

A useful analogy here might be drawn with the efforts during the 1970s and 1980s to free the Soviet Union's Jews, its 'refuseniks' and 'prisoners of conscience'. Endeavour on behalf of Soviet Jewry became, for nearly twenty years, one of the two central unifying political campaigns among Diaspora Jewry, second only to support for Israel against the Arabs. The Soviet Jewry campaign was headed by American Jewry, then at the peak of its influence, and enjoyed the support of every Western government and all opinion-makers, without exception. Anti-semitism of the kind common in the West during the 1930s and 1940s had virtually disappeared. The Soviet government of this period, while both anti-semitic and totalitarian, can obviously not be compared with Hitler's obsessively genocidal regime. Yet, with the exception of the 250,000 Soviet Jews allowed to emigrate during the Nixon presidency, the Soviet Jewry campaign was a total failure, Russia's two million Jews remaining imprisoned and persecuted until shortly before the collapse of the Soviet Union itself. Was this failure of the Soviet Jewry campaign until the late 1980s due to American anti-semitism or any of the other factors so often suggested about the lack of success achieved by Western Jewry during the Holocaust – or was it not entirely due to the impossibility of changing Soviet policy in this area?

The story of Britain's plans for rescue is depressingly similar to America's. Naturally there were important differences between the Jewish communities and the political processes in the two countries, but the outcomes were extraordinarily similar, and efforts to contrast the British response negatively with that of America, as some recent historians have done, are certainly misleading if the merits of America's plans for 'rescue' are objectively considered.[150] Curiously, some American historians have contrasted Britain's response favourably with America's, especially the sympathetic activism of a major segment of the British 'Establishment' in British 'rescue' efforts.[151]

Superficially, the two communities had little in common and demonstrated many differences. The American Jewish community, numbering about 5 million, was perhaps thirteen times larger than the Anglo-Jewish community of about 380,000. In contrast to the multiplicity of competing groups and leaders within American Jewry, Anglo-Jewry had a clearly established and universally recognised structure of governance, with the Board of Deputies of British Jews acknowledged by the government and the media as speaking on behalf of Anglo-Jewry, and the Chief Rabbi of the United Synagogue recognised as the community's religious head.[152]

The United Synagogues and the Board of Deputies have often been seen as having adopted, over many generations, a particular and characteristic style, emphasising decorum, conservatism and British patriotism, and often in a mock-Anglican way. It has often been suggested that before the 1930s the Anglo-Jewish community was led by Britain's wealthy Anglo-Jewish 'grandee' families such as the Montefiores, Rothschilds and Montagus, and that its elite structure remained far more impervious to penetration by the eastern European newcomers than American Jewry's. Anglo-Jewry had also long since put its faith in British liberalism and tolerance, and in a view of British society, sometimes termed 'meliorism', which viewed Britain's traditions of toleration as so strong as to prove superior to any underlying anti-semitism, at least in the long run. Notwithstanding the fact that Chaim Weizmann lived in Manchester and the Balfour Declaration was addressed to Britain's Lord Rothschild, the Anglo-Jewish elite was notably cool to any concept of 'political Zionism' which entailed the breaking of links between Britain and the Jewish community of Palestine. While social anti-semitism was arguably less significant in Britain than in America, and while Mosley and the British Fascist Movement remained on the outer fringes of British political life, during the 1930s Anglo-Jewry was, it is often suggested, acutely aware of rising anti-semitism and was extremely reluctant to 'rock the boat' or demonstrate on behalf of persecuted Jewry in a visible way.[153] Significant sections of the British 'Establishment' are often seen as anti-semitic in at least a mild way, while the Foreign and Dominions Offices were, during the 1930s, ever-increasingly pro-Arab and anti-Zionist in an undisguised fashion.

Unlike America, Britain faced the imminent prospect of a German invasion in 1940–1, and, temporarily at least, all minorities, especially Jews and in particular Jewish refugees, became the object of deep suspicion and general fear and hostility. Historians have cited all these factors as significant reasons for the alleged failure of Anglo-Jewry to respond adequately to the Holocaust, and for the alleged indifference, if not overt hostility, on the part of the British government to rescuing Europe's Jews from mass murder. These points have been made so often and by so many historians that it is difficult to believe they can possibly be anything other than true and accurate.

In reality, however, once again it is the tacit assumption underlying the widespread perception of British inaction – that, during the Holocaust, rescue on a significant scale was possible – which is erroneous. An appreciation of this fact, I would suggest, will make virtually everything concerning the British response to the plight of the Jews appear in a new light.

After admitting at least 50,000 German Jewish refugees between 1933 and 1939, the great majority in the two years preceding the outbreak of the war (in addition to 35,000 who migrated to other parts of the Commonwealth and 55,000 to Palestine), Britain abruptly closed its doors to further Jewish (and non-Jewish) refugee migration in September 1939. In retrospect this obviously appears harsh and regrettable, although the apparently imminent and very real danger of a German invasion made it appear, to virtually all contemporaries, as an obvious necessity. By the time that a more tolerant attitude towards would-be refugees became more general, after the threat of invasion had receded, the Nazis had made impossible any further Jewish *emigration* from German-occupied Europe.

In any case it is most significant to note clearly that this 'limbo' period – that is, after the outbreak of the war but *before* the gates to Jewish *emigration* from Europe had shut in late 1940 to 1941 – occurred *before* the genocide of European Jewry began in mid-1941 (early 1942 in Poland). It also took place at a time when Britain's officials had absolutely no way of knowing what Hitler had in mind for the Jews. Yet it is this period which is almost invariably highlighted by critics of Britain's refugee policy.[154] It is this confusion over dates, combined with the general illogicality that besets this whole subject, which perhaps accounts for some of the more egregious comments which have been made even by first-rate historians on the topic. Professor Bernard Wasserstein, for instance, is an internationally known historian and biographer of great sophistication and intelligence. Yet he can make the following statement, with evident reproach to the British government, that 'before the war some 90 per cent of refugees from Nazism admitted to Britain were Jews. During the war more than 80 per cent were non-Jews', without noting (or perhaps even perceiving) the fact that before the war the policy of the Nazis was to expel the Jews of the *Reich*, while during the war it was their policy to imprison them, prior to genocide.[155]

A comparison of the American and British Jewish communities also reveals a number of other differences between the two which might be relevant to their respective responses during the Holocaust. As noted, while the American Jewish community contained a plethora of independent, sometimes competing and hostile groups and organisations, Anglo-Jewry's central representative body, the Board of Deputies of British Jews, was universally recognised as such: this, in itself, deterred the formation of groups outside the Board of Deputies' structure which claimed to speak on behalf of the whole Jewish community or which expected themselves to be recognised as speaking on behalf of Anglo-Jewry. While the Board of Deputies had frequent access to government ministers and other public officials when the Jewish viewpoint had to be put, bodies outside the Board's structure were unlikely to gain such access easily.

Another important contrast between the two communities lay in their respective relationship to their governments and heads of state. In America, Franklin D. Roosevelt had held the office of President since 1933 and enjoyed the overwhelming support of America's Jews, who viewed Roosevelt and his New Deal in glowing personal terms, with Jewish leaders such as Rabbi Stephen Wise having personal access to the President. The relationship of Anglo-Jewry to the British government was subtly different. Because of the National Government's Appeasement policies and the 1939 MacDonald White Paper on Palestine, Anglo-Jewry's leaders had clearly felt alienated from Neville Chamberlain's administration – even those Jews who were normally avid Tories – and notwithstanding the government's excellent record, from 1938, on the admission of refugees. Most Jews greeted Winston Churchill's accession to power in May

1940 as almost a divine deliverance. Churchill was a lifelong philo-semite and pro-Zionist, leader of the anti-Hitler forces in Britain and pledged to continue the war until victory. His government consisted of anti-Appeasement Conservatives and, as co-equal partners, the Labour Party, perceived at the time as automatically anti-Nazi and pro-Zionist.

As noted in Chapter 1, the tributes paid by Anglo-Jewry's leaders to Churchill and his government were indeed fulsome, There was thus a profound sense that the Churchill wartime government was as 'pro-Jewish' a government as Britain could ever see, and that its policies must have represented the militarily and politically feasible limits of the rescue of Europe's Jews. Indeed, this was the case, but the esteem in which Churchill was held itself discouraged independent proposals for rescue, especially from within the Jewish mainstream.

British Jewry produced much less in the way of point-by-point plans for rescue than did American Jewry; it held fewer rallies (or none at all), and lobbied the British government much less often than did America's Jewish bodies. Possibly more than in the United States, proposals for 'rescue' seemed to emerge from marginal individuals within the community (and outside it) and from *ad hoc* groups independent from the mainstream. Nevertheless, the British pattern of rescue proposals and groups is recognisably similar to that in America, above all in the sense that in neither country was any practical scheme for rescue actually put forward by anyone.

News of the extermination of Europe's Jews reached Britain at the same time as America, with reports of slaughters by the *Einsatzgruppen* being reported in late 1941 and the Nazi campaign of genocide throughout Europe reported at the end of 1942. By 11 December 1942 the *Jewish Chronicle*, the Anglo-Jewish community's weekly newspaper, headlined 'Two Million Jews Slaughtered/Most Terrible Massacre of All Time/Appalling Horrors of Nazi Mass Murders'. In its editorial comment on confirmation of the Holocaust, the *Jewish Chronicle* offered no sweeping proposals for rescue, making tentative suggestions similar to those proposed in America.

> What is to be done in face of this unparalleled disaster? The masses here – those who don't yet know or won't believe – must, in their own interests, have the hideous truth hammered home to them. Those who shrink from the truth must be told, not merely by recital of revolting facts but by the gripping manner in which they are narrated, why it is an imperious duty to themselves and their own clearest interests to know these sickening facts. Public opinion having thus been stimulated, much more remains to be done. After 2,000 years of Christendom, the home of Martin Luther exhibits to the gaze of the world a staggering reversion to naked savagery. Is this blank denial of Christianity, this reduction of human progress to a hollow

mockery, this threat to the foundation of human society, to be met with only feeble laments of impotence or finnicking talk about legal punctilio? The blood of the Jewish martyrs calls out, if not for vengeance, then at least for retribution. Can the United Nations refrain from solemnly announcing that the assassins who participated in the slaughtering will be held to account and meet a just punishment – as the Archbishop of York pleaded in a House of Lords that ardently supported him, and as M. Masaryk, with characteristic warm-hearted honesty, has proclaimed as far as Czechoslovakia is concerned? If only one Nazi thug were deterred in this way from his bestial murders, the step would be worth while. Can nothing again, absolutely nothing, be done to succour the victims? The Primate suggests that at least an offer might be made to receive here those few Jews who might be able to escape the Nazi clutches. Must the doors of the Jewish homeland be closed, even if difficulties of transportation could be overcome? Can we not undertake to indemnify neutral countries affording haven to fugitives against the expenditure they would incur? If only a few were thus plucked from the holocaust, the Christian conscience could at any rate proclaim that it had tried, and done its best.

We are constantly being told that there is a large section of Germans who are entirely out of sympathy with Nazi brutalities. Why cannot they be enlightened as to the cruelties being wrought in their names? A systematic broadcast campaign to bring the enormity of this crime home to the German people, a few more million leaflets fluttering down on German soil could do no harm. It would at least reveal whether this alleged remnant of decent Germans is a fact or a myth. It might also seep through to some of the poor wretches in the European dungeon to bring a little ray of comfort – the knowledge that they are not altogether forsaken by men. And there is one act of redress that still remains to be done to stricken Jewry. Challenged in body and soul, it has begged and implored, again and again, for the right to answer its enemies in the only way its enemies understand, by the creation of a Jewish Army. The Jew wishes to confront them as Jew, sword in hand. That would at least be balm to his wounded spirit, and it would be none the less valuable if it presented to this and the other nations the spectacle of the Jew fighting his own battles in the belief that God helps those who help themselves.

Above all, we ask that the conscience of the free nations having been somewhat aroused, its response should not be allowed to die away in a fleeting spasm of indignation and protest. The murderers will not relax their sinister work. The extermination of the Jews is one of those promises which the Nazis will inflexibly pursue, and every day more and more victims pile up in their lethal chambers or fill the graves which their digging machines excavate. The credit of the Christian peoples is at stake, as well as all that they have ever preached. Their Churches, which have done well hitherto, should surely from now onwards be ranged in a sustained campaign for the destruction of that particular manifestation of the Kingdom of Satan on earth, the anti-Semitic cult. This is, primarily, a fight for elementary spiritual values. In this doing to death of 2,000,000 Jews the world can see the logical climax of the brutal anti-Jewish creed. It is up to the statesmen and leaders of civilisation to ensure that against this insidious disease, now exposed in all its inherent horrors and dangers to national solidarity, a sanitary cordon be drawn. Statesmen have also to grasp the truth that if the German conspiracy to brutalise and decimate, or annihilate millions of Jews and other Europeans and extinguish their potential leaders, should succeed, Nazidom in all its filthy array will be left lord of the Continent, whatever victory we may achieve. For the relative numerical superiority of Germans to any other European nation will sooner or later give them mastery. No, the Nazi plot against the Jews, and other peoples, has to be squarely faced and frustrated one way or another beyond all hope of revival. Either that, or good-bye to hopes of New Orders and enduring peace.[156]

A week later, the *Jewish Chronicle* editorially called for the creation of a Jewish army, and praised a letter in *The Times* urging a joint approach by the three Allied powers 'to give shelter to all Jews who are allowed to leave the Nazi-dominated Continent', although the editorial also noted that 'the writer admits that it is more than doubtful whether Hitler will let any Jews go'.[157] On 17 December 1942 the House of Commons heard Anthony Eden, the Foreign Secretary, confirm the news of the extermination of European Jewry. It was on this occasion, following Eden's speech and the ensuing debate, that the House spontaneously rose and 'stood in silence', for one minute, a gesture without precedent in parliamentary history.[158]

The fullest parliamentary discussion of rescue occurred in the House of Lords on 23 March 1943, in reply to a motion by William Temple, the Archbishop of Canterbury, that

> the House desires to assure His Majesty's Government of its fullest support for immediate measures, on the largest and most generous scale compatible with the requirements of military operations and security, for providing help and temporary asylum to persons in danger of massacre who are able to leave enemy and enemy-occupied countries.[159]

The debate in the Lords, chiefly conducted on behalf of the government by Viscount Cranborne (later the fifth Marquess of Salisbury, an anti-Appeasement ally of Anthony Eden during the 1930s), emphasised how little could, in fact, be done. The Archbishop, a liberal philo-semite and a Christian socialist, made the accurate point that 'We know of course that the German Government will not give exit permits', but that a 'steady stream, or perhaps more accurately a steady trickle' of Jews reached Spain or Switzerland from France, and that more could perhaps be done to make Europe's neutral countries more receptive to refugees. He also proposed that 'through some neutral Power an offer should directly be made to the German Government to receive Jews in territories of the British Empire', although 'very likely it would be refused, and then Hitler's guilt would stand out all the more evidently'.[160] Everyone who spoke – indeed, everyone present in the Lords – agreed with him, and his motion was carried unanimously. Needless to say, it had no effect whatsoever on Hitler, and no one had anything new or cogent to contribute.

The Board of Deputies turned its attention to the rescue of European Jews almost at once. Its Joint Foreign Committee suggested, in February 1943, that Britain and the Allies provide asylum for Jewish refugees; 'adequate recognition of the specially favourable position of Palestine for refuge'; that Germany be approached so that 'Jews under German control should be allowed to leave'; and that neutral governments approach Germany 'for the same purpose.' A final suggestion was that 'Perhaps the Pope would agree to associate himself with the neutrals' approach'.[161] On this occasion, Professor Selig Brodetsky, President of the Board, also expressed 'a certain amount of dissatisfaction' with the British government while admitting that 'they realised that the problem was one of very great difficulty'.[162] These suggestions emerged from a special conference held by the Board on 24 January 1943 to consider how European Jewry could be helped.[163]

A further conference, called by the Deputies and chaired by Brodetsky, was held in April 1943.[164] At this meeting, the 'suggested measures for rescue' included an announcement by the government of asylum for refugees; the provision of visas by British consuls in neutral countries; the establishment of camps for refugees in territories under the government's control; 'the utmost use of Palestine' and 'speedy transport' for those already granted Palestine visas; 'additional transport from the Balkans and shipping also for transfers from Spain and Portugal'; 'suitable assurances' to neutral countries regarding the 'transfer and feeding' of refugees; 'the exchange of refugees with Axis nationals'; and an approach by the government to the Axis governments 'to allow the Jews to leave'.[165]

Most of these suggestions had been made before, while virtually all foundered upon the fact that Jews at risk were unable to leave (if indeed they were still alive). For instance, the suggestion of the provision of visas for Jews by British consuls 'in neutral countries' could have no effect upon the Jews of Nazi-occupied Europe, while Jews actually in neutral countries were not at risk. Conceivably, the only practical suggestion was for 'the exchange of refugees with Axis nationals', one made from time to time throughout the war. Very limited exchanges were carried out during the war, but the numbers involved always diminished as negotiations proceeded because of Nazi intransigence; in any case the number of 'Axis nationals' in the democracies who were willing to be repatriated to Nazi Germany and its allies was obviously much smaller than the number of Jews under Nazi control.

Delegates to this conference derived from a very wide variety of Jewish communal bodies including the Revisionist Zionists and the Agudas Israel movement; Brodetsky stated that eighty-one organisations were represented. Participants demonstrated despair at the prospect in front of them, but repeatedly called for 'bold action' and 'united action'. There was an undercurrent of impatience with – but never overt hostility towards – the British government. Indeed, the government's attitude, while obviously anti-Nazi, seemed to many (but certainly not most) Jews to be strangely torpid. Its stance throughout the war was a simple one: that no realistic proposals for rescue had been made and that – in the words of Osbert Peake, Under-Secretary of State for Home Affairs – 'The Government had their programme, which was victory'.[166]

The official efforts at rescue by the Anglo-Jewish community were paralleled by the unofficial endeavours of activists, deeply concerned with the genocide of Europe's Jews, lacking direct connection with the Jewish community's organised structure. The best known of the extra-communal bodies concerned with rescue, then and now, was the National Committee for Rescue From Nazi Terror, founded in March 1943.[167] Its chief organisers were two remarkable campaigners on behalf of Jewish and other causes: Eleanor Rathbone (1872–1946), Independent MP for the Combined English Universities and Victor Gollancz (1893–1967), the publisher and left-wing activist.

Rathbone, who came from a wealthy Unitarian family of Liverpool shipowners, was one of the first women in Parliament, and was an active and effective social campaigner on behalf of feminism, colonial independence and, after 1933, for Jewish refugees, emerging as perhaps their most vocal champion in Parliament.[168] Gollancz, the founder and head of the famous publishing house, emerged from the Anglo-Jewish upper middle class, but was, in religious outlook, a genuine eccentric, proclaiming himself to be, at the same time, a Jew, a Christian and an agnostic; he is best known, perhaps, for helping to found the Left Book Club; he was probably the greatest disseminator of socialist ideas in Britain and one of the principal intellectual sources of Labour's sweeping victory in 1945. Although never a communist and never politically naive, he spent much of the 1930s producing book after book which lauded every aspect of Soviet policy, a stance occasioned by his loathing of Nazism and fascism.[169]

Both Gollancz and Rathbone felt the catastrophe then unfolding in Europe to their cores. Gollancz may well have been the first man in England to have fully internalised the Holocaust. In 1942–3, as news of the Nazi genocide filtered back to Britain, he gave talk after talk on the Holocaust to English audiences.

> Fearing that his speech might become stale, he took too literally for comfort the advice he had given in *Let My People Go!* and began a practice of arriving at the speaking venue half an hour early. He would spend the time 'feeling myself, with all the wholeness I could manage, into the situation of people at Dachau or Buchenwald. One night I was being gassed in a gas chamber; the next I was helping others dig our own mass grave, and then waiting for the splatter of the machine gun.'[170]

By June 1943, this practice had led Gollancz to a serious nervous breakdown, incapacitating him for more than six months. When news of the Holocaust arrived in Britain, Rathbone redoubled her efforts on behalf of the Jews, working day and night without respite on their behalf, leading delegations, organising letters of protest and button-holing ministers. 'The appalling evidence that came before the National Committee haunted Rathbone for the rest of her life.'[171]

It is difficult to imagine two more dedicated champions of the Jews in Britain than those two, who were at once both outsiders in the sense of belonging to no orthodox faction, and insiders in their access to the powerful. Contrary to the popular myth of universal indifference to the fate of European Jews during the war, the National Committee's office-bearers constituted a 'Who's Who' of the British Establishment. Among its vice-presidents were the Archbishops of Canterbury and York, the Moderators of the Church of Scotland and the Free Church of Scotland, and such notables as Sir William Beveridge, Lady Violet Bonham-Carter, Lord Sankey the Lord Chancellor, Harold Nicolson and Quintin Hogg (later Lord Hailsham). Despite the bodies for rescue formed by the Board of Deputies, the National Committee also numbered among its office-bearers many leaders of the Jewish community, including Chief Rabbi Joseph Hertz, Professor Brodetsky, Herbert Samuel and spokesmen for diverse tendencies within Anglo-Jewry such as Harry Goodman and Berl Locker. Another important office-bearer was Revd James Parkes, the Anglican vicar who was probably the leading Christian philo-semite in Britain.[172]

The Committee took evidence, produced fourteen booklets and pamphlets on the Holocaust, and presented several detailed plans for rescue. From September 1943 until January 1946 it published forty-seven issues of a monthly *Bulletin From Hitler's Europe*, demonstrating its considerable knowledge of the Holocaust, although of course the whole story was not fully pieced together until the Nuremberg Trials.

Before considering these plans, we should perhaps note that the National Committee operated in an atmosphere of very considerable public goodwill: the notion that anti-semitism was both widespread and increasing in Britain during the war is directly contradicted by the reception accorded the National Committee and by other evidence. The National Committee's pamphlet of early 1944, *Continuing Terror*, referred to a Gallup poll taken during the spring of 1943, which asked 'Do you think that the British Government should or should not help any Jews who can get away [from Europe]?' Seventy-eight per cent of respondents answered 'yes', 'this being almost the largest majority ever recorded in a Gallup Poll'.[173] Gollancz's pamphlet on the Holocaust, *Let My People Go!* published in January 1943, sold 150,000 copies within six months.[174]

The National Committee noted an extraordinary response to their publicity:

A member of the R.A.F. drew up a strongly worded petition and set himself to collect signatures from officers and men of his Unit, stopping when he had easily reached his target of 1,000 signatures. The head of an Anglican sisterhood wrote to twenty similar communities suggesting that they guarantee between them maintenance for a number of children. A lady living on a small income in two rooms rushed off a cheque for £50, 'in haste to catch the post,' apologising for the meagreness of her contribution. A lady pledged herself to raise £50 a week and wanted to go 'anywhere in Europe' to collect the children. Many households volunteered to keep one or two refugees on their present rations without asking for more. Whole-time workers offered their week-ends and evenings for secretarial work. A resident in a poor neighbourhood, shocked at the charge of anti-Semitism, started to test feeling by collecting signatures to a petition for the admission of Jewish refugees and reported hardly a single refusal from 250 houses. A meeting in a strongly Conservative rural neighbourhood resulted in an offer to establish and maintain a camp for refugees. And so on.

More formal demonstrations have included meetings in numerous cities chaired by the Mayor or University Vice-Chancellor and supported by leaders of all political parties, Trade Unions and Religious Organisations. A debate in the Oxford Union resulted in the two selected opponents crossing the floor and supporting an almost unanimous resolution. The under-graduate societies of Conservatives, Labour and Liberals then formed a Committee to raise funds, collecting within a week nearly £500. A public meeting in Oxford, chaired by Sir William Beveridge and addressed by the Vice-Chancellor, the Master of Balliol and the Bishop passed a remarkably strong resolution expressing disappointment with the meagre action taken by the Government. This was subsequently signed by ninety of the best-known Oxford names, including the heads of many of the Colleges. A letter in the 'Times,' of February 16th, bore the signatures, among others, of Professor Carr Saunders, Sir Wyndham Deed[e]s, Professor Gilbert Murray, the Hon. Harold Nicolson, Sir John Orr, G. Bernard Shaw,

Professor Tawney, Mrs. Beatrice Webb, Lady Rhondda, Lord Sankey. It asked boldly for the following measures:

'(1) To make representations by the United Nations to the German Government to permit Jews to leave the Occupied countries of Europe. (2) To offer the joint protection of the United Nations to Jews liberated or escaping from the occupied territories. (3) To facilitate the transfer of Jews to, and their asylum in, the territories and colonies of the United Nations. (4) To urge on neutral countries the desirability of receiving as many Jewish refugees as possible until, with victory, it is possible to consider ways and means of their permanent settlement. Where food and finance raise difficult problems for neutral countries willing to assist, the United Nations should agree to make these available to them. (5) To make available the fullest possible facilities for the immigration of Jewish refugees into Palestine.[175]

From virtually the moment that news of the Holocaust reached Britain, the magnitude of the evil being perpetrated by the Nazis was understood by Britain's opinion-leaders in almost uncannily accurate terms. 'The greatest crime in history is now being perpetrated, the murder of a nation and the deliberate extermination of the Jews in Europe', wrote the Archbishop of York, Dr Cyril Garbett in his 1943 New Year's Message to his congregants. 'We may now look upon our people and our allies as united in a crusade to deliver our fellow-men from a sub-human barbarism.'[176] Sir David Ross, the Vice-Chancellor of Oxford University, stated as early as February 1943 at a rally to condemn the Nazi atrocities, that 'In the whole course of human history there was no such destruction of human beings and on such a scale'.[177] Earlier that week, the Oxford Union, the University's famous debating society, had debated the motion that 'The House urges that a more energetic and practical policy be pursued by the Government towards the rescuing of the Jews of Europe'. After a moving and passionate speech for the affirmative by Victor Gollancz, the principal speakers against the motion 'decided to cross the floor and associate themselves with him', the only time in the history of the Oxford Union that this has happened.[178]

Of Winston Churchill's sincere and deeply felt sympathy for the plight of the Jews under Hitler, there can simply be no doubt: with his historical imagination, Churchill grasped the singularity of the Holocaust at once. His celebrated marginal comment of July 1944 to Anthony Eden – 'there is no doubt that this is probably the greatest and most horrible single crime in the whole history of the world' – was in no way uncharacteristic of Churchill's views on the Holocaust. In July 1942 Harold Laski complained to Churchill that a recent speech contained no reference to the Jews. Churchill replied:

Although in my speech at the Guildhall I referred only to the wrongs inflicted by Hitler on the Sovereign States of Europe, I have never forgotten the terrible sufferings inflicted on the Jews, and I am constantly thinking by what means it may be in my power to alleviate them, both during the war and in the permanent settlement which must follow it.[179]

In November 1947 Churchill experienced an apparently genuine occult or hallucinatory experience in which he saw and spoke to his father, Lord Randolph Churchill, the Tory politician, who had died in 1895. Churchill was asked by his father about the major historical events which had happened since his death.

> Did Russia still have a tsar? Yes, his son replied, 'but he is not a Romanoff. It's another family. He is much more powerful, and much more despotic.' But as a result of the most recent war, Europe was a ruin. 'Many of her cities have been blown to pieces by bombs.' Thirty million people had been killed in battle and seven million in cold blood. 'They made human slaughter-pens like the Chicago stockyards.'[180]

In 1943–4 the National Committee for Rescue From Nazi Terror produced a series of rescue proposals. The earliest is a typewritten draft statement, dated 5 April 1943, which illustrates how the thinking of the Committee had evolved at this point.

NATIONAL COMMITTEE FOR RESCUE FROM NAZI TERROR

TWELVE-POINT PROGRAMME
FOR RESCUE MEASURES.

I. REVISION OF REGULATIONS FOR U.K. VISAS, including:-

    A. Grant of visas for those with special claims on this country, based on near relatives already here, previous residence, or useful work awaiting them.

    B. Supply of blocks of unnamed visas to British Consuls in neutral European countries, especially Spain and Portugal.

    C. Removal of the condition for a visa that the refugee must already have left enemy-controlled territory.

    NOTE: The above three concessions would together meet hard cases (e.g. the present exclusion of parents of Service men), encourage neutral countries to admit more refugees, and stimulate Allied countries to similar action. The numbers of admissions involved would be at most a few thousand. Abundant offers of hospitality are available but for those for whom that is judged unsuitable on security grounds, accommodation could be provided in the Isle of Man internment camps, which have now less than half their population of two years ago, i.e. 4,600 fewer . . . .

II. ENCOURAGEMENT TO NEUTRAL STATES TO ADMIT MORE REFUGEES by:-

    A. Guarantees by Great Britain and/or the United Nations that refugees would – to an extent defined by numbers or date of reception – be removed after victory or sooner wherever practicable.

    B. Gifts of and/or facilities for obtaining food, clothing and other requisites, navicerts &c.

    C. Financial aid: immediately where practicable, otherwise promised after victory.

NOTE: The form of assistance could vary with the conditions of the country concerned, e.g. for Spain and Portugal early evacuation is essential and practicable; less so for Sweden and Switzerland.

III. PROVISION OF NEW REFUGE CAMPS AND USE OF THOSE ALREADY AVAILABLE

    (a) for the temporary disposal, pending dispersion, of refugees collected from neutral or enemy-occupied countries in places easily accessible under British or Allied control (e.g. N. and E. Africa, Cyprus, Palestine, Isle of Man); and

    (b) in the same or more distant places (e.g. the West Indies) for the longer-term disposal of those considered unsuitable on grounds of security, ill-health &c. for release for employment or for private hospitality.

IV. INCREASED TRANSPORT FACILITIES FOR EVACUATING REFUGEES by:-

    A. The use of neutral or other ships as ferry boats between ports in neutral or enemy countries where refugees could be congregated and ports under British or Allied control.

    B. The use of ships which have brought troops, supplies &c. to Allied ports or food to Greece for taking refugees to places of safety on their homeward journey.

    C. Other help to neutrals in transporting refugees, e.g. coal and rolling stock to Turkey.

V. ADMISSIONS TO PALESTINE through:-

    A. Speeding up of the arrangements for the selection and transport of the children and adults agreed to be admitted from Bulgaria, Hungary and Roumania.

B. Removal of the condition, implied in the Colonial Secretary's Statement of February 3rd but unjustified by the terms of the White Paper, that the majority of those admitted under the Immigration Quota ending April 1944 must be children.

C. Without prejudice to the question of whether the immigration limits laid down in the White Paper are justified, consideration of the admission to temporary refuge camps in Palestine of refugees in excess of the quota limit.

VI. <u>PRESSURE ON THE AXIS SATELLITES</u>, including the Balkan States, Italy and Finland, to refrain from cruelties and deportations and to let their victims go, by making it known that not only – as already promised – would the perpetrators be punished, but that behaviour in this matter would be taken into account in the post-war settlement.

VII. Following the precedent of arrangements already made with Bulgaria, Hungary and Roumania, for the release of refugees to Palestine, <u>CONSIDERATION OF FURTHER OFFERS TO ANY OR ALL OF THE ENEMY AND ENEMY-OCCUPIED COUNTRIES</u>, to take over refugees from them under specified conditions as to numbers, categories, time and places of taking over.

VIII. <u>EXPLORATION OF THE POSSIBILITIES OF EXCHANGING CIVILIAN INTERNEES WITH AXIS SYMPATHIES</u> now under British or Allied control (e.g. Italians in North Africa and German internees in the Isle of Man who were previously approved for exchange) <u>FOR JEWISH OR POLITICAL REFUGEES</u> under enemy control.

IX. <u>FREQUENT APPEALS, BY RADIO AND LEAFLET, TO THE PEOPLES OF ALL ENEMY AND ENEMY-OCCUPIED COUNTRIES</u>, making known the facts of the persecution, urging the peoples on grounds of humanity and religion to resist by succouring the victims and promising both punishments and rewards.

<u>NOTE</u>: It is known that the B.B.C. European Service has already done much on this question. But the imminent threat of further large-scale deportations from Holland, the Balkans, France &c. makes further efforts necessary. Yet the recent utterance by Dr. Goebbels: 'We are not opposed to the creation of a Jewish State. This world problem must be solved, but the solution may be carried out by humanitarian methods'

indicates that the Nazis are anxious about the effect of their atrocities on their own public opinion and/or world opinion.

X. THE FORMATION OF A NEW ORGAN WITHIN THE BRITISH GOVERNMENT, such as will ensure that the whole problem of rescue measures will receive the undivided attention of at least one or two persons of high calibre and with authority, and is no longer left to the occasional and un-coordinated efforts of overburdened departmental Ministers.

XI. THE APPOINTMENT ON BEHALF OF THE UNITED NATIONS OF A HIGH COMMISSIONER OR OTHER EMISSARY ('a new Nansen'), who could visit the neutral and Allied countries principally concerned in the refugee problem, negotiate the carrying out of measures already approved and explore further possibilities.

XII. ADOPTION OF THE PRINCIPLE THAT, WHATEVER OTHER NATIONS MAY DO OR LEAVE UNDONE, THE BRITISH CONTRIBUTION TO THE WORK OF RESCUE SHOULD BE THE SPEEDIEST AND MOST GENEROUS POSSIBLE WITHOUT DELAYING VICTORY.[181]

This document contains a number of proposals not given similar centrality in American schemes for rescue made up to that point. 'Pressure on the Axis satellites', embodying both a post-war stick – punishment of the perpetrators – and a post-war carrot, that 'their behaviour in this matter would be taken into account in the post-war settlement', was an innovation. The possibility of 'exchanging civilian internees with Axis sympathies' for 'Jewish or political refugees' was given high priority, as it was in the Board of Deputies' proposals. The most interesting feature of this document, however, is probably point (X), recommending that 'a new organ within the British government' devoted to 'rescue measures' be established. This suggestion came several months in advance of any *American* proposal for a specialised body to be established by the United States government. But it bore no fruit in Britain, where no 'organ' was ever established to parallel the War Refugee Board.[182]

For the most part, however, these draft proposals were every bit as useless and misguided as their American counterparts. Manifestly, they centrally conceived of the task of 'rescue' as the reception of refugees rather than the liberation of captives of the Nazis. In 1943–4, the British government, with the best will in the world, had precisely as much ability to liberate the Nazis' remaining Jewish captives as they had to influence events on Mars. Nevertheless, the typescript's first five points specifically concern greater generosity regarding the admission of refugees to Britain, neutral states and Palestine: this was, alas, not the dilemma confronted by Hitler's Jews. The final point in the draft, that the British contribution 'should be the speediest and most generous possible *without delaying victory*' potentially left the way open to negating any rescue measures which 'delayed victory'. The alleged quotation from Goebbels, that he was 'not opposed to the creation of a Jewish state' and that 'the solution may be carried out by humanitarian measures[!]' shows the extent to which the National Committee was grasping at straws, and how incompletely even Gollancz, Rathbone and its other members understood the diabolical evil they were attempting to ameliorate.

The National Committee's most considered plans appeared in early 1944, when it published *Continuing Terror: How to Rescue Hitler's Victims – A Survey and a Programme.*[183] This pamphlet contained a revised 'ten-point programme' for rescue which, in its words, 'superseded' the previous twelve-point plan.[184] The scheme, published shortly before the SS invaded Hungary to begin the extermination of the largest surviving European Jewish community in the Axis, comprised the following planks:

TEN POINT PROGRAMME FOR MEASURES OF RESCUE FROM NAZI TERROR

1.

RESCUE IN LANDS COMING UNDER ALLIED CONTROL.

Instructions should be given to all Allied Commanders wherever operating, and requests made to chiefs of Guerilla Forces, to do everything possible, without hindering military operations, to rescue Jews and political prisoners. These should be transferred with the minimum of formality to countries of safety.

Similarly, immediate arrangements should be made to ensure that wherever there is a landing in Europe, military commanders should regard it as an urgent duty to do everything practicable to rescue those likely otherwise to be massacred.

To facilitate evacuation of those rescued, there should be extended provision of refuge camps and use of those already available, in places easily accessible under Allied control for the temporary disposal of refugees collected from enemy-occupied or neutral countries.

2.

ENCOURAGEMENT TO NEUTRAL STATES TO ADMIT MORE REFUGEES, by:

a) Gifts of and/or facilities for obtaining food, clothing, fuel, etc; and/or financial aid now or after victory.

b) Guarantees by the United Nations, or those willing to cooperate, that the refugees will, to an extent defined by numbers or date of reception, be evacuated after victory or sooner where practicable; such guarantees to be formally conveyed to the Neutral Governments.

c) H.M.'s Government to take the initiative by promising to find homes post-war for a substantial number of those refugees who prove to be non-repatriable and to invite the Dominions to do the same.*

3.

RECONSIDERATION OF REGULATIONS FOR UNITED KINGDOM VISAS in order to include:

a) Greater liberality in the admission of refugees. The present strictly utilitarian tests of usefulness for the war effort should be supplemented by the humanitarian tests of rescue from Nazi terror, both subject to precautions for security.

b) Removal of the present rule that a visa cannot be promised for any refugee while still in enemy-occupied territory, in cases where there is reason to believe that the promise would facilitate the refugee's escape or admission to a neutral country.

4.

WORKERS EXPERIENCED IN DEALING WITH REFUGEES, with the appropriate linguistic and other qualifications, should be sent to assist the British Authorities in all countries where such assistance may be needed.

Supplementary Passport Control Officers should be appointed to Consulates in Neutral countries, to relieve the greatly over-worked officials.

5.

INCREASED TRANSPORT FACILITIES FOR EVACUATION [OF] REFUGEES, including:

a) The use of neutral or other ships as ferry boats between ports in neutral or enemy countries where refugees could be congregated and ports under British or Allied control.

b) The use of ships which have brought troops, supplies etc, to Allied ports or food to Greece, for taking refugees to places of safety on their homeward journey.

6.

THE ADMISSION OF JEWISH REFUGEES TO PALESTINE should be facilitated by:

a) The removal of the restriction, announced by the Colonial Secretary but unjustified by the terms of the White Paper of May, 1939, that the 34,000 certificates still available under the immigration quota of the White Paper must be used mainly for children.

b) The supply of unnamed certificates to the British representatives at Ankara, to be filled up on nomination by the representative of the Jewish Agency for Palestine, for refugees whether already in neutral territory or to facilitate their escape thereto.

c) Extended arrangements, if permitted by the Turkish Government, for the accommodation within their territories, without expense to them, of refugees in transit, and for facilities for transport.

7.

CONTINUED PRESSURE ON GERMANY AND ITS SATELLITES (including Vichy) to refrain from cruelties and deportations and to let their victims go; making it clear that those responsible for these cruelties will be considered as war criminals.

8.

FREQUENT APPEALS, THROUGH RADIO AND LEAFLETS, TO THE PEOPLES OF ENEMY AND ENEMY-OCCUPIED LANDS, making known the facts and urging them to resist deportations and cruelties, politically and by succouring the victims.

9.

RECOGNITION OF THE EXTREME URGENCY AND IMPORTANCE OF THE PROBLEM. The position should be frequently reviewed by the Cabinet. Parliament should be kept fully informed of the activities of the Inter-Governmental Committee and of U.N.R.R.A. The British representatives on these bodies should take the initiative in proposing all possible measures of rescue.

10.

Adoption of the principle that, whatever other Nations may do or leave undone, the British Contribution to the work of Rescue should be the speediest and most generous possible without delaying victory.

*[as in text of original]:

The above assurances should be given publicly or privately, as discretion requires. The contributions promised would necessarily vary with the circumstances both of the States giving and the States receiving the assurances. Their purpose is to encourage the Neutral States to make offers which may depend on how far they can count on the necessary aid. Assurances have already been officially given of help both in maintenance and in evacuation. (See the Foreign Office statement issued December 10th.) The task will, we gather be shared between U.N.R.R.A. and the Inter-Governmental committee on refugees; the former being concerned chiefly with post-war maintenance and the repatriation of those who can return to their home lands; the latter assuming responsibility for finding homes for those who cannot return. The numbers of these non-repatriables may be substantial, owing to racial and political difficulties and the fear of being permanently encumbered with them may deter the Neutral States from making large offers. Hence the importance of Point 2(c).

This final plan differed little from the National Committee's earlier twelve-point scheme, although there was now clearly a sense that the Allies would soon be dealing with the Jewish survivors of Nazi rule. The two proposals dealing with the treatment of Jews in newly-liberated areas, (1) and (4), possessed (at last) some potential practical value. Immediate attention paid by the Allied armies, while liberating France, Belgium or the concentration camps in Germany, to the desperate medical, physical and psychological needs of the Jewish survivors might well have made the difference between life and death for the living skeletons they were about to liberate. Additionally, since the Nazis' murderous hatred of the Jews, and their insatiable lust for Jewish victims, continued literally until the moment they surrendered to the armies of freedom, a greater awareness of this fact on the part of the Allied military commanders might – conceivably – have saved some Jewish lives.

The other points, however, are simply a rehash of all the misconceived notions of 'rescue' in the past: the central confusion between 'refugees' and prisoners had not been corrected during four-and-a-half years of the war. 'Continued pressure' on Germany's satellites did indeed work to save the Jews of south-eastern Europe (and was indeed being pursued by the Allies). It worked – as in Hungary – up until the moment that Hitler and the SS decided to take matters into their own hands, at which point the opposition of the rulers of the Nazi satellites to deportation and genocide became irrelevant: they were simply powerless to prevent Hitler's intentions. It must also be clearly noted that the 'ten-point programme' did *not* include the bombing of Auschwitz or any other extermination camp (or the rail lines leading to them), despite the fact that it was, by early 1944, given the capture of Foggia Airfield in Italy in late 1943, at least theoretically possible for the Allies to have bombed them (although the full story, discussed later in this book, is much more complicated). The bombing of Auschwitz had not been proposed by anyone in Britain (or, indeed, in America) even by March 1944.

As with the American proposals for 'rescue' which appeared during the war (and which, of course, these closely resembled), the impression made by the 'ten-point programme', when seen in the light of the impossibility of rescue, is that they are a total and pathetic confession of impotence by men and women who felt the catastrophe of European Jewry to the depths of their souls. One must also certainly point out that there were no magical panaceas proposed and discussed by 'outsiders' or by figures or activists mistrusted by the 'Establishment': these *were* the proposals of 'outsiders'; there were no others. In fact they were virtually identical to the proposals discussed and approved by the 'Establishment' British Board of Deputies and by America's rescue bodies. That the proposals offered by these groups, too, were virtually useless reflects the impossibility of the dilemma they were attempting to solve, rather than either the level of goodwill or the level of concern of those who devised these proposals, or their knowledge of the situation of Europe's Jews.

Rescue proposals also appeared elsewhere in the democracies, for example in Australia. There, a United Emergency Conference to 'Save the European Jews' was organised on 29 December 1942, only twelve days after Anthony Eden's declaration in the House of Commons which confirmed genocide.[185] It was led by Zionists and recent refugees from Europe, but enjoyed the support of the largely non-Zionist leadership of the Australian Jewish community. Remarkably full and horrifying reports of the extermination of Soviet Jews by the *Einsatzgruppen* had appeared in both Jewish and general newspapers in Australia by the end of 1941.[186] A Second Emergency Conference was held in February 1943, and an intense campaign of reporting on the plight of Europe's Jews to non-Jewish bodies throughout Australia was begun.[187] As in America and England, these efforts were actively supported by many non-Jewish leaders and opinion-makers.[188] The Australian United Emergency Committee for European Jewry adopted its own ten-point programme for rescue in mid-1943, shortly after the Bermuda Conference. Its main points were that 'Palestine should be opened forthwith to all Jewish refugees who can be saved'; that the United Nations 'approach Germany and other enemy countries . . . to allow Jews . . . to emigrate'; that Jews be exchanged 'for . . . similar categories of enemy nationals'; and that 'the

International Red Cross should be approached to undertake the supervision of the work of evacuating refugees'.[189] Most of the points were 'extracted verbatim' from Gollancz's pamphlet *Let My People Go!*, which itself repeated most of the points made by the British National Committee for Rescue.[190]

It has been necessary to record in precise detail *all* of the proposals made by anyone in the democracies during the war in order to demonstrate beyond cavil how futile such ideas were, and how little anyone, even the most truly committed (or the most marginal), was able to offer a single practical suggestion. Until the bombing of railway lines to Auschwitz was first mooted in May 1944 – a topic discussed in a separate chapter – *no other* proposals for rescue were made by anyone in the democracies.

There is one other subject which might usefully be discussed here as well, the attitude of the Jewish *Yishuv* in Palestine towards the rescue of European Jews. This topic has presented a veritable minefield to the Israelis since the creation of the State, and even today is seldom examined with objectivity by its citizens, who are only too well aware that the phoenix of Israel arose in large part from the ashes of European Jewry, whose slaughter they were powerless to prevent. Most debate on the stance of the *Yishuv* during the Holocaust has centred upon the question of why so 'little' was 'done' by them, closely paralleling the debates in the American and British Jewish community, with even more passion but with even less reason. If the Jewish communities of America and Britain were powerless to halt the Holocaust (because their countries were powerless to halt it), the *Yishuv* was without any direct influence whatever. Remote from Europe and without any real mastery of its own destiny, lacking an army, fearing Arab attack and British repression, and dreading, above everything, the not unrealistic possibility of a German victory during the first three years of the war – a victory which would have assuredly seen the extermination of the Jews of the *Yishuv* – Palestinian Jewry could not possibly have done more than they actually did to have saved the Jews of Europe. This is the conclusion very sensibly reached by the two outstanding works of recent Israeli scholarship on this subject available in English, Dina Porat's *The Blue and Yellow Stars of David* and Dalia Ofer's *Escaping the Holocaust*, while the inability of the *Yishuv* to facilitate rescue is a highlight of Tom Segev's account of the impact of the Holocaust upon Israeli society during the war and since, *The Seventh Million: The Israelis and the Holocaust*.[191]

A few important points about the *Yishuv* and the Holocaust are, however, worth making. There is general agreement among scholars that the attitude of David Ben-Gurion and most other leaders of the *Yishuv* to news of the Holocaust as it unfolded was extremely curious, hallmarked by disbelief and something resembling inertia.[192] The puzzling stance of Ben-Gurion has been seen as a result of his unwillingness to face unpleasant facts, his alleged belief in 'beneficial disasters' throughout Jewish history and his sheer inability to comprehend the

Map 5 Location of concentration camps. All of the extermination camps were in Poland; the German camps were primarily used to house prisoners and slave labourers, although tens of thousands of Jews were killed by the S.S. *Einsatzgruppen* through mass shootings in the USSR, or perished through disease or malnutrition in ghettos. (From D. Cohn-Sherbok, *Atlas of Jewish History*, 1996. Reproduced by permission of Routledge.)

magnitude of the catastrophe in Europe. Against this must be set, as always, the fact that Ben-Gurion and the other leaders of the *Yishuv* were simply powerless to affect events in Nazi-occupied Europe.

Some telling examples of this are to be found in *aliyah* to Palestine during the period of the Holocaust. Although the British apparently reduced the volume of Jewish immigration to that land to absurdly low levels, in fact about 15,000 *fewer* Jews legally migrated to Palestine during the Second World War than was permitted by the 1939 MacDonald White Paper. In October 1943, the Jewish Agency still had 30,000 entrance certificates unallocated from the 75,000 limit imposed by the White Paper.[193] From September 1939 until the end of 1944, only 37,451 legal immigrants reached Palestine, in addition to about 11,600 'clandestine immigrants' who were allowed to migrate there without hindrance.[194] During this period about 52,650 immigration permits were issued by the British authorities.[195] In the period from mid-1941 to the end of 1944, the number of immigrants to Palestine arriving by ship totalled only 4,565, compared with 5,694 in the month of August 1939 alone.[196] The great majority of these arrivals came from Rumania after March 1944, that is, after it had signalled its intentions of joining the Allies and ending German domination. Not one ship carrying immigrants, legal or illegal, reached Palestine between September 1942 and March 1944.[197]

That it was chiefly the Nazi imprisonment of the Jews prior to genocide, and not Allied restrictions on immigration to Palestine, which explains the low figures of *aliyah* after 1940, was readily admitted by Zionist spokesmen during the war, for example, E. Dobkin at the Third Zionist Conference at Tel Aviv on 6 October 1943. In a wide-ranging discussion of 'Immigration and Rescue of Jews' he noted, concerning 'Permission to leave enemy-occupied territory', that:

> The enemy is determined to exterminate Jews wherever he finds them. For more than a year the Nazi authorities have perfected a policy forbidding Jews to leave the country. In countries directly under German rule such as Germany, Czechoslovakia, Poland and Greece, not only are Jews forbidden to leave the country, but they cannot make use of any means of transport, the sealed doomed waggons carrying them eastwards to their death excepted. The situation varies in the satellite countries, particularly in the Balkans. In most of these countries Jews, in principle, are allowed to leave. Not long ago the Hungarian Premier announced that his Government decided to allow Jews to leave the country. However, such concessions are weakened by pressure brought to bear by the Germans, who wish to forbid Jewish emigration. About half a year ago German pressure made impossible the departure of Jews from the Balkan countries via Bulgaria. Tremendous efforts are being exerted to overcome this main difficulty. All means at our

disposal are being used in the various capitals, particularly in Constantin-ople, where a representative of the Immigration Department permanently resides, and which has been visited during the past six months by repre-sentatives of the Jewish Agency Executive. Only in the last few days have we seen a ray of hope, and we trust we shall not be disappointed. Some progress has also been made regarding questions of safe transport.

The question as to whether during the war we may be fortunate enough to meet our brethren from the German occupied countries, as well as from the Balkan countries, still remains. Have not the 30,000 permits for immigrants from enemy-occupied countries, which were placed at our disposal after a two-and-a-half years of discussion, come too late? But we must not despair. We must continue to make every effort, for all hope is not yet lost.

It can be assumed that every additional allied victory will influence the satellite countries to review their attitude and seek more humane methods of 'solving' the Jewish problem, so as to make their own lot easier after the war. Were the Allied Powers to be more emphatic and specific as regards punishment for the persecution of Jews, the position of our brethren in these countries would be better, and more sincere attempts would be made to enable them to leave.[198]

As much as in the Western democracies, the Jews of the *Yishuv* remained passive onlookers in both the war against the Nazis and the struggle to save European Jewry. Only a few dramatic gestures were possible; for the most part these proved to be theatrical failures. Perhaps the most tragic (and famous) such gesture was the parachuting of *Yishuv* volunteers behind the Axis lines in mid-1944; of these the heroine Hannah Senesh, executed by the Hungarian fascists, is the most celebrated.[199] After a great deal of prevarication and opposition by both Ben-Gurion and the British, a group of thirty-two volunteers, mainly young Zionist enthusiasts from the *kibbutzim*, were selected from 200 volunteers for parachuting behind enemy lines in Rumania, Hungary and Yugoslavia. The British instructed them to aid the partisans and Allied prisoners of war. The leaders of the *Yishuv* had little or no idea of what they were supposed to do.

On the eve of their departure, the paratroopers met with the leaders of the yishuv, among them Berl Katznelson, David Ben-Gurion, and Golda Meir. They tried to learn what was expected of them, but instead of operational instructions they received only words of inspiration and encouragement. Ben-Gurion told them to make sure 'that the Jewish people recognize the Land of Israel as their land and fortress,' so that after the war they would come by the thousands. Eliahu Golomb told them that their goal was to show the Jewish people how to 'stand proud.' One Jewish Agency official told them to bring the 'Messiah' to the Jews of the Exile; Golda Meir just wept, paratrooper Yoel Palgi later recalled.[200]

Segev describes the mission as one of 'national Zionist awakening, to save the souls of the remnant of the Jewish people, rather than a military mission to save their lives'.[201] Senesh, who had volunteered chiefly in order to bring her mother, in Budapest, to Palestine, was captured, tortured and judicially executed at the age of 23. Her renowned poem 'Blessed is the Match that is Consumed in Kindling Flame', has become perhaps the most famous poem written in Hebrew in this century; in 1950 she was reburied, as a national hero, in Jerusalem, hailed as a Jewish Joan of Arc.[202] While Senesh was executed, her mother, ironically, survived the war. The mission, if not a fiasco — the parachutists were often a valuable, if minor part of the underground — did little, other than to create a legend. Marie Syrkin 'asked each of the parachutists: "What did you accomplish?" Each . . . said to me, "The mere fact of our presence was important."'[203] It need not be observed that none of the parachutists came close to Auschwitz or interfered with the extermination process. Other Jews employed by the *Yishuv* to assist with rescue could do little or nothing. For instance, the Jewish Agency employed agents in Istanbul to try to assist refugees and escapees who had passed from Nazi-occupied Europe to Turkey on the way to Palestine. Historian Dina Porat asked Venya Pomerantz, one of the agents in Turkey, what they had done there. 'Nothing', he answered.[204]

There is a final point about rescue and *aliyah* which is of very considerable importance indeed. It is this: throughout the literature of rescue there is a central confusion between the democracies allowing Jews who escaped from Nazi-occupied Europe to remain *somewhere*, in security, in the lands of the Allies, and allowing them to migrate to Palestine, the primary intention of many who escaped. It is perfectly true that some Jews who escaped from Nazi-occupied Europe were not permitted to settle in Palestine, although their numbers, especially after 1942, were smaller than one might suppose and many were indeed allowed to migrate there despite the 1939 White Paper.[205] It is, however, *not* true that those Jews who escaped from Nazi-occupied Europe were returned to the Nazi realms. A most extraordinary and crucial fact about the policies of the democracies toward the Jews of Europe is that, so far as I am aware, after the genocide of Europe's Jews began, no Jew who escaped from Nazi-occupied Europe was ever forced by the democracies to return.[206] This remarkable fact was asserted in the House of Commons in May 1943 by Osbert Peake, Under-Secretary at the Home Office, in his reply to critics of the Bermuda Conference.[207] Escaping Jews who intended to migrate to Palestine, but were prevented from so doing by Britain's enforcement of the White Paper, were interned for the duration of the war in such places as Cyprus and Mauritius, where they were as secure from harm at the hands of the

Nazis as they would have been in Palestine, however galling to Zionists and arguably quite unfair this was.

Repeatedly we return to the central point: it was not the Allies' refusal to admit more Jewish refugees which was the problem, but the Nazis' refusal to let the Jews depart. An interesting and very typical example of this can be seen in the case of Spain during the war, a country whose policies were philo-semitic, despite its fascist regime headed by Franco. In November 1942 Spain (which remained neutral during the war) altered its border policies so that *all refugees without exception* would be allowed to enter and remain.[208] Germany soon pressured Spain to close its borders to refugees, which it then did. But 'Germany's political success provoked sharp Allied reaction', according to historian Haim Avni.[209] The American ambassador placed strong pressure on the Franco government to rescind this order. As well:

> Winston Churchill now took up the cause of the refugees' plight. On April 7, 1943 he warned the Spanish ambassador in London that if the Spanish government went to the length of preventing these unfortunate people seeking safety from the horrors of Nazi domination and if they went further and committed the offence of actually handing them back to German authorities, that was a thing which would be the destruction of good relations.[210]

These protests achieved their objective, and Spain reversed its policy, such that from April 1943, 'in future all refugees who reached Spain would be allowed to remain there', a policy continued by Franco until the end of the war.[211]

How many Jews did this remarkably generous policy actually save? Estimates vary, but the number might well have been no more than 7,500 persons.[212] The reasons why so few Jews were saved, despite the fact that Spain abutted directly onto Nazi-occupied Europe, are clear: when Vichy came to power in 1940 it immediately closed its border with Spain to departing refugees. Germany stationed two divisions of troops in south-western France throughout the war.[213] Most centrally, the Spanish border was hundreds of miles from the nearest significant Jewish population centre, and to reach Spain from the ghettos of Poland or the attics and cellars of Amsterdam or Berlin was utterly impossible. For Jews in those places, nothing whatever could be done by the Allies, apart from winning the war as quickly as possible and annihilating the Nazis.

DIGEST OF SUGGESTIONS SUBMITTED TO THE
WAR REFUGEE BOARD BY VARIOUS PRIVATE ORGANIZATIONS
IN RESPONSE TO A CIRCULAR LETTER.
[Compiled by the U.S. War Refugee Board in c. March 1944]

I Direct appeals to Germany for cooperation in evacuation.
(Valuable for morale of persecuted peoples, even if no concrete results are
forthcoming – American Friends.)

A. Release of entire Jewish minority – American Friends
   1. Approach through Vatican and Neutrals –
      Joint Emergency Committee.

   2. Through Red Cross and Neutrals, using every avenue of propaganda,
      directed particularly to the German people rather than the govern-
      ment.
      American Jewish Conference.

B. Release children and aged persons, if not all Jews.
   American Friends
   H.I.A.S.
   American Committee of O.S.E.
   Jewish Labor Committee

   1. Request permission for free passage of trains through Hungary,
      Roumania and Bulgaria.
      Jewish Labor Committee.

   2. Include 10 % of Germans in bad health, as inducement to German
      government. – American Friends.

C. In interim, have Red Cross conduct a census of Jews in Poland, and feed
   those awaiting evacuation.
   Jewish Labor Committee.

D. Request safe-conduct for trains full of refugees from Switzerland to
   Spain, to relieve pressure in Switzerland, since evacuation is otherwise
   impossible.
   American Friends and H.I.A.S.
   (Passage of sealed cars on other occasions has been permitted – H.I.A.S.).

E. Negotiate exchanges against Nazi internees.
   Agudas Israel of America.

1. Don't request particular persons, since that might endanger their safety. – American Friends.

2. Include rabbis, scholars, and families of persons in America (whether citizens or not).
   Union of Orthodox Rabbis.

3. Exchange Dutch and Belgian Jews, and those at Camps Vittel and Titmoning for Germans on the Isle of Man and elsewhere.
   World Jewish Congress.
   Netherland Jewish Society.

4. (Related subject) – Include Polish Jews in Shanghai in Japanese exchanges. – Union of Rabbis.

II Warnings to German people and officials, and to satellites generally.
   A. Counteract official German propaganda alleging anti-Semitic feeling and disregard for plight of Jews on the part of the people of the United Nations, and bring full gory details of Nazi persecution to the attention of the German people.
      American Jewish Conference.
      Agudas Israel of America.
      World Jewish Congress.

   B. Warn that perpetrators of acts of persecution will be held guilty of murder.
      World Jewish Congress.
      Union of Rabbis.

      1. Stimulate action by the Commission for the Investigation of War Crimes. Hold more trials immediately – (Prosecute particularly perpetrators of such acts as the deportation of the Benghasi Jews) – and publicize highly. – World Jewish Conference.

   C. Propaganda methods.
      1. Short-wave radio and leaflets dropped by plane.
         World Jewish Congress.
         Union of Rabbis.
         American Jewish Conference.

      2. Procure cooperation of neutral countries, governments-in-exile, and all religious groups.
         Union of Rabbis.

      3. Repeated official warnings, particularly by Roosevelt and Churchill.
         World Jewish Congress.

III Efforts directed specially toward satellite countries.

  A. Encourage aid, clemency and relaxation of border controls generally.
American Friends.

    1. Get exit and transit visas from Bulgaria.
American Jewish Conference.

    2. Get Russia to intercede with Bulgaria.
Union of Rabbis.

    3. Enlist cooperation of Holy See for Slovakia and Hungary, and the Exarchate in the case of Bulgaria.
World Jewish Congress.

    4. Take advantage of the apparent willingness of the satellite governments to permit the Red Cross to operate within their borders.
World Jewish Congress.

  B. Threaten post-war repercussions.

    1. Future consideration will be governed by present behavior.
Union of Rabbis.

    2. Inform Rumania that ransom and punitive taxes will be charged against it in post-war accounting.
American Jewish Conference.

  C. Appoint special Board attachés in Switzerland and/or Turkey to keep watch over situation in Hungary.
World Jewish Congress.

IV Relations with neutral European countries.

  A. Helping to maintain refugees in these countries, and trying to evacuate them as soon as possible will create more favorable attitude toward admitting additional numbers. Since re-evacuation of Switzerland is impossible now, guarantee post-war action.
Joint Distribution Committee.
American Jewish Conference.
Union of Rabbis.
Agudas Israel.
American Friends.

    1. Persuade Switzerland to stop turning back adults not accompanied by children.
World Jewish Congress.

    2. Encourage Sweden and Finland to take in Jews in the Baltic States in

path of German withdrawal.
Union of Rabbis.

V Suggested places to which refugees may be taken.
  A. Temporary havens in neutral countries and allied territory.
    1. Large camps in Turkey, Sweden, Spain and Switzerland.
       Jewish Labor Committee.

    2. Canada, Mexico, Cuba, etc.
       H.I.A.S.

    3. England, and British territories in Africa and the Caribbean area.
       Joint Emergency Committee.

    4. Iran, Iraq and Egypt (plus those listed supra).
       American Friends.

    5. Russia.
       American Friends.

    6. Southern Italy.
       Joint Distribution Committee.

    7. Transfer from liberated areas to places safer from recapture (e.g. Isle
       of Rab).
       World Jewish Congress.

  B. Permanent resettlement projects.
    1. Remove all restrictions on immigration into Palestine.
       American Jewish Conference.
       World Jewish Congress.
       Joint Emergency Committee.

    2. Use all available Palestine certificates, at least.
       Joint Distribution Committee.
       H.I.A.S.

    3. Have all United Nations make public announcement of willingness to
       take in all refugees reaching their borders.
       World Jewish Congress.

    4. Relax United States, Great Britain and Latin American immigration
       policies.
       Joint Emergency Committee.

    5. Get Mexican visas for Spanish Republicans.
       American Friends.

6. Permanent visas, definitely committed, for Jewish children, for use now and in post-war period, following example of Australia.
American Committee of O.S.E.

7. Request Russia to grant exit visas to rabbis now there, Iran to grant temporary refuge, and U.S. to issue visas to several hundred of them.
Union of Rabbis.

8. Act on specific commitments made by various countries in connection with old project of evacuating children from France.
Union of Rabbis.

C. Relax United States immigration laws and/or policy.
1. Liberalize U.S. visa policy 'quietly', dropping 'relatives clause', and simplifying procedure, particularly with respect to transit visas.
American Friends.

2. Temporary U.S. visas with a general revision of immigration laws at the proper time, to be initiated by the War Refugee Board.
Council of Jewish Women.

3. Change administration of U.S. laws to permit full use of present quotas.
World Jewish Congress.

VI Implementing evacuation.
A. Coordinating efforts.
1. Seek cooperation of French Committee of Liberation and governments-in-exile generally to include Jews with their nationals being evacuated by the underground sponsored by each.
Union of Rabbis.

2. Cooperate generally with underground movements.
Joint Distribution Committee.
American Jewish Conference.
H.I.A.S.
Council of Jewish Women.

3. Appropriate funds to smuggle out refugees.
Agudas Israel.
World Jewish Congress.
Union of Rabbis.

4. Assign to attaché of the Board to North Africa to supervise evacuation and welfare of refugees.
Union of Rabbis.

5. Assign special representatives to Switzerland and/or Turkey to aid work in Hungary.
World Jewish Congress.

6. Procure Turkish visas for Jews in Bulgaria and Rumania.
Union of Rabbis.

7. Follow up request made by Sweden to Germany to release 20,000 Jewish children.
World Jewish Congress.

8. Insure renewable visas for children to be taken in by Switzerland (to be granted by U.S.).
Joint Distribution Committee.

9. Follow up old project of evacuating children from France to United Nations countries.
Union of Rabbis.
H.I.A.S.

B. Shipping problems.
1. Shipping in Black Sea urgently needed.
Joint Distribution Committee.
Union of Rabbis.

2. Provide Red Cross with additional ships.
American Jewish Conference.
World Jewish Conference.

3. Lease Portugese, Swedish and Turkish ships.
World Jewish Congress.

4. Use empty ships returning to U.S., and Swedish ships returning from relief missions to Greece.
H.I.A.S.
World Jewish Congress.

5. Make use of Army and Navy facilities.
Union of Rabbis.

VII Program for persons who cannot be evacuated.
A. Diplomatic aid to those in Axis territory.
1. Induce Turkey to issue certificates to Turkish Jews in France.
American Jewish Conference.
H.I.A.S.

2. Act with regard to threatened voiding of illegal Latin American passports held by persons interned in Europe, and urge Swiss to stop blocking issuance of additional such papers.
World Jewish Conference.

3. Give Stateless refugees identification papers analogous to 'Nansens'.
Joint Emergency Committee.

4. Press and support I.G.C. in procuring documentation and representation for Stateless. If no results are forthcoming, U.S. should assume diplomatic responsibility, issuing temporary identification papers through Switzerland, as protecting power for U.S. interests. This action should be supplemented by Swiss or Swedish assumption of responsibility. If neither of these plans are carried out, could private groups (e.g. American Friends) assume responsibility, much as has been done in Madrid?
American Friends.

5. Give Jews the status of prisoners-of-war, or that of civilian internees.
Joint Emergency Committee.
World Jewish Congress.
Union of Rabbis.

6. Granting of visas (not intended to confer any rights as against country of issue) would provide basis for claim to status of civilian internees.
Union of Rabbis.

7. Have Red Cross approach German government to clarify status of Jews.
World Jewish Conference.

8. U.S. and Great Britain should revise strict interpretation of status, for blockade purposes.
World Jewish Conference.

9. Having established a satisfactory status, Red Cross could inspect ghettos and Jewish camps, and pass food through blockade.
World Jewish Conference.

B. Material aid.
1. Expedite proposed financial aid to Red Cross by U.S. and Great Britain, now in hands of IGC.
World Jewish Conference.

2. Send food (package or bulk), medical supplies and clothing into Axis territory.

Agudas Israel.
Joint Emergency Committee.
Joint Distribution Committee.
Union of Rabbis.
American Jewish Conference.
American Friends.
League for Liberation of Lithuanians.

3. Send mercy ships to ghettos.
   Union of Rabbis.

4. Increase package reserve of Intercross to make supplies available for civilians.
   American Friends.
   (W.J.C. claims large surpluses in Switzerland now, not available under blockade rules.)

5. Permit transmittal of funds for purchase of food in Europe.
   American Friends.

6. Use underground to get food to those in hiding.
   Union of Rabbis.

7. Furnish refugees in hiding with money, food ration books and identification papers, through underground.
   World Jewish Conference.

8. Smuggle in weapons for last ditch stand by condemned Jews in Poland.
   World Jewish Conference.

9. Send money to bribe officials not to deport Jews.
   World Jewish Conference.

10. Swiss program of taking children for several months at a time to rehabilitate them is criticized on ground that to date only German children have been taken for a 'Bomb-free vacation.'
    World Jewish Congress.

11. Shanghai – Extend Red Cross facilities to Jews.
    American Jewish Conference.
    Jewish Labor Committee.

12. Shanghai – License $50,000, and urge neutral countries to support Vatican in plea to Japan.
    Union of Rabbis.

VIII General suggestions re implementing work of Board, financially, and through cooperation with others.

A. International solidarity.

   1. Call immediate conference of United Nations to announce world-wide unanimity of purpose.
   Council of Jewish Women.

   2. Urge full cooperation of British in Board's work.
   Union of Rabbis.

   3. Establish inter-governmental agency.
   Joint Emergency Committee.
   (The plan submitted by this organization was the one submitted to the Bermuda Conference.)

   4. Expenses of refugee work should be underwritten by the United Nations.
   Joint Emergency Committee.

   5. The Swiss should be urged to co-operate more fully with private organizations.
   Union of Rabbis.

B. Financing War Refugee Board's work.

   1. Follow plan used for UNRRA.
   American Jewish Conference.

   2. Use Lend-Lease funds.
   Union of Rabbis.

   3. Use Intergovernmental Committee funds.
   Union of Rabbis.

   4. Get Congressional appropriation, or amend UNRRA law to make its funds available.
   Union of Rabbis.

   5. Have UNRRA take over administration of refugee camps.
   American Friends.

C. General cooperation with private agencies.

   1. Request reports and suggestions.
   Joint Distribution Committee.

   2. Encourage evacuation efforts.
   American Friends.

3. Lend political and diplomatic backing, license private funds, and make W.R.B.'s funds available.
Union of Rabbis.

4. Designate persons to work with rescue committees.
Union of Rabbis.

D. Specific aids to work of private agencies.
1. Permit transmittal of funds.
American Friends.
Union of Rabbis.

2. Permit agents of private organizations to go to Europe to make contacts.
Agudas Israel.

3. Permit 'religious rescue squads' to visit liberated territories to furnish religious comfort.
Agudas Israel.

4. Permit augmentation of staffs (locally or from here?).
American Friends.

5. License communications, including sending lists of names, to neutral countries.
Joint Distribution Committee.
Agudas Israel.

6. Urge relaxing of censorship rules generally, to permit greater efficiency of operations. Reports now are often obsolete before received.
World Jewish Conference.

4

THE MYTH OF BOMBING
AUSCHWITZ

Unquestionably, when the subject of what the Allies should have done but neglected to do is raised today, the failure to bomb Auschwitz is the suggested lost opportunity which is most often put forward. I might personally note that whenever I have lectured on the topic of rescue, either before scholarly or non-scholarly audiences, the bombing of Auschwitz has always and invariably been aired in question time. If I have spoken on another aspect of 'rescue', for instance the schemes for rescue actually proposed during the war, and failed to discuss the bombing of Auschwitz, someone will be sure to mention it; if I have discussed the bombing of Auschwitz in my talk, members of the audience are absolutely certain to question my remarks in detail, often with a wealth of understanding of its military dimensions – more, in fact, than is often possessed by some historians who have written on this subject.

It is easy to understand why this is so. The bombing of Auschwitz, if successful, would seemingly have provided a dramatic and sudden end to the extermination process itself. Bombing Auschwitz appears to have been quite feasible: as is well known, Allied strategic bombing took place only a few miles from Auschwitz in 1944 when Jews were being murdered there. There is, seemingly, enough evidence of bad faith on the part of the Allies when the bombing of Auschwitz was allegedly proposed to make it look not merely like a lost opportunity, but an indication that the Allies had no real interest in saving Jews. Those historians who imagine that large-scale rescue was possible, especially those who believe the inability to rescue was rooted in anti-semitism, overt or disguised, have naturally had a field-day with the failure of the Allies to bomb Auschwitz; perhaps because of the dramatic and seemingly easily understood nature of any Auschwitz bombing mission, it has probably entered the popular consciousness more fully than any other aspect of the question of the rescue of Jews during the war.

In reality, however, there is as little in the way of a valid critique of Allied policy in respect to bombing Auschwitz as there is to any other part of the myth of rescue: indeed, arguably there is much less, and the notion that the Allies genuinely lost an opportunity – still less that they lost it through ill-disguised anti-semitism – appears to be even more dubious than the other components of an historiographical argument not notable for its cogency. There is, indeed, rather less to say about the bombing of Auschwitz than perhaps any other aspect of the question of rescue during the war.

There is one basic and underlying reason why the question of bombing Auschwitz can be dismissed with some brevity: *virtually no one in the United States proposed bombing it, or any other extermination camp, while significant numbers of Jews were imprisoned there, or were being sent there*; in particular, the War Refugee Board failed to suggest it. (There are, as well, a host of subsidiary reasons why no successful bombing of Auschwitz could have occurred.) As we have seen from the detailed discussions of the plans for 'rescue' actually put forward during the war, the bombing of Auschwitz was never, at any time, included among the proposals made by Jewish or non-Jewish groups concerned with the plight of Europe's Jews. No suggestion for bombing Auschwitz, or any other extermination camp, was included among the more than one hundred ideas advanced by every American group concerned with the rescue of the Jews to the newly created War Refugee Board early in 1944. For whatever reason, no person or group in the democracies, however deeply they felt the sufferings of Europe's Jews, proposed the destruction of any extermination camp.

The bombing of Auschwitz, or any other camp in eastern Europe was, in fact, logistically impossible for Allied bombers before December 1943. Only from that time, with the capture of Foggia airbase in southern Italy, did it become logistically possible for the Allies to mount any air strike of any kind against Auschwitz, even if this had been proposed and adopted as Allied policy.[1] Prior to late 1943 Auschwitz (and the other extermination camps, all situated in Poland) were simply too far away for Allied bombers, necessarily accompanied by fighter-interceptors for protection, to raid. Before the capture of southern Italy (and, even more emphatically, prior to D-Day in June 1944), the closest the Western Allies were to Auschwitz was Dover, Kent, roughly a thousand miles away. Until 1944 Allied bombers could travel – with considerable difficulties – only as far as, roughly, Berlin, about 400 miles north-west of Auschwitz. Until late 1943, too, the Soviet front line was just as far from Auschwitz as was the Anglo-American front line: a thousand miles away.

The first suggestion made by anyone which resembled a proposal to 'bomb Auschwitz' was that put by Rabbi Michael Dov Ber Weissmandel (1904–57), a Slovakian rabbi who was deported to Auschwitz but managed to jump from the train (his family perished). After the war, he emigrated to the United States and founded the Nitra Yeshivah in Mount Kisco, New York; he has become a considerable hero to America's growing Agudas Strictly Orthodox community, both because of his wartime activities and his subsequent role in American Jewry.[2]

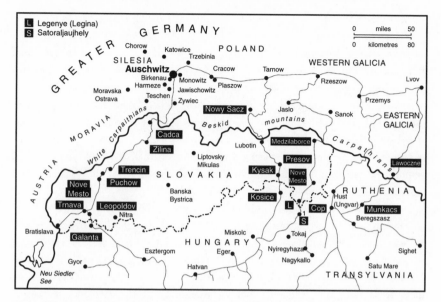

Map 6 The principal railway lines from Hungary to Auschwitz. Only the proposal to bomb one railway line, between Presov (Preskov) and Kosice, was discussed by the US War Refugees Board. (From M. Gilbert, *Auschwitz and the Allies*, 1991. Reproduced by permission of Mandarin.)

On 16 May 1944 he sent a telegram (in code) from Bratislava to Swiss Orthodox Jewish leaders, for transmission to the United States, urging the Allies to bomb the railway lines between Kosice (also known as Kaschau, Kassa, Kelse and Kelsice) and Preskov in Slovakia, in order to impede the transport by rail to Auschwitz of Hungary's Jews. He had learned that the SS, under Himmler and Eichmann, had begun the deportation of Hungarian Jews from ghettos (in which they had been confined since March 1944) to Auschwitz on the previous day, 15 May 1944.[3]

Weissmandel's message (and a second one sent by him on 24 May) reached Isaac Sternbuch, the representative in Switzerland of the Union of Orthodox Rabbis of the United States. Sternbuch relayed the message to Jacob Rosenheim, President of the Agudas Israel World Organization in New York, who, in turn, sent it to Roswell McClelland, an official of the War Refugee Board.[4] McClelland passed the telegram on to Lieutenant-Colonel Alfred de Jong (an American army officer) on 25 May 1944.[5] On 2 June Leland Harrison, United States Minister to Switzerland, sent a telegram to the American State Department with a detailed message from Sternbuch concerning conditions in Hungary and a request that 'airmail [*sic*] be sent to the towns of Munkacs, Kaschau, and Presov [Preskov]' as '15,000 Jews daily are deported over this route to Poland since May 15th', obviously a plea for Allied bombing.[6] That same day, Lowell Pinkerton, American

Consul-General in Jerusalem, sent a telegram to Cordell Hull, the United States Secretary of State, relaying a statement from the Jewish Agency on the Hungarian situation which included the following: 'Suggest deportation would be much impeded if railways between Hungary and Poland could be bombed.'[7] Pressure was thus emerging from a number of rescue groups for some of the *rail lines* to Auschwitz to be bombed. Those demands, it must be appreciated, emerged from only a handful of the rescue groups, and from only one American organisation, the Agudas Israel World Organization in New York, a body which would have been regarded by many American Jewish groups as small and quite marginal. *No* request for bombing the rail lines was made at this time from America's best-known and largest Jewish organisations.

All of the requests for bombing which reached the War Refugee Board specifically asked that the rail lines – and, in particular, the line from Kosice to Preskov – be bombed, *not* Auschwitz. When a proposal to bomb the camp itself was first made to the Board is unclear. A typescript memorandum dated 22 May 1944 exists in the Board's files at the Franklin D. Roosevelt Library at Hyde Park, New York. It was written by Rabbi Weissmandel and Mrs Gizi Fleischmann of the Jewish underground in Slovakia, and contains a remarkably detailed report on the deportation process in Hungary and extermination process at Auschwitz. The recommendations of this memorandum included one calling upon Jews in the West to demand the 'bombarding [of] the "death halls" in Auschwitz', which would be 'easily recognizable' from the crude sketch map of Auschwitz drawn by the escapees (and since frequently reproduced).[8] When John Pehle first saw this typescript – if, indeed, he did at this time – is unclear; the document's historical importance is that it was the first proposal ever made to bomb Auschwitz itself.[9] (Clearly, a memorandum from Slovakia dated 22 May 1944 would not have reached Washington until some later time.)

It is also interesting to note that the War Refugee Board issued, between February 1944 and June 1945, a detailed typescript 'Weekly Report' of its plans and activities. The earliest specific mention of any bombing proposal is to be found in that of 26 June–1 July 1944 where (buried on page 6, in an account headed 'Report From Bern'), it is stated that

> The particular stretches of railroad used in these deportations [from eastern Hungary] were indicated to McClelland, who relayed to us without recommendation the fact that all his sources of information in Slovakia and Hungary had urged that vital sections of these lines, especially bridges, be bombed as the only possible means of slowing down or stopping future deportations.[10]

The next mention is in the 'Weekly Report' of 10–15 July 1944, where it is noted, in an Appendix 'Summary of Steps Taken With Respect to the Jews of

Hungary', that the Board 'has received several proposals that certain military operations might take place with the possible purpose of forestalling or hindering German extermination operations. One . . . was . . . that the railways leading from the points of deportation to the camps be bombed.'[11] For the first time the bombing of Auschwitz was specifically mentioned:

It has been suggested that the concentration and extermination centres be bombed in order that in the resultant confusion some of the unfortunate people might be able to escape and hide. It has also been suggested that weapons be dropped simultaneously with such bombings. Finally, it has been proposed that some parachute troops be dropped to bring about disorganization and escape of the unfortunate people.[12]

The only proposal officially discussed with America's military officials by the War Refugee Board at this time was one specifically 'to bomb the railroad line between Kassa [Kosice] and Presov [Preskov] being used for the deportation of Jews from Hungary to Poland'. As is well known, Pehle discussed this proposal – and no other – for 'exploration' with Assistant Secretary of War John J. McCloy on 24 June 1944.[13] (Pehle apparently did not actually receive any suggestion to bomb the rail lines before 18 June 1944.[14]) He expressed considerable reservations about the viability of this plan, doubting whether it would be an appropriate use of military force, whether the line could actually be put out of commission and whether it would help Hungarian Jewry.[15] He also 'made clear to Mr McCloy that I was not, at this point at least, requesting the War Department to take any action on this proposal other than to appropriately explore it'.[16]

On 26 June an official reply was received from that body saying that the

suggested air operation is impractical for the reason that it could be executed only by diversion of considerable air support essential for the success of our forces. . . . The War Department fully appreciates the humanitarian importance of the suggested operation. However, after due consideration of the problem, it is considered that the most effective relief to the victims . . . is the early defeat of the Axis.[17]

No further proposals were made by Pehle about bombings until 3 October 1944. In the meantime, however, suggestions to bomb both the rail lines and the extermination camps were now made by other Jewish groups, including a proposal from the New York Office of the World Jewish Congress on 9 August 1944 advocating 'the destruction of gas chambers and crematoria in Oswiecim [Auschwitz] by bombing', which

would have a certain effect now. Germans are now exhuming and burning corpses in an effort to conceal their crimes. This could be prevented by destruction of crematoria and then Germans might possibly stop further mass exterminations especially since so little time is left to them.[18]

On 14 August McCloy responded that 'the diversion of considerable air support essential to the success of our forces . . . would not warrant the use of our resources . . . at least at this time'.[19] Pehle's reluctance to recommend the bombing of Auschwitz was of great importance. As Richard H. Levy has noted, the War Refugee Board 'seems to have acquired a virtual monopoly on the trans- mission of appeals to the War Department'.[20] While the American government was willing to consider proposals for rescuing Jews from other sources, the War Refugee Board was officially mandated to do so, and its views were naturally very important.

Those historians who have examined these proposals and concluded that, through inaction, America shamefully missed a golden opportunity to halt the extermination process, have in my opinion given sufficient thought neither to what was actually suggested nor to when these ideas occurred. The timing of any proposed bombings was all-important. The deportation of Jews from Hungary to Auschwitz began on 15 May 1944 and was completed on *9 July* 1944; no deportations occurred after that date.[21] Pehle's official proposal to consider the bombing of one rail line was made on 24 June 1944, and officially denied two days later. In other words, even if it had been enthusiastically received and endorsed at the highest level, *there was a period of no more than fifteen days during which operations could have proceeded with any hope of rescuing Hungarian Jewry*. This time-period was almost certainly inadequate, in the real world of the European conflict as it was being conducted in 1944, to have mounted even a simple bombing mission, which normally required an absolute minimum of two weeks to plan prior to execution, as well as an enormous amount of preparatory work such as dedicated photo reconnaissance and the preparation of a model of the target. Any such raid was also crucially dependent upon the weather.[22] It also cannot be emphasised too much that this operation would have been planned only three weeks after D-Day, when the Allied High Command was still totally preoccupied with the success of the Normandy landing and its aftermath.

There is, however, much more to say about the proposal that was actually made – the only one put forth at the time – to bomb the railway line from Kosice to Preskov. There are two vital reasons why any such bombing mission, even if carried out successfully, would have failed to halt the deportation of Jews to Auschwitz. In the first place, *there were no fewer than seven separate railway lines from Hungary to Auschwitz*, each of which fed into the Lvov–Auschwitz trunk route at different points. (It might be noted that before the First World War, Auschwitz (Osweicim) was in Galicia, in Austria-Hungary, not in Russian Poland. Adjacent to the border with Germany, it was a major railhead; indeed Auschwitz was chosen as the site of the most infamous death camp precisely because it was a major railhead junction for eastern and south-central Europe.) The Kosice–Preskov rail line is simply one of many branch feeder lines from Hungary to southern Poland, which criss-crossed each other. It was not the main line, merely a local branch. Even if it had been successfully bombed, Jews would simply have been transported over a different route.[23] It is *not* immediately apparent why the Kosice–Preskov route was given such prominence: apparently, however, the Agudas organisation learned that it was being used *at that time* to deport Hungary's Jews. This brings us to the second vital point. *By late June–early July 1944 the Kosice–Preskov route was only a minor one* among those used by the death trains. The Jews of its region of central-eastern Hungary had already been sent to Auschwitz, and Eichmann and the SS were then chiefly working on deporting Jews further to the West. (Eichmann divided Hungary into regions and deported Jews starting with the east, those most likely to be liberated by the advancing Soviet armies.)

It is also important to realise that bombing the Kosice–Preskov rail link would have had absolutely no effect upon any deportation of Jews to Auschwitz from any other part of Europe. For instance, bombing this line would not have affected in any way the deportation and extermination of the 70,000 Jews of Lodz, the last remaining Polish ghetto, between 6–30 August 1944. Lodz lies *north* of Auschwitz while the Kosice–Preskov line is situated to its south-east. Bombing could not have affected the final deportations from France or Italy, nor the 'death marches' in the closing stages of the war. It might be argued that if the Kosice–Preskov line was successfully bombed, others might have followed, but no such proposals were actually made, and the abbreviated time-frame would have made any further raids of that sort most improbable.

Pehle not only recommended no further bombing action of any kind until much later in 1944, but *specifically rejected* the possibility of bombing Auschwitz until November 1944. On 11 August 1944 representatives of several major American Jewish organisations, including the American Jewish Congress and the American Jewish Committee, met Pehle in Washington, DC. He 'flatly rejected as unfeasible the proposal that the extermination camps in Osweiczym [Auschwitz] and elsewhere should be destroyed by bombers or parachutists', on the grounds that it 'had been objected to by Jewish organizations because it would result in the extermination of large numbers of Jews there'.[24] He suggested that 'an underground detachment' be sent to Auschwitz, but 'expressed doubts that the Poles could muster the strength' for such an operation.[25] *No Jewish leader present at this meeting objected to Pehle's rejection of the 'bombing Auschwitz' option.*[26]

On 1 October 1944, Pehle wrote to McCloy, bringing to his attention a cable from James Mann, Assistant Executive Director of the War Refugee Board, in which Polish underground groups 'urged . . . again to explore with the Army the possibility of bombing the extermination chambers and German barracks' at

Auschwitz.[27] Finally, on 8 November 1944, Pehle wrote to McCloy officially advocating the bombing of Auschwitz itself, the first time the War Refugee Board had officially called for the camp to be bombed.[28] Pehle was apparently motivated by detailed eye-witness accounts of Auschwitz which had just become available. He stated that

> until now, despite pressure from many sources, I have been hesitant to urge the destruction of these camps by direct military action. But I am convinced that the point has now been reached where such action is justifiable if it is deemed feasible by competent military authorities.[29]

Pehle cited as goals the heightened 'morale of underground groups' and the possible liberation of 'people confined in Auschwitz and Birkenau', and drew a parallel with the bombing of Amiens prison in February 1944 by Royal Air Force Mosquitos, an action which liberated '100 French patriots'.[30] McCloy rejected both of these proposals, citing as reasons arguments which subsequent authors have claimed lacked merit, and for which he has been consistently criticised by recent historians of 'rescue'.[31] (McCloy did not directly point out the highly pertinent fact that Amiens, situated between Paris and the English Channel, is only seventy-five miles from Britain's south coast, while Auschwitz was roughly one thousand miles from the Allied front lines.)

Once again, however, this assumption needs to be looked at critically. What strikes one most forcefully about Pehle's November 1944 recommendation is that it came far too late to have saved anyone, even if it had been acted upon immediately and was entirely successful in its aims. The last gassings at Auschwitz occurred on 28 November 1944, *twenty days* after Pehle made his first official proposal to bomb the crematoria.[32] Twenty days (a maximum figure, from which the time necessary to secure military approval and pass the orders through the European war theatre's chain of command must be deducted) was simply too little time to mount a raid on Auschwitz from scratch.

It is often noted that American heavy bombers were carrying out raids at this time on industrial targets only a few miles away from the Auschwitz gas chambers, an observation made over and over again in the literature of 'rescue' which criticises the Allies.[33] This point is, however, extremely misleading, regardless of how often it has been repeated. *All* such strategic raids on military-industrial bases proceeded only after months of preparatory intelligence work, entailing the creation of a target folder with specific information about the size, hardness, structure placement, defences and so on, of the target and detailed aerial photography. However, *the United States Air Force totally lacked the intelligence base necessary to plan and execute a bombing raid against the Auschwitz extermination camp.*[34] This information – even if such a raid were enthusiastically endorsed at the most senior military levels – could simply not have been procured for months.

It would have been difficult enough to effect in the best of circumstances, but it would have been especially difficult in the late autumn–winter of 1944–5 and bearing in mind (as will be discussed) that the essential aims of bombing an extermination camp are entirely different from bombing an industrial plant. Furthermore, as Dr James H. Kitchens has remarked, the raid itself would also have required perfect weather, since the bombing would have to be carried out visually.[35] 'I leave you to ponder how frequently such perfect weather occurred over southern Poland; how accurately such weather in the interior of Europe could have been predicted from southern Italy given 1944 state of the art; and how many abortive raids might have been launched before the necessary meteorological conditions materialised over the targets', Dr Kitchens has added.[36] Self-evidently, it is exceedingly doubtful, starting from scratch in November 1944, whether any such bombing raids could have been accomplished before the Soviet army liberated Auschwitz on 27 January 1945.

It is also often contended that at least a part of the target information necessary for a bombing raid on Auschwitz did indeed already exist, namely aerial photographs of Auschwitz taken by Allied air reconnaissance missions. This claim, so often repeated, is also entirely misleading and ought to be examined with some care.

What are probably the best-known and most widely publicised aerial photographs of Auschwitz were taken by an Allied air crew on 25 August 1944. These have been published and republished, generally as enlargements, during the past two decades. Even now, few apart from specialist historians realise that these aerial photographs *remained in negative form until 1978*, and were not seen by anyone until 1978–9. In 1978, two American historians of aerial photography in the Second World War, Dino A. Brugioni and Robert Poirier, discovered these undeveloped films while researching in government photographic intelligence files.[37] As a result of publicity generated by the American television series *The Holocaust*, American aerial photograph analysts were given permission to use modern microstereoscopes to reexamine precise photographic enlargements of the original films.[38] It was these enlarged, cropped and newly captioned photographs which were published and republished in the press. They had never been seen before. Especially poignant is the overhead enlargement of several columns of prisoners, captioned 'Group on Way to Gas Chambers', which has been frequently reprinted.

There is no evidence that these photographs were seen by anybody before 1978, let alone by trained photointelligence officers during the war who realised their significance. Indeed, no one could have seen the columns of prisoners on the way to the gas chambers because no aerial imagery photoenlargement techniques available in 1944 could have spotted those columns. As Colonel Roy M. Stanley II noted in his work *World War II Photo Intelligence*:

A report based on postwar ground information that no World War II P.I. [Photo Interpreter] had available, on modern enlargements that no World War II photo lab could have made, and all of the postwar sophistication developed in the P.I. trade could unintentionally mislead the layman. Because of their advantages, this 1978 photo analysis contains an understanding and correlation of what was happening on the ground that would have been impossible for a 1945-vintage interpreter.[39]

Moreover, no one ever asked the Allied photointelligence operatives to search for extermination camps. This failing was not the result of some anti-semitic cover-up (as might well be alleged by adherents of the proposition that rescue was possible): no Jewish individual or group recommended a search by photographic specialists, and nor did the War Refugee Board. This failure arose simply from the nature of the tasks and priorities assigned to Allied photography interpreters in the context of the European war situation in 1944. Dino A. Brugioni, who, as noted, decades later rediscovered the wartime aerial photographs of Auschwitz, was himself a member of a Second World War bomber crew and then a senior photography interpreter for the CIA who conducted extensive research on Second World War photographic intelligence files. In 1983 Brugioni explained the failure in these terms:

> Whenever I have shown the photographs of the extermination complex, the most frequently asked questions have been: Why did not or why could not the World War II photo interpreters identify the horrifying activities perpetrated at this complex? How could something so hideous have been overlooked? Why did not the photo interpreters note the unusually large size and unique configuration of Birkenau and know that it was not a conventional 'prison camp'? Why were the large number of boxcars on the Birkenau sidings never questioned, considering the obvious lack of industrial installations within the camp? Most importantly, why did not the photo interpreters spot the four separately secured extermination areas, each of which contained unique facilities – an undressing room, a gas chamber and a crematorium?
>
> I have gone back and searched the records and reports produced by the concerned reconnaissance units and interpretation organizations. I have also analyzed the interpretation practices and priorities of the time and have concluded that five major factors influenced these shortcomings:
>
> 1. Tasking – This is a military intelligence term meaning requirements imposed – on a photo interpreter, for instance, to procure specific information needed to formulate intelligence about a specific enemy target or targets. During World War II, photo interpreters operated under an

elaborate tasking and priority system to produce intelligence from aerial photography. Searching for or doing detailed analysis on concentration camps was not a specific task. Photographs were searched to find any indication of enemy build-up or military movements. . . . Of prime concern were concentrations or movements of troops which posed threats to Allied operations, either current or planned. In addition, the photographs were scanned for evidence of reprisal weapons (V-1 and V-2 rocket sites), flak and searchlights, coastal defenses, materiel dumps and depots, camps and barracks, fieldworks and defense lines, construction work or demolition activity, and road, rail, port and inland waterway transport activity. . . .

Photo interpreters were also tasked to perform detailed analysis on a variety of significant tactical and strategic targets. Concentration and extermination camps were not considered significant targets. . . .

The target chart for the Auschwitz (Oswiecim) area was centered on the I.G. Farben 'Buna' Synthetic Fuel and Rubber Plant and did not include either the Auschwitz I or Birkenau camps. The specific detailed interpretation tasking was to report on the progress of the construction of the plant. Later, an added requirement was to report on the extent and effect of Allied bombing. A review of all the photo interpretation reports created on the Farben plant reveals that interpreters' principal concern was the bomb damage and production stoppages at the synthetic fuel plant. There is not a single reference to either the Auschwitz or Birkenau camps, which were covered on the same photographic runs. The Monowice camp, next to the Farben Plant, was correctly identified as a concentration camp.

2. Priority Projects – The principal units performing interpretation of the photographs taken over Germany and German-occupied territories were the Allied Central Interpretation Unit at the Royal Air Force Station Medmenham in England and the Mediterranean Allied Photo Reconnaissance Wing in Italy. These organizations worked on a 24-hour-a-day basis and in 1943 and 1944 were heavily involved in the planning of the Normandy and Southern France landings. Support to the Normandy landings alone required an estimated half-million photo interpretation manhours. The stepped-up Allied bombing offensive of German strategic industries in 1944, which included synthetic fuel plants, also involved extensive photographic analysis and assessments. Other high priority projects included the searching for and destruction of V-1 and V-2 rocket sites, jet aircraft plants, and submarine production facilities. Photo interpreters were also employed in the planning and execution of special bombing missions against critical targets. The volume of materials being received for photo interpretation must also be considered. The daily intake

for the Allied Central Interpretation Unit averaged 25,000 negatives and 60,000 prints. By V-E Day, over five million prints were in storage. More than 40,000 reports had been prepared from these prints.

3. Training – Interpreter trainees were normally sent to a four-to-six-week course which explained the identification of military equipment – airplanes, tanks, artillery, ships and the like. Senior photo interpreters, organized in sections, worked on more specific subjects such as strike photography, bomb damage assessments, rail and road transportation, ports and shipping, military installations, inland waterway transportation, aircraft plants and airfields, radar and electronics, underground installations, V-1 and V-2 installations, enemy defenses, armor and artillery and petroleum refineries. No photo interpreters were assigned to do detailed interpretation on concentration or extermination camps. As nearly as I can determine, no tasking was ever imposed to conduct aerial reconnaissance of such camps. Photography that was acquired of these camps was a by-product of the reconnaissance of nearby strategic installations.

Since photo interpreters were not directed to locate or interpret such camps, they did not try to determine which camps were unique or different, that is, those which contained gas chambers and crematoriums.

Photo interpreters were provided with hundreds of so-called photographic keys to aid them in identification of newly photographed targets. These keys were manuals, each containing photographs of a previously identified target. Annotations and text provided guidance on the unique characteristics (called 'indicators' or 'signatures') of targets which could be used to identify a newly photographed target. No such keys were prepared about any of the various types of installations involved in what is now known as the Holocaust. For that matter, no photo interpreters experienced in identifying such installations were available to compile such keys.

No detailed photo intelligence study was ever done on any of the major concentration camps; in truth, no distinctions were ever made among the various types of camps. A variety of descriptive terms were used indiscriminately, although some of the camps were much larger and more complex than others. The following terms were used to describe these camps: slave labor camps, labor camps, construction camps, forced labor camps, prisons, concentration camps and internment camps. The most frequent and descriptive term used, however, was 'hutted camp.' This term, of British derivation, was originally used to describe a series of prefabricated buildings similar in appearance to British Nissen huts or the later American quonset huts, and was carried over into the interpretation field. The term 'extermination camp' was never used in any of this reporting . . . The main effort in World War II, with respect to camps, was to locate those which contained Allied prisoners of war. In this effort, the photo interpreters were provided pertinent data and the locations of specific camps. In addition to the barracks and security features, other indicators were provided which the interpreters could use in making identification. . . .

4. Precedence – Photo interpreters depend heavily on precedence or existing knowledge about a subject or installation. I did not find a single reference in which interpreters were told to look for the gas chambers and crematoriums that were killing thousands each day. There simply was no historical or intelligence precedence for genocide on such a scale. Most World War II interpreters I have spoken to found the concept unbelievable, unimaginable and completely incongruous. For that matter, most of the general public of Allied countries were unaware of the genocide activities during the war.

It must be quickly added, however, that during World War II information from human sources and communication intelligence was not available to most interpreters. Photo interpreters, for the most part, worked in a vacuum while interpreting and reported only what they saw on the photography. *My research also confirms that the information about Auschwitz provided by two escapees, Rudolf Vrba and Alfred Wetzler, was never made available to those interpreting the I.G. Farben Plant photos.* [Italics added.] It is my professional opinion that had such information been provided to the photo interpreters, they would have quickly located the gas chambers and crematoriums.

5. Photo Interpretation Equipment – By modern standards, the photo interpretation equipment used in World War II can only be classified as primitive. Photo interpreters used stereoscopes with lenses capable of magnification four times the original imagery (about like that of a magnifying glass). In addition, tube magnifiers with a seven-time magnification capability were also used in scanning the aerial photos. Photo interpreters performed the interpretation from contact paper prints rather than film duplicates. We know today that the negatives from which some of the Auschwitz contact prints were made in World War II could have been enlarged up to 35 times.

Concomitant with the tragic failure of photo interpreters to identify the Auschwitz-Birkenau Extermination Complex was the equally tragic failure of major Allied air commands to be aware that aerial photography of the complex existed. There had been numerous appeals from many sources to bomb the complex, the railyards, the rail bridges and rail lines leading to Auschwitz. . . . In fact, such photos were readily available at the Allied

Central Interpretation Unit at Royal Air Force Station Medmenham, 50 miles outside of London and at the Mediterranean Allied Photo Reconnaissance Wing in Italy. The ultimate irony was that no search for the aerial photos was ever instituted by either organization.[40]

The essential reason for the failure to identify Auschwitz or to bomb the rail lines leading to it was thus rooted overwhelmingly in an entirely different perception of the use to which strategic air power was to be put at the height of the war than would apply today. It is therefore worth considering in more detail the nature of what Allied bombers were engaged in doing in German-occupied Europe in 1944–5, and how the strategy for bombing evolved and was viewed *at the time*. Strategic bombing of German cities by the Royal Air Force began in 1940 and had as its aim the destruction of Germany's cities and the demoralisation of its civilian population. Under the celebrated and controversial leadership from 1942 of Air Chief Marshal Sir Arthur ('Bomber') Harris Germany's cities were indeed relentlessly destroyed, such that 'Berlin 1945' is a synonym for total urban destruction. Nevertheless, it is agreed by historians that the Royal Air Force campaign had remarkably little effect on Germany's military output or upon her ability to manufacture the weaponry or infrastructure for continuing the war.

America's bombing campaign, in contrast, was, from the first, aimed at an entirely different strategy for ending the war as quickly as possible, specifically at using 'air operations . . . against [Germany's] sustaining sources' of its 'war effort'.[41] In December 1942, a Committee of Operations Analysis (COA) of the US Army Air Force, headed by Colonel Byron E. Gates, was established. It specifically and intentionally limited its brief to finding ways to bring Nazi Germany to her knees by destroying her military-industrial base. Seventeen COA sub-committees were established to draw up strategic bombing plans to destroy the most important sectors of the German war machine (for example, petroleum, aircraft production, electric power, electric equipment, motor vehicles and the like).[42] From the first, it was decided that any strategic bombing plan, to be effective, had to be stringently and relentlessly maintained. An interim report on German synthetic oil plants (which recommended the destruction of twenty-eight German synthetic oil plants at Ploesti, Rumania) prepared in January 1943 stated that:

It is clear that it is better to use a high degree of destruction in a few really essential industries or services than to cause a small degree of destruction in many industries.

It is clear that results are cumulative and that a master plan, once adopted, should be adhered to with relentless determination.

It is clear that our day operations and the night bombing of the Royal Air

Force should be correlated so that both may be applied to the same system of targets, each at the point where it is most effective.

It is already clear that with the force available during 1943, concentrated on the right targets, very grave injury can be done to the Western Axis economic system.[43]

In March 1943 the COA formulated a list of nineteen types of industrial targets, in descending order of importance, to be bombed by the Allies. Top priority was given to fighter aircraft, ball bearings, petroleum, abrasives, non-ferrous metals, rubber and tyres, and submarine construction yards.[44] This American list was then approved by the Royal Air Force, and became operational in May 1943, when it became known as the Combined Bomber Offensive (CBO) plan.[45] (The British also continued their massive night bombings of German cities.)

The CBO master plan was thus 'set in concrete' in May 1943, and, while varied according to the success achieved against each type of military target, it was not altered in any way in its underlying premise of using bombing raids solely to destroy Germany's military capability. It will be seen that absolutely no thought was given to the 'rescue' of civilians (including Jews) who suffered under Nazism, and it will be recalled from the previous chapter that no individual or group in the Western democracies proposed that the US Army Air Force or the Royal Air Force should be doing this.

An indication of the rigidity of the Allies' post-1943 strategic bombing of Germany might be gleaned from the areas in which this programme – with hindsight – clearly failed, neglecting strategic targets which, if destroyed, might well have significantly shortened the war. Two areas, in particular, stand out. The first was the German electricity grid. As astonishing as it may seem, the Allies failed to destroy that grid (which was omitted from the May 1943 list of targets). No more than one hundred power stations in Germany provided over 56 per cent of all electricity generated; a further 300 supplied another 25 per cent.[46] Both the power stations and the lines of the grid were extremely vulnerable, the location of the stations was well known and, most importantly of all, since electricity cannot be stored, the Germans would have had no way of compensating for the losses endured. Albert Speer later stated that the loss of about 60 per cent of German electricity capacity – something the Allies could have accomplished within a few months, at most – would have brought German industry to a standstill. Despite the extremely promising nature of these targets, however, the power grid was 'almost totally ignored', with only 0.12 per cent of Allied bombs being expended on the German power grid.[47]

Second, the Allies also failed to bomb any of the very limited number of plants in Axis Europe (two in Germany) which produced ethyl fluid, an 'indispensable constituent' of high-grade aviation fluid.[48] Ethyl fluid was made by combining two chemicals, one of which, ethylene dibromide, was supplied by only one plant in Germany. Only four plants – whose locations were known to the Allies – produced aviation fluid, without which no modern aircraft can be operated. A history of the strategic bombing efforts produced by the American government as early as October 1945 concluded, regretfully, that 'these plants were not bombed, although the equipment and the processes were such as to make them highly vulnerable to air attack . . . A major opportunity in the Allied air offensive against oil was unexploited.'[49]

On the other hand, and paradoxically, at the same time as the rigid structure of the Allied strategic bombing campaign resulted in significant lost opportunities, the campaign which had been decided upon and was being waged was relentlessly grinding many other key aspects of Germany's military machine to a virtual halt. Almost every significant statistic of Germany's industrial and military-related output showed a sharp and critical reduction due to Allied bombing. German production of synthetic fuel, for example, declined from 348,000 tons to a mere 26,000 tons between April and September 1944; aviation fuel production declined from 175,000 tons to only 17,000 tons in the same five-month period (which coincided with the deportation of Hungarian Jewry to Auschwitz).[50] Albert Speer noted in late January 1945 that, because of Allied bombings, in 1944 Germany had produced 35 per cent fewer tanks than planned, 31 per cent fewer aircraft, and 42 per cent fewer lorries.[51]

Apart from strategic bombing of German military-industrial complexes, the Allies were also engaged at this time – June–August 1944 – in 'carpet bombing' in support of the Normandy invasion. A total of 12,837 aircraft (including 5,400 fighters) was assigned to Eisenhower's Supreme Headquarters to support the invasion.[52] Every surviving German veteran of the invasion has stressed the utterly impressive role of Allied aircraft employed in a ground support role for the invasion.[53] One ordinary German soldier later recalled that 'Unless a man has been through these fighter-bomber attacks he cannot know what the invasion meant . . . Not until they've wiped out everything do they leave . . . Ten such attacks in succession are a real foretaste of hell.'[54] Typical of the subsequent comments of Germany's military officers were the remarks of the commander of the 116th Panzer division: 'the enemy airforce paralysed every movement on the battlefield, especially those of the tanks . . . [It] also decisively impeded the command of the conflict on and behind the front by destruction or crippling of command means'.[55]

The third use of Allied air power at this time entailed the controversial night-time bombing raids of Germany carried out by the British under Sir Arthur Harris. These were much more equivocal in their effect. There is general agreement that they did virtually nothing to cut German military production. Their effect, if it existed at all, came in destroying German morale: 600,000

Germans, chiefly civilians, were killed in these raids, which also destroyed 2.3 million houses in what became West Germany alone.[56] Harris persisted in these policies, oblivious – rightly or wrongly – to any criticism. The American-led CBO was, in effect, engaged in a rivalry with the British Strategic Command, pitting the effectiveness of its scientifically-based destruction of Germany's military-industrial complex against the night-time bombing raids, aimed at civilian targets, pioneered and carried out by the British. Week after week, month after month, in 1944 and 1945, it appeared absolutely clear to America's Army Air Force and other military leaders that they, with their scientific strategy, were winning the war with ruthless effectiveness, destroying Germany's ability to wage modern warfare. It is not surprising that, *ipso facto*, America's military leaders were reluctant to divert their bombers to any other purpose, however deeply-based in humanitarian ideals this might have been. To them, in the cold wartime light of mid-1944, any such diversion meant a slowdown in the quick and ruthless destruction of the German military machine, and a violation of the plans for strategic bombing, evidently successful, which had been formulated the year before.

Proposals to bomb Auschwitz were also made at the same time – June 1944 – in Britain. Unlike the suggestions made to and by the American War Refugee Board, these occasionally included a recommendation to bomb Auschwitz itself, rather than the Kosice–Preskov rail line. On 30 June 1944, Moshe Shertok, Head of the Political Department of the Jewish Agency (and subsequently Prime Minister of Israel in 1955–6) spoke officially to George Hall, MP, Under-Secretary of State at the Foreign Office, about the situation facing Hungarian Jewry. One of several proposals made by him was that 'death camps should be bombed'.[57] The British investigated this possibility, but concluded that only American bombers could undertake the daylight raids required for such a mission while the Royal Air Force bombers could attack only at night, and lacked the range for a precision night-time raid to southern Poland.[58] The British government continued to take this possibility seriously, with Air Commodore 'Tubby' Grant requesting, on Anthony Eden's instructions, 'photographic cover of the camps and installations in the Birkenau area' as a matter of urgency. Nothing was done about this request, in part owing to the normal confusion of wartime, in part because the British government believed that 'the very great technical difficulties involved' precluded British bombing of the camps.[59] No attempt was made by Jewish or non-Jewish sources to coordinate the proposals to the American and British governments (which were made in virtual independence of each other). The British proposals came much too late to help Hungarian Jewry, and were fraught with the same technical difficulties (discussed below) facing any proposal to bomb Auschwitz itself, raids which could probably be carried out only by American planes in any case.

Central to the claims of an appalling missed opportunity for bombing is the contention that the Auschwitz extermination camp itself could have been bombed, destroying the gas chambers and saving the lives of tens of thousands of Jews and others. David S. Wyman has contended that:

> Available figures indicate that some 100,000 Jews were gassed at Auschwitz in the weeks after the August 20 air raid on the camp's industrial sector. If the date is set back to July 7, the time of the first attack on Blechammer, the number increases by some 50,000. Requests for bombing Auschwitz did not arrive in Washington until July. If, instead, the earliest pleas for bombing the gas chambers had moved swiftly to the United States [sic], and if they had drawn a positive and rapid response, the movement of the [Hungarian Jews] would most likely have been broken off.[60]

Wyman made several suggestions as to how Auschwitz itself could have been bombed. First, 'by heavy bombers on one of the large Auschwitz [industrial plant] strikes to swing over to the Birkenau [extermination] side and blast the killing facilities'.[61] He concedes that heavy bombers 'flying at 20,000 to 26,000 feet' would not have accurately bombed these buildings, while 'some of the bombs probably would have struck nearby Birkenau, itself a heavily populated concentration camp'.[62] He therefore argued that either 'a small number of Mitchell medium bombers [with] greater accuracy' should have flown with the bombing missions, hitting Auschwitz from 'lower altitudes', or that either 'a few lightning (P-38) dive-bombers' or 'about twenty British Mosquitoes' should have been despatched, missions which he claims would have been technically feasible.[63]

There are several major difficulties with these assertions made by Wyman and the other historians who regard bombing Auschwitz as a classic lost opportunity. In the first place, no detailed suggestions as to how the bombings should be carried out were made by anyone until much later. With the hindsight of many decades, schemes such as these can readily be devised by armchair historians and strategists, but no one did so *at the time*, and it is therefore utterly pointless to attach blame for the failure to bomb Auschwitz or to regard it as in any sense a lost opportunity. Second, and even more importantly, Wyman and his school are not military historians, and have made no effort to take the realities of military strategy into accurate account. Their knowledge of military history, as seen by professional military historians, is superficial, out of date and decontextualised.[64]

Recent military historians have looked at Wyman's claims about the possibility of bombing Auschwitz with critical eyes, and concluded that the options put forward were highly impractical and most unlikely to have succeeded.[65] Kitchens' analysis, 'The Bombing of Auschwitz Re-examined', is the most thorough, and refutes Wyman's suggestions as unrealistic at every point: it should be required reading for every student of this topic. For instance, concerning Wyman's contention that Mosquitos could attack Auschwitz's gas chambers and crematoria, Kitchens has this to say:

> Of all tactics for camp attacks, however, it is a daring surgical strike by De Havilland D.H.98 Mosquito bombers that has attracted the most attention. In 1984 Wyman wrote that 'the most effective means of all for destroying the killing installations would have been to dispatch about twenty British Mosquitos to Auschwitz.' . . . On the surface, the Mosquito's potential indeed might seem impressive. Capable of carrying a ton of bombs at nearly three hundred mph close to the ground, the all-wood Mosquito was one of World War II's wonder planes. Highly versatile, it was built in over two dozen versions and performed well in many roles. Its most impressive – though not necessarily most important or successful – operations were a handful of split-second treetop attacks on high-priority pinpoint targets in Western Europe conducted between September 1942 and March 1945. . . . In the famous Amiens operation, nineteen D.H.98 F.B. Mk. VIs flying as low as fifteen feet breached the prison walls and released 258 resistance fighters, many of whom were later recaptured and shot; over 100 others were killed by the bombs or while escaping.
>
> The similarity of the dramatic Mosquito operations to the problem of attacking Auschwitz's gas chambers and crematoria, however, is vague at best, and in a close comparison, Auschwitz emerges as a well-nigh invulnerable target. All of the notable low-level Mosquito raids from England were conducted across the North Sea or relatively flat northwestern Europe, and none had to contend with navigating long mountainous stretches while flying at maximum range. Few, if any, of the special Mosquito raids attacked more than one building, while there were *five* discrete objectives at Auschwitz. Mosquito fighter-bombers had no defensive armament and could not dogfight with interceptors; flying unescorted they relied solely on surprise and lightning speed for success. These advantages would have been very hard to achieve and maintain while attacking multiple objectives with a force of perhaps forty aircraft, and in fact even the later special low-level Mosquito operations in Western Europe were escorted by P-51 Mustangs. Thus, flying over 620 miles in radio silence, crossing the Alps in some semblance of cohesion at low altitude, then sneaking through German air defenses with enough fuel to make a coordinated precision attack on five targets and return home beggars belief.
>
> Ironically, the astonishing standards of flying that characterized special Mosquito operations put further limitations on the possibility of such operations out of Italy. In the *Abandonment of the Jews* [p. 303 n. 63], Wyman asserts than 'At least 44 Mosquitos (and probably more), were stationed at

Allied air bases in Italy in June 1944.' His authority for this is a letter from archivist Eric Munday of the RAF Historical Branch. But in fact, as MAAF orders of battle at the USAF Historical Research Center show, all forty-four of these Mosquitos were N.F. Mk. XII and XIII night fighters (108 and 256 Squadron) and Mk. IX and XVI photo reconnaissance aircraft (60 South African Squadron) which could carry no bombs. Furthermore, no Mosquito fighter-bombers were stationed in the Mediterranean in the summer of 1944, and none could be moved there. There were good reasons for this. The USAAF had no Mossie fighter-bombers, and though after mid-1944 the RAF had six or seven squadrons available in Great Britain, it entrusted only four squadrons with the most exacting missions against Gestapo head-quarters and prisons. These units, all concentrated in 140 Wing, were Nos. 21, 464, 487, and 613 Squadrons. Their elite crews were priceless human assets, made all the more so by continuous demand and high losses.

During 1944–45, 140 Wing typically employed from six to twenty aircraft against single-building targets on its most demanding low-level strikes. About one-third of the force was usually launched as a reserve. If one assumes a strike force of just eight aircraft to destroy each target at Auschwitz, a strike force of forty aircraft, or two full squadrons, would have been required. In 1944–45, this amounted to one-half of the very best Mosquito fighter-bomber crews in Britain. Had such a force been transferred to the Mediterranean Theater for a death camp raid, numerous sorties against NOBALL (V-1 rocket) sites, barges, petroleum-oil-and-lubricant depots, roundhouses, airfields, power stations and other German military installations would have been sacrificed, and some of the special pinpoint humanitarian missions might have been delayed or given up. How many innocents in occupied countries – some of them Jews – would then have perished because Gestapo headquarters or the Dutch Central Population Registry might have gone unattacked? Such agonising questions of asset allocation lay at the heart of military science, and Allied air leaders probably had them in mind when they responded negatively to pleas for an attack on Auschwitz-Birkenau in mid-1944.[66]

Kitchens (and other recent military historians who have examined this question) shows, with proposal after proposal made by Wyman and others, that these were simply impractical and made by non-specialists with no real knowledge of Second World War military history.

There is also another matter, ethical and moral in nature, which must characterise any proposal to bomb Auschwitz: the fact that many Jewish and other prisoners held there would certainly have been killed in any bombing raid on the camp. Normally, this objection is dismissed on two grounds: they were going to die anyway, while Jews and others suffering under the Nazi yoke would have welcomed any bombing raid as evidence that the Allies had not forgotten their plight, even if it meant death for some in the short term.[67] While there may be a hindsighted element of truth in these claims – hindsighted because no one at the time either proposed bombing Auschwitz or consulted its victims and prisoners – other realities have also to be kept clearly in mind. Bombing the gas chambers and crematoria at Auschwitz was *not* like bombing a German armaments factory: its essence was fundamentally different. In bombing raids on a German factory, any damage caused, even to minor components of the plant such as its warehouse or transport facilities, impeded that factory's output. Moreover, in terms of killing or injuring the workers at a factory, the more Germans who were killed, the better, while foreign slave labourers were – tragically – regarded as fair game since they were aiding the military output of the enemy.

A bombing raid on a death camp was, however, an entirely different matter: the central aim of any raid was to halt the extermination process (and, presumably, kill as many German and other guards as possible) without harming the camp's prisoners. To accomplish this aim, however, a degree of pinpoint accuracy was required which simply did not exist at the time. Because raids were often so inaccurate, the real possibility loomed, in any raid, of a 'worst case scenario' in which the Allies killed numerous Jewish and other prisoners while failing to halt the murders in any way: for example, by Allied bombs falling on the camp's barracks rather than on the gas chambers. In 1944 there was every likelihood in the world of something such as this actually happening. In March 1944 – after a marked degree of improvement in bombing accuracy during visual attacks – only *13 per cent* of bombs dropped in an average American Air Force bombing raid fell within *500 feet* of their intended targets, and only 34 per cent *within 1,000 feet.*[68] Accuracy then increased still further, but even in August 1944 only 44.5 per cent of all bombs dropped by the US Eighth Air Force landed within 1,000 feet of intended targets.[69] (Most of even these targets, it must be realised, were in western Germany, much closer to the Western Allies, and not in remote southern Poland.)

That any bombing raid on Auschwitz might well have killed its prisoners without necessarily halting the extermination process is at the heart of accurately assessing any such proposal in the context of what was actually proposed at the time. The central assumption made by Wyman and others is that proposals to bomb Auschwitz were repeatedly made by Jewish groups and individual activists, and these were rejected by the American government on a variety of inadequate and even malevolent grounds. In fact, however, many Jewish groups *specifically opposed the bombing of Auschwitz*, when the issue was raised in mid-1944, precisely because any such raid was likely to kill the camp's imprisoned Jews. Furthermore, other proposals for 'dramatic' action against Germany, to be made as a specific response to the killing of Jews, *but unrelated to the bombing of Auschwitz*, were also to be made at this time.

On 1 July 1944 A. Leon Kubowitzki, Head of the Rescue Department of the World Jewish Congress in New York, sent the following letter to John Pehle:

May I come back to the suggestion I made to Mr. Lesser in the course of the conference I had with him on June 28.

Discussing the apparent determination of the German Government to speed up the extermination of the Jews, I wondered whether the pace of the extermination could not be considerably slowed down if the instruments of annihilation – the gas chambers, the gas vans, the death baths – were destroyed. You will remember that in August and October, 1943, respectively, revolting Jews set fire to installations in Treblinka and Sobibor. The revolt culminated in the escape of a large number of Jews from these camps.

Three governments are directly interested in stopping the massacres: the Soviet Government, whose captured soldiers are being exterminated in the Oswiecim gas chambers, according to a cable received by the Polish Information Center on June 22, a copy of which is attached; the Czechoslovak Government, whose citizens are being murdered in Birkanau; and the Polish Government, for obvious reasons.

<u>The destruction of the death installations can not be done by bombing from the air, as the first victims would be the Jews who are gathered in these camps, and such a bombing would be a welcome pretext for the Germans to assert that their Jewish victims have been massacred not by their killers, but by the Allied bombers.</u>

I submitted to Mr. Lesser that the Soviet Government be approached with the request that it should dispatch groups of paratroopers to seize the buildings, to annihilate the squads of murderers, and to free the unfortunate inmates. Also that the Polish Government be requested to instruct the Polish underground to attack these and similar camps to destroy the instruments of death.

May I add that I think it would be useful to approach also the Czechoslovak Government, so that it may use its influence with the Soviet and Polish Governments to support our request.

May I express the hope that you will consider the suggestion made in this letter as deserving to be acted upon without delay.[70]

In November 1944, Kubowitzki may have changed his mind and recommended the bombing of Auschwitz to Pehle, but by that time, the gas chambers had already been shut down. On the same date Kubowitzki wrote another letter, in which he claimed, even more pointedly, that bombing Auschwitz 'would be a welcome pretext for the Germans to assert that their Jewish victims have been massacred not by their killers, but by Allied bombings'.[71] Bombing Auschwitz

was also specifically opposed on 11 July 1944 by the Jewish Agency's representatives in London (a few days after Weizmann and Shertok had tentatively
and half-heartedly proposed bombing 'the death camps' to Eden) as 'hardly likely
to achieve the salvation of the victims to any appreciable extent'.[72] Moreover,
virtually all of the members of the Rescue Committee of the Jewish Agency in
Palestine, including David Ben-Gurion, *specifically opposed the bombing of Auschwitz*
on the same grounds – that Jews would be unnecessarily killed and that the Allies,
rather than the Germans, would be blamed for killing Jews. As early as 11 June
1944, perhaps a month before proposals for bombing Auschwitz itself had reached
the War Refugee Board in Washington, the following remarkable discussion of the
issue of an air strike on Auschwitz took place at the Executive of the Jewish
Agency in Palestine:

> Provisional and partial translation of the minutes of the meeting of the
> Executive of the Jewish Agency held June 11, 1944.
>
> Present: Ben-Gurion – Chair, Mr. Gruenbaum, Dr. Senator, Rabbi
> Fischman, Mr. Kaplan, Dr. Schmorek, Dr. Joseph, Mr. Schapira, Mr. Ben-
> Tzvi, Dr. Hantke, Dr. Granovsky, Mr. Eisenberg.
>
> Agenda:
>
> 1. Matters of rescue
> 2. Discussion of Mr. Gruenbaum with Mr. Pinkerton on matters of rescue
> 3. The department of immigrant absorption
>
> Item 2, Discussion of Mr. Gruenbaum with Mr. Pinkerton on matters of
> rescue.
>
> Mr. Gruenbaum: Sent to the members of the board a protocol of his
> discussion with the U.S. Consul General on matters of rescue. Among
> other things he (Gruenbaum) suggested that the Allies should bomb the
> communication lines between Hungary and Poland. If they destroy the
> railway line, it would be impossible to carry out, for a definite period of
> time, their vicious plans. Mr. Pinkerton promised to transmit the suggestion
> to the War Refugee Board.
>
> Mr. Gruenbaum also suggested that airplanes of the Allies should bomb
> the death camps in Poland, such as Auschwitz, Treblinka etc. Mr Pinkerton
> argues that if this were done the Allies would be blamed for the murder of
> Jews, so he asked for the suggestion to be put in writing. Mr. Gruenbaum
> promised to consult with his colleagues on the matter.
>
> According to the news available, every day thousands of Jews are being
> murdered in the death camps. Only the 'Ordung-Dienst' remain alive for a
> short period of time. They do not wait long before they kill the victims.

Even if we assume that they will bomb the camps while there are Jews in them, and some of them will get killed, the others could disperse and save themselves. By destroying the buildings they will not be able to murder, by means of the techniques they use, for months. We have received news today that, in the course of ten days, 120,000 Jews were expelled from Hungary.

Ben-Gurion: We don't know what really is the situation in Poland, and it seems that we could not offer (propose) anything with regard to this matter.

Rabbi Fischman: Concurs with Ben-Gurion's opinion.

Dr. Schmorek: Here we hear that in Auschwitz there is a large labor camp. We cannot take upon ourselves the responsibility of a bombing which would cause the death of a single Jew.

Dr. Joseph. He too opposes the suggestion to ask the Americans to bomb the camps, and so to murder Jews. Mr. Gruenbaum does not speak as a private individual, but as the representative of an institution. He (Joseph) thinks that the institution to which we are linked should not suggest such a thing.

Dr. Senator: Concurs with the view of Dr. Joseph. It is regrettable that Mr. Gruenbaum spoke of it with the American Consul.

Ben-Gurion: The view of the board is that we should not ask the Allies to bomb places where there are Jews.[73]

Nor was the bombing of Auschwitz the only dramatic proposal for direct action made by Jewish groups at this time. Other proposals, entirely unrelated to the bombing of Auschwitz (and apparently offered as 'rival' proposals for drastic action) were also voiced, with high-level lobbying undertaken on their behalf. On 16 September 1944 Peter Bergson, head of the Hebrew Committee of National Liberation, wrote to the Joint Chiefs of Staff to 'request that a specific warning be issued' to the Nazis, 'stating that unless the practice of using poison gas against the Hebrew people ceases forthwith, retaliation in kind will be immediately ordered against Germany'.[74] The Joint Chiefs took that plainly absurd proposal with great seriousness, sending Bergson a lengthy letter of rejection three days later.[75] Bergson's letter to the Joint Chiefs said nothing whatever about bombing Auschwitz.

Because of the inaccuracy of bombing raids in 1944, if a raid had somehow been launched against Auschwitz in 1944 it is probable – even likely – that such a mission would have been seen, then and now, as a complete fiasco, an ill-considered and dubious exercise, carried out for political rather than for military reasons, in which many hundreds of Jewish and other captives were killed but which utterly failed to halt the Nazi death machine. If (as is likely) this proved to be the case, one can readily imagine what the attitude of today's historians of 'rescue' would have been: the Allies would now be *blamed* for 'killing Jews' in a foolish and unnecessary way. Indeed, it seems to me to be a near-certain bet that many of today's historians who are loudest in their criticism of the Allies for failing to bomb Auschwitz, seeing it as evidence (if for them any were needed) of Western anti-semitism and complicity in genocide, would then be equally vocal – or, probably, even more vocal – in criticising the Allies for having bombed Auschwitz and 'killed Jews' without reason, seeing it as evidence (if for them any were needed) of Western anti-semitism, complicity in genocide and assisting the Nazis to kill the Jews.

5

THE MYTH OF THE WAR
REFUGEE BOARD

The United States War Refugee Board, which existed from January 1944 until 14 September 1945, was the only body ever established by any Allied government with the specific aim of rescuing Jews from the Nazis. Founded by an Executive Order issued by President Franklin D. Roosevelt on 22 January 1944, it was given a very wide brief, including, without limitation,

> the development of plans and programs for the inauguration of effective measures for (a) the rescue, transportation, maintenance and relief of the victims of enemy oppression, and (b) the establishment of havens of temporary refuge for such victims.[1]

By Roosevelt's Executive Order, it was deemed to 'be the duty of the State, Treasury, and War Departments, within their respective spheres, to execute at the request of the Board, the plans and programs which the Board developed.[2] Moreover, the State Department was empowered to 'appoint special attachés with diplomatic status, on the recommendation of the Board . . . where it is likely that assistance can be rendered to war refugees', and the Board was authorised 'to accept the services or contributions' of any private person or organisation.[3]

All these specific privileges were highly unusual – indeed, perhaps unique – and were the result of pressures, from Jewish groups and from influential government sources such as Secretary of the Treasury Henry Morgenthau, which many historians have seen as belated. The first Executive Director of the Board was John W. Pehle (b. 1909), a committed New Dealer and liberal who had served directly under Morgenthau in the Treasury as Director of the Foreign Funds Control. Pehle, a non-Jew, was only 33 years old at the time of his appointment. There can be absolutely no doubt as to his remarkable energy, intelligence and grasp of the urgency of the situation, and the assessment of the War Refugee Board presented here is in no sense a criticism of him or his staff, whose dedication cannot reasonably be faulted.[4]

Pehle served until January 1945, and formulated the Board's basic policies and programmes. (From November 1944 he held his appointment on a half-time basis.) He was replaced on 27 January 1945 by Brigadier-General William O'Dwyer (1890–1964), colourful Irish-born former District Attorney of Brooklyn (King's County) New York, whose unexpected military rank came after he entered the United States Army in 1942 and was appointed head of the economic section of the Allied Government in Italy. O'Dwyer spent only three days a week as Executive Director, commuting from his normal base in Brooklyn.[5] He was an excellent relief administrator and, from his home in New York, was close to many influential Jewish leaders. His primary handicap lay in his overriding political ambitions, and he was, in fact, elected Mayor of New York City in November 1945.

The War Refugee Board operated with a small staff in Washington, never exceeding thirty in number, and consisting of 'highly-trained professional people including several refugee specialists'.[6] Allocated a fund of $1 million from the President's Emergency Fund the Board, remarkably, had spent only $465,000 by 31 December 1944. It was granted another $150,000 to cover the period from January–June 1945, but spent only $82,000.[7] It maintained close contact with Jewish and other private agencies concerned with rescue, and received nearly $20 million for relief purposes (including the bribery of Nazi officials) from Jewish organisations, including $15 million from the American Jewish Joint Distribution Committee, $1 million from the Va'ad Hahatzala [Strictly Orthodox] Distribution Committee and $300,000 from the World Jewish Congress.[8]

The Board's central claim to close analysis and scrutiny flows from the very remarkable assertions made on its behalf by subsequent historians, especially by Professor David Wyman. According to him, 'The War Refugee Board . . . managed to help save approximately 200,000 Jews and at least 20,000 non-Jews'.[9] Wyman's *The Abandonment of the Jews* later offers a tentative breakdown of the figure of 200,000 Jews which the Board saved. The two largest categories of Jews saved wholly or primarily by the Board were the 120,000 Jews of Budapest – credited by Professor Wyman with having been spared owing to War Refugee Board 'diplomatic pressures' and by the intervention of Board-approved representative Raoul Wallenberg – and the 48,000 Jews in Transnistria, Rumania, 'moved to safe areas of Rumania' through Board exertion.[10] Additionally, 15,000 Jews 'were evacuated from Axis territory' by the Board (as were 20,000 non-Jews), while 10,000 'and probably thousands more' were 'protected within Axis Europe by [Board]-financed underground activities and by the Board's steps to safeguard holders of Latin American passports'.[11]

Professor Wyman's estimate of the number of Jews rescued by the Board has found its way into standard reference works dealing with America's role during the Holocaust. In the article on 'America's Response to the Holocaust' in *The*

Reader's Companion to American History, a work found on most university library reference shelves, the statement that 'Estimates indicate that the War Refugee Board may have saved as many as 200,000 Jews', probably based on the figure found in Wyman's book, is made without further qualification.[12] If valid, the estimate of 200,000 Jews saved certainly marks the War Refugee Board out as having saved the lives of more Jews in Nazi-occupied Europe than any single body at work during the war. The validity of the Board's claims to having saved the lives of 200,000 European Jews hinges crucially upon what are by far the two most important components of its alleged achievements: saving the lives of about 50,000 Transnistrian Jews and of 120,000 Jews in Budapest. Unfortunately, both assertions in my view are wholly fallacious.

The fate of the Transnistrian Jews comprises part of the saga of Rumanian Jewry during the Second World War. The situation of the Rumanian Jewish community during the war is, arguably, the most anomalous and in some ways mysterious single episode of the Holocaust. Although Rumania was ruled throughout the war by a brutal, anti-semitic fascist, an ally of the Nazis for the first four years of hostilities, no deportations to extermination camps occurred from Rumania, and the Jews of Old Rumania – the central core of the Rumanian nation – survived the war virtually intact, with perhaps as many as 400,000 alive in 1945.[13] On the other hand, in the initial phases of the conflict tens of thousands of Rumanian Jews died in Rumanian-led pogroms and massacres, or from starvation and disease in the concentration camps of Transnistria, while tens of thousands more found themselves in the territories of Transylvania ceded to Hungary in 1940, and were deported to Auschwitz as part of the Nazi extermination of Hungarian Jewry in 1944.[14]

Briefly to summarise a very complex situation, the relatively liberal King Carol II of Rumania headed a royal dictatorship between February 1938 and September 1940. Trying to steer a midcourse between Nazi Germany and Soviet Russia, he executed the leaders of the pro-fascist Iron Guard in November 1938, then joined in the Second World War as an ally of Nazi Germany in May 1940, and finally found himself ceding Bessarabia and Bukovina to the Soviet Union in June 1940, a result of the Nazi–Soviet Pact, as well as being compelled to give up most of Transylvania to Hungary a month later. By then desperately unpopular, Carol was compelled to abdicate in favour of his son in September 1940, appointing as Prime Minister the leader of the Rumanian fascists, the Iron Guard, Ion Antonescu (whom he had imprisoned two months before).[15] Antonescu became dictator of Rumania (officially termed 'Leader of the Country'), ruling it until Soviet troops entered Rumania four years later.

Antonescu and the Iron Guard were furious anti-semites, and initiated a series of Nazi-style measures depriving Rumania's Jews of their rights and property. Rumania also became a valuable ally of Nazi Germany in a fuller sense, with two

German divisions occupying Rumania's oil fields and thousands of Rumanian troops fighting alongside Germans in the invasion of Russia. In mid-1941 tens of thousands of Jews perished at the hands of a joint Rumanian-German offensive to reconquer Bukovina, lost to the Soviet Union a year earlier. Additionally, in late June 1941 a notorious pogrom was carried out by Iron Guardists at Jassy, Rumania, in which 10–12,000 Jews were slaughtered, while over 10,000 other Jews in northern Rumania were murdered by Rumanians in July 1941.[16] The survivors – now officially in Rumanian hands – were then rounded up and deported to ghettos in Transnistria, a region of the southern Ukraine adjacent to Rumania which was ceded to Rumania following the invasion of the Soviet Union.

Transnistria (meaning 'across the Dniester') was proclaimed a Rumanian province on 17 October 1941.[17] Transnistrian Rumania consisted of what had been, the previous year, the Moldavian Soviet Socialist Republic, plus adjacent parts of the Ukraine, including the seaport of Odessa.[18] In the latter part of 1941 Antonescu deported virtually all the surviving Jews from the northern Rumanian provinces of Bessarabia and Bukovina to Transnistria. Their number has been estimated at 185,000.[19] In Transnistria they joined about 25,000 Jews who remained alive and resident (out of 330,000 present in this region in 1939) after the *Einsatzgruppen* massacres and the flight of many others ahead of the Nazi advance. Another 25,000 Rumanian Jews were deported to Transnistria in October 1942.[20]

Although the Jews deported to Transnistria were not exterminated as such, many thousands died of disease, especially typhoid and dysentery, malnutrition, starvation, overwork and brutal treatment by the Rumanian regime.[21] Only about 77,000 Transnistrian Jews remained alive in March 1943.[22] By late 1943, how-ever, Antonescu sensed that the Allies rather than the Axis were likely to win the war (with the Soviet Union likely to become hegemonic in the Balkans), and he began to go to great lengths to forestall German plans to deport and exterminate the Jews of Transnistria (and 'Old Rumania', as the core area of Rumania is known). The remaining Jews of both Transnistria and Old Rumania did in fact survive the war. By May 1945 Rumanian Jewry had become the largest surviving Jewish community in any country occupied by Nazi Germany. Most authorities believe that between 380,000 and 400,000 Jews were alive in Rumania at the end of the war.

The claims made by the War Refugee Board on its own behalf about rescuing Transnistrian Jewry concern its role during the closing stages of the war, when the German armies were retreating before the forces of the Soviet Union. These alleged achievements were among the earliest which the Board believed it had accomplished. At the end of March 1944, less than two months after the Board's establishment, the London *Jewish Chronicle* reported the following:

RESCUING EUROPE'S JEWS/40,000 ESCAPE FROM TRANSNISTRIA.

More than 40,000 civilian victims of the Nazis, the majority of them Jews, reached Rumania from Transnistria, before the retreat of the German Army from Transnistrian cities, it was announced by the War Refugee Board in Washington on Tuesday in last week.[23]

Following the war's end, the Board again claimed the rescue of the Jews of Transnistria from massacre at the hands of the Germans as one of its major achievements. In the typescript 'Final Summary Report of the Executive Director, War Refugee Board', dated 15 September 1945, the Board stated the following:

Approximately 150,000 Jews had been deported in October 1941 from Bessarabia and Bocovina [Bukovina] to Transnistria, a German-controlled area between the Dniester and Bug Rivers. They were housed in deplorable camps in a territory virtually destroyed in the course of the German-Russian fighting. Epidemics broke out and thousands died. At the time of the Board's creation, reports were received that some 50,000 Jews still alive in Transnistria were in the direct line of the retreating German armies. Despite the fact that the United States and Germany were at war, the Board's representative in Ankara, with the approval of [American] Ambassador Steinhardt, undertook direct negotiations with Alexander Cretzianu, the Rumanian Minister to Turkey, to induce the Rumanian Government to transfer these people from Transnistria to Rumania and later facilitate their emigration from Rumania. Rumania finally agreed, and late in March 1944, 48,000 Jews were moved from Transnistria to Rumania. Many of them, mostly children, were transferred with other refugees from Rumania to Palestine.[24]

The Board's assertions on behalf of itself may thus be divided into three basic components. It claimed to have saved the Transnistrian Jews from massacre by 'the retreating German armies', that those Jews were transferred from Transnistria to Old Rumania and that this transfer occurred because of War Refugee Board intervention with the Rumanian government to bring it about. Unfortunately, none of these claims appears to be valid.

It is perfectly true that the Jews of Transnistria were in mortal danger in early 1944 from the 'retreating German armies' – as they had been at every moment after the German occupation of Rumania in 1940, and certainly since the beginnings of genocide in mid-1941, but – just as they had avoided deportation to extermination camps in 1942–3 – they now escaped massacre at the hands of the 'German armies'. They managed the latter because of vigorous action by the Rumanian government *before the War Refugee Board was established* in early 1944. As Schechtman explains it:

In the fall of 1943, the relentless advance of the Soviet troops forced the German-Rumanian armies to abandon considerable areas of occupied Soviet Ukraine. The situation of the Jews became exceedingly dangerous since it became known that the German command intended to murder all the Jews in localities from which they had to withdraw. Antonescu was apparently scared by this prospect. Anticipating the defeat of the Axis, he was anxious not to be made responsible for the final extermination of the Transnistrian deportees. The minutes of the meeting of the Rumanian cabinet which took place on *November 17, 1943* give evidence of his eagerness to prevent this German move. During the course of this meeting Antonescu indicated several times that he was opposed to the German plan to exterminate all the remaining Jews in Transnistria and he ordered General [P.Z.] Vasiliu to present this view to the Germans in no uncertain terms.[25]

The sequence of events here – and throughout the Rumanian phase of the Holocaust – raises a much more fundamental question, namely, how did several hundred thousand Rumanian Jews escape extermination? This fundamental question has never been satisfactorily answered. Most attempts at explanation centre around the surprising (in view of his fierce anti-semitism) refusal of Antonescu to agree to the deportation of Rumania's Jews to extermination camps, fully planned by the SS to begin in the period August–November 1942. Most discussion has focused on the motives behind Antonescu's extraordinary defiance of the Nazi regime.[26] While this question is significant, highlighting it has concealed a much more important and much less explicable puzzle: namely, why the Nazis allowed Antonescu to get away with saving the Jews. Why did the Nazis – with thousands of troops in Rumania – not deal with Antonescu in the same manner as they did with Horthy in Hungary in 1944? Why did they not establish a ferociously genocidal regime in Bucharest as they were to do in Budapest? It is this vital question which has not properly been addressed or answered. Without detailed new knowledge of Nazi intentions, no complete answer is yet available, but one might point to a number of possible suggestions.

In 1942, when SS plans to deport and exterminate Rumanian Jewry were drawn up, Germany expected to win the war, and would therefore view Rumania's refusal to acquiesce in these plans as only temporary, something which could be corrected a year or two later when Germany had defeated its foes and was undisputed master of Europe. In contrast, the deportation and extermination of Hungarian Jewry came as an act of desperation nearly two years later, when it was apparent to everyone that the war was going badly for Germany: their fate represented a last attempt to 'root out the biological bases of Jewry' in the largest remaining European Jewish community, while this was still possible. By 1944, too, Rumania had ceased to be under effective German military control, and a parallel action to Hungary was no longer possible. Second, the political positions of Horthy and Antonescu differed in several salient respects. Admiral Horthy was the Regent of the Kingdom of Hungary (a temporary substitute for a restored Hapsburg monarch who, in Kafkaesque fashion, had been prevented from resuming his throne by the self-same Admiral Horthy). He was, in other words, Hungary's head of state, not its head of government. In contrast, the Rumanian head of state was King Michael, while Antonescu was, officially, its head of government.

If the Nazis wished to install a puppet ruler in Rumania in a manner parallel to the Arrow Cross in Hungary, while preserving the appropriate Rumanian legal niceties, they would have had to pressure the Rumanian king to dismiss the country's strongman Antonescu, replacing him with an even more fanatical pro-Nazi without disrupting the country's war efforts, oil production or loyalties to the Axis. But no super-fanatical replacement for Antonescu (along the lines of Szalasi in Hungary) existed; the pre-war royal dictatorship and Antonescu himself had crushed all opposition from the extreme right as well as from the liberal left. In January 1941, in fact, Antonescu had crushed a rebellion by independent Iron Guard elements, angered by his policy of disarming the Guard and strengthening the regular army. At the time, Antonescu's actions actually enjoyed the support of Hitler, who was anxious to see a stable, pro-German regime in power in Rumania as his plans for the invasion of the Soviet Union approached fruition.[27]

The third point which may be relevant here is a more technical one: extermination camps existed only in Poland, not in Germany's semi-independent allies and satellites, and the Jews of Rumania would presumably have been deported, in sealed trains, to Auschwitz had the SS had its way. But any deportations from Rumania required extremely long and roundabout rail journeys *across Hungarian territory* into southern Poland. The Germans remained strangely punctilious in officially securing governmental permission for the deportation trains in their semi-independent satellites, and it was at least problematical that, *in 1942*, the Horthy government would have given its permission, especially once the fate of the Jews became known. A corollary of this is also appropriate to considering why the Jews of Transnistria survived: it was the SS, not the German army, which murdered Jews, and in 1943–4 this occurred chiefly by deportation to an extermination camp rather than through mass executions on the spot. The SS might well have lacked the infrastructure, *especially the rail lines* and other forms of transport, to send large numbers of Jews from Transnistria (north of the Black Sea) to southern Poland. Finally, if the Nazis had truly intended, in late 1943 or 1944, either to kill, or to deport and kill, the Jews of Transnistria, obviously Antonescu could not have prevented them, any more than Horthy was able to do in Hungary, or any other local leader in any Nazi puppet state, and no amount of negotiations with representatives of the War Refugee Board would have given him that power, whatever his intentions or fears. Furthermore, if the Nazis had actually put in place a scheme to kill the Jews of Rumania, it is unlikely that residence in Old Rumania or Transnistria would have made the slightest difference to their fate; indeed, since Transnistria was so isolated (especially from rail links to Auschwitz), the Jews who had been expelled there would, if anything, have been marginally safer than those in Old Rumania.

For whatever reason, however, by late 1943 or 1944 the Jews of Transnistria (and, of course, of Old Rumania) were evidently safe from mass deportation to Auschwitz, whether the War Refugee Board existed or not. In fact, however, the claims made by the War Refugee Board concerning Transnistria were almost wholly inaccurate. In the first place, the Board's statement that '48,000 Jews' had been moved from Transnistria to Old Rumania 'in March 1944' appears to be flatly wrong. As Schectman put it in an article first published in 1953:

> Two months later [in March 1944] the War Refugee Board . . . surprisingly announced that 'more than 40,000 Jews interned by the Rumanians in Transnistria have been removed to comparative safety out of the way of retreating Nazi armies because of the pressure exerted by the War Refugee Board' . . . [but] the number of 40,000 'repatriated' Jews was obviously an overstatement. Several months later, when the Antonescu regime collapsed, the total number of Transnistria Jewish repatriates in Rumania were reliably estimated at between 15,000 and 17,000 . . .
>
> A considerable number of Rumanian Jews remained in Transnistria when this area was reconquered by Soviet troops. After the establishment of a pro-Allied government . . . they were given the right to return to Rumania. By the end of December 1944, 564 Jewish families, totalling 2,000 persons, decided to do so. Simultaneously, a Jewish delegation, headed by Dr. Filderman, visited General Sergei Vinogradov, chief of the Russian Armistice Commission in Rumania, and submitted to him a memorandum requesting that 9,000 Rumanian Jews who at that time were still in Transnistria be repatriated by the Soviet authorities to their home towns in Rumania. It is obvious that the 9,000 in question were deportees from south Bukovina or old Rumania; Jews deported to Transnistria from north Bukovina and Bessarabia [i.e. areas annexed to the Soviet Union prior to June 1941] were considered as Soviet citizens. . . .
>
> About 15,000 Bukovina Jews were repatriated in the spring and 5,000 in the *fall of 1945*; some 15,000 followed in the *spring of 1946*. An estimated total of 40,000 survivors of the Transnistria reservation found their way back to Rumania.[28]

The '15,000' or '17,000' Jews who actually returned from Transnistria to Old Rumania, moreover, did so *after* that region had ceased to be subject to Nazi rule. The Russian Army had reached the Dneister (i.e., the *western* boundary of Transnistria) on *22 March 1944*, that is, just *before* Pehle's dramatic announcement.[29] (The Rumanian leadership, well aware of the likely outcome of the war, had been seriously considering disengagement from the conflict as early as January 1943.)

Finally, it is doubtful that representatives of the War Refugee Board played more than a marginal part in any decision by Antonescu to allow the Transnistrian Jews to be repatriated, even after taking into account the facts that they were in no danger of being deported to Auschwitz in any case, and that only minimal numbers returned from Transnistria to Old Rumania before the end of the war. According to Professor Radu Ioanid, the Antonescu government started 'in 1943 . . . to consider the repatriation of the Jews deported to Transnistria'.[30] After a year of 'orders and counterorders; commissions . . . [and] other commissions', Antonescu 'refused to allow the general repatriation of Jews from Transnistria' on 6 February 1944, 'but he changed his mind again in March'.[31] This scholar sets the number of Transnistrian Jews repatriated before the Red Army reached the Dneiper on 22 March 1944 at only 2,518.[32] Representations by the War Refugee Board might well have played a role in Antonescu's decision of March 1944, but it is clear that he was seriously considering it long before the Board was formed and that his primary aim was to avoid post-war punishment; in addition, most of Hitler's eastern European quislings, as fanatically anti-semitic as they were, simply drew the line at wilful genocide.

It seems abundantly clear from all of this that the War Refugee Board's assertions about its role in saving the lives of 50,000 Transnistrian Jews are untrue and unsustainable in the light of careful historical evidence. The obvious question is why it made such exaggerated claims on its own behalf, claims which were made both during the heat of the war and repeated after the war had ended, in its 'Final Summary Report'. A likely explanation is that John Pehle and the other officials of the Board actually believed that it had saved the lives of Transnistria's Jews, drawing this conclusion from inaccurate information coming to it from remote Transnistria in early 1944, and inferring its success from Antonescu's March 1944 change of policy towards repatriation. There is a good deal of evidence for this view. The Board's typescript 'Weekly Report' for 20–25 March 1944 explicitly noted, citing information received from the Rumanian Ambassador to Turkey, that the Rumanian government had decided to transfer the Transnistrian Jews to Rumania proper, and that the International Red Cross 'reported that this movement from Transnistria had already begun and that 48,000 Jewish refugees had been moved up to March 20th'.[33] The Board was thus able to boast of a striking success within seven weeks of its establishment. Nevertheless, the Board made no effort to modify its original claims in the light of later, more accurate information, which must have been available when it was compiling its 'Final

Summary Report' in mid-1945. More disturbingly, subsequent historians such as Professor Wyman, writing decades later, have accepted the Board's early claim uncritically, rather than assessing it in the light of evidence available after the war.

The second, better known, area where the War Refugee Board claimed success in saving the lives of very large numbers of Jews was in Hungary. The Board has been seen as instrumental in securing the cessation of the deportation of Hungarian Jewry on 9 July 1944, and of great importance in assisting Raoul Wallenberg, the celebrated Swedish diplomat, to save the lives of Budapest's Jews in the closing phases of the Holocaust, as well as in exerting 'pressure' which 'helped end the Hungarian deportations'.[34] The Board itself was more modest in its claims on its own behalf than have been later historians. The Board, in its 'Final Summary Report', stated that 'in all, approximately 20,000 Jews received the safety of Swedish protection in Hungary'.[35] Additionally, it took credit for assisting '7,000 Jews' to escape from Hungary to liberated Yugoslavia and Italy, and helping unspecified 'thousands of Jews' to return from 'hiding places or from German labor camps'.[36] Nothing daunted by these fairly modest figures, Professor Wyman has asserted that 'W.R.B. diplomatic pressures . . . helped end the Hungarian deportations. Ultimately, 120,000 Jews survived in Budapest.'[37] These 120,000 Jews must perforce have been the single largest component of the 'approximately 200,000 Jews' which he credits the Board with having 'played a crucial role in saving'.[38]

Very similar claims have been made, too, on behalf of Raoul Wallenberg in other, often unexpected sources. *The Guinness Book of Records* is the world's standard reference work for superlative achievements of all kinds. For the past fifteen years or so, each annual edition of this book has carried the following entry, surely one of the more surprising notices to find in the same volume as discussions of the world's heaviest-ever man, the longest snake and the best cricketing innings: '*Saving of Life.* The greatest number of people saved from extinction [sic] by one man is estimated to be nearly 100,000 Jews in Budapest, Hungary from July 1944 to January 1945 by the Swedish diplomat Raoul Wallenberg.'[39] Raoul Wallenberg's career was, self-evidently, altogether praiseworthy. He was an authentic – and very typical – secular saint of the twentieth century who met with a terrible and totally undeserved fate, and no person of goodwill would wish to belittle his record of saving Jewish lives in Budapest in 1944–5. Nevertheless, his achievements should also not be exaggerated, especially when the limitations on his ability to influence the situation in Budapest in an essential way are realised. In particular, his actual accomplishments should not be inflated to score points on behalf of an American government body with which he was only indirectly connected.

No fewer than 110–120,000 Budapest Jews survived the war, and Budapest Jewry was certainly, in May 1945, one of the largest urban Jewish communities remaining in any place actually occupied by Nazi Germany. While Budapest Jewry largely survived the war, and were never deported to Auschwitz, the reasons for this are complex, and Wallenberg's role in their rescue (and, as well, the part played by the War Refugee Board) should be considered objectively. There is a series of separate questions which need to be addressed: what was the connection between Wallenberg and the War Refugee Board? To what extent did Wallenberg's efforts save Budapest Jewry? Conversely, were there other reasons, unrelated to any efforts made by the War Refugee Board, why so many Budapest Jews survived the war?

That the War Refugee Board greatly facilitated Wallenberg's mission to Budapest in 1944 is indisputable. The Board's representative in Sweden, Iver Olsen (who was officially attached to the American Embassy in Stockholm) was instrumental in selecting Wallenberg as a Swedish diplomat who, with War Refugee Board backing, would attempt to rescue as many Hungarian Jews as possible.[40] Wallenberg's appointment came despite the opposition of much of the Swedish Jewish community, who feared that this 33-year-old diplomat was a 'lightweight' and would have preferred Count Folke Bernadotte (who, ironically, was assassinated by Zionist extremists in Jerusalem four years later). Bernadotte's appointment was vetoed by the Hungarian government, and Wallenberg was appointed after Olsen, and the American Ambassador to Sweden, Herschel V. Johnson, met him and were impressed by his energy and courage.[41]

The War Refugee Board thus, certainly, must take a good deal of the credit for Wallenberg's appointment. Nevertheless, in its 'Final Summary Report' the Board heavily qualified its relationship with Wallenberg:

> The Swedish Government granted him diplomatic status and stationed him in Budapest for the sole purpose of rendering protection to [Hungarian Jewry]. The Board furnished Wallenberg with detailed plans of action, but made it clear that he could not act in Hungary as a representative of the Board.[42]

The Board also provided him with some funding, but most – $100,000 – came from the American Jewish Joint Distribution Committee, a long-existing relief organisation founded in New York in 1914.[43] Wallenberg's posting was also the result of pressure by the World Jewish Congress (based in New York) and the US State Department.[44] While in Budapest, Wallenberg derived his authority not from his associations with the War Refugee Board, but from his diplomatic status as First Secretary of the Swedish Embassy. The fact that the Allies were soon bound to win the war, with Nazi murderers and war criminals held fully accountable for their wartime slaughter, he used as a weapon to good measure and as best he could; yet the Nazis and their Hungarian allies were fully aware of this fact without Wallenberg's reminders.

Wallenberg was chosen for his mission on 9 June 1944 and was given Swedish Foreign Office approval on 13 June. He was, most unusually, given explicit *carte blanche* to use any means he saw fit to rescue Jews, including bribery and direct intercession with Horthy (a privilege usually reserved for the Ambassador).[45] All this took time, and Wallenberg did not actually reach Budapest until 9 July 1944, the *day the deportation of Hungarian Jews to Auschwitz ceased*. The ending of the deportation of Hungarian Jewry came on instructions from Admiral Horthy, who had become convinced, from a variety of foreign reports and representations, that Jews were deported not to work in factories (as stated by the Germans) but to meet their deaths. A relatively liberal government, bent upon making a separate peace with the Allies, was in power in Hungary between July and October 1944; during that period anti-semitic excesses decreased sharply. By the time Ferenc Szalasi, the pro-Nazi head of the Arrow Cross, had been installed as leader of Hungary in late October 1944, deportations to Auschwitz were no longer a goal of Nazi policy: Jews were now needed as slave labourers, and Himmler had determined to end the extermination camps, probably fearing retribution by the Allies.[46] Thus Wallenberg did *not* save the Jews of Budapest from deportation to Auschwitz. His efforts were aimed, first, at preventing Jews from being murdered by marauding gangs of Arrow Cross anti-semites; second, at creating 'safe houses', organised by foreign embassies and hence under foreign protection where Jews could live without fear; third, by deterring the Nazi-organised 'death marches' begun by Eichmann in November 1944; and fourth, by allegedly preventing a massacre, by Nazis and Arrow Cross men, of the Budapest ghetto shortly before its liberation by Soviet troops in January 1945.

Wallenberg acted with super-human dedication and energy in all of these endeavours, and significant numbers of Hungarian Jews owe their lives to his efforts. Yet virtually all the claims made on his behalf appear to be exaggerations of his actual role. For instance, much of Wallenberg's efforts at saving Jews revolved around the issuance of protective passports (*Schutzpässe*) by the Swedish embassy to Hungarian Jews giving their bearers a kind of temporary Swedish citizenship. They were also issued by other neutral governments. These protective passports were recognised by both the Hungarian and German governments. The German forces, who had previously treated such obviously fraudulent and contrived documents with contempt, now at least temporarily recognised their validity in order to avoid diplomatic unpleasantness with the Swedish and other neutral governments.[47] By country, the number of protective passports issued in 1944 was as follows:

Switzerland   7,800
Sweden   4,500

Vatican	2,500
Portugal	698
Spain	100
El Salvador	1,600
Total	17,198[48]

As will be seen, fewer protective passports were issued by Wallenberg than by Switzerland's Ambassador to Hungary, Charles Lutz, a professional diplomat who had also spent time in Palestine, but was unconnected with the War Refugee Board.

Furthermore, in the closing months of Nazi occupation, the Szalasi government refused to recognise these documents, and Germany, too, changed its policy so that, as Hilberg put it, these 'protective passports . . . offered very little protection'.[49] The protective passports 'were only occasionally respected by the Hungarian [Arrow Cross] gendarmes and hardly ever by the Germans', the editors of the published transcripts of Adolf Eichmann's interrogation by the Israeli authorities have stated.[50] The innumerable massacres and slayings of 'protected' Jews by Arrow Cross murderers and terrorists occurred during the last months prior to the liberation of Budapest.[51] Despite doing his utmost, Wallenberg could save only a small fraction of the 50,000 Jews sent on 'death marches' to German slave labour camps by Eichmann in November 1944.

Whatever success Wallenberg enjoyed came, at base, from the ending of the Nazi policy of mass deportation to Auschwitz, a change in policy which occurred on the day he first arrived in Budapest. Had that policy continued, there is no reason to suppose that the Jews of Budapest would have survived the war in greater numbers than the Jews of rural Hungary. With the abandonment of the policy of deportation – that is, of the Nazis' conveyor-belt murder machine – the Nazis and the Arrow Cross were forced to rely upon cruder, less thorough methods of killing even when the mass killing of Jews remained their short-term policy. Indeed – as disturbing as this thought might seem to many – given the fact that foreign 'protective passports' were *not* honoured by either the Nazis or the Arrow Cross, it is difficult to see how Wallenberg actually saved the lives of *any* significant number of Budapest Jews, let alone 100,000, although he almost certainly prevented the deaths of many of those he managed to remove from the 'death marches' and those for whom he provided food, medicine and shelter in the international houses and the Budapest ghettos.[52]

Professor Wyman's claim that it was the Board's 'diplomatic pressures' which 'helped end the Hungarian deportations' is also very dubious and in serious need of amendment.[53] On 24 March 1944, President Roosevelt directly warned the Hungarian government that the persecution of Jews in Hungary would not be tolerated.[54] This warning obviously had no effect. Shortly thereafter the Board persuaded Switzerland and the International Red Cross to contact Admiral Horthy in an attempt to stop the deportations. Their overtures were useless. In late June members of Hungary's ruling circles, including Horthy's son (a relatively philo-semitic figure who was in touch with members of Budapest's Jewish Council) were given authoritative information, provided by Auschwitz escapees, that Jews deported from Hungary were being sent to their deaths rather than – as Horthy had believed – to work in German factories.[55] On 25 June 1944 Horthy received an appeal from Pope Pius XII (the first issued by the pontiff during the war), which Yehuda Bauer has seen as 'influenced perhaps by the liberation of Rome by the Allies on June 6', while Roosevelt sent a second warning to Horthy on 26 June. On 30 June, Sweden's King Gustaf sent a telegram to Horthy requesting a halt to deportation, following his receipt of accurate information regarding the fate of Hungary's Jews from the Jewish Council in Hungary (by way of the Swedish Foreign Ministry), from the chief rabbis of Zurich and Sweden and from the Zionist Executive in Jerusalem.[56] On 2 July 1944, American Air Force planes bombed Budapest heavily, an act Horthy became convinced was in retaliation for the deportation of Hungary's Jews.[57]

Despite all these pressures, Horthy hesitated another week before finally ordering a halt to the further deportation of Jews from Hungary on 9 July. By this time, too, Eichmann and the SS were preparing to round up and deport the Jews of Budapest, a group whom Horthy and Hungary's ruling elite had always seen as 'better' and more magyarised than those of the rural areas, and whose deportation would have entailed a highly visible disruption to the life of the Hungarian capital. It seems apparent that the War Refugee Board's role in Horthy's decision was minimal, except perhaps in procuring Roosevelt's second warning. The Board obviously played no role whatever in the 2 July air attack on Budapest, or in Horthy's misperceptions of the purpose of the raid.

The remainder of the claims made by Professor Wyman on behalf of the Board also appear to be highly questionable, with most being prime examples of what has previously been termed 'pseudo-rescue': the removal of Jews *who were no longer in danger of being killed by the Nazis* to Western or neutral countries distant from the war zone. Professor Wyman has, for instance, asserted that 4–5,000 Jews 'evacuated via Turkey' were 'rescued' by the Board.[58] Omitting entirely any consideration of the Board's actual responsibility for their migration, all of these evacuated Jews came from Bulgaria and Rumania, countries from which no Jews were deported or killed, certainly not after January 1944. (Rumania formally changed sides in the war on 26 August 1944. From then on, she was officially an ally of America, Britain and the Soviet Union and at war with Nazi Germany. Bulgaria followed suit on 5 September 1944.)

Wyman also claims as an example of the Board's success at rescuing Jews the fact that its representative in Sweden, Iver Olsen, 'persuaded the Swedish government to bring in the 150 Jewish refugees in Finland. This was a precaution against possible danger in Finland.'[59] But no Jews, citizens or refugees, had ever been deported from Finland; in 1944 they obviously faced no Nazi threat and were no safer in Sweden than in Finland. Wyman's contention that '8000 and up' Jews were 'protected' by money provided by the Board's discretionary fund, used to provide 'undercover protection' and goods for survival for Jews and Resistance fighters in Axis territory, may well contain an element of truth, but the numbers assisted are unknowable. Similarly, his endorsement of the Board's own claim that it assisted 'nearly 8000 Jewish orphans who were hidden in France in Christian homes, schools, and convents' might be wholly or partly accurate, as might be the inference that the Board had saved the lives of many of these hidden Jews from murder by the Nazis.[60] On the other hand, no more than about 8,200 Jews were deported from all parts of France to Auschwitz between the time of the establishment of the Board in January 1944 and the last French deportations prior to liberation in August 1944 (some of whom survived the war): thus the Board's claim ought at least to be queried.[61] As elsewhere in the War Refugee Board's 'Final Summary Report', just how the total number of Jews allegedly rescued by the Board was arrived at is unclear. The 'Final Summary Report' was completed on 15 September 1945, only four months after V-E Day, and before the Nuremberg Tribunal (let alone subsequent historians) had pieced together the infrastructure of the Holocaust. Regrettably, Professor Wyman has accepted many of the Board's claims made on its own behalf at face value, with no effort to provide independent confirmation of their accuracy.[62]

What, then, is an accurate estimate of the number of Jews whom the War Refugee Board actually rescued from death at the hands of the Nazis? In my view, a very generous estimate, one which credits to the Board all the 'death march' Jews Wallenberg rescued in Hungary as well as those he saved from starvation, and all those, such as a reasonable component of the 8,000 French orphans whom the Board's actions were likely to have saved from deportation or murder by the Nazis and their allies, might amount to 20,000 persons. Naturally, the survival of 20,000 Jews, marked for certain death by the Nazis, is wholly meritorious, and no one ought now to denigrate this achievement. On the other hand, it represents only 10 per cent of the numbers asserted by Wyman and other historians. So small a figure is plainly not evidence of any lack of energy or zeal for rescue by the Board, but striking proof of the virtual impossibility of the task the Board had set itself. This figure of 20,000 Jews rescued by the War Refugee Board should, moreover, be regarded in my opinion as an upward limiting figure, not a minimal estimate or even a median one. It is entirely possible that a searching and critical view of the role of the Board would conclude that the War Refugee Board *actually rescued no Jews at all*, especially after the complex issues of historical causality entailed in assessing the real responsibility for achieving rescue, and the multiplicity of actors and circumstances involved, are accurately analysed, and once the claims made by the Board during and immediately after the war are subject to close scrutiny in the light of evidence available today.[63]

6

THE MYTH OF NEGOTIATIONS WITH THE NAZIS

It is often alleged that the Nazis conducted negotiations with Jewish individuals and groups with the aim of agreeing to free significant numbers of Jews in exchange for ransom.[1] Most of these alleged negotiations for ransom occurred in Hungary, during the later stages of the war, and were initiated by Heinrich Himmler, the head of the SS, or by his deputies such as Adolf Eichmann. The best known (or most infamous) instance was the so-called 'blood-for-trucks' proposal made by Eichmann to Joel Brand (1906–84) a former communist turned adventurer, a German Jew who migrated to Budapest in the 1930s, and was involved in the rescue of Jews from the Nazis. Eichmann famously proposed to Brand, on 25 April 1944, that 1 million Jews be exchanged for 10,000 trucks and other wartime supplies, to be used exclusively on the eastern front against the Soviet Union. The Jews were to be released in 'batches' as the supplies were received, and were to be allowed to emigrate to the West, but not to Palestine, where Hitler had promised the pro-Nazi, anti-semitic Grand Mufti of Jerusalem that no Jewish emigration would be permitted. Despite some efforts by Jewish groups and the West to string the Nazis along, obviously nothing came of this proposal.[2]

Shortly thereafter, complicated negotiations continued between the Nazis, especially Kurt Becher, an Assistant to Himmler, and Rudolf (Rezso) Kastner, a leading Budapest Zionist (assassinated in Israel in the 1950s following a celebrated libel trial over his role in these negotiations), between the Nazis and Saly Mayer, a Swiss Jewish businessman who played a key role in the 'blood-for-trucks' negotiations, and later, during the final six months of the war, between Himmler himself and a pro-Nazi Swiss politician, Jean-Marie Musy (acting as an intermediary for the American Union of Orthodox Rabbis). In April 1945, during the last month of the war, discussions took place between Himmler and a Swedish representative of the World Jewish Congress, Norbert Masur. The net result of all these 'negotiations' was that up to 20,000 Jews survived the war (often in concentration camps), kept alive while these 'negotiations' were proceeding and liberated by the Allies because these events took place just prior to the successful advance of the Allied armies.

Many (but certainly not all) historians of the Holocaust have dismissed these alleged attempts at ransom with derision. This is a verdict with which I agree, although it will become clear that I do so for one central, all-important reason which has not been considered before. There are, however, other fundamental reasons for believing that until the latter months of 1944, the Nazis were not serious in these 'negotiation' offers. The most striking (and seemingly irrefutable) grounds for arriving at the conclusion that they were never serious is that the Nazis continued relentlessly to kill Jews during the very period of the 'offer' to Joel Brand, beginning the deportation of Hungarian Jewry to Auschwitz and their extermination there on 15 May 1944, at the very time when Brand, in the Middle East, was attempting to secure some financial backing for the 'offer'. During these months the extermination process in Hungary proceeded methodically and without respite, as quickly as Eichmann and the SS could organise it. Jews were also brought to Auschwitz from all other parts of Nazi-occupied Europe where they still remained. On the other hand, it is possible that, from late 1944 until the end of the war, Himmler, seeking to make a separate peace with the Allies and to succeed Hitler as Germany's ruler, might have been more serious than he was earlier in 1944, but by this time the gassings had come to an end in any case (although not the mass murder of Jews by other means, such as shootings, forced marches and deliberate starvation).

If the Nazis were not serious about their 'blood-for-trucks' ransom proposal, why did they make it? There is no way to answer this question definitely at the present time, but such historians as Martin Gilbert and Randolph L. Braham believe that the proposal was essentially a deliberate attempt to deceive the leadership of Budapest Jewry, lulling it into inaction.[3] The later attempts at 'ransom' initiated by Himmler might well have been less disingenuous, with Himmler aiming at recognition by the Allies as leader, post-Hitler, of an anti-Bolshevik, independent *Reich* which was anti-Soviet but not necessarily anti-semitic and certainly not genocidal. There is considerable evidence that Himmler was, at the very least, toying with such an outcome and was deliberately trying to camouflage his previous genocidal record.[4] Professor Yehuda Bauer, the eminent Israeli expert on the Holocaust, has long argued that the negotiations with Himmler were potentially fruitful, and that the West arguably missed the opportunity to save 'maybe thousands, maybe tens of thousands, maybe hundreds of thousands' of Jewish lives by not vigorously pursuing these 'ransom' proposals.[5]

This briefly summarises the state of the historical debate at the present time. Although many historians reject the possibility of the 'ransom' negotiations as a genuinely realistic possibility, the failure of such negotiations to achieve more than minimal concrete results is certainly accepted by other historians as another major lost opportunity to save Jewish lives during the Holocaust. As noted, I personally agree with the former school of historians, those who argue that rescue by

'ransom' was never a feasible option. I do not believe, however, that the fundamental reason why the rescue of large numbers of Jews by negotiation with the
Nazis was not merely unlikely, but quite impossible, has been explicitly noted
before by any historian (although it has been hinted at several times). This unnoted
fundamental fact is indeed of such crucial importance as simply to rule out the
success of any proposal for rescue by ransom, whether suggested by Himmler or by
anyone else in the Nazi hierarchy. The central fact is this: *Hitler almost certainly knew
nothing whatever about the negotiations tentatively undertaken by Himmler and others for
the release of Jews by 'ransom' and it is inconceivable that he would have given his agreement
for any such 'deal' to proceed, certainly not for any agreement entailing the release of large
numbers of Jews. All* of the negotiations carried on by Himmler and other members
of the SS acting upon Himmler's orders were conducted *behind Hitler's back.* There
is no explicit evidence that Hitler ever learned of the 'blood-for-trucks' deal or any
other, and a good deal of indirect but telling evidence that Hitler was deliberately
kept completely in the dark by Himmler about these negotiations.

In October 1944 Jean-Marie Musy, the Swiss politician who acted on behalf
of Rabbi Isaac Sternbuch of the Union of Orthodox Rabbis, visited Himmler
and Walter Schellenberg (1900–52), a Major-General in the *Waffen SS* who
conducted many negotiations for Himmler in the latter phases of the war, when
'Schellenberg and Himmler estimated that there were 600,000 Jews under his
[Himmler's] rule, and Himmler could free them *without asking Hitler*'.[6] Why
should Himmler have made a point of noting that he need not 'ask Hitler' if Hitler
had known and approved of the plan? Would not the liberation of 600,000 Jews
– a figure higher than the total number of Jews in Germany in 1933, or
in Palestine in 1944 – have most certainly required Hitler's explicit and direct
agreement to occur?

In June 1944, Joel Brand reached Cairo and explained the 'blood-for-trucks'
proposal to members of the British Secret Service. A 1956 book by Alex
Weissberg, *Advocate For the Dead: The Story of Joel Brand,* claims to contain a virtually
verbatim account of the conversations which Brand had on his mission, drawn
from extensive interviews which Weissberg had with Brand. The latter was
reportedly asked in Cairo: 'Now, tell me one other thing, Mr. Brand. If the
German Government is really behind this offer why don't they communicate it
officially to the Allies through some neutral country?' He allegedly replied: 'I've
already told you that up to now *Himmler is probably the person behind this proposal,*
and the SS leaders are hoping to win over Hitler and Goebbels to the scheme later
on.'[7] According to Felix Kersten, the physician-masseuse who treated Himmler
and became the recipient of his confidences, Himmler was terrified of Hitler's
response were he to permit a wholesale release of Jews; the implication is
therefore very strong that Himmler had not breathed a word of his proposals to
the *Führer.*[8]

As well, there is not a single direct piece of evidence, in all of the innumerable accounts of Hitler's life, that he knew of the 'blood-for-trucks' proposal or any other significant proposal to 'ransom' Jews. Hitler's attitude towards the freeing of Jews, with the exception of the most limited numbers in the most exceptional of circumstances, was one of unremitting, unchanging, unyielding hostility and opposition from the moment the mass slaughter of Jews began in mid-1941 until literally the minute he killed himself in April 1945. Hitler's ceaseless hatred of the Jews – the central obsession of his life – and his desire to blot out once and for all the biological bases of Jewry in Europe as his lasting legacy to the Aryan race if anything only intensified from 1944 onwards, and particularly after his attempted assassination in July 1944. According to a statement made by SS Colonel Kurt Becher, another Assistant to Heinrich Himmler, at his trial after the war, when in February 1945 Hitler heard (by reading reports in Swiss newspapers) that on the sixth of that month Himmler had allowed 1,200 Jews to enter Switzerland from Theresienstadt – the fruit of one of Himmler's later attempts at negotiation and ransom – the *Führer* made such a violent scene in front of Himmler that Himmler was forced to revoke all measures of relief for the Jews. Himmler proceeded to give instructions to Hermann Pister, the commandant of Buchenwald concentration camp, not to allow any concentration camp prisoners in southern Germany to pass into enemy hands alive.[9] On 14 April 1945, a fortnight before Hitler's suicide, a somewhat similar incident occurred.

> Himmler nominated Becher to supervise the handing-over of the camps at Flossenburg, Dachau (in Bavaria), Mathausen (in Austria), and Theresienstadt (in Bohemia) [to the Allies]. Himmler withdrew this concession the next day after a row with Hitler; the Führer had heard of the surrender of Buchenwald to the Americans with all the inmates of the camp . . . Hitler's intention was clear: not to leave any enemy of the Reich alive in the hands of the Allies, and all camp inmates were, by definition, Reich enemies.[10]

There is much further evidence of the same kind from the final eighteen months of the war that Himmler was conducting these negotiations *behind Hitler's back*. In support of the contrary position, that Himmler actually informed Hitler and had received his explicit permission to proceed, there is simply no direct evidence whatever. Yet many historians have tacitly assumed that Hitler *must* have known of Himmler's 'ransom' attempts, especially his 'blood-for-trucks' proposal. Again, so far as can be determined, such a view is pure supposition, made without any direct supporting evidence; it is contradicted by everything we know about Hitler's mind.

Some historians such as Professor Bauer have made a good deal of one or two statements made by Hitler which seemed to imply that 'ransom', in some circumstances, might be politically possible in the Nazi wartime world-order. On

10 December 1942 Himmler wrote an *aide-memoire* to himself, described by Professor Bauer as 'crucially important', which stated: 'I have asked the Führer with regard to letting Jews go in return for ransom. He gave me full powers to approve cases like that, if they really bring in foreign currency in appreciable quantities from abroad.'[11] Bauer notes that there were 'a number of such cases, especially after 1942', but it must be realised that 'ransom' in exchange for foreign currency was, with the rarest of exceptions in the most unusual of circumstances, never at any time an option for Jews in Nazi-occupied Europe. There were surely plenty of Jews in Poland, Czechoslovakia, Hungary and elsewhere whose wealthy relatives in the West would have gladly paid a king's ransom for their safe release; if the wartime embargo on trading with Germany precluded American, British or Canadian Jews from redeeming their relatives (and many Western Jews would surely have found ways and means of ransoming their relatives illegally), wealthy Jews in neutral Latin American countries would still have been able and ready to enter into deals of this kind, given that they were literally matters of life or death. Needless to say, no such offer was ever made to Jews being sent to extermination camps: Jews could not buy their lives. It seems clear that Himmler's *aide-memoire* did *not* foreshadow any widespread attempt to trade captive Jews for foreign currency, and it is difficult to see how this note can accurately be termed 'crucially important'.

So far as I am aware, after mid-1941 Hitler voluntarily consented to the emigration from Nazi-occupied Europe of Jews on only one occasion. On 16 July 1944 Hitler conveyed to Horthy, via a message from von Ribbentrop (Germany's Foreign Minister) to Edmund Veesenmayer, Germany's Ambassador to Hungary, his expectation that 'now measures will be taken against the Budapest Jews, with those exceptions that the Reich government had conceded to the Hungarian government', a reference to a total of 7–8,000 Jews who had been previously granted exit visas by the Hungarians.[12] Hitler was willing to allow this fortunate group to emigrate if Horthy agreed to the deportation to Auschwitz of the remaining 120,000 Jews of Budapest. Von Ribbentrop's message added for good measure that

> the Regent should not be intimidated by any ridiculous Jewish-American threats. These are familiar to us, and they should not impress him any more than they do us, since at the end of the war, Germany and its allies, not America, will stand victorious in Europe.[13]

To my knowledge, there is no other single case in which, after June 1941, Hitler explicitly agreed to the release of Jews from Nazi-occupied Europe.

If Himmler, the second most powerful man in Nazi Germany and the very head of the Nazi death machine, wished, from 1944, to ransom Jews, what was stopping him? The answer is simple: he had sworn absolute and total obedience to Hitler – whose word was, literally, unbreakable law – and he could not be disobedient to Hitler so long as the *Führer* was alive and in power.[14] It has also been noted repeatedly by historians that Himmler was desperately afraid of Hitler, afraid (in common with most other Nazi leaders) of falling from the *Führer's* good graces, afraid for his very life if Hitler came to regard him as a traitor.[15] Only if Hitler had been assassinated, or if the *Führer's* mental or physical health deteriorated to the point of unsustainability, could Himmler act in contradiction to Hitler, and even then he would have plenty of potential opposition from other top Nazi leaders.

Given Hitler's implacable hostility to Jews and his near-certain ignorance of the 'blood-for-trucks' proposal and the other suggestions for the ransom of Jews, it seems impossible that any *large-scale* ransom proposals could have succeeded. Any *substantial* proposal for 'ransom' was, sooner or later, certain to come to Hitler's attention, and the larger in scope any ransom scheme, the more certain Hitler was to hear about it. Self-evidently, it is inconceivable that a million Jews – or a fraction of that number – could have safely reached the West while Hitler remained unaware of this fact. If Hitler reacted with venomous fury when he learned that Himmler had permitted 1,200 Jews to reach Switzerland, his response on hearing of a deal to free most of the Jews in Nazi-occupied Europe would assuredly be indescribable; it is also a certainty that Himmler would have been removed from his post, if not executed forthwith. Indeed, one might tentatively suggest that *if* Himmler were even remotely serious about the 'blood-for-trucks' suggestion, he chiefly saw in the receipt of 10,000 trucks and other war material a concrete way of appeasing and palliating Hitler when he, Himmler, was forced to break the news to the *Führer* of the deal he had just concluded. In the final analysis Himmler was simply unable to bring himself to be serious about the ransom of Jews precisely because of the shattering effect this would have had upon Hitler.

An important corollary of the fact that Hitler almost certainly remained totally ignorant of Jewish 'ransom' proposals is that only very small-scale and very limited attempts by Jews in the West (or in Nazi-occupied Europe) to 'ransom' Jews in Nazi-occupied Europe could conceivably have succeeded, precisely because anything of a larger scale would inevitably have come to Hitler's attention, and would inevitably have been vetoed, with venom and indescribable fury. One might also view other alleged examples of 'ransom', particularly the events in Slovakia, an independent, pro-Nazi, anti-semitic state headed by Jozef Tiso, an extreme right-wing Catholic priest whose regime was not dissimilar to those in Rumania and Hungary, in light of these conclusions. Between March and October 1942, 58,000 Slovakian Jews (out of 90,000 Jews in the country) were deported to Auschwitz. In October 1942, remaining Jewish leaders in Slovakia paid a bribe of $40–50,000 to Dieter Wisliceny (hanged in 1948), a major in the SS who was in charge of Slovakian Jewry, with the aim of halting further Jewish deportations. Indeed, most deportations (though not all) were then stopped until a Slovakian uprising in August 1944 led to the sending of at least 13,500 Slovakian Jews to Auschwitz and the killing of many more within the country itself.[16]

Some subsequent writers have accepted without question that the bribes halted the deportations; there is an especially strong tendency in recent Strictly Orthodox accounts of the Holocaust to take the efficacy of bribery at face value because of the prominent role played by Slovakian Orthodox Rabbi Michael Dov Ber Weissmandel in this affair.[17] Most academic historians have, however, discounted the importance of the bribes, with *The Encyclopedia of the Holocaust* noting that 'there is no evidence that it was Wisliceny's intervention that brought the deportations to an end, or that there was any such intervention on his part, but [Slovakian Jewish leaders] believed that this was the case'.[18] Yehuda Bauer believes that the bribes might have comprised a minor element among the reasons why most further deportations were halted: bribes to Wisliceny were less signifi-cant in Bauer's view, than bribes to Slovak officials.[19] As in pre-1944 Hungary and in Rumania, the semi-independence of the Tiso regime gave it an ability to halt deportations so long as the SS, acting on Hitler's instructions, did not directly intervene.

Other factors entailed in halting the deportations from Slovakia certainly included a growing awareness by the anti-semitic but not genocidal Slovakian government that the Jews were being sent not as labourers to Germany — the account which the Nazis gave to Slovakia's leaders concerning the 1942 deporta-tions — but to their deaths, and concentration by the SS on other matters, especially the deportation of Warsaw's Jews.[20] The attitude of Slovakia's church leaders was also important. Wisliceny was, at best, a middle-ranking SS official with absolutely no independent authority. Jewish bribes to him may have been of marginal but perceptible importance in preserving the lives of the remaining 30–40,000 Slovakian Jews for two years, but this could have been effective only up to the moment when higher authorities in the Nazi regime (including, most particularly, Adolf Hitler) heard of these transactions and put an immediate halt to them — as, indeed, occurred in August 1944.[21] The hiatus to the extermination of Slovakia's Jews should also, most certainly, be viewed in the context of Germany's pre-occupation with other matters. Had Germany won the war, there is no reason to suppose that the remainder of Slovakia's Jews would not have been exterminated. At the end of the war, it would seem that of the 25–30,000 Slovakian Jews who remained alive, only 4–5,000 survived in Slovakia itself, with 10,000 or so being concentration camp survivors and the others chiefly those who escaped to Hungary or elsewhere.[22] Nazi genocide in Slovakia was just as thorough as anywhere else in central Europe.

On 21 May 1945, after wandering around Germany disguised as a junior

Gestapo agent accompanied by two adjutants, Heinrich Himmler was arrested by British troops. Two days later he revealed himself to be 'der Reichsführer-SS' to startled British officers.[23] Himmler apparently had not even remotely grasped that one moral universe, that of the Nazi regime and genocide, had passed into history, and another, that of the Western democracies, had taken its place. A British intelligence officer (acting against instructions that Himmler was not to be interrogated before Field-Marshal Bernard Montgomery's Chief of Intelligence arrived) could not resist showing Himmler photographs of corpses and skeleton-like survivors taken at Buchenwald and asked Himmler for his comments. In total contradiction to the *Führerprinzip* by which he had sworn to live since he joined the Nazi party, Himmler responded to the photographs by asking the officer, 'Am I responsible for the excesses of my subordinates?'[24] These are Heinrich Himmler's only recorded remarks, after the German defeat, about the Holocaust. That evening Himmler was contemptuously treated by Britain's senior intelligence officer on the spot, Colonel Michael Murphy, and by his deputy, Sergeant-Major Austin, who ordered the mass murderer to strip in order to search for poison. A British army doctor, C.J.L. Wells, who performed another body search, noticed a vial of potassium cyanide in a gap in Himmler's teeth, but was unable to remove it before the former *Reichsführer* was able to crush it between his teeth and lost consciousness. Despite frantic attempts over the next fifteen minutes to save his life, Himmler's efforts to commit suicide were successful.

7

THE MYTH OF RESCUE

Do what? What could the Allies have done, what should the Allies have done, to rescue Jews from the Nazi Holocaust? A number of historians have made quite specific proposals and these should be carefully considered in the light of the arguments of this work. In considering any such proposal, one must at all times be aware of a crucial distinction between *what was actually proposed at the time* in the West and what has since been proposed, often many decades later, by historians who are able coolly to reflect on the events of the Holocaust, possessing knowledge well known today but unknown at the time. Proposals for rescue first made many decades later — that is, suggestions not actually made by anyone during the war itself — are *ipso facto* highly suspect if not historiographically illegitimate. An historical actor cannot reasonably be criticised by later observers for failing to do what no one thought of at the time; it is so easy to be wise after the event. Many of the proposals made by later historians fall into the category of those first proposed and advanced after the war ended. But it must be emphasised that no proposal for rescue advanced by later historians was actually practical, or represented a likely way to save the lives of any European Jews, even if it had been taken up and acted upon with gusto by the Allies.

The most complete list of suggestions of what might have been done was advanced by David S. Wyman in the conclusion of *The Abandonment of the Jews*.[1] This list has been reprinted several times and is often taken by other historians to represent a realistic programme of regrettable missed opportunities. In my opinion, however, not one of the points made by Wyman is valid: not one could have been implemented during the war, and most were only proposed, with hindsight, many years later. Professor Wyman's catalogue of lost opportunities is as follows:

(1) Most important, the War Refugee Board should have been established in 1942. And it should have received adequate government funding and much broader powers.

(2) The U.S. government, working through neutral governments or the

Vatican, could have pressed Germany to release the Jews. If nothing else, this would have demonstrated to the Nazis – and to the world – that America was committed to saving the European Jews. It is worth recalling that until late summer 1944, when the Germans blocked the Horthy offer, it was far from clear to the Allies that Germany would not let the Jews out. On the contrary, until then the State Department and the British Foreign Office feared that Hitler might confront the Allies with an exodus of Jews, a possibility that they assiduously sought to avoid.

In a related area, ransom overtures might have been much more thoroughly investigated. The use of blocked funds for this purpose would not have compromised the war effort. Nor, by early 1944, would payments of limited amounts of currency have hurt the progress of the war. In particular, the Sternbuch–Musy negotiations could have received fuller American backing.

(3) The United States could have applied constant pressure on Axis satellites to release their Jews. By spring 1943, the State Department knew that some satellites, convinced that the war was lost, were seeking favorable peace terms. Stern threats of punishment for mistreating Jews or allowing their deportation, coupled with indications that permitting them to leave for safety would earn Allied goodwill, could have opened the way to the rescue of large numbers from Rumania, Bulgaria, Hungary, and perhaps Slovakia. Before the Germans took control of Italy, in September 1943, similar pressures might have persuaded the Italian government to allow its Jews to flee, as well as those in Italian-occupied areas of Greece, Yugoslavia, and France.

(4) Success in setting off an exodus of Jews would have posed the problem of where they could go. Strong pressure needed to be applied to neutral countries near the Axis (Spain, Portugal, Turkey, Switzerland, and Sweden) to take Jews in.

(5) Locating enough outside havens, places beyond continental Europe where refugees could safely await postwar resettlement, would have presented difficulties.

[But] ample room for camps was available in North Africa. In the United States, the immigration quotas were almost untouched; in addition, a government committed to rescue would have provided several camps besides Fort Ontario. A generous response by the United States would have put strong pressure on the Latin American nations, Canada, the British dominions, and Palestine.

(6) Shipping was needed to transfer Jews from neutral countries to outside havens. Abundant evidence proves that it could have been provided without interfering with the war effort.

The preceding steps, vigorously pursued, might have saved scores or even hundreds of thousands. Early in 1943, the United States turned its back on the Rumanian proposal to release 70,000 Jews. It was a pivotal failure; seizure of that chance might have led to other overtures by Axis satellites.

At the same time, Switzerland was willing to accept thousands of children from France if it had assurance of their postwar removal. After refusing for more than a year, the State Department furnished the guarantee. But by then the main opportunity had passed. During the summer of 1943, the way opened for evacuating 500 children from the Balkans. But a boat had to be obtained within a month. The State Department responded with bureaucratic delays. Allied actions, instead of encouraging neutral countries to welcome fleeing Jews, influenced them to do the opposite. For instance, it took more than a year to move a few hundred refugees out of Spain to the long-promised camp in North Africa. With a determined American effort, these failures, and others, could have been successes.

(7) A campaign to stimulate and assist escapes would have led to a sizable outflow of Jews. Once the neutral nations had agreed to open their borders, that information could have been publicized throughout Europe by radio, airdropped leaflets, and underground communications channels. Local currencies could have been purchased in occupied countries, often with blocked foreign accounts. These funds could have financed escape systems, false documentation, and bribery of lower-level officials. Underground movements were willing to cooperate. (The WRB [War Refugee Board], in fact, carried out such operations on a small scale.)

(8) Much larger sums of money should have been transferred to Europe. After the WRB was formed, the earlier, tiny trickle of funds from the United States was increased. But the amounts were still inadequate.

(9) Much more effort should have gone into finding ways to send in food and medical supplies. The American government should have approached the problem far sooner than it did. And it should have put heavy pressure on the International Red Cross and British blockade authorities on this issue.

(10) Drawing on its great prestige and influence, the United States could have applied much more pressure than it did on neutral governments, the Vatican, and the International Red Cross to induce them to take earlier and more vigorous action. By expanding their diplomatic missions in Axis countries, they would have increased the numbers of outside observers on the scene and perhaps inhibited actions against Jews. More important, the measures taken by Raoul Wallenberg in Budapest should have been implemented by all neutral diplomatic missions and repeated in city after city throughout Axis Europe. And they should have begun long before the summer of 1944. . . .

The United States could also have pressed its two great allies to help. The Soviet Union turned away all requests for cooperation, including those from the WRB. An American government that was serious about rescue might have extracted some assistance from the Russians.

Britain, though more responsive, still compiled an abysmal record. . . . (11) Some military assistance was possible. The Air Force could have eliminated the Auschwitz killing installations. Some bombing of deportation railroads was feasible. The military could have aided in other ways without impeding the war effort. It was, in fact, legally required to do so by the executive order that established the WRB. . . .

(12) Much more publicity about the extermination of the Jews should have been disseminated through Europe. Allied radio could have beamed the information for weeks at a time, on all possible wave-lengths, as the Germans did regarding the alleged Russian massacre of Polish officers at the Katyn forest. This might have influenced three groups: the Christian populations, the Nazis, and the Jews. Western leaders and, especially, the Pope could have appealed to Christians not to cooperate in any way with the anti-Jewish programs, and to hide and to aid Jews whenever possible. . . .

Roosevelt, Churchill, and the Pope might have made clear to the Nazis their full awareness of the mass-murder program and their severe condemnation of it. If, in addition, Roosevelt and Churchill had threatened punishment for these crimes and offered asylum to the Jews, the Nazis at least would have ceased to believe that the West did not care what they were doing to the Jews. That might possibly have slowed the killing. And it might have hastened the decision of the SS, ultimately taken in late 1944, to end the extermination. Even if top Nazis had brushed the threats aside, their subordinates might have given pause.

The European Jews themselves should have been repeatedly warned of what was happening and told what the deportation trains really meant. (With good reason, the Nazis employed numerous precautions and ruses to keep this information from their victims.) Decades later, Rudolf Vrba, one of the escapees who exposed Auschwitz to the outside world, remained angry that the Jews had not been alerted. 'Would anybody get me alive to Auschwitz if I had this information?' he demanded. 'Would thousands and thousands of able-bodied Jewish men send their children, wives, mothers to Auschwitz from all over Europe, if they knew?'

Each of these suggestions deserves specific commentary, bearing in mind the points which have been repeatedly raised in this book:

Point (1): no one advocated the establishment of the War Refugee Board in 1942, or at any time before about July 1943. Professor Wyman has, in my opinion, exaggerated the number of Jews rescued by the Board by a factor of at least 90 per cent. Even if the Board had come into existence in 1942, it is extremely difficult to see what it could have accomplished, given that Nazi-occupied Europe was entirely beyond the reach of the Allies at that time.

Point (2): Adolf Hitler's aim was to exterminate European Jewry, and it is inconceivable that he would have agreed to releasing them at any time after late 1940. It was precisely upon Hitler's instructions that the Nazi policy of exiling its Jews was transformed into one of imprisoning them, prior to genocide. Professor Wyman evidently does not really believe that 'pressing Germany' to release its Jews would have had the slightest effect, and is reduced to urging that this would have 'demonstrated to the Nazis' that America was 'committed' to saving Jews. But Hitler believed that America (as well as Britain and Russia) was *controlled* by its Jews; every air raid on a German city surely demonstrated the Allies' commitment to 'international Jewry'.

The fact that until mid-1944 'it was far from clear to the Allies that Germany would not let the Jews out' is a manifest *non sequitur*. From late 1940, it was Germany's policy 'not to let the Jews out'; it is also difficult to see why Professor Wyman believes that the blocking of the Horthy offer marked a turning-point in Allied thinking.

'Ransom overtures', even if vigorously pursued, would inevitably have failed for the reason examined in Chapter 6: Hitler would, sooner or later, have heard of them and instantly stopped their continuation. And the more Jews who were likely to be ransomed, the more likely Hitler was to have learned of any negotiations.[2]

Point (3): greater pressure *might* have been brought upon the Axis satellites, but it is difficult to see what this could conceivably have achieved. No Jews were deported from Rumania or Bulgaria to extermination camps; no Jews were deported from Hungary to extermination camps until May 1944, when the Nazis convinced Horthy that they were being sent to Germany to work for the *Reich*. When, through precisely the kind of campaign that Wyman implies was never made, Horthy became convinced that Hungary's Jews were being sent to their deaths, he halted the deportations; for his efforts, the Nazis staged a *coup d'état* in large part because of his lack of cooperation over the Jewish question. If Horthy had put a stop to the deportations before, Hitler would have staged the *coup* earlier. Indeed, an earlier pro-Nazi *coup* would almost certainly have seen the deportation and extermination of Budapest's Jews, who were spared chiefly because the Soviet armies were closing in on Auschwitz. One of Hitler's few explicit statements on the Holocaust is that he was extremely keen to deport Budapest's Jews to their deaths. Since *no* Italian Jews were deported to Auschwitz before the Nazi seizure of power there in September 1943, while Mussolini appeared to be protecting them from deportation, Italy's Jews seemed to be safe

from extermination. Mussolini, by the outbreak of the war a convinced anti-
semite (if not yet genocidal) and a pro-Nazi, was certain to reject any entreaties
by the Allies: he had declared war on the United States, not the other way round.

Points (4), (5), (6), (7) and (8) require little comment, predicated as they are
on the Jews being allowed to emigrate from Nazi-occupied Europe in significant
numbers during the war, something which was *ipso facto* impossible without a
total change of heart by Adolf Hitler. It is worth reiterating that no Jews who
successfully fled from Nazi-occupied Europe to the democracies were ever
returned to Nazi-occupied Europe, Jews fleeing to Switzerland being the sole
possible exception to this generalisation. Perhaps more pressure might have been
brought to bear on Switzerland to take more refugees, but – despite its age-old
history of neutrality – that country, surrounded on all sides by Axis Europe, was
desperately afraid of a Nazi invasion, and there is no reason to suppose that, for
fleeing Jews, the borders to Switzerland were any less well guarded by the
Germans than anywhere else.

The 70,000 Jews of Transnistria survived the war, but, ironically, any sign
that Antonescu was actually in the process of allowing them to emigrate would
certainly have come to Hitler's attention and led to an immediate despatch
of Eichmann and the SS. The Jews of Spain were safe from the Nazis, whether
they remained in Spain or in a 'long-promised camp in North Africa'. This is a
particularly egregious example of illogical 'pseudo-rescue'.

There were repeated messages and warnings, on the BBC and by underground
sources, of what the Nazis had in mind for Europe's Jews. The central difficulty
with all such warnings is that Jews in Nazi-occupied Europe could do nothing to
heed them.

Point (9) in Wyman's list, concerning food and medical aid, is yet another
example of egregious illogicality. Neither food nor medical aid could have
been brought to Jews in Nazi-occupied Europe. As equivocal as the role of
the International Red Cross during the Holocaust may well have been, it had
no powers to enter any ghetto or concentration camp. Contrary to Professor
Wyman's assertion, the Jews of Europe suffered not from a 'British blockade'
but from a Nazi blockade; short of defeating the Nazi scourge, this particular
blockade was unlikely to end.

Point (10) is similar to point (3) and is fallacious for the same reason: the Nazis
would not have allowed it. There were no 'neutral diplomatic missions' in Poland,
the German-occupied territories of the Soviet Union, or indeed virtually anywhere from where Jews were deported to extermination camps; had there been
any neutral diplomats in these places, it is extremely difficult to see what they
might have done, since Hitler, the absolute master of continental Europe, saw
the extermination of European Jewry as arguably the central goal of his life. As
was discussed in Chapter 5, Raoul Wallenberg was successful – in so far as he was

successful at all – in saving Budapest's Jews from the Hungarian Arrow Cross (and, occasionally, from the Nazi death marches). He did not save any of Hungary's Jews from deportation to Auschwitz, for the deportation of Hungarian Jewry to Auschwitz had ceased just as he arrived in Hungary.

Professor Wyman's point (11), about bombing Auschwitz, has been fully discussed above. Briefly, virtually no one in the United States proposed the bombing of Auschwitz, (as opposed to one particular rail line, of little or no importance to the deportation process when it was suggested) while significant numbers of Jews were being transported there; the War Refugee Board most certainly did not. There are, as well, a host of military operational reasons why the bombing of Auschwitz was a virtually impossible task in mid–late 1944.

Wyman's final point falls into the same category as the others, a curious mixture of criticising the Allies for what they actually did and urging the egregious. The Allies repeatedly made clear their 'full awareness of the mass-murder program', and were bombing Germany by day and by night. Professor Wyman's suggestion that Jews in Nazi-occupied Europe somehow volunteered for transport to Auschwitz is the most curious point of all. Jews had absolutely no choice in the matter: the Germans may have depicted their fate as working for Germany in factories or as 'transportation to the east', but whatever their purported destination, the SS was, ultimately, there to enforce the deportation of Jews with their full terror, brutality and utterly relentless inhumanity.

It must finally be noted that few (perhaps none) of the points on this list were made by any person, Jewish or non-Jewish, or by any organisation at the time, certainly not in the form suggested by Professor Wyman, whose proposals represent his thinking when he wrote *The Abandonment of the Jews* in 1984. As such, they are similar to any counterfactual historical speculation – what if Napoleon had won the Battle of Waterloo or if Lee had been victorious at Gettysburg?: food for endless, fascinating debate, but remote from the historian's task. In this case their pointlessness is compounded by the fact that not one suggestion, even with the superior wisdom provided by forty years' hindsight, was likely to have been successful. Professor Wyman may well recognise this, for immediately after presenting his list, he is careful to note that

> None of these proposals guaranteed success . . . There was a moral imperative to attempt everything possible that would not hurt the war effort. If that had been done, even if few or no lives had been saved, the moral obligation would have been fulfilled.[3]

In my opinion, given what was either possible or actually proposed *at the time*, this moral obligation was being fulfilled every day the war continued and brought Europe closer to liberation.

Other suggestions, different in kind from those made by Professor Wyman, have also been made by others. It has been suggested by several historians that the Western Allies could have launched D-Day a year earlier, in mid-1943, when Germany was allegedly in a weaker position to resist an invasion than in June 1944, and swept on to Berlin in time to prevent the genocide of Hungarian Jewry. This possibility was put most clearly in 1980 by John Grigg in his *1943: The Victory That Never Was*.[4] According to this view, America had favoured a 1943 invasion and was forced into foot-dragging by Churchill and the British strategists; in 1943 Germany's Atlantic Wall and its designs for maintaining an impregnable 'Fortress Europe' were less well advanced, while landing craft for an invasion could have been found by diverting these from the Pacific and the Mediterranean theatres. *If* D-Day had occurred a year earlier, and *if* its success had brought about a German surrender a year earlier, the lives of perhaps 600–700,000 Jews who perished during the last year of the war would have been spared.[5]

There are, however, many reasons for questioning whether it was logistically possible for the Western Allies to have initiated a successful Second Front a year earlier, and more fundamental reasons for doubting whether this could have saved Hungarian Jewry. The weight of very recent military history has been to emphasise the enormous strength of the Nazi military regime and the equally enormous difficulties facing the Western Allies as they prepared for Operation Overlord, the Normandy invasion. Nazi submarine warfare was a real danger to Allied shipping until mid–late 1943; Nazi Germany was highly successful in its efforts to organise an economically unified Axis Europe; there were too few American troops in Britain and no 'Mulberry' harbours to facilitate a cross-Channel invasion until 1944; most of all, perhaps, American strategic bombing of Germany's military-industrial infrastructure had not yet brought the Nazi war machine to its knees: its success began only in 1944.[6]

Churchill and his British advisors, who controversially wished to delay a direct invasion of Europe until the last possible minute, were chiefly motivated by perceptions of the extraordinary fighting ability of the German military, and (with memories of the 1914–18 trenches clearly in mind) the near-certainty that Britain would bear tremendous casualties in any invasion which was premature. In 1945, when Germany was reduced to conscripting 15-year-olds and was utterly out-numbered and outclassed in every phase of warfare by the Allies, it still took the Soviet Union (with 12 million battle-hardened soldiers under arms) nearly 100 days to advance the 200 miles from central Poland to Berlin, a gain of just two miles per day; the Soviet conquest of Berlin cost the lives of 300,000 Russian soldiers. It is well known, too, that the Normandy invasion succeeded as well as it did because of wholly fortuitous factors (Erwin Rommel, the Nazi commanding general, was away in Berlin celebrating a birthday party) and through the efforts of a far-reaching attempt at deceiving the Nazis as to the main thrust of the Allied invasion whose success was certainly not guaranteed in advance.

More significant, however, is the fundamental fact that it was not the Western Allies who liberated either Hungarian Jewry or the extermination camps in Poland, but the Soviet army, and in mid-1943 – or even mid-1944 – the Soviet Union's front line was literally hundreds of miles to the east of these places. Soviet troops liberated Kiev, the capital of the Ukraine, only in December 1943 and did not reconquer even one inch of Polish territory until July 1944. Neither Auschwitz nor Budapest were liberated until January 1945. Even if a Second Front had been opened a year earlier, and even if it had proved remarkably successful at thrusting into German territory, the Nazis would have had ample time to exterminate virtually every Jew who actually perished during the war; indeed Hitler might well have speeded up the extermination process if he suspected that the end was approaching. Only an advance of the Soviet armies at a rate paralleling that of an imaginary Western thrust a year earlier than actually occurred, and vastly more rapid than in the actual course of the war as it unfolded, could have guaranteed the liberation of the surviving remnants of eastern European Jewry. Given the stubbornness of Nazi resistance, and such factors as the Russian winter, it is most unlikely, even in the most optimistic plausible scenario, that the Soviet armies could have regained eastern Europe before the SS had done its work.

Regret has also been expressed that Hitler was not assassinated. 'Had Hitler been assassinated in 1943 or 1944, hundreds of thousands of Jews – if not more – would have been saved, so pivotal was his input in the Holocaust policy', Yehuda Bauer has written, and it is impossible to disagree with this assertion other than to add that without Hitler's ordering of the Holocaust, it would not have occurred at all.[7] It is indeed puzzling that no well-planned, well-financed attempt at assassinating Hitler was ever made by either a Jewish source or by the Western Allies: while several rather amateurish efforts were made to assassinate Hitler, only the famous 'Officers' Plot' of July 1944, headed by Lieutenant-Colonel Klaus von Stauffenberg, had an even remotely professional air about it. Had Jewish or anti-Nazi sources financed six or eight separate, unconnected assassination squads, cleverly organised and properly financed, it is difficult to believe that one of these would not have succeeded. Since 1950, four American presidents have been the victims of serious assassination attempts – one, of course, a successful attempt – despite massive security protection. Hitler, obviously, was at the centre of a totalitarian, militarised society, closely guarded by an elite secret service whose members were sworn to lay down their lives for the *Führer*. Yet Hitler also appeared continuously in the open air, and relied heavily upon public appearances and speeches for his continuing authority and mass appeal. Perhaps those who would have loved to see Hitler dead assumed that his successor would be even worse, but in fact it is unlikely in the highest degree that his probable successors such as Goering, Hess or even Goebbels would have ordered the Holocaust. Presumably, too, the wartime Allies feared that Hitler's assassination, if carried out under Allied instructions, would invite retaliation against Churchill and Roosevelt. Yet of all the roads not taken, assassinating Hitler would have been the most certain way of preventing the Holocaust or of stopping it once it began: even if Goebbels or Himmler had succeeded Hitler during the war, it is likely – as Yehuda Bauer has rightly argued – that they would not have murdered Jews with the single-mindedness of Hitler, if they continued to kill Jews at all. To be sure, if a Jew had assassinated Hitler, it is certain that the Nazis would have carried out a pogrom of unprecedented violence against any and all Jews they could find, although no amount of Nazi vengeance against the Jews could have been worse than what actually occurred. The fact that no serious, carefully planned attempts were made by Jewish or Western anti-Nazi groups is evidence of how little the true menace of Hitler, or his utter centrality as the driving force in the Holocaust, was appreciated.

If the State of Israel had come into existence ten or fifteen years earlier, would this have helped in a central way? Self-evidently, a very significant number of Jews trapped in Nazi-occupied Europe would have fled there prior to Hitler's invasions of their countries; if Palestine/Israel had survived the war unscathed, presumably those Jews, too, would have survived the war. Yet, as we have seen previously, it is easy to overestimate the potential clientele for Zionism among eastern European Jewry prior to the Holocaust; *at the time, even when* Nazi Germany existed, most Jews were adherents of other ideologies – Bund Socialism, Strict Orthodoxy, Marxism – which were explicitly anti-Zionist, and showed no interest in migrating to the Hebrew-speaking *Yishuv*, economically primitive and under constant Arab threat. Some historians have also argued that had Israel existed during the war, it might have saved Europe's Jews in other ways. For instance, Lucy S. Dawidowicz, seldom a proponent of overly sanguine 'might-have-beens' of Holocaust rescue, nevertheless stated without qualification that:

> Without political power Jews had no chance for survival. Had a Jewish state existed in 1939, even one as small as Israel today, but militarily competent, the terrible story of six million dead might have had another outcome. As a member of the Allied nations, contributing its manpower and military resources to the conduct of the war, a Jewish state could have exercised some leverage with the great powers in the alliance. Even though it would not have diverted Hitler from his determination to murder the Jews, a Jewish state might have been able to wield sufficient military and political clout to have inhibited Slovakia, Rumania, and Croatia from collaborating with the Germans in that murder. A Jewish state could have persuaded neutral countries to give Jewish refugees safe passage. A Jewish state would have ensured a safe haven. A Jewish state would have made the difference.[8]

It is genuinely surprising to read – alas – such a naive and improbable state-ment in the writings of an author as astute and intelligent as Lucy S. Dawidowicz. Unfortunately, even if Israel had existed and attempted to use its 'military and political clout' to change the anti-semitic policies of 'Slovakia, Rumania, and Croatia', it was Hitler and Hitler alone who had the final say about the fate of the Jews in these places: he could – and doubtless would – have intervened to ensure the deportation of Jews from these countries, just as he did in Hungary. Indeed, had an independent Jewish state existed in Palestine during the war, the fate of the Jews might have been very different, but not in the way imagined here: Hitler might well have made its conquest and destruction a much higher priority than it was actually given. Rommel had only ten divisions in North Africa; with the destruction of Israel and the extermination of perhaps 1 million Jews there as his goal, Hitler might have agreed to give him twenty, thirty or whatever number of Axis divisions was necessary for a successful drive through Egypt (incidentally seizing the Suez Canal) to Palestine, doubtless fanning Arab anti-British and anti-Jewish nationalism every inch of the way. Given what we know about Hitler, which possibility was the more likely?

With great and genuine regret, we reach the final conclusion of this work: turn where you will, turn to any proposal for rescue you wish, one will invariably find either that it was wholly impractical (and, very likely, irrelevant) or not actually proposed by anyone at the time. I simply know of no exceptions to this con-clusion, and certainly of no plans for rescue action which were actually capable of saving any significant number of Jews who perished. While this conclusion must be deeply depressing to some readers, it also suggests very strongly that both the governments of the Western democracies and the Jewish communities of the democracies must be viewed much more favourably: no rescue action was taken because no one, anywhere, had anything genuinely practical or effective to suggest, apart from winning the war even more quickly. Those excuses which are sometimes offered for the lack of a rescue policy – ignorance of genocide, Jewish community powerlessness, anti-semitism and anti-Zionism in the democracies, and so on – were, even if true, essentially irrelevant to the basic fact that rescue was impossible. Conversely, it cannot be emphasised too strongly that the respon-sibility for the Holocaust lies solely and wholly with Adolf Hitler, the SS and their accomplices, and with no one else. In searching for a rational explanation of modern history's greatest crime, it is important that we not assign guilt to those who were innocent.

NOTES

1 THE HISTORIOGRAPHY OF RESCUE

1 Chief Rabbi Hertz, '70th Birthday Message to Churchill', *Jewish Chronicle*, 8 December 1944.

2 Henry L. Feingold, 'Jewish Leadership During the Roosevelt Years', in Henry L. Feingold, *Bearing Witness: How America and Its Jews Responded to the Holocaust* (Syracuse, 1995), p. 241.

3 Melvin I. Urofsky, *We are One! American Jewry and Israel* (Garden City, NY, 1978), p. 46.

4 Arthur Schlesinger Jr, 'Did FDR Betray the Jews? Or Did He Do More than Anyone Else to Save Them?', in Verne W. Newton (ed.), *FDR and the Holocaust* (New York, 1996), p. 159.

5 In 1963, however, Dr Emanuel Scherer, Secretary of the *Bund* World Coordinating Committee in New York, stated that

> Today, in the light of various facts and available documents (inaccessible during the war), it is perfectly clear that only forces outside the [Warsaw] ghetto, the democratic and more humanitarian countries, could have restrained the Nazis and their collaborators by means of specific military steps undertaken with the deliberate aim of saving the Jews.
>
> Such help could only have been given to Jews during the fourteen months between the first mass slaughter in Chelmno and the creation of the Warsaw ghetto [i.e., roughly from December 1941 to February 1943].
>
> During this period necessary, and in our opinion, feasible acts of effective help were possible.
>
> (*Socialist International*, 27 April 1963, cited in Wladyslaw Bartoszewski,
> 'The Martyrdom and Struggle of the Jews in Warsaw Under
> German Occupation 1939–43', in Wladyslaw T. Bartoszewski and
> Antony Polonsky (eds.), *The Jews in Warsaw: A History*
> (Oxford, 1991), p. 332)

Scherer does not state what these 'specific military steps' were, or how they could have been achieved with the Allied front lines a thousand miles to the east and west.

6 I mention the fact of Wyman's background only because he himself deliberately makes it known, and plainly regards it as important. In *The Abandonment of the Jews* Wyman states

I have written not as an insider, I am a Christian, a Protestant of Yankee and Swedish descent . . . American Christians forgot about the Good Samaritan . . . The Holocaust was certainly a Jewish tragedy. But it was not *only* a Jewish tragedy. It was also a Christian tragedy . . . The bystanders most capable of helping were Christians.

(New York, 1984, pp. ix, xii)

7　*Ibid.*, p. 335.

8　Seymour Maxwell Finger (ed.), *American Jewry During the Holocaust* (New York, 1984).

9　*Ibid.*, pp. 11–14.

10　Lucy S. Dawidowicz, 'Indicting American Jews', in Lucy S. Dawidowicz, *What Is the Use of Jewish History?*, ed. Neal Kozodoy (New York, 1992), pp. 179–201; Yehuda Bauer, 'The Goldberg Report', *Midstream*, February 1985. (Dawidowicz's essay originally appeared in *Commentary*, June 1983.)

11　Michael R. Marrus, *The Holocaust in History* (London, 1989), p. 173. By the late 1980s it had become difficult to find a work on the Holocaust, or even touching on the subject, which did not take it for granted that the Allies were at fault for failing to rescue more Jews. Two examples will illustrate this. In a collection of essays by leading historians on Nazi Germany (H. W. Koch (ed.), *Aspects of the Third Reich* (London, 1985)), an essay by W. Carr entitled 'The Hitler Image in the Last Half-Century' states (p. 486) that

Before the war Hitler seems to have gone along with the emigration policy favoured by Himmler, a rising star in the Nazi firmament. The outbreak of war put a stop to that policy but opened the door to other 'solutions'.

At this point in the text, and most unusually, the editor has placed the following in square brackets:

In practice a stop had been put to emigration prior to the outbreak of war. The USA were not prepared to relax their immigration quota in favour of a large influx of German and European Jews. Emigration to Palestine was cut by the British mandatory power, in response to an Arab wave of protest and violence against the 'undesired' immigrants.

The editor's comments here are flatly false. More Jews emigrated from Germany in the ten months after *Kristallnacht* than in any other period; their emigration continued at a record pace from Germany, Austria and Czechoslovakia until the outbreak of the war and, indeed, beyond.

Another example of how widespread is this notion may be found in Adrian Hastings' widely praised and outstanding *A History of English Christianity, 1920–1990* (London, 1991), which makes the response of English Christians to the Holocaust one of its main areas of discussion. The book refers (p. 377) to Anglican Archbishop William Temple's speech in the House of Lords on 23 March 1943 in favour of giving 'temporary asylum' to all Jews able to escape from the Nazis.

It had next to no effect. The British Government – at one moment Foreign Office staff, at another the Colonial Office, at a third the Cabinet – steadily blocked every proposal to help the Jews, whether it be to bomb the railway lines going to Auschwitz or the gas chambers themselves, to admit children to Palestine (beyond the highly limited quotas drawn up in quite other circumstances), or even the Swedish proposal to take in twenty thousand Jewish children until after the war.

Each of these claims is extremely dubious. No proposals to bomb either Auschwitz or the rail lines were made by anyone until May or June 1944, and (as shown in Chapter 4) could not have been successfully mounted until after the deportations had ceased; they were also opposed by many Jewish leaders in Palestine. The other two examples cited by Hastings show the central, fundamental confusion demonstrated by so many writers on this subject between refugees and prisoners. More Jews could not be admitted to Palestine, Sweden, etc., because they were prisoners of the Nazis: they were not 'refugees'.

12 Rafael Medoff, *The Deafening Silence: American Jewish Leaders and the Holocaust* (New York, 1987), p. 183 and dust-jacket.

13 *Ibid.*, pp. 165–7.

14 Medoff seems to suggest that American Jewry should have lobbied Roosevelt to compel Britain to admit more Jewish refugees to Palestine (*ibid.*, pp. 175–7). As will be repeatedly stressed in this work, the admission of refugee Jews to Palestine during the war is irrelevant to the question of rescue, since the dilemma facing Jews in Nazi-occupied Europe was that they could not escape from Hitler.

15 David Kranzler, *Thy Brother's Blood: The Orthodox Jewish Response During the Holocaust* (Brooklyn, 1987), p. 1.

16 See, for instance, Joseph Friedenson, *Dateline: Istanbul – Dr Jacob Griffel's Lone Odyssey Through a Sea of Indifference* (Brooklyn, 1993), and David Kranzler and Eliezer Gevirtz, *To Save a World: Profiles in Holocaust Rescue*, 2 vols (New York, 1991). In *Thy Brother's Blood* the claim is made (p. 177) that Rabbi Dr Solomon Schonfeld, a Strictly Orthodox rabbi in London 'managed to save more than 3,700 children, adolescents, and adults in Central Europe before, *during* and after the Holocaust' (my italics). I wrote to David Kranzler to ask for details of the persons Schonfeld saved 'during' the Holocaust, but did not receive a reply. It would also be interesting to learn what Rabbi Schonfeld saved these Jews from 'after' the war.

17 Yehuda Bauer, *Jews For Sale?: Nazi-Jewish Negotiations, 1933–1945* (New Haven, 1994), pp. 258–9.

18 It is important, however, to bear in mind that Professor Feingold now believes that 'after many years of working with this problem, my conclusion is that what American Jewry did and did not do is perhaps 5 percent of the problem' ('Rescue and the Secular Perception', in *Bearing Witness: How America and Its Jews Responded to the Holocaust* (Syracuse, 1995), p. 252). Professor Feingold and I are thus only 5 per cent apart in our views.

19 'Who Shall Bear Guilt for the Holocaust?', in *Bearing Witness*, p. 265. This article was originally published in *American Jewish History*, 48(3), March 1979. The article by Roger M. Williams appeared in *Commonweal* (an American Catholic magazine) on 24 November 1978, pp. 746–51.

20 Bauer, *Jews For Sale?*, pp. 252–60.

21 Henry L. Feingold, *The Politics of Rescue: The Roosevelt Administration and the Holocaust, 1938–1945* (New Brunswick, NJ, 1970), p. 307; Wyman, *Abandonment of the Jews*, p. 331.

22 Frank W. Becher, 'David Wyman and the Historiography of America's Response to the Holocaust: Counter-considerations', *Holocaust and Genocide Studies*, 5(4), 1990, pp. 423, 431.

23 *Ibid.*, p. 431.

24 See, in particular, Dawidowicz's essay 'Could America Have Rescued Europe's Jews?', in Dawidowicz, *What Is the Use of Jewish History?*

25 The classical artefact of the previous tolerant interpretation of Anglo-Jewish history was Cecil Roth's *History of the Jews in England*, first published in 1941, the year the Holocaust began, and clearly intended to mark Anglo-Jewish history off from the tragic history of European Jewry.

26 Richard Bolchover, *British Jewry and the Holocaust* (Cambridge, 1993), p. 146.

27 The closest we come in Bolchover's work to actually learning what these plans for rescue were occurs on p. 186, n. 27, where we learn that 'the twelve-point plan of the National Committee for Rescue From Nazi Terror', the chief rescue body of the 'exceptions', may be found in the Parkes Papers at the University of Southampton Library (*ibid.*).

28 Geoffrey Alderman, *Modern British Jewry* (Oxford, 1992), pp. 301–2.

29 Many of Alderman's claims about this question are erroneous or misleading. For example, he states that Churchill and Eden 'favoured the plan' of bombing Auschwitz, but were 'outmanoeuvred by Foreign Office officials' (*ibid.*, p. 302). Yet their main objection to *British* forces bombing Auschwitz was that British bombers could only attack Auschwitz at night, when any raid requiring pinpoint accuracy would be impossible, and only the Americans could bomb Auschwitz by day. The 'excuse' that 'it was understood that deportations of Hungarian Jews to Auschwitz had come to a halt' (*ibid.*) was perfectly valid. (Alderman here relies chiefly on Wasserstein's work.) Alderman's account of 'the efforts of Dr. Solomon Schonfeld' (*ibid.*, pp. 303–5), drawn exclusively from Kranzler's book, is almost wholly inaccurate. See my *A History of the Jews in the English-Speaking World: Great Britain* (London, 1996), pp. 356, 505, n. 329.

30 'Rules of the Game,' in Tony Kushner, *The Holocaust and the Liberal Imagination* (Oxford, 1994), esp. pp. 187–201.

31 *Ibid.*

32 For instance Werner E. Mosse (ed.), *Second Chance: Two Centuries of German-Speaking Jews in the United Kingdom* (Tübingen, 1991).

33 One must also mention the review of Wasserstein's book and the subsequent exchange with Wasserstein by the British historian John P. Fox, *European Studies Review*, 10, January and October 1980. Fox is also critical of the notion of 'rescue'.

34 See Michael Blakeney, *Australia and the Jewish Refugees, 1933–1948* (Sydney, 1983); Suzanne Rutland, *Edge of the Diaspora* (Sydney, 1987); Paul R. Bartrop, *Australia and the Holocaust, 1933–1945* (Melbourne, 1994); Hilary L. Rubinstein, *The Jews in Australia: A Thematic History, 1788–1945* (Melbourne, 1991); and W.D. Rubinstein, 'Australia and the Refugee Jews of Europe, 1933–1955: A Dissenting View', *Australian Jewish Historical Society Journal*, 10(6), 1985.

2 THE MYTH OF CLOSED DOORS, 1933–9

1 Michael Berenbaum, *The World Must Know* (Boston, 1993), p. 56.

2 Michael R. Marrus, *The Holocaust in History* (London, 1987), pp. 164–5.

3 Herbert A. Strauss (ed.), *Jewish Immigrants of the Nazi Period in the U.S.A., Volume 6: Essays on the History, Persecution and Emigration of German Jews* (New York, 1987), p. 144. The data in this work by Strauss originally appeared in 'Jewish Emigration

From Germany: Nazi Policies and Jewish Responses (I)', in *Year Book XXV of the Leo Baeck Institute* (London, 1980) and '(II)', in *Year Book XXVI of the Leo Baeck Institute* (London, 1981.)

4 Ninety-one Jews were killed during *Kristallnacht* (9–10 November 1938) and another 244 died in Buchenwald during the following months (Martin Gilbert, *The Dent Atlas of the Holocaust* (London, 1993), pp. 27–8). The excess of Jewish deaths over births during the period from 1933–40 was certainly very considerable. It is estimated by Strauss at perhaps 55,000 or more (Strauss, *Jewish Immigrants*, Table VII, p. 151). *Kristallnacht* is the term given to the unprecedented pogroms throughout Germany on 9–10 November 1938, after which it was clear that Jews had no place in Nazi Germany and would have to emigrate *en masse*; *Kristallnacht* means 'the night of broken glass', and refers to the destruction of Jewish property which took place. *Kristallnacht* is usually seen as a crucial turning-point on the way to genocide. See, for instance, Rita Thalmann and Emmanuel Feinermann, *Crystal Night* (New York, 1974).

5 Strauss, *Jewish Immigrants*, p. 151.

6 Reworked from *ibid.*, Table IIIa, p. 145.

7 *Ibid.*, Table V, p. 207 and Table II, p. 197.

8 *Ibid.*, Table I, p. 144, Table VII, pp. 151, 152. See Jeremy Noakes, 'The Development of Nazi Policy Towards the German-Jewish "Mischlinge", 1933–1945', and Ursula Büttner, 'The Persecution of Christian-Jewish Families in the Third Reich', both in *Leo Baeck Institute Year Book XXXIV* (London, 1989). Most bizarrely, Hitler personally 'Aryanised' 263 Jews, chiefly Jews who had joined the Nazi Party prior to 1933, without being aware of their 'racial' origins (Noakes, 'Development of Nazi Policy', p. 319). It is quite possible that 'Aryanisation' was more widespread than this, as the American researcher Bryan Rigg has recently suggested. Several of the Austrian relatives of Ludwig Wittgenstein, the famous philosopher, were declared to be 'Aryans' in exchange for the transfer of their foreign assets to the Nazis (Ray Monk, *Ludwig Wittgenstein: The Duty of Genius* (London, 1990), pp. 397–400). The half-Jewish Otto Warburg (of the famous banking family), who won the 1931 and 1944 Nobel Prizes for medicine, 'received a personal order from Hitler's Chancellery to resume his work on cancer research' in 1941, and was 'up-graded' by Goering to being only one-quarter Jewish. He lived in Germany until his death in 1970 (Ron Chernow, *The Warburgs: The Twentieth-Century Odyssey of a Remarkable Jewish Family* (New York, 1993), pp. 540–1). Some estimates of the number of German Jews who perished in the Holocaust are lower still. For instance in his 'Statistics of Jewish Dead', in the revised edition of *The Destruction of European Jewry*, 3 vols (New York, 1985), Raul Hilberg places the number of Jews who died in Germany at 'over 120,000' and in Austria at 'over 50,000' (vol. 3, p. 1220). Hilberg's statistical approach differs from that normally employed in estimating the total number of deaths in each type of Nazi action against the Jews, rather than by comparing 1939 and 1945 Jewish population estimates (as is normally done). Hilberg's overall figure, of 5.1 million Jewish deaths in the Holocaust is, of course, significantly lower than the commonly accepted figure of 5.7–6 million. It is important to realise, however, that his estimates for some phases of the Holocaust are higher than those currently accepted, e.g., his estimate (p. 1219) that '1,000,000' Jews died at Auschwitz, which is higher than the now generally accepted best estimate of 900,000.

9 From Strauss, *Jewish Immigrants*, Table VII, p. 151.

10 Berenbaum, *The World Must Know*, p. 56.

11 Geoffrey Alderman, *Modern British Jewry* (Oxford, 1992), p. 273.

12 Fay Kesacoff, 'The Kibbutz Guard', in Louise Hoffman and Shush Masel (eds), *Without Regret* (Perth, 1995), p. 179. (*Without Regret* is a volume of twenty-eight interviews with German and other central European Jewish refugees in Western Australia.)

13 Erna Sarah Lessheim, 'Top Hat and Tails', in Hoffman and Masel (eds), *Without Regret*, p. 205.

14 Robert Exiner, 'From the Spree to the Yarra: Memoirs of an Emigration', *Australian Jewish Historical Society Journal*, 12(3), November 1994, p. 546.

15 Betty Lipton, 'At Home in Berlin', in John Foster (ed.), *Community of Fate: Memoirs of German Jews in Melbourne* (Sydney, 1986), pp. 28–9.

16 Herbert Liffmann, 'The Riddle of Identity', in Foster (ed.), *Community of Fate*, p. 51.

17 Marion Berghahn, *Continental Britons: German-Jewish Refugees from Nazi Germany* (Oxford, 1988), pp. 71–2. A recent account of this subject may be found in John V. H. Dippel, *Bound Upon a Wheel of Fire: Why So Many German Jews Made the Tragic Decision to Remain in Nazi Germany* (New York, 1996). Dippel, however, focuses chiefly on six very prominent German Jews (among them Nobel Prize winner Richard Willstatter, Rabbi Leo Baeck and banker Max Warburg), who assumed that they could not be touched by any regime. Most German Jews remained because they assumed that Nazi anti-semitism would reach distinct limits, and then possibly recede.

18 See, for example, Karl A. Schleunes, *The Twisted Road to Auschwitz: Nazi Policy Towards German Jews, 1933–1939* (Urbana, Ill., 1970), pp. 62–91.

19 *Ibid.*, pp. 187–8; Yehuda Bauer, *A History of the Holocaust* (New York, 1982), p. 123.

20 For a useful summary of this topic see Konrad Kwiet, 'To Leave or Not to Leave: the German Jew at the Crossroads', in W.H. Pehle (ed.), *November 1938: From 'Reich Kristallnacht' to Genocide* (New York, 1991). The genuine reluctance of so many Germans to leave, and their perceptions that Nazi anti-semitism was profoundly anomalous, should be contrasted with the thesis presented in Daniel Jonah Goldhagen's highly dubious work *Hitler's Willing Executioners: Ordinary Germans and the Holocaust* (London, 1996), that anti-semitism was all-pervasive in German society. Germany's *Jews* simply did not perceive their own society in this way. And why should they? Weimar Germany was a golden age of German Jewish freedom; as late as 1928, the Nazi Party received only 3 per cent of votes cast in the German general election. Goldhagen's thesis also seems grossly inconsistent with the degree of secrecy with which the Holocaust was surrounded when the top Nazis addressed memoranda to *each other*, with the killings invariably referred to as 'evacuation to the east', 'special actions' or some other euphemism.

21 Lucy S. Dawidowicz, *The War Against the Jews, 1933–45* (London, 1987), p. 220.

22 Kwiet, 'To Leave or Not to Leave'.

23 Dawidowicz, *War Against the Jews*, p. 447.

24 *Ibid.*

25 *Ibid.*, p. 449. An additional 60,000 Jews lived in the Sudetenland, annexed by Germany in September 1938, and 135,000 in Slovakia, which declared its independence in April 1939 under the pro-Nazi, anti-semitic Tiso regime.

26 Louise London, 'Immigration Control Procedures', in Werner E. Mosse (ed.), *Second Chance: Two Centuries of German-Speaking Jews in the United Kingdom* (Tübingen, 1991), p. 489.

27 *Ibid.*

28 Sir John Hope Simpson, *The Refugee Problem: Report of a Survey* (Oxford, 1939), p. 339.

29 *Ibid.*

30 *Ibid.*, p. 340.

31 *Ibid.*, p. 343.

32 *Ibid.*, p. 344.

33 *Ibid.*

34 *Ibid.*

35 *Ibid.*

36 Berghahn, *Continental Britons*, p. 75.

37 A.J. Sherman, *Island Refuge: Britain and Refugees From the Third Reich, 1933–39*, 2nd edn (London, 1994), p. 271; Berghahn, *Continental Britons*, p. 75. In the second edition of his work Sherman places the figure at 'between 60 and 70,000' (*Island Refuge*, p. 7).

38 Sherman, Island Refuge, p. 7.

39 On the response to the refugees see the chapter 'Anglo-Jewry and the Holocaust' in my *A History of the Jews in the English-Speaking World: Great Britain* (London, 1996).

40 Margaret Thatcher, *The Path to Power* (London, 1995), p. 27.

41 Sherman, *Island Refuge*, p. 215.

42 *Ibid.*, pp. 242–51.

43 *Ibid.*, Appendix I, p. 270. Sherman (p. 269) cautions against the literal acceptance of these figures, which are probably underestimates.

44 *Ibid.*, p. 270.

45 *Ibid.*, p. 267.

46 Reworked from Strauss, *Jewish Immigrants*, p. 197. The figures here for 'illegal immigrants' are considerably lower than in other sources. The Assistant Commissioner for Migration at the American Consulate in Jerusalem, M.I. Mindel, estimated in August 1938 that 'over 25,000' illegal immigrants were then resident in Palestine, while Malcolm MacDonald, Britain's Colonial Secretary, claimed that 4,000 more had entered Palestine in the six months from April–September 1939 (Francis R. Nicosia, *The Third Reich and the Palestine Question* (London, 1985), p. 162). It is debatable, of course, whether 'illegal' immigration should be included in these tables.

47 Nicosia, *Third Reich*, is the most complete study of this matter; see also Strauss, *Jewish Immigrants*, pp. 195–206.

48 Strauss, *Jewish Immigrants*, p. 196.

49 Nicosia, *Third Reich*, p. 136.

50 *Ibid.*, p. 264, n. 83.

51 Among the numerous works on this subject are Henry L. Feingold, *The Politics of Rescue: The Roosevelt Administration and the Holocaust* (New York, 1980); David S. Wyman, *Paper Walls: America and the Refugee Crisis, 1938–1941* (New York, 1985); and Barbara M. Stewart, *United States Government Policy on Refugees From Nazism, 1933–1940* (New York, 1984). Henry L. Feingold's *A Time For Searching: Entering the Mainstream, 1920–1945* (Baltimore, 1992), pp. 225–66, part of a five-volume history of the American Jewish community, provides an excellent and sensible overall view, although its conclusions are still far less positive than those presented here. See also Sheldon Morris Neuringer, *American Jewry and United States Immigration Policy, 1881–1953*, (New York, 1980).

52 Figures from *The Annual Report of the Secretary of Labor, 1939* (Washington, DC, 1939), p. 99, supplied by the Historical Reference Library of the Immigration and Naturalization Service, US Department of Justice, Washington, DC.

53 *Ibid.*

54 Feingold, *Politics of Rescue*, p. 16.

55 *Ibid.*

56 *Annual Report*, p. 99.

57 Letter to the author from Elizabeth A. Berrio, Chief of the Historical Reference Library of the Immigration and Naturalization Service, US Department of Justice, Washington, DC, dated 2 June 1994.

58 'Designation of Race in Immigration Procedures', Instruction No. 177, Immigration and Naturalization Service, US Department of Justice, 8 November 1943.

59 'Immigrant Aliens Admitted . . . 1931 to 1941, by Races or Peoples', typescript, Immigration and Naturalization Service, US Department of Justice, and *ibid.* for 'Year ended June 30, 1942'. The figures given here differ significantly from those presented in many other accounts of Jewish refugee migration to the United States.

60 *Annual Report*, p. 99.

61 Strauss, *Jewish Immigrants*, p. 207.

62 Hope Simpson, *Refugee Problem*, p. 473, citing *New York Times*, 18 November 1938.

63 That is, fourteen twelfths of 27,360.

64 Yehuda Bauer, *American Jewry and the Holocaust: the American Jewish Joint Distribution Committee, 1939–1945* (Detroit, 1981), p. 51. His figures differ from those presented above in this work.

65 Anthony Heilbut, *Exiled in Paradise: German Refugee Artists and Intellectuals in America, from the 1930s to the Present* (New York, 1983), p. 78.

66 Strauss, *Jewish Immigrants*, p. 225. Elsewhere in his work, Strauss puts the Latin American total at '80–85,000' (*ibid.*, p. 340).

67 *Ibid.*, pp. 216–21. Some of these totals include all Jewish immigration from the Nazi period, not just German Jewry.

68 Jeffrey Lesser, *Welcoming the Undesirables: Brazil and the Jewish Question* (Berkeley, 1985), p. 119.

69 *Ibid.*, Appendix 5, p. 183.

70 *Ibid.*, Appendix 6, p. 184.

71 Eric D. Kohler, 'Byways of Emigration: Panama, the Canal Zone and Jewish Rescue Efforts, 1939–1941', in Sanford Pinsker and Jack Fischel (eds), *Holocaust Studies Annual*, vol. 1 (Greenwood, Florida, 1983), p. 91.

72 *Ibid.* Haim Avni notes that the total *official* number of Jews who migrated to Argentina between 1933 and 1945 was 24,488, a figure which excludes 'first-class passengers, except for 1944 and 1945, or those who declared themselves to be Catholics or Protestants in the hope of better treatment . . . quite a few "Catholic" immigrants [had] typically Jewish names' (Haim Avni, *Argentina and the Jews: A History of Jewish Immigration* (Tuscaloosa, Alabama, 1991), p. 170). The actual total of Jewish migrants during this period may in fact have been considerably higher. In 1936, a 'comprehensive socioeconomic survey of the Argentine Jewish community' stated that 39,441 migrants had arrived since 1933, 'approximately 40–50 percent' of whom 'were German-speaking and the remainder, East Europeans' (*ibid.*). Immigration to Argentina was tightened up on 1 October 1938 (immediately before *Kristallnacht*) so that the officially known total of Jewish migrants to Argentina

totalled 4,919 in 1938 but only 1,873 in 1939. However, these official figures do not account for all the Jews immigrating to Argentina, Avni states. Jewish bodies 'had inside knowledge of at least a thousand Jewish tourists who never returned home. Another fifteen hundred Jews crossed the borders from neighbouring countries or remained in Argentina after stopping there in transit. If these figures are taken into consideration, the number of Jewish immigrants in 1939 was actually 4,373' (*ibid.*, p. 150).

73 'Dominican Republic', in *Encyclopaedia Judaica*, vol. 6 (Jerusalem, 1972), p. 160.

74 *Ibid.* This was not necessarily because of pervasive philo-semitism in the Dominican Republic, but because votes in the Dominican 'parliament' when Trujillo was the country's dictator tended to be unanimous.

75 *Ibid.*, and Mark Wischnitzer, 'The Historical Background of the Settlement of Jewish Refugees in Santo Domingo', *Jewish Social Studies*, 4(1), January 1972, p. 47; and Nicholas Ross, 'Sousa: A Colony of Hope', *American Jewish History*, 82, 1994.

76 'Dominican Republic', p. 160.

77 *Ibid.* It should be noted that Argentina's policies toward Jewish refugees was unusually harsh. See Leonardo Senkman, 'Argentina's Immigration Policy During the Holocaust (1938–1945)', in *Yad Vashem Studies XXI* (Jerusalem, 1991), pp. 155–88.

78 Senkman, 'Argentina's Immigration Policy', pp. 216–21. Some of these totals include all Jewish immigration from the Nazi period, not just German Jewry.

79 *Ibid.*

80 Strauss, *Jewish Immigrants*, p. 100.

81 Hope Simpson, *Refugee Problem*, p. 297.

82 *Ibid.*

83 *Ibid.*, p. 298.

84 *Ibid.*, p. 322–3.

85 *Ibid.*, p. 323.

86 *Ibid.*, p. 322.

87 Strauss, *Jewish Immigrants*, Table 1, p. 191.

88 The figure of 40,000 is from Michael R. Marrus, *The Unwanted: European Refugees in the Twentieth Century* (New York, 1985), p. 149, citing Hope Simpson. Professor Marrus' contention that France was an example of 'Closing Doors' (*ibid.*, p. 145–9) in this period is simply not borne out by the facts. The decrees of 1938–9 intended to keep out illegal refugees had little effect on their number. According to Michael Schapiro:

> Expulsion orders were frequently issued, but rarely carried out unless the police . . . could furnish definite proof that the refugee in question was undesirable. At times, the refugee who was served with an expulsion order could not obey it because he had no country to which to return. In such cases the Ministry of the Interior was authorised to determine the department of the country in which the refugee was to reside while reporting to the police at regular intervals.
>
> ('German Refugees in France', *Contemporary Jewish Record*, 3, 1940, p. 137)

89 Schapiro, 'German Refugees'.

90 Marrus, *Unwanted*, pp. 190–2.

91 *Ibid.*, pp. 156, 158. Despite Switzerland's notoriety in barring the doors to refugee migration during the war, about 21,000 Jewish refugees survived the war in that country (*ibid.*, p. 195).

92 Paul R. Bartrop, '"Good Jews" and "Bad Jews": Australian Perceptions of Jewish Migrants and Refugees, 1919–1939', in W.D. Rubinstein (ed.), *Jews in the Sixth Continent* (Sydney, 1987); Hilary L. Rubinstein, *The Jews in Australia: A Thematic History, Volume 1: 1788–1945* (Melbourne, 1991), pp. 145–234 and Paul R. Bartrop, *Australia and the Holocaust, 1933–1945* (Melbourne, 1994), provide overviews.

93 W.D. Rubinstein, 'The Attitude of the Australian Jewish Community and of Non-Jewish Opinion Leaders to the Rise of Nazi Germany and Nazi Anti-Semitism in 1933', *Australian Jewish Historical Society Journal*, 12 (1), November 1993, p. 105, citing Geoffrey Serle, *John Monash: A Biography* (Melbourne, 1982), p. 526.

94 Strauss, *Jewish Immigrants*, p. 227.

95 *Ibid.*, p. 229; Irving Abella and Harold Troper, *None is Too Many: Canada and the Jews of Europe, 1933–1948* (Toronto, 1983).

96 Hilary L. Rubinstein, *Jews in Australia*, pp. 170–9. Australia admitted 5,080 refugees in 1939 (*ibid.*, p. 178). Of the 15,000 refugees Australia agreed to admit, 3,000 were to be 'non-Aryan Christians'.

97 For essays on this topic see Paul R. Bartrop (ed.), *False Havens: The British Empire and the Holocaust* (Lanham, Maryland, 1995).

98 Strauss, *Jewish Immigrants*, p. 226.

99 *Ibid.*, p. 227. By that time there had been an excess of deaths over births among Shanghai Jewry of about 1,300 persons (*ibid.*, p. 226).

100 Cited in Marrus, *Unwanted*, p. 142.

101 Read Lewis and Marian Schibsby, 'Status of the Refugee Under American Immigration Laws', *Annals of the American Academy of Political and Social Sciences*, 203, May 1939, p. 77.

102 Eric D. Kohler, 'Relicensing Central European Refugee Physicians in the United States, 1933–1945', in *Simon Wiesenthal Center Annual*, 6 (Los Angeles, 1989), pp. 4–6.

103 Kwiet, 'To Leave or Not to Leave', p. 147.

104 *Ibid.*

105 Doron Niederland, 'Areas of Departure From Nazi Germany and the Social Structure of the Emigrants', in Mosse, *Second Chance*, Table V, p. 65.

106 Henry R. Huttenbach, 'The Emigration of Jews From Worms (November 1938–October 1941): Hopes and Plans', in Yisrael Gutman and Efraim Zuroff (eds), *Rescue Attempts During the Holocaust* (Jerusalem, 1977), p. 273.

107 *Ibid.*, pp. 273–5. The pattern of emigration in Worms, it must be noted, differed markedly from Germany as a whole (where most emigrated *after* November 1938).

108 *Ibid.*, p. 278.

109 *Ibid.*, pp. 278–9.

110 *Ibid.*, p. 285.

111 *Ibid.*, p. 283.

112 George H. Gallup, *The Gallup Poll: Public Opinion 1935–71, Volume 1: 1935–1948* (New York, 1972), p. 128. The results were released on 9 December 1938. At the same time, another question was also asked: 'Do you approve or disapprove of the treatment of Catholics in Germany?' The results here were: Approve, 3 per cent; Disapprove, 97 per cent (*ibid.*). The insignificant difference between the two results may highlight the true extent of theological anti-semitism. It should be noted that before 1950 Gallup Polls were not taken on the strictly random sample basis which has been employed since, but based upon a quota of representative cities, towns and

rural areas in the country, and, within them, on representative quotas of individuals based upon age, sex and socio-economic group (*ibid.*, p. vii).

113 *Ibid.*, pp. 128–9. The interviews for this question were conducted on 16–21 November 1938 and released on 11 December 1938.

114 *Ibid.*, p. 125. Interviews conducted 19–24 October 1938 and released on 11 November 1938. It will be seen that the 'Don't knows' have been ignored, a procedure which would not be permitted today.

115 *Ibid.*, p. 126. Interviews conducted 3–8 October 1938 and released on 20 November 1938.

116 *Ibid.*, p. 130. Interviews conducted 24–29 November 1938 and released on 18 December 1938. 'Others' (not further defined) split 50–50 on a boycott.

117 *Ibid.*, p. 177. Interviews conducted 8–24 August 1939 and released on 1 September 1939.

118 *Ibid.*, p. 179. Interviews conducted 1–6 September 1939 and released on 8 September 1939.

119 *Ibid.*, p. 186. Interviews conducted 5–10 October 1939, and released on 23 October 1939.

120 Wayne S. Cole, *Charles A. Lindbergh and the Battle Against American Intervention in World War II* (New York, 1974), p. 161. For good measure, Lindbergh added 'capitalists, anglophiles, and intellectuals . . . who believe that . . . the future of mankind depend[s] upon the domination of the British Empire' and 'Communistic groups' as significant (*ibid.*).

121 Gallup, *Gallup Poll*, p. 278. Interviews conducted 27 April–1 May 1941 and released on 9 May 1941.

122 *Ibid.*, p. 119. Survey released 23 September 1938. No information was provided in this survey as to which lawyers were surveyed, how they were selected or when the survey was administered.

123 *Ibid.*, p. 137. Interviews conducted 12–17 January 1939 and released on 29 January 1939.

124 *Ibid.*, p. 67. The results of this survey were not released until 15 August 1937.

125 *Ibid.*, p. 74.

126 *Ibid.*, p. 86.

127 *Ibid.*, p. 472. Interviews conducted 17–22 November 1944 and released on 4 December 1944.

128 *Ibid.*, p. 504. Interviews conducted 4–9 May 1945 and released on 20 May 1945.

129 Moshe R. Gottlieb, *American Anti-Nazi Resistance, 1933–1941: An Historical Analysis* (New York, 1982), p. 261.

130 *Ibid.*

131 Cited in Hadley Cantril (ed.), *Public Opinion, 1935–1946* (Westport, Conn., 1951), pp. 381–2. Note that the April 1938 responses add up to more than 100 per cent.

132 It should be noted that all final Gallup polls of voting intention at presidential elections of this period were within the 2–4 per cent range of accuracy found today. The final Gallup survey of voting intentions at the 1940 election, taken on 26–31 October 1940, showed Roosevelt defeating Willkie by 52–48 per cent, understating the former's actual share of the vote by 2.5 per cent (*ibid.*, pp. 249–50).

133 In *Beyond Belief: The American Press and the Coming of the Holocaust, 1933–1945* (New York, 1986) Deborah E. Lipstadt mentions (pp. 114–15) 'a January 1939 Gallup Poll' which 'found 66 per cent opposed to the plan to allow 10,000 refugee children from

Germany' to come to America, citing Henry Cantril's *Public Opinion* (Princeton, 1951), p. 1081. Most recent historians of American anti-semitism and American attitudes towards Jews in this period have simply ignored the wealth of positive indices of overwhelming American hostility to Nazi anti-semitism: for example, Leonard Dinnerstein, *Anti-Semitism in America* (Oxford, 1994), which systematically exaggerates the amount of anti-semitism throughout American history by ignoring all evidence of philo-semitism.

134 *Fortune*, July 1938, p. 80.

135 *Ibid.*

136 'The Fortune Survey and How it is Conducted' (Time Inc. Archives, 1939), supplied by Herbert W. Hooper, of Time Inc. Archives; Robert T. Elson, *Time Inc.: The Intimate History of a Publishing Enterprise; 1923–41* (New York, 1968), pp. 222–4.

137 Elson, *Time Inc.*, p. 224.

138 On this topic see Wayne S. Cole, *Charles A. Lindbergh and the Battle Against American Intervention in World War II* (New York, 1974), and Wayne S. Cole, *America First: The Battle Against Intervention, 1940–1941* (New York, 1971).

139 Cole, *Lindbergh*, pp. 172–3.

140 Cited in *ibid.*, pp. 171–2.

141 *Ibid.*

142 *Ibid.*, p. 173.

143 Cited in *ibid.*, p. 175.

144 *Ibid.* Even before the Des Moines speech, (non-Jewish) New Deal liberals had denounced Lindbergh in language which was remarkably extreme. In December 1940 the playwright and speechwriter Robert E. Sherwood had termed Lindbergh 'a Nazi with a Nazi Olympian contempt for all democratic processes – the rights of freedom of speech and worship, the right to select and criticise our own government and the right of labor to strike' (cited in Cole, *America First*, pp. 142–3).

145 See, for example, *Congressional Quarterly's Guide to U.S. Elections* (Washington, DC, 1976), p. 83.

146 *Ibid.*, p. 84.

147 *Ibid.*, p. 290.

148 Guy Stern, 'The Burning of Books in Nazi Germany, 1933: The American Response', *Simon Wiesenthal Center Annual*, 2, 1985, p. 96.

149 Lipstadt, *Beyond Belief*, p. 104.

150 George H. Gallup, *The Gallup International Public Opinion Polls: Great Britain, 1937–1975, Volume 1: 1937–1964* (New York, 1977), p. 7.

151 *Ibid.*, p. 22.

152 *Ibid.*, pp. 8–9.

153 *Ibid.*, p. 9.

154 *Ibid.*, p. 10.

155 *Ibid.*, p. 16.

156 *Ibid.*, p. 17.

157 *Ibid.*, p. 22.

158 See, for example, Peter and Leni Gillman, *'Collar the Lot!': How Britain Interned and Expelled its Wartime Refugees* (London, 1980).

159 Gallup, *Gallup Polls: Great Britain*, p. 34.

160 *Ibid.*, p. 94.

161 Cited in Cantril, *Public Opinion*, p. 382.

162 *Jewish Chronicle*, 23 September 1933. See the chapter 'Anglo-Jewry and the Holocaust' in my *History of the Jews* for many similar examples.

163 Charles Osbourne, *The Life and Crimes of Agatha Christie* (Chicago, 1990), pp. 88–9.

164 Robert Barnard, *A Talent to Deceive: An Appreciation of Agatha Christie* (New York, 1987), p. 17.

165 Anne Sebba, *Enid Bagnold: The Authorised Biography* (London, 1986), p. 139.

166 *Ibid.*, pp. 139–41, 172.

167 Figures from Simon Haxey, *Tory M.P.* (London, 1939), pp. 198–9, and my *History of the Jews*, pp. 309–12.

168 W.J. West, *Truth Betrayed* (London, 1987), pp. 15–21; Robert Skidelsky, *Sir Oswald Mosley* (London, 1990 edn.), p. 371.

169 See also Andrew Sharf, *The British Press and Jews Under Nazi Rule* (Oxford, 1964), for an analysis of the British press in the Nazi period, which shows that Nazi atrocities were, by and large, fully reported and condemned.

170 Cited in Robert Shepherd, *A Class Divided: Appeasement and the Road to Munich, 1938* (London, 1988), p. 273.

171 Angela Lambert, *1939: The Last Season of Peace* (London, 1989). Ellipses and emphases as in the original. Angela Lambert conducted oral interviews with these ex-debutantes in the mid-1980s, and, obviously, they may well be hindsightedly false and self-justificatory. Nevertheless, similar attitudes were expressed by many of those she interviewed.

172 On Australia, see my 'Attitude of the Australian Jewish Community'.

173 Berenbaum, *The World Must Know*, p. 58.

3 THE MYTH OF PLANS FOR RESCUE

1 On this 'debate', see, for instance, David Cesarani, 'Introduction', in David Cesarani (ed.), *The Final Solution: Origins and Interpretation* (London, 1994), and Christopher R. Browning, 'Beyond "Intentionalism" and "Functionalism": The Decision for the Final Solution Reconsidered', in Christopher R. Browning, *The Path to Genocide* (Cambridge, 1992).

2 See Philippe Burrin, *Hitler and the Jews: The Genesis of the Holocaust* (London, 1994) and Arno Mayer, *Why Did the Heavens Not Darken?* (New York, 1988).

3 Adolf Hitler, *Mein Kampf*, trans. by Ralph Manheim (London, 1974), p. 356.

4 *Ibid.*, p. 357.

5 *Ibid.*, p. 365.

6 *Ibid.*, p. 367. Each of these passages appears in *Mein Kampf* in italics.

7 See Z. Sternhall, 'Fascist Ideology', in Walter Laqueur (ed.), *Fascism: A Reader's Guide* (Harmondsworth, 1979); Roger Griffin, *The Nature of Fascism* (London, 1991), pp. 110–12.

8 Hitler, *Mein Kampf*, p. 393.

9 *Hitler's Table Talk, 1941–1944* (London, 1953), pp. 313, 562.

10 *Ibid.*, p. 409.

11 *Ibid.*, p. 548.

12 Lucy S. Dawidowicz, *The War Against the Jews, 1933–45* (London, 1986), pp. 47–8. One of the best of innumerable studies of Hitler's anti-semitism is Robert Wistrich, *Hitler's Apocalypse: Jews and the Nazi Legacy* (London, 1985), esp. pp. 48, 135.

13 The best of several psychological investigations of this question is Robert G.L.

Waite's outstanding book *The Psychopathic God: Adolf Hitler* (originally 1977; revised edn, New York, 1993). Waite's characterisation of Hitler as a 'borderline personality' (in the clinical psychiatric sense) is flawed, however, by the fact that this is no longer accepted as a valid psychiatric category. (I am grateful to Dr Paul Brown of Melbourne for his discussions with me of this question.)

14 So far as I am aware, the only time Hitler met a known Jew during his period as *Führer* was in April 1933, when he officially received the Ambassador of the USSR, Lev Khinchuk, who was Jewish (Wistrich, *Hitler's Apocalypse*, p. 109).

15 Karl A. Schleunes, *The Twisted Road to Auschwitz: Nazi Policy Toward German Jews, 1933–39* (originally 1970; Urbana, Ill., 1990). On the other hand, as a young man in Vienna Hitler appears to have had many Jewish friends, and even business partners, according to the Austrian historian Brigitte Hamann ('Some of his Best Friends were Jews', *Jerusalem Report*, 12 December 1996). If this is true, more weight must be placed upon the effects of the First World War on the evolution of history's greatest anti-semite. Hitler appears to have suffered a nervous breakdown in November 1918 when he learned of Germany's sudden defeat; he emerged as a raving demagogue soon afterwards.

16 Christopher R. Browning, 'Nazi Resettlement Policy and the Search for a Solution to the Jewish Question, 1939–1941', in Browning, *Path to Genocide* pp. 3–23. See also Saul Friedlander, 'From Anti-Semitism to Extermination: A Historiographical Study of Nazi Policies Toward the Jews and an Essay in Interpretation,' *Yad Vashem Studies XVI* (Jerusalem, 1984).

17 Cited in *ibid.*, p. 23.

18 The argument made here is rather different from that which is now frequently encountered in works on the origins of the Holocaust, that Hitler decided upon extermination because there were, with the invasion of Russia, simply too many Jews to deport to Madagascar or elsewhere (options which were now closed off, in any case, by the progress of the war). The argument made here is that Hitler's fundamentally demographic and biological world-view seized upon genocide as a golden opportunity to finish off European Jewry for once and for all *because* so many Jews had come under Nazi domination, especially the 'biological' centre of Jewry in the former Pale of Settlement, the western area of Czarist Russia to which Jews were confined until the end of the regime.

19 Waite, *Psychopathic God*, pp. 19–20.

20 Cited in *ibid.*, p. 19.

21 Cited in *ibid.*, p. 20.

22 *Ibid.*, p. 353.

23 Albert Speer noted that in the autumn of 1943, when reading reports of air raids on German cities 'Hitler was in the habit of raging against the British government and the Jews, who were to blame for these air raids' (*Inside the Third Reich: Memoirs by Albert Speer* (London, 1970), p. 299). In his so-called 'Last Will', Hitler specifically stated that the killing of the Jews was in part revenge for Allied air raids against 'Aryan' civilians. Josef Goebbels, a fanatical advocate of the 'deportation' of all Jews during the war, also claimed that 'the Jews were the force behind the British and American raids'. (Jay W. Baird, *To Die For Germany: Heroes in the Nazi Pantheon* (Bloomington, Ind., 1990), p. 237).

24 John Ellis, *Brute Force: Allied Strategy and Tactics in the Second World War* (London, 1990), pp. 167, 169.

25 Alexander Werth, *Russia At War, 1941–45* (New York, 1964), p. 122.

26 See e.g. the 'Introduction' by Saul Friedlander in Burrin, *Hitler and the Jews* pp. 1–15.

27 From Alfred Franke-Gricksch, 'From the Diary of a Fallen SS Leader' (dictated 1948), quoted in Gerald Fleming, *Hitler and the Final Solution* (Berkeley, 1984) p. 147. The German word *Judentum* can be translated as either 'Judaism' or 'Jewry': clearly the latter translation, rather than the former, was more accurate here.

28 Cited in Dr Joseph Billig, 'The Launching of the "Final Solution"', in Serge Klarsfeld, *The Holocaust and the Neo-Nazi Mythomania* (New York, 1978), p. 40.

29 *Ibid.*

30 Jochen von Lang (ed.), *Eichmann Interrogated: Transcripts from the Archives of the Israel Police* (New York, 1983), p. 119.

31 It is worth noting that in the period 1881–1924, when the United States and many other countries permitted virtually unrestricted Jewish immigration, while approximately 3–3.5 million Jews emigrated from the Russian Pale of Settlement, nearly twice that number remained where they were, despite both the lure of the democracies and the burden of oppression and poverty at home. Many Strictly Orthodox Jewish leaders actually advised Jews in the Pale to avoid migrating to 'godless' places such as America while Bundists and other Yiddish culturalists would have feared, rather than welcomed, the prospect of their children assimilating the cultural values of America and other new countries of settlement. Finally, during this period *aliyah* to Palestine was derisory, Palestine's Jewish population rising only from perhaps 50,000 in the mid-1890s to only 175,000 in 1933.

32 'Anzahl der Schekelzahler in der Nachkriegszeit': Table provided by Central Zionist Archives, Jerusalem. A 'shekel' was the term given to the payment of the small fee (about 50 cents in the United States and two shillings in Britain) required for official membership in the Zionist movement. This was solicited by the various Zionist groups and parties. So far as I am aware, the only previous published work to highlight the international weakness of Zionism in the inter-war years is Ezra Mendelsohn, 'Zionist Success and Zionist Failure: The Case of East Central Europe Between the Wars', originally in R. Kozodoy *et al.*, (eds), *Vision Confronts Reality: Historical Perspectives on the Contemporary Jewish Agenda* (Rutherford, NJ, 1989); reprinted in Jehuda Reinharz and Anita Shapira (eds), *Essential Papers on Zionism* (London, 1996). On the failure of the Zionist movement to foresee the Holocaust, see the very useful article by Anita Shapira, 'Did the Zionist Leadership Foresee the Holocaust?', in Jehuda Reinharz (ed.), *Living With Antisemitism: Modern Jewish Responses* (Hanover, NH, 1987).

33 Reinharz and Shapira, *Essential Papers.*

34 Moreover, the figures for shekel-holding cited here represent the periodic *maximum* figures in a year of a Zionist General Congress, when great efforts were made by Zionist groups to increase their numbers and, hence, their voting bloc at the Zionist Congress. In 1929–30, for instance, an 'off-year' when no Zionist Congress was held, the world-wide total of shekel-holders was only 201,250.

35 Joseph Marcus, *Social and Political History of the Jews in Poland, 1918–1939* (Berlin, 1983), p. 264.

36 *Ibid.*, p. 283. On this election, which became internationally renowned in socialist circles, see Robert Moses Shapiro, 'The Polish *Kehilla* Elections of 1936: A Revolution Reexamined', in Anthony Polonsky, Ezra Mendelsohn and Jerzy

Tomaszewski (eds), *Polin: Studies in Polish Jewry – Jews in Independent Poland 1918–1939* (London, 1994).

37 Celia S. Heller, *On the Edge of Destruction: Jews of Poland Between the Two World Wars* (New York, 1977), p. 264. This author's views on the weakness of Bundism is directly contradicted by the evidence presented by Marcus. See also Arthur Ruppin, *The Jewish Fate and Future* (London, 1940), p. 278, for further statistics on the weakness of Polish Zionism.

38 'Anzahl'; Harry M. Rabinowicz, *The Legacy of Polish Jewry: A History of Polish Jews in the Inter-War Years 1919–1939* (New York, 1965), p. 109.

39 Joseph B. Schectman, *Fighter and Prophet: The Vladimir Jabotinsky Story, Volume 2, The Last Years* (New York, 1961), p. 345. In 1931, during the compilation of the Polish census of that year, the Zionist movement requested that its followers declare Hebrew to be their native language, not Yiddish, Polish or some other language. About 7.8 per cent of Polish Jewry – approximately 243,000 among 3,114,000 Polish Jews – 'obeyed the command of the Zionist movement' (Ezra Mendelsohn, *The Jews of East Central Europe Between the World Wars* (Bloomington, Ind., 1983), p. 30). Hebrew was, of course, not a vernacular language of Polish Jewry.

40 Mendelsohn, 'Zionist Success', p. 180. Professor Mendelsohn attributes some of this decline to the defection of the Zionist Revisionists from the World Zionist Organization (*ibid.*, p. 181).

41 Marcus, *Social and Political History*, p. 410.

42 D. Ben-Gurion, 'The Zionist Organisation And Its Tasks', *Zionist Review* (London), April 1936, p. 31.

43 *Ibid.*

44 *Ibid.*, p. 32.

45 'Anzahl'. According to Mendelsohn ('Zionist Success', p. 181) the number of Hungarian shekel-holders rose to 21,562 in 1939.

46 'Anzahl'. This figure rose to 53,350 in 1935 and to 60,013 in 1939 (Mendelsohn, 'Zionist Success', p. 111), whose figures differ from those of the 'Anzahl'.

47 Mendelsohn, 'Zionist Success', p. 186.

48 See Ben-Cion Pinchuk, *Shtetl Jews Under Soviet Rule: Eastern Poland on the Eve of the Holocaust* (Oxford, 1990).

49 *Ibid.*, pp. 117–19.

50 'Annual Quotas and Quota Immigrants Admitted . . . 1925 to 1944, By Countries', *Monthly Review* of the Immigration and Naturalization Service, US Department of Justice, June 1945, p. 48. I am most grateful to Professor David Wyman for providing me with this table.

51 *Ibid.*

52 'Surinam', in *Encyclopaedia Judaica*, vol. 15, (Jerusalem, 1971), p. 531. How these refugees fled from the Netherlands 'during World War II' is not explained. There was, similarly, no notable Jewish emigration to the other Dutch colony in the Caribbean, the Netherlands Antilles, during this period ('Netherlands Antilles', in *ibid.*, vol. 12, pp. 993–5).

53 Take, for instance, this statement by Professor Henry L. Feingold (normally an excellent and very balanced historian of America's response to the Holocaust):

The Roosevelt Administration could have offered a safe haven between the years 1938 and 1941. Had that been done, there is some reason to believe that the

decision for systematic slaughter taken in Berlin might not have been made or
at least might have been delayed.

('Who Shall Bear the Guilt for the Holocaust?' American Jewish History,
48, March 1979, p. 122)

This claim in my opinion is supremely misleading. There is no evidence for such a
view, and Feingold provides none. The great majority of the Jews murdered by the
Nazis were in Poland, the Soviet Union, and south-eastern Europe, not in Germany,
and no one proposed that Roosevelt should have provided a 'safe haven' for them
in 1938–41, i.e. before or just after they came under Nazi control. It was the
Nazis (as will be shown), who forbade Jewish emigration; the Allies did not prohibit
immigration. Professor Feingold's claim is another example of statements about
'rescue' during the Holocaust where even excellent historians clearly seem to be
making dubious statements.

54 From Yitzhak Arad, Yisrael Gutman and Abraham Maragoliot (eds), *Documents on the Holocaust: Selected Sources on the Destruction of the Jews of Germany and Austria, Poland, and the Soviet Union* (Jerusalem, 1981), pp. 219–20. The 'Reich Security Main Office' was the central organ of the SS bureaucracy, and shows the evolution of the attitude of the SS from enforced emigration to enforced imprisonment by this date. The editors of *Documents on the Holocaust* note that this memorandum was 'addressed to District Governors in the Government-General' (*ibid.*, p. 220).

55 Fleming, *Hitler and the Final Solution*, pp. 44–5. From the summer of 1940 and the division of newly conquered France into an occupied and unoccupied zone, civilian travel outside of France was forbidden, except for diplomats and other officials. 'French Jews were therefore unable to flee impending doom at the hands of the Nazis', although a considerable illegal movement from occupied to unoccupied France, and then to Spain and Italy, did occur (Stanford J. Shaw, *Turkey and the Holocaust* (New York, 1993), p. 135).

56 Cited in Wistrich, *Hitler's Apocalypse*, p. 124.

57 Ruth Zariz, 'Officially Approved Emigration From Germany After 1941: A Case Study', *Yad Vashem Studies XVIII* (Jerusalem, 1987), p. 276. Zariz states that she found three categories of Jews allowed to emigrate in very limited numbers: foreign nationals exchanged for Germans living overseas; holders of Palestinian residence certificates, also exchanged for Germans residing in Palestine and the British Empire, in 1943; and a group of approximately one dozen German Jews aged 65 or more exchanged for a German property owner in Guatemala in 1944 (a deal approved by Himmler against the strenuous objections of Goebbels) (*ibid.*).

58 Friedlander, 'Anti-Semitism to Extermination', p. 41.

59 Dalia Ofer, *Escaping the Holocaust: Illegal Immigration to the Land of Israel, 1939–1944* (New York, 1990), pp. 184–5.

60 *Ibid.*, p. 185. However 'a small but steady trickle of Jewish refugees continued to leave Rumania on yachts and small vessels throughout 1942' (*ibid.*).

61 *Ibid.*

62 Michael R. Marrus and Robert O. Paxton, *Vichy France and the Jews* (New York, 1981), p. 266.

63 Livia Rothkirchen, 'Hungary – An Asylum For the Refugees of Europe', *Yad Vashem Studies VII* (Jerusalem, 1968), as reprinted in Michael R. Marrus (ed.), *The Nazi Holocaust: Part 4: The 'Final Solution' Outside Germany, Volume 2* (Westport, Conn., 1989), p. 525, n. 7.

64 Pinchuk, *Shtetl Jews*, p. 12.

65 Ben-Cion Pinchuk, 'Jewish Refugees in Soviet Poland, 1939–1941', *Jewish Social Studies*, 40, 1978, reprinted in Marrus, *Nazi Holocaust: Part 8, Volume 3: Bystanders to the Holocaust*, p. 1038.

66 Selig Brodetsky, *Memoirs: From Ghetto to Israel* (London, 1960), p. 218.

67 Lipstadt, *Beyond Belief* (New York, 1986) p. 270.

68 *Ibid.*, p. 1. Professor Lipstadt states that this failure occurred 'during the 1930s and 1940s' (*ibid.*) Of course, if she means only that America might have admitted more Jews as refugees prior to the war, this is certainly true, especially if American opinion-makers of the time possessed crystal balls with which to see the Holocaust that began several years later.

69 See e.g. Freda Kirchway, 'State Department Versus Political Refugees', *Nation*, 26 December 1940, pp. 648–9; Norbert Engels, 'Refugee Scholars Welcome in Our American Colleges', *America*, 27 September 1941.

70 See Lipstadt, *Beyond Belief*, pp. 142–9. These reports were publicised throughout the world and appeared in Australian newspapers soon afterwards. One remarkable fact about the speed with which knowledge of Nazi genocide spread should be noted: by September–October 1941 remarkably accurate reports of the activities of the *Einsatzgruppen* in the USSR were widely reported in the Jewish underground press in the *Warsaw Ghetto*, although the ghetto had been sealed from outside contact a year earlier. See Leni Yahil, 'The Warsaw Underground Press', in Reinharz, *Living with Antisemitism*, pp. 433–442.

In November 1996 many newspapers around the world, including the London *Times* and the *New York Times*, carried reports that the release of new documents by the British government showed that it knew of the killings in the Soviet Union in 1941. But those press claims are misleading in that it is well known that the British government knew of the killings, which were reported throughout the world at the time.

71 *Ibid.*, p. 151.

72 Eliyho Matzozsky, 'The Response of American Jewry and Its Representative Organizations Between November 24, 1942 and April 19, 1943 to the Mass Killing of Jews in Europe', unpublished MA thesis, 1979, p. 6; Yehuda Bauer, 'When Did They Know?' *Midstream*, April 1968. See also Walter Laqueur, *The Terrible Secret: Suppression of the Truth About Hitler's Final Solution* (Boston, Mass., 1980). American and British newspapers had carried unconfirmed reports of Nazi mass murders in Poland from late 1941.

73 John S. Conway, 'The First Report About Auschwitz', in Alex Grobman (ed.), *Simon Wiesenthal Center Annual*, 1 (Chappaqua, NY, 1984).

74 David S. Wyman (ed.), *America and the Holocaust: A Thirteen-Volume Set Documenting the Acclaimed Book The Abandonment of the Jews, Volume 1: Confirming the News of Extermination* (New York, 1990), p. vii. (This series is henceforth cited as Wyman, *AH*, followed by the particular volume and page reference.)

75 *Ibid.*, p. vii.

76 *Ibid.*

77 Yehuda Bauer, 'The Goldberg Report', *Midstream*, February 1985, pp. 27–8. Professor Bauer here refers to the 'Finger Report' as the 'Goldberg Report'. The 'blood libel' is the allegation that Jews kidnapped and murdered Christian children at Passover, a stock-in-trade of religious anti-semitism since the Middle Ages. Saul

S. Friedman's essay in that report is 'The Power and/or Powerlessness of American Jews, 1939–1945'.

78 Wyman, *AH*, vol. 2, p. 72.

79 Matzozsky, 'Response', p. 12.

80 *Ibid.*, p. 16.

81 *Ibid.*, p. 23.

82 Wyman, *AH*, vol. 2, p. 73.

83 *Ibid.*, pp. 73–4.

84 *Ibid.*, p. 73.

85 *Ibid.*, p. 111.

86 'Governing Council Meeting Held Thursday, December 10, 1942', in *ibid.*, pp. 92–3.

87 *Ibid.*, p. 121.

88 'Strictly Confidential/Activities of the American Jewish Congress and the World Jewish Congress With Respect to the Hitler Program of Exterminating the Jews', in *ibid.*, pp. 128–33. This document has no date, but someone – presumably an archivist – has written 'Prob[ably] mid-Jan '43 (after 1/6/43 [i.e., 6 January], anyway)' on the document.

89 Yehuda Bauer, *American Jewry and the Holocaust: The American Jewish Joint Distribution Committee, 1939–1945* (Detroit, 1981), pp. 320–1.

90 *Ibid.*

91 'The "Stop Hitler Now" Demonstration', *Congress Weekly*, 10 (10), 5 March 1943, p. 15.

92 Freda Kirchway, 'While The Jews Die', *Nation*, 13 March 1943, p. 367, in Wyman, *AH*, vol. 2, p. 181. Wyman also reprints a longer typescript version of these resolutions, in *ibid.*, pp. 169–75.

93 Matzozsky, 'Response', pp. 39–40.

94 *Ibid.*, p. 40.

95 *Ibid.*, p. 39.

96 Wyman, *AH*, vol. 2, pp. 182–3, '"We Will Never Die!"' letterhead.

97 *Ibid.*, p. 189.

98 Matzozsky, 'Response', p. 40.

99 *Ibid.*, p. 41.

100 'Action Not Pity Can Save Millions Now!' full-page advertisement in *New York Times*, 8 February 1943, in Wyman, *AH*, vol. 2, p. 162.

101 *Ibid.*

102 Over 1.1 million Jews served in the armies of the three great Allies during the Second World War – about 550,000 in the American military, 500,000 in the Soviet Union's and nearly 100,000 in the forces of Britain and the Commonwealth (see Israel Guttman, *The Heroism of the Jewish People in the Second World War* (Tel Aviv, 1985), pp. 119, 120, 127).

103 The United States government officially rejected the idea of a Jewish Army along the lines proposed by Bergson in January 1943, American Under-Secretary of War Robert P. Patterson writing to Bergson that the proposals 'are not practical from a military standpoint' (Matzozsky, 'Response', p. 44).

104 *Ibid.*, p. 48, citing *New York Times*, 7 December 1942.

105 *Ibid.*, p. 49, citing *New York Times*, 16 February 1943.

106 Ofer, *Escaping the Holocaust*, pp. 187–94.

107 Edward Pinsky, 'American Jewish Unity During the Holocaust – The Joint Emergency Committee, 1943', *American Jewish History Quarterly*, 72, (4) 1983.

108 *Ibid.*, p. 481. Zygelbojm's dramatic suicide two months later, caused by his despondency over the Western world's alleged indifference to the fate of Warsaw's Jews, is well known.

109 These organisations were the American Jewish Congress, B'nai B'rith, the Jewish Labor Committee, the American Emergency Committee for Zionist Affairs, the American Jewish Committee, Agudath Israel of America, the Union of Orthodox Rabbis of America and the Synagogue Council of America. 'Program For the Rescue of Jews From Nazi Occupied Europe', *Congress Weekly*, 30 April 1943, p. 11.

110 From *ibid.*, pp. 11–12.

111 On this subject see e.g. Owen Chadwick, *Britain and the Vatican During the Second World War* (Cambridge, 1986), pp. 198-221.

112 Reprinted in Wyman, *AH*, vol. 3, pp. 51–2.

113 *Ibid.*, p. 51.

114 Wyman, *AH*, vol. 3, pp. v–vi.

115 Bauer, *American Jewry*, p. 195.

116 Legitimate criticisms of Bermuda might, of course, be made, especially of the fact that non-governmental bodies were not directly represented and that its final report remained secret.

117 'Note on Measures For the Rescue of Refugees From Axis Persecution', 24 March 1943, in Wyman, *AH*, vol. 3, p. 65. Emerson (1881-1962) was an administrative civil servant who was the head of Britain's refugee administration.

118 *Ibid.*

119 *Ibid.*, p. 66.

120 'Confidential Memorandum For the Chairman', 20 April 1943, in *ibid.*, pp. 77–8.

121 'Report of the Interim Committee . . . to . . . the American Jewish Conference', 1 November 1944, reprinted in Wyman, *AH*, vol. 5, p. 157. It was widely seen as a counterweight to the American Jewish Committee, a group perceived as either hostile to or lukewarm towards Zionism.

122 *Ibid.*, p. 13. This Commission appointed 'a small executive committee' of eight persons in February 1944.

123 *Ibid.*, p. 167.

124 See e.g. 'Introduction' to Wyman, *AH*, vol. 5, p. v; David Kranzler, *Thy Brother's Blood: The Orthodox Jewish Response During the Holocaust* (Brooklyn, NY, 1987), pp. 83, 100. Kranzler's book claims that the idea originally came from Rabbi Solomon Schonfeld, who suggested it to his father-in-law, British Chief Rabbi Joseph Hertz (*ibid.*, p. 298, n. 70). Schonfeld, an Agudas Israel Strictly Orthodox rabbi, was very active in rescue activities, though the claims made on his behalf by his later admirers such as Kranzler are clearly exaggerated. Agudas Israel had a friendly relationship with Revisionist Zionism and the Bergson group at this stage.

125 *Answer*, 1(1), 5 July 1943, pp. 10, 19.

126 From Wyman, *AH*, vol. 5, pp. 30–1, reprinted from *Answer*, 1 (7–8), August 1943.

127 Henry L. Feingold, *The Politics of Rescue: The Roosevelt Administration and the Holocaust, 1938–1945* (New Brunswick, NJ, 1970), points out (pp. 211–12) that the Bergsonite proposals omitted any reference to the Palestine question, a strange omission for a Revisionist Zionist-based body, which led to much hostility to its proposals from mainstream Zionist groups.

128 Kranzler, *Thy Brother's Blood*, p. 100; Wyman, 'Introduction', to *AH*, vol. 5, p. vi.

129 See the collection of such editorials and newspaper comments published by the Emergency Committee, *The American Press and the Rescue Resolution* (New York, n.d. [early 1944]).

130 *Ibid.*, p. 6. Defenders of the Bergson group have missed this distinction.

131 'Is Dr. Wise Right?' (editorial), *Daily Jewish Courier* (Chicago), 7 December 1943, reprinted in *American Press*, p. 41. Wise, in testimony to the House of Representatives Foreign Affairs Committee, proposed that the Allies 'discuss with, and convince, the countries which are [allied] with Hitler that they should allow the Jews to leave', that a United Nations' agency undertake rescue work, that food be sent to the ghettos and that Palestine open its doors to Jews (*ibid.*).

132 Bauer, *America and the Holocaust*, p. 401.

133 The organisations submitting suggestions for rescue were Agudas Israel of America, American Committee of OSE, American Friends Service Committee, American Jewish Conference, American Jewish Joint Distribution Committee, HIAS, Jewish Labor Committee, the Joint Emergency Committee for European Jewish Affairs, the League for the Liberation of Lithuania, National Council of Jewish Women, Netherlands Jewish Society, Refugee Economic Corporation, the Union of Orthodox Rabbis of the United States and Canada, and the World Jewish Congress (Wyman, *AH*, vol. 13, pp. 159–69).

134 Reported in *ibid*. This document is undated, but was apparently typed in early March 1944. Most of the responses received from Jewish organisations date from the last week of February up to 1 March 1944.

135 Eliyo Matz, '"The American Jewish Press and Its Reaction to the Mass Killing of Jews in Europe: November 24, 1942 – March 4, 1933," An Analysis With Emphasis on the Yiddish Daily Papers of New York', unpublished typescript, p. 8, reprinted in Wyman, *AH*, vol. 2, p. 14.

136 'Petition of American Scholars to the President Concerning Nazi Persecutions of the Jews', *Newsletter of the Yivo*, 1, September 1943, p. 3.

137 See Efraim Zuroff, 'Rescue Priority and Fund Raising as Issues During the Holocaust: A Case Study of the Relations Between the Vaad Ha-Hatzala and the Joint, 1939–1941', *American Jewish History*, 68(3), 1979; Efraim Zuroff, 'Rabbis' Relief and Rescue: A Case Study of the Activities of the *Vaad ha-Hatzala* (Rescue Committee) of the American Orthodox Rabbis, 1942–1943', *Simon Wiesenthal Center Annual*, 3, 1987; and Kranzler, *Thy Brother's Blood*. Zuroff, it should be noted, is a careful and scholarly historian who has made no extravagant claims in his works. This subject is examined objectively in Meir Sompolinsky, 'Jewish Institutions in the World and the Yishuv as Reflected in the Holocaust Historiography of the Ultra-Orthodox', in Yisrael Gutman and Gideon Greif (eds), *The Historiography of the Holocaust Period* (Jerusalem, 1988).

138 Kranzler, *Thy Brother's Blood*, pp. 1–2.

139 To take one very typical example, Kranzler's book contains a section (*ibid.*, pp. 84–9) on 'Food to the Ghettos', noting that the Strictly Orthodox Agudah organisation continued to send food to the ghettos throughout 1941, despite intense pressure by mainstream Jewish bodies wishing to boycott Nazi-occupied Europe. Almost completely lost in this discussion is the fact that the Nazis forbade the shipment of food to the ghettos in late 1941 and exterminated their Jews in 1942–3. This discussion – like the rest of Kranzler's book – contains a lengthy gratuitous attack on non-Strictly Orthodox Jews for attempting to stop the 'flow of food'.

140 On the uniqueness of the Holocaust, see, for example, Michael R. Marrus, *The Holocaust in History* (London, 1987) pp. 18–25; Henry L. Feingold, 'How Unique Was the Holocaust?', in Alex Grobman and Daniel Landes (eds), *Critical Issues of the Holocaust* (Los Angeles, 1983), pp. 397–401; Steven T. Katz, 'The "Unique" Intentionality of the Holocaust', *Modern Judaism*, 1(2), 1981, and, especially, his monumental *The Holocaust in Historical Context, Volume 1: The Holocaust and Mass Death Before the Modern Age* (Oxford, 1994). For a vigorous and highly controversial collection of essays on this topic, see Alan S. Rosenbaum (ed.), *Is the Holocaust Unique? Perspectives on Comparative Genocide* (Boulder, Col., 1996), which is remarkable for the significant number of contributors who argue with great passion that the Holocaust was not unique, and for a Foreword (by Israel W. Charny) which criticises many of the contributions!

141 Max Lerner, 'Not Easy – But Possible,' *Answer*, August 1943, pp. 7–8.

142 *Ibid.*, pp. 8–9. Lerner, it should be pointed out, also said the following (p. 8):

> I am confident when I say that there is not a person in this group who would for a moment consider rescuing the Jews of Europe if it meant prolonging the war, strengthening the enemy, or endangering or qualifying victory. There is not one among us who does not hold a speedy victory and an unconditional surrender of the enemy higher than any human life, including his own.

143 'What Can We Do?', *Jewish Comment*, 17 December 1943, p. 1. It need not be pointed out that 'providing food' to the 'incarcerated Jews' was impossible and would not have prevented their murders, nor that the Nazis slammed the door on Jewish *emigration*.

144 *Ibid.*, p. 3. Throughout this article, the Jews of Europe are continuously referred to as 'refugees', and their dilemma conceptualised as the relief of 'refugees'.

145 *Nation*, 9 January 1943, pp. 48–51. This was the second of three articles by Bernstein on the future of Europe's Jews.

146 According to Bernstein (*ibid.*, p. 50), although 'without any guarantees, many thousands of fleeing Jews have crossed the Pyrenees into Spain, the Danube into Hungary [etc.] . . . Their numbers have been limited largely by the unwillingness of other countries to accept escaping Jews.' The role of the Nazis in 'limiting' their numbers has disappeared from Bernstein's analysis (as from so many others).

147 Edward Pinsky, 'American Jewish Unity', p. 477.

148 Pinsky (*ibid.*, p. 494), sensibly notes that proposals for rescue were 'hardly distinguishable from one another'.

149 'Fort Ontario', in Israel Gutman, *Encyclopedia of the Holocaust*, vol. 2 (New York, 1990), pp. 503–4; S. Lowenstein, *Token Refuge: The Story of the Jewish Refugee Shelter at Oswego, 1944–1946* (Bloomington, Ind., 1986). Instances of 'pseudo-rescue' being portrayed as genuine examples of rescue by the Allies abound in the literature of this topic. A recent example is Alexis P. Rubin, 'The Schleifer Children: A Special Holocaust Rescue Case', *American Jewish History*, 84, March, 1996.

150 On Britain and its response to the Holocaust see Tony Kushner, *The Holocaust and the Liberal Imagination: A Social and Cultural History* (Oxford, 1994), esp. pp. 146–204; Richard Bolchover, *British Jewry and the Holocaust* (Cambridge, 1993); Geoffrey Alderman, *Modern British Jewry* (Oxford, 1992), pp. 265–305; and Bernard Wasserstein, *Britain and the Jews of Europe, 1939–1945* (Oxford, 1979); and Monty Noam Penkower, 'Great Britain and the Holocaust', in Saul S. Friedman (ed.),

Holocaust Literature: A Handbook of Critical, Historical and Literary Writings (Westport, Conn., 1993). All these works, in different ways and from differing perspectives, may fairly be described as unrelentingly negative about the response of mainstream British Jewry to the plight of Europe's Jews, in a manner very reminiscent of the American historical literature on the American response. Some balance is provided by Martin Gilbert, *Auschwitz and the Allies* (London, 1981). My book, *A History of the Jews in the English-Speaking World: Great Britain* (London, 1996), pp. 280–7, disputes the mainstream interpretation root and branch.

151 See e.g. Deborah E. Lipstadt, *Beyond Belief: The American Press and the Coming of the Holocaust, 1933–1945* (New York, 1986), pp. 189-92.

152 The Board of Deputies was established in the eighteenth century. It originally consisted (and consists) of representatives ('deputies') chosen by Britain's Orthodox synagogues. In the twentieth century, representation has been broadened to include non-Orthodox synagogues, and many secular Jewish bodies (the Zionist Federation, youth and women's groups, etc.). The Board of Deputies, it should be noted, consists only of delegates representing a member body, who have been chosen by that body. It includes no independent members and its representatives are not selected by a community-wide poll (although member bodies may well select their 'deputies' by an internal election).

153 See e.g. Alderman, *Modern British Jewry*, pp. 265–305; Bolchover, *British Jewry*, pp. 31–53; and Tony Kushner, *The Persistence of Prejudice: Antisemitism in British Society During the Second World War* (Manchester, 1989).

154 See e.g. Wasserstein, *Britain and the Jews of Europe*, p. 52 *et seq.*, which in effect holds Britain's policies in 1940–1 to blame for Nazi policies which came into effect a year later (and were unknown to anyone in the West until even later).

155 Bernard Wasserstein, 'Patterns of Jewish Leadership in Great Britain During the Nazi Era', in R.L. Braham (ed.), *Jewish Leadership During the Nazi Era* (New York, 1985), p. 36.

156 'The Slaughter of European Jewry' (editorial), *Jewish Chronicle*, 11 December 1942.

157 'Answers to the Mass Murders' (editorial), in *Jewish Chronicle*, 18 December 1942.

158 Hansard, *House of Commons Proceedings*, 17 December 1942, columns 2082–7. One observer present on this occasion wrote to the *Jewish Chronicle* that

> the House had listened in an almost overpowered silence, broken, at moments, with gasps . . . Suddenly, from the obscure corner near the Speaker's chair, the quivering voice of a small man was barely heard to ask that the House of Commons might rise in sympathy with the Jewish people and in protest against Nazi infamy. A murmur swept through the packed benches. – a murmur of approval, as well as of sheer surprise that so great a gesture should have come from a man – a working man – so unobtrusive. The House of Commons rose. The British Cabinet, complete save for the Prime Minister himself, rose. The Distinguished Strangers, conspicuous by the tall, gaunt figure of Lord Simon, the Lord Chancellor, rose. The visitors in the Gallery rose. With bowed heads 300 men and women stood in silence.
>
> (Letter from A.L. Easterman, 25 December 1942. The MP who suggested that the House of Commons rise was W.S. Cluse, Labour Member for Islington South.)

159 Hansard, *Parliamentary Debates, House of Lords*, 23 March 1943, column 812. An

identical motion was also introduced into the Commons signed by 277 MPs. Bolchover (*British Jewry*, pp. 37–8) exaggerates the importance of this resolution, while Alderman (*Modern British Jewry*, p. 304), following Kranzler (*Thy Brother's Blood*, p. 181) misstates its intentions.

160 Hansard, *Parliamentary Debates*, columns 817–19.

161 'The Deputies/Rescue of European Jews', *Jewish Chronicle*, 26 February 1943.

162 *Ibid.*

163 *Ibid.*

164 'European Rescue Conference', *Jewish Chronicle*, 9 April 1943.

165 *Ibid.*

166 'Rescue of Hitler's Victims/Commons "After-Bermuda" Debate', *Jewish Chronicle*, 21 May 1943, reporting on the debate in the House of Commons of 19 May 1943 on the Bermuda Conference and refugees.

167 There is unfortunately no comprehensive study of this body, whose papers are deposited at the Parkes Library at Southampton University. See, however, Bolchover, *British Jewry*, pp. 114–18, Kushner, *Holocaust and Liberal Imagination*, pp. 183–91 and my *History of the Jews*, pp. 352–61.

168 Mary Stocks, *Eleanor Rathbone* (London, 1949) remains, regrettably, the only full-length biography of this remarkable woman. See also Martin Pugh, 'Eleanor (Florence) Rathbone', in Keith Robbins (ed.), *The Blackwell Biographical Dictionary of British Political Life in the Twentieth Century* (Oxford, 1990), pp. 352–3. Rathbone is probably most famous for introducing the concept of family allowances paid to the mother rather than to the father. Until 1950, Britain's universities returned their own MPs to Parliament, elected by graduates of each institution.

169 Ruth Dudley Edwards, *Victor Gollancz: A Biography* (London, 1987), is an outstanding work.

170 *Ibid.*, p. 377

171 *Ibid.*

172 See *Continuing Terror: How to Rescue Hitler's Victims – A Survey and a Programme*, produced by the National Committee in early 1944, esp. pp. 25–6.

173 *Ibid.*, p. 19. This poll surveyed 2,450 adult civilians in 175 parliamentary constituencies. See also Charles Solomon, 'Hitler Killed Anti-Semitism in Britain', *Jewish Bulletin* (London), 10 June 1943, pp. 2–3.

174 Victor Gollancz, '*Let My People Go!': Some Practical Proposals For Dealing With Hitler's Massacre of the Jews* (London, 1943), facing p. 1.

175 *Continuing Terror*, pp. 20–1.

176 'Archbishop on "History's Greatest Crime"', *Jewish Chronicle*, 25 December 1942. Garbett added that 'it is only by victory that we shall be able to save the victims of this awful tyranny'.

177 'Oxford Urges Rescue of Nazi Victims', *Jewish Chronicle*, 5 February 1943. (It might be pointed out for American readers that a Vice-Chancellor in the British university system is the equivalent of a college or university president.)

178 *Ibid.*; Christopher Hollis, *The Oxford Union* (London, 1965), pp. 206–7.

179 Cited in Martin Gilbert, *Auschwitz and the Allies* (London, 1981), p. 148.

180 Martin Gilbert, *In Search of Churchill* (London, 1994), p. 315.

181 From Parkes Papers 15/57, Southampton University Library Archives and Manuscripts Department. The National Committee published this twelve-point programme as a pamphlet in April 1943.

182 See Kushner, *Holocaust and Liberal Imagination*, pp. 187–95 on this point, although (to reiterate) Kushner exaggerates the extent of 'rescue' actually carried out by the Board.

183 This was apparently published in February or March 1944. It contains material on the creation of the War Refugee Board by Roosevelt in late January 1944.

184 *Continuing Terror*, p. i.

185 J.M. Machover, 'Towards Rescue', *Australian Jewish Historical Society Journal*, 7(1), 1971, p. 16.

186 W.D. Rubinstein, 'The Revolution of 1942–44', *Australian Jewish Historical Society Journal*, 11(1), 1990.

187 Machover, 'Towards Rescue', pp. 25–9.

188 Obviously, these efforts had absolutely no direct impact upon European Jewry, but did have one perhaps too little-known but most important consequence after the war. Australia's Foreign Minister, Dr.H.V. Evatt, became a dedicated pro-Zionist largely as a result of sympathy for Jewish suffering occasioned by the Holocaust, in particular as a result of many meetings with leaders of 'rescue' bodies during the war. Evatt became President of the *Ad Hoc* United Nations Committee on Palestine which decided on Partition in 1947, and was President of the UN General Assembly in 1949 when Israel was admitted as a member state, always using his influence in a pro-Zionist direction. Australia's stance was in clear opposition to that taken by Britain, probably the first time Australia had adopted a position directly at variance with Britain's on a major international issue.

189 *'And They Went Out Into the Wilderness': The Bermuda Conference on Refugees* (Sydney and Melbourne, n.d. [1943]), pp. 10–12.

190 *Ibid.*, p. 12.

191 The works by Porat and Ofer are, in my opinion, superior in their grasp of historical realities to virtually anything published on this subject by American or British scholars; Dina Porat, *The Blue and Yellow Stars of David* (Cambridge, Mass., 1990) and Ofer, *Escaping the Holocaust*.

192 See e.g. Shabatai Teveth, *Ben-Gurion: The Burning Ground, 1886–1948* (Boston, 1987), pp. 849–50; Dina Porat, 'The Historiography of the Yishuv and the Holocaust', in Yisrael Gutman and Gideon Greif (eds), *The Historiography of the Holocaust Period* (Jerusalem, 1988); Dina Porat, 'Ben-Gurion and the Holocaust', in Ronald W. Zweig (ed.), *David Ben-Gurion: Politics and Leadership in Israel* (London, 1991); Yechiam Weitz, 'Jewish Refugees and Zionist Policy During the Holocaust', *Middle Eastern Studies*, 30(2), 1994; and Yechiam Weitz 'The Positions of David Ben-Gurion and Yitzhak Tabenkin vis-à-vis the Holocaust of European Jewry', *Holocaust and Genocide Studies*, 5, 1990. For a revisionist view of Ben-Gurion's stance, see Tuvia Frieling, 'Ben-Gurion and the Holocaust of European Jewry, 1939-1945: A Stereotype Reexamined', *Yad Vashem Studies XVIII* (Jerusalem, 1987).

193 Address by E. Dobkin at the Third Zionist Conference, Tel Aviv, 6 October 1943, in 'The Jewish Agency For Palestine Information Section', 1 December 1943, typescript, reprinted in Wyman, *AH*, vol. 5, p. 106.

194 Porat, *Escaping the Holocaust*, Appendix A, p. 319. This includes *aliyah* from all parts of the world, of course.

195 *Ibid.*, Appendix B, p. 320.

196 'List of Boats', in *ibid.*, pp. 323–7. In addition to the 4,565 Jews who arrived safely, 1,148 others drowned, 769 on the *Struma* in February 1942 and 379 on the *Mefkura* in August 1944.

197 *Ibid.*

198 Dobkin, in Wyman, *AH* vol. 5, pp. 107–8.

199 There is a large literature on Senesh and the paratroopers, e.g. Peter Hay, *Ordinary Heroes: Chana Szenes and the Dream of Zion* (New York, 1986); Marie Syrkin, *Blessed is the Match: The Story of Jewish Resistance* (London, 1948), pp. 12–57; Antony Masters, *The Summer That Bled: A Biography of Hannah Senesh* (London, 1972).

200 Tom Segev, *The Seventh Million: The Israelis and the Holocaust* (New York, 1993), p. 87.

201 *Ibid.*

202 Syrkin, *Blessed is the Match*, p. 18; Hay, *Ordinary Heroes*, p. 254.

203 Syrkin, *Blessed is the Match*, p. 55.

204 Segev, *Seventh Million*, p. 89.

205 On this topic, and key changes by the British in the direction of greater liberalisation after the *Struma* disaster, see Ofer, *Escaping the Holocaust*, pp. 157–82.

206 The only exception to this known to me is the case of Switzerland which, although it did admit thousands of Jews fleeing Nazi Germany, also turned many away. Switzerland was, of course, neutral during the war and was deeply concerned about a possible German invasion.

207 'No refugee who had reached this country without a visa had been turned back', 'Rescue of Hitler's Victims/Commons "After Bermuda" Debate,' *Jewish Chronicle*, 21 May 1943.

208 Haim Avni, *Spain, the Jews and Franco* (Philadelphia, 1982), pp. 100–3.

209 *Ibid.*, p. 104.

210 *Ibid.*

211 *Ibid.*

212 *Ibid.*, p. 186. Spain gave refuge to about 30,000 Jews in the early days of the war and another 4,035 who were protected diplomatically (*ibid.*).

213 *Ibid.*, p. 104; Chaim U. Lipshitz, *Franco, Spain, the Jews and the Holocaust* (New York, 1984), p. 48.

4 THE MYTH OF BOMBING AUSCHWITZ

1 Martin Gilbert, *Auschwitz and the Allies* (London, 1991 edn), p. 190. Gilbert's excellent book is notable for its outstanding common sense, and clearly shows that bombing Auschwitz was impossible prior to late 1943. Unfortunately, much of the book deals with how fragmentary news of Auschwitz came to the West before 1943, with Foreign Office intransigence over Palestine and with alleged German proposals for the 'ransom' of Jews, all giving the impression – unless very carefully and critically considered – that much more could have been done than it was possible to do. One very early proposal to bomb Auschwitz, unrelated to those made in 1944, must be noted. On 4 January 1941 [*sic*], Captain Count Zamoyski, of the Polish government-in-exile in London, proposed that the RAF launch an air attack on 'the concentration camp at Oswiecim' in order to free Polish prisoners there. (The use of Auschwitz as a death camp for Jews did not, of course, begin until 1942.) This proposal was discussed by British military leadership, including Air Marshal Sir Charles Portal, who officially rejected it, according to a letter to General W. Sikorski, leader of the Polish government-in-exile in London, dated 15 January 1941. The proposal was rejected as impractical and unlikely to destroy the camp's defences.

See Richard Peirse to General Sikorski, 15 January 1941, in *Armaia Krajowa w Dokumentach 1939–1945, Tom VI* (London, 1989), document 1647. (I am most grateful to Ms Barbara Rogers for this reference.)

2 On Weissmandel see Gilbert, *Auschwitz and the Allies*, pp. 354–5 and David Kranzler and Eliezer Gevirtz, *To Save a World: Profiles of Holocaust Rescue* (New York, 1991), pp. 31–82.

3 Gilbert, *Auschwitz and the Allies*, p. 209.

4 *Ibid.*, p. 209, and David S. Wyman (ed.), *America and the Holocaust: A Thirteen-Volume Set Documenting the Acclaimed Book The Abandonment of the Jews, Volume 12: Bombing Auschwitz* (New York, 1990), pp. 87–8. (This series is henceforth cited as Wyman, *AH*, followed by the particular volume and page reference.)

5 *Wyman, AH*, vol. 12, p. 88.

6 *Ibid.*, p. 89.

7 *Ibid.*, p. 93. This came in the middle of a series of other suggestions by the Jewish Agency about emigration from Rumania, warning the Hungarian government, etc. Other messages to bomb the Kosice–Preskov rail line reached the War Refugee Board at this time. (See Gilbert, *Auschwitz and the Allies*, pp. 237–8 and Wyman, *AH*, vol. 12, pp. 104–5 *et seq.*)

8 Wyman, *AH*, vol. 12, pp. 95–6. This typescript is held in Box 61: 'Miscellaneous Documents and Reports *re* Extermination Camps', of the War Refugee Board archives, rather than in Box 62, which contains the correspondence of McClelland and the Union of Orthodox Rabbis.

9 A summary of the Auschwitz escapees' reports by Gerhart Riegner, of the World Jewish Congress in Geneva, sent under the cover of R.E. Schoenfeld, US chargé to the Czech government-in-exile in London to Cordell Hull, US Secretary of State, dated 5 July 1944, also contains a proposal to bomb 'the crematoria' at Auschwitz, as well as the rail lines, and other suggestions (*ibid.*, p. 102). This document is held with the Morgenthau Diaries at the F.D. Roosevelt Library; there is no evidence as to when or whether Pehle saw it.

10 Wyman, *AH*, vol. 11, p. 228.

11 *Ibid.*, p. 270.

12 *Ibid.*, p. 271. It will be seen that the proposed bombing of Auschwitz was *not* suggested in order to put the gas chambers out of commission, but to enable some prisoners to escape.

13 'Memorandum For the Files', Wyman, *AH*, vol. 12, p. 104; Gilbert, *Auschwitz and the Allies*, p. 228. ·

14 Wyman, *AH*, vol. 11, p. 289.

15 *Ibid.*

16 *Ibid.*

17 Major-General J.E. Hull for Major-General Thomas T. Hardy to Civil Affairs Division, 26 June 1944, in *ibid.*, p. 107.

18 Letter from A. Leon Kubowitzki, Head, Rescue Department, World Jewish Congress, New York, 9 August 1944, to John J. McCloy, in *ibid.*, p. 104.

19 *Ibid.*, p. 165.

20 Richard H. Levy, 'The Bombing of Auschwitz Revisited: A Critical Analysis', in Verne W. Newton (ed.), *FDR and the Holocaust* (New York, 1996), p. 223.

21 Two trainloads, carrying 4,000 Jews, were sent to Auschwitz on 27–28 August 1944.

22 Letters to the author from Dr James H. Kitchens III (Archivist of the US Air Force

Historical Research Center, Maxwell, Alabama) of 13 February and 12 March 1995. I am deeply grateful to Dr Kitchens for responding to my questions with such expert knowledge. Dr Kitchens is the author of the important article 'The Bombing of Auschwitz Re-examined', *Journal of Military History*, 58(2), April 1994. He also emphasised in his letter of 13 February 1995 that any raid against Auschwitz itself 'would also have required perfect weather, since the bombing would have to be done visually'.

23 The best maps of the rail situation are in Martin Gilbert, *The Dent Atlas of the Holocaust* (London, 1993 edn), maps 241 and 255, and in his *Auschwitz and the Allies*, p. 247.

24 Rafael Medoff, *The Deafening Silence: American Jewish Leaders and the Holocaust* (New York, 1987), pp. 158–9, citing two memoranda in the File 'Hungary 1944, 1949–50', Box 6, American Jewish Committee Archives, YIVO Institute, New York.

25 *Ibid.*, p. 159.

26 *Ibid.*

27 Wyman, *AH*, vol. 12, p. 169.

28 *Ibid.*, pp. 175–6.

29 *Ibid.*, p. 175.

30 *Ibid.*

31 For instance, McCloy (citing verbatim reasons provided by Major-General J.E. Hull) stated (*ibid.*, p. 184) in reply (18 November 1944) that 'the target is beyond the maximum range of medium bombardment, dive bombers and fighter bombers located in United Kingdom, France, or Italy', without noting as such that it was not beyond the reach of heavy bombers (bombardment by heavy bombers was rejected for other reasons). Because of his cool response to the War Refugee Board proposals and, later, his alleged softness on former Nazis during his time as Administrator of the American Zone in occupied Germany, McCloy is sometimes seen as a quasi-anti-semite, but this is very dubious. McCloy was extremely sympathetic to Jewish Displaced Persons streaming into the American Zone after the war and in August 1949 stated that the 'yardstick by which the progress' of the newly formed Federal Republic of Germany was to be measured 'would be its attitude toward the Jews' (*American Jewish Year Book 1951* (New York, 1951), pp. 310, 317). He also 'denounced all the anti-Semitic acts' of neo-Nazi groups in West Germany (*Ibid.*, p. 320).

32 Gilbert, *Atlas of the Holocaust*, p. 210. A total of 8,000 Jews were gassed at Auschwitz in November 1944.

33 See e.g. Wyman, *AH*, vol. 12, pp. vii–viii, and even Gilbert, *Auschwitz and the Allies*, pp. 282–3 *et seq*.

34 Letter to the author from Dr James H. Kitchens III, 13 February 1995.

35 *Ibid.*

36 *Ibid.*

37 Dino A. Brugioni, 'Why World War II Photography Interpreters Failed to Identify Auschwitz-Birkenau', *Martyrdom and Resistance*, September–October 1983. This publication is the Newsletter of the American Federation of Jewish Fighters, Camp Inmates and Nazi Victims, Inc. Colonel Roy M. Stanley gives this version:

When the mini-series 'Holocaust' was aired on television, it fired the imagina-tion of a pair of CIA PI's [photo interpreters] with an interest in history. They wondered if there was any imagery available, and sure enough, a search turned up over twenty cans of film as covering the area. Bob Poirier . . . eventually found that twelve of those twenty cans actually showed the Auschwitz camps . . . [During] the Camp David Middle East peace talks (of 1978) I [Stanley] had found six more cans of film containing some coverage of those camps . . . including film of 31 May 1944 showing (apparent) ongoing cremations . . . Allied imagery was next searched for Chelmno, Treblinka and other camps in Eastern Europe, but they were not located.

(Roy M. Stanley, *World War II Photo Intelligence* (London, 1981), p. 348)

38 Robert Wolfe, 'Nazi Paperwork For the Final Solution', in James S. Pacy and Alan P. Wertheimer (eds), *Perspectives On the Holocaust: Essays in Honor of Raul Hilberg* (Boulder, Col., 1995), pp. 9–10.

39 Stanley, *Photo Intelligence*, p. 348.

40 Brugioni, 'Why World War II Photography Interpreters Failed to Identify Auschwitz-Birkenau'. Brugioni's claim that these particular photographs were available at both Medmenham Air Force base in England and in Italy is made without sufficient evidence. How does he know that these particular photographs were in both places at this time?

41 General Arnold to General Gates, 8 December 1942, quoted in Charles W. McArthur, *History of Mathematics, Volume 4: Operations Analysis in the U.S. Army Eighth Air Force in World War Two* (Providence, RI, 1990), p. 9.

42 *Ibid.*, p. 9.

43 Cited in *ibid.*, pp. 10–11.

44 *Ibid.*, p. 11. It might be mentioned here that no military officer below General Eisenhower had the authority to order a raid on Auschwitz, given the nature of the Allied chain of command. In practice, only President Roosevelt could have ordered such a novel bombing mission. No request came to either Eisenhower or Roosevelt to bomb Auschwitz from any source. (I owe this point to Dr Richard H. Levy.)

45 *Ibid.*

46 John Ellis, *Brute Force: Allied Strategy and Tactics in the Second World War* (London, 1990), p. 218.

47 *Ibid.*, pp. 218–19.

48 *Ibid.*, p. 217.

49 Ellis, *Brute Force*, pp. 217–18, citing *The Effects of Strategic Bombing on the German Economy* (Washington, October 1945), p. 162.

50 Ellis, *Brute Force*, p. 207, and Appendix, Table 48. The tonnage of Allied bombs dropped on these two types of targets increased from zero in March 1944 to about 6,000 tons in April 1944, 17,000 tons in May 1944, 21,000 tons in June 1944 and 27,000 tons in July 1944. This volume of bombing cut German synthetic and aviation fuel production by approximately 90 per cent (*ibid.* Table 44).

51 Richard Overy, *Why the Allies Won* (London, 1995), p. 131. Overy (pp. 101–33) presents a wealth of related evidence.

52 Ellis, *Brute Force*, p. 361.

53 *Ibid.*

54 Cited in *ibid.*, p. 366.

55 Cited in *ibid.*, p. 367.

56 *Ibid.*, p. 220. The air crew of the British Bomber Command suffered a casualty rate

of 47.5 per cent *killed* over the whole war, an incredible figure, with fatality rates of up to 65 per cent prior to D-Day (*ibid.*, p. 221).

57 Gilbert, *Auschwitz and the Allies*, p. 255.

58 *Ibid.*

59 *Ibid.*, p. 305, citing a letter of 1 September 1944 from Richard Law, MP, Minister of State at the Foreign Office, to Chaim Weizmann.

60 David S. Wyman, *The Abandonment of the Jews: America and the Holocaust, 1941–1945* (New York, 1984), p. 304. Wyman's claims strike me as misleading on several grounds. First and most importantly, while many suggestions for bombing the Kosice–Preskov rail lines had reached 'Washington', it is problematical that suggestions to bomb Auschwitz itself had done so. European Jews themselves consistently gave a higher priority to bombing the rail lines than to bombing Auschwitz. Second, Pehle and the War Refugee Board made no recommendation to bomb Auschwitz itself until November: it was the War Refugee Board which filtered out any official proposal to bomb Auschwitz until months later.

61 *Ibid.*, p. 302.

62 *Ibid.*

63 *Ibid.*, p. 303. Wyman (pp. 303–4) cites the Amiens mission, without pointing out the vast difference in the distances involved. (Amiens is located half-way between Paris and the English Channel.) Even so, the Amiens raid took three weeks from proposal to execution, and 100 of the Allied prisoners who escaped from the Amiens prison were later killed by the bombs or while escaping, in addition to many prisoners recaptured and shot (Kitchens, 'Bombing of Auschwitz', p. 260.)

64 An expert professional military historian and archivist, Dr James Kitchens has cogently summarised this failing in Wyman's best-known work, *The Abandonment of the Jews*, as follows (Kitchens, 'Bombing of Auschwitz', pp. 242–3):

> Not surprisingly, Wyman based *Abandonment* largely on ethnic and socio-political sources and personal papers, and considering the criticality of the bombing question to the book's thesis, its air power bibliography is astonishingly anemic. Of five books on air power, two are elderly USAAF and RAF official histories, the first thirty years old, the second twenty years old in 1981. The age factor is particularly significant in such sources because over time the declassification of documents makes them obsolete; one instance of this is mentioned below in connection with the AZON bomb. Of other books cited, one is a buff's book, one an examination of the Poltava affair, and one a 1963 mélange of unannotated articles and extracts about diverse aspects of the European air war. Not a single reference to the B-17, B-24, B-25, or P-38 is listed, even though the combat capabilities and tactical employment of these machines are quintessential to the bombing dialectic. Wyman's remarks about the D.H.98 Mosquito are scarcely better supported, resting on nothing but Birtles's pictorial history – a far cry from Bowyer and Sharp's definitive 494-page treatment of the machine – and on one apparently misunderstood letter from an RAF Air Historical Branch archivist. Some tangible consequences of this faulty documentation of the Mosquito will be seen shortly. *Abandonment*'s bibliography includes nothing on German air defenses, nor are any works on Ploesti raids listed, even though Fifteenth Air Force experiences against this target usefully illuminate the camp-bombing problem. Finally, not a single article entry out of fifty-eight seems to

relate to aircraft, air power, air leaders, or air operations per se, although two essays do address aerial photo intelligence about Auschwitz. Of ten booklets, just one, the Fifteenth Air Force's *Historical Summary: First Year of Operations* (1944) documents that Air Force's operations.

Primary sources are even weaker. The bibliography, for example, simply lists the USAF Historical Research Center as an Institution, and nothing indicates which of the facility's files were actually examined. In fact, there is strong inferential evidence that the author never visited the Center, or that if he did, dozens of entries in its finding aids were overlooked or ignored.

65 The best full discussion of this is to be found in Kitchens, *ibid.*, an utterly devastating critique of Wyman's recommendations from a military historical viewpoint. See also Richard Foregger, 'The Bombing of Auschwitz', *Aerospace Historian*, 34, Summer 1987; Richard Foregger, 'Technical Analysis of Methods to Bomb the Gas Chambers at Auschwitz', *Holocaust and Genocide Studies*, 5(4), 1990. Critical analysis of the notion that Auschwitz could have been bombed has become so widespread in recent years that it became a front-cover (and very valuable) featured story in the *Jerusalem Report* (Israel's English-language equivalent of *Time* magazine) in 1995, in David Horovitz's 'Why the Allies Didn't Bomb Auschwitz' (12 January 1995). A wide-ranging, very important essay which is also key reading on this question is Richard H. Levy, 'The Bombing of Auschwitz Revisited: A Critical Analysis', in Verne W. Newton (ed.). *FDR and the Holocaust* (New York, 1996). Levy's analysis (which I read only after completing this chapter) parallels many of the points made here. The other essays in this book are also valuable, and represent a welcome reaction to the ahistorical criticism of Roosevelt. Kitchens' remarkable essay cited above is reprinted in this collection.

66 Kitchens, 'Bombing of Auschwitz', pp. 259–61.

67 See e.g. Wyman, *Abandonment of the Jews*, pp. 302–3, n.; Gilbert, *Auschwitz and the Allies*, p. 301. According to her *Diary*, Anne Frank had a different view. She saw the Allied invasion of Normandy on 6 June 1944 as a portent that the Jews were about to be liberated.

68 McArthur, *Operations Analysis*, Tables 6.1 and 6.2, pp. 112–13.

69 *Ibid.*, p. 214. No statistics are presented here of bombs landing within 500 feet of target. The two sets of two gas chambers and crematoria at Auschwitz were each less than 1,000 feet across. They were set adjacent to prisoners' quarters, but about a mile away from the SS barracks and camp commandant's headquarters. (See map in Kitchens, 'Bombing of Auschwitz', p. 255.)

70 Kubowitzki to Pehle, 1 July 1944, in FDR Library Collection: War Refugee Board, Box 35, No. 5. Emphasis as in original. I am most grateful to William vander Heuvel, head of the Roosevelt Institute, for a copy of this letter, which is not mentioned in Wyman's *Abandonment of the Jews* and does not appear in Wyman's *America and the Holocaust* series (or in any other source).

71 Cited in Gilbert, *Auschwitz and the Allies*, p. 256. See also Michael R. Marrus, *The Holocaust in History* (London, 1987), p. 194.

72 Levy, 'Bombing of Auschwitz Revisited', p. 233.

73 From Newton, *FDR and the Holocaust*, pp. 271–2. Agenda items one and three are not included here.

74 Bergson to the Joint Chiefs, 16 September 1944, reprinted in John Mendelsohn (ed.), *The Holocaust, Volume 14: Relief and Rescue of the Jews from Nazi Oppression*

1943–1945 (New York, 1982), p. 129. Bergson had previously made this proposal to the War Refugee Board, which advised him that 'since the proposal is one involving military considerations, the Board is not prepared to comment on it' (*ibid.*). As with Kubowitzki's letter reprinted above, this proposal is not mentioned either in Wyman's *Abandonment of the Jews* or in his documents collection, *America and the Holocaust*, nor in any other work critical of America's response to the Holocaust.

75 Reply signed by Brigadier-General A.J. McFarland, 19 September 1944, in Mendelsohn, *Holocaust*, vol. 14, pp. 133–5. The use of poison gas on civilians, apart from being outlawed by the rules of war, invited retaliation on civilians in Allied countries; there is no reason to suppose that the use of poison gas on Germany's cities would have been more effective in stopping Hitler from killing Jews than dropping bombs on Germany's cities had been.

5 THE MYTH OF THE WAR REFUGEE BOARD

1 'Final Summary Report of the Executive Director, War Refugee Board – Washington, September 15, 1945', in David S. Wyman (ed.), *America and the Holocaust: A Thirteen-Volume Set Documenting the Acclaimed Book The Abandonment of the Jews, Volume 10: Token Shipment (Oswego Camp) – War Refugee Board 'Summary Report'* (New York, 1990), p. 113. This series is henceforth cited as Wyman, *AH*, followed by the particular volume and page reference. This 'Final Summary Report' is anonymous, but is written as from the Board's second Executive Director, William O'Dwyer. This 'Final Summary Report' is seventy-six pages long. A much longer typescript 'History of the War Refugee Board with Selected Documents' exists at the F.D. Roosevelt Library in Hyde Park, New York. It consists of 448 pages of text and over 800 further pages reproducing the cables, letters, memoranda and other material issued or received by the Board. There is no comprehensive scholarly history of the Board, and the longer typescript 'History' remains little-known to historians. It will be noted that the Board was not explicitly given the task of rescuing Jews as such, merely 'victims of oppression'. Despite this, probably well over 95 per cent of the Board's activities consisted of attempting to rescue Jews. A number of other groups, such as exiled Spanish Republicans, occasionally received the Board's attention, but for all practical purposes the War Refugee Board was an American government body intended to rescue Jews from the Nazis.

2 'Final Summary Report,' 'Executive Order No. 9417', p. 185.

3 *Ibid.*, pp. 185–6.

4 On the other hand, one must also bear in mind that Pehle, a professional civil servant, was precisely the kind of 'chairborne' Washington bureaucrat unlikely to influence America's military leaders, especially in view of his youth (Pehle was certainly of age for conscription). Moreover, the fact that Pehle did not appear to speak for or represent an obvious political interest may well have proved a handicap. One might contrast the lack of success and delay experienced by Pehle in obtaining US Army Air Force agreement to bomb the Kosice–Preskov rail line leading to Auschwitz with the correspondence which passed between the US Hebrew Committee of National Liberation and the Joint Chiefs of Staff in September–October 1944. As noted in Chapter 4, on 16 September 1944, the Hebrew Committee recommended the threatened use of poison gas against German cities as 'retaliation in kind' for the gas chambers in a letter to the Joint Chiefs of Staff. This

obviously absurd proposal was taken with considerable seriousness by the Joint Chiefs and was carefully considered before being rejected. It would seem here as if the fact that the Hebrew Committee spoke directly for a visible American constituency led to it being taken seriously.

5 David S. Wyman, *The Abandonment of the Jews: America and the Holocaust, 1941–1945* (New York, 1984), pp. 284–6.

6 'Final Summary Report,' p. 116.

7 *Ibid.*, p. 124.

8 *Ibid.*, p. 123. On 24 June 1944, Dr Gerhart Riegner presented to Roswell McClelland, the War Refugee Board's representative in Berne, a much longer list of rail lines from Hungary to Auschwitz to be bombed. In every memorandum emanating from the War Refugee Board, however, and in every discussion of this question by the Board or by Jewish groups, it was only the Kosice–Preskov route which was specifically mentioned. For Riegner's original proposals see Martin Gilbert, *Auschwitz and the Allies* (London, 1991 edn), pp. 245–7 (which contains a good map).

9 Wyman, *Abandonment of the Jews*, p. x.

10 *Ibid.*, p. 285.

11 *Ibid.* Professor Wyman (*ibid.*, pp. 405–6, n. 129), carefully offers an approximate estimate of these lesser categories, as follows. Evacuation: via Turkey, 4–5,000; via Spain, 1,000; from Finland 150; to Switzerland, 4,250; to Switzerland by negotiations, 2,896; Hungary to Rumania, 2,000; Hungary to Yugoslavia, some [*sic*]. Protection: McClelland's Fund 8,000 and up; exchanges and Latin American document recognition, 2,000.

12 Aaron Berman, 'America and the Holocaust', in Eric Foner and John A. Garraty (éds), *The Reader's Companion to American History* (Boston, 1991), p. 508. Wyman's *Abandonment of the Jews* is one of the three books cited in the bibliography accompanying this article. *The Reader's Companion* states on its title page that it is 'sponsored by the Society of American Historians'.

13 The Jewish population of Rumania in its post-1945 boundaries was estimated by the *American Jewish Year Book 1950* (New York, 1950) at 'about 350,000' in January 1949 (p. 365). Its Jewish population had, by then, been diminished by some emigration to Palestine and elsewhere after May 1945. *However*, this estimate *excludes* the post-1945 Jewish population of Moldavia (returned to the USSR in 1945) or of the other areas of the southern USSR which comprised the wartime Rumanian province of Transnistria. In 1959, the first post-war Soviet census found that the Jewish population of Moldavia (by nationality definition) was 59,000, with another 121,000 Jews found in the District of Odessa, 20,000 in Nikolayev, 10,000 in Kherson and 26,000 in Crimea, all areas which comprised parts of wartime Rumanian Transnistria (A. Nove and J.A. Neuth, 'The Jewish Population: Demographic Trends and Occupational Patterns', in Lionel Kochan (ed.), *The Jews in Soviet Russia Since 1917* (Oxford, 1978), map facing p. 149). These Soviet figures must include a very significant number of Jews who fled to the east ahead of the German army, as well as those settling in these regions for the first time after 1945. Owing to boundary changes and migrations, the demographic losses to Rumanian Jewry because of the Holocaust can only be estimated, but it seems clear that a figure of 400,000 surviving Jews seems, if anything, cautious. The fact that no Jews were deported from Old Rumania, and that virtually all survived the war, is important when considering the

fate of the *Struma*, the ill-fated unseaworthy Panamanian ship which sailed from Rumania with 767 Jews in late 1941, and sank, with the loss of virtually everyone on board, in the Black Sea off Istanbul on 25 February 1942, probably torpedoed by a Soviet submarine. The *Struma* was headed for Palestine, but only succeeded in reaching Turkish waters, remaining in Istanbul, its Jews in wretched conditions, for six weeks. It seems clear that official British pressure on Turkey, especially from Lord Moyne (formerly Walter Guinness MP) Secretary of State for the Colonies, was responsible for the attitude of Turkey. Moyne's successor as Colonial Secretary, appointed on 22 February 1942, Lord Cranborne (later the fifth marquess of Salisbury), a notable philo-semite, reversed most features of his predecessor's harsh policy, in part because of the widespread outcry when the *Struma* was torpedoed. The *Struma* incident is one of the few examples of Allied policy towards Jews during the war which might remotely be termed inhuman, and it is mentioned in virtually every account of Western policy which is critical of its attitude towards the Jews during the war. Yet several facts about the *Struma* should be considered carefully. The *Struma* was in the Black Sea. It was not near Palestine (as many believe) and had not been turned back from landing on the coast of Palestine. The identity of the vessel which torpedoed it is unknown, but was most probably a Soviet submarine rather than a German (or British) ship. The *Struma* was denied permission to sail to Palestine many months before news of the extermination camps was known in the West; indeed, the Nazi genocide of Polish Jewry had only just begun when the *Struma* sank. At the last minute, Britain agreed to allow the children on board the *Struma* to enter Palestine. Most of all, had the Jews who embarked on the *Struma* simply stayed in Rumania, they were very likely to have survived the war, and the statement (p. 161) in Dalia Ofer's otherwise excellent *Escaping the Holocaust: Illegal Immigration to the Land of Israel, 1939–1944* (Oxford, 1990) that 'there was every possibility that the Nazi-influenced governments [of the Balkan countries] . . . would have the passengers killed. Indeed the Rumanians were explicit about their intention to do just this' appears extremely dubious. Neither Old Rumania nor Bulgaria 'killed' any Jews (the murderous pogroms carried out by the Iron Guard in Rumania having ceased before the *Struma* sailed), and Dr Ofer's reference to the fact that Rumania intended to kill the *Struma* Jews is to a British Foreign Office document (FO 371/29162, W2093) which could hardly be privy to the Rumanian regime's actual intentions towards its Jews.

14 Apart from the standard accounts of the Holocaust, the following specialist books and articles are useful: Randolph L. Braham (ed.), *The Tragedy of Romanian Jewry* (New York, 1994); Julius S. Fisher, *Transnistria: The Forgotten Cemetery* (Cranbury, NJ, 1969); Jean Ancel, 'Plans For the Deportation of the Rumanian Jews and their Discontinuance in Light of Documentary Evidence (July–October 1942)', *Yad Vashem Studies XVI* (Jerusalem, 1984); Th. Lavi, 'The Background to the Rescue of Romanian Jewry During the Period of the Holocaust', in Bela Vago and George L. Mosse (eds), *Jews and Non-Jews in Eastern Europe, 1918–1945* (New York, 1974); Dora Litani, 'The Destruction of the Jews of Odessa in the Light of Rumanian Documents', *Yad Vashem Studies VI* (Jerusalem, 1967); Dalia Ofer, 'The Holocaust in Transnistria: A Special Case of Genocide', in Lucjan Dobroszycki and Jeffrey S. Gurock (eds), *The Holocaust in the Soviet Union* (Armonk, NY, 1993); Dina Porat, 'The Transnistria Affair and the Rescue Policy of the Zionist Leadership in Palestine, 1942–1943', in M. Marrus (ed.). *The Holocaust: Other Rescue Options*, pp. 223–48;

Alexandre Safran, 'The Rulers of Fascist Rumania Whom I Had to Deal With', *Yad Vashem Studies VI* (Jerusalem 1967); Joseph B. Schectman, 'The Transnistria Reservation', originally in *YIVO Annual of Jewish Social Science*, 8, 1953, reprinted in Marrus, vol. 4, part 2; Bela Vago, 'Political and Diplomatic Activities For the Rescue of the Jews of Northern Transylvania (June 1944–February 1945)', *Yad Vashem Studies VI* (Jerusalem, 1967); Bela Vago, 'The Destruction of Romanian Jewry in Romanian Historiography', in Yisrael Gutman and Gideon Greif (eds), *The Historiography of the Holocaust Period* (Jerusalem, 1988). A gripping account of the life of an ordinary Jewish doctor in Bucharest during the war, demonstrating its terrible hardships (if not murder), is Emil Dorian, *The Quality of Witness: A Romanian Diary, 1937–1944* (Philadelphia, 1982).

15 Fisher, *Transnistria*, pp. 22–7.

16 Radu Ioanid, 'The Antonescu Era', in Braham, *Tragedy of Romanian Jewry*, pp. 131–46.

17 Schechtman, 'Transnistria Reservation', p. 374.

18 *Ibid.* Moldavia was receded to the USSR in 1944 and since 1991 has been an independent republic.

19 *Ibid.*, pp. 376–7.

20 *Ibid.*

21 *Ibid.*, pp. 378–83. Thousands of Jews had also perished on the forced marches from Rumania to Transnistria.

22 *Ibid.*, p. 383.

23 *Jewish Chronicle*, 7 April 1944.

24 'Final Summary Report', in Wyman, *AH*, vol. 10, p. 133.

25 Schechtman, 'Transnistria Reservation', p. 389 (my italics). The War Refugee Board was established in late January 1944.

26 See, for instance, Jean Ancel, 'German-Romanian Relations During the Second World War', in Braham, *Tragedy of Romanian Jewry*, esp. pp. 70–3.

27 Dennis Deletant, 'Romania', in I.C.B. Dear (ed.). *The Oxford Companion to the Second World War* (Oxford, 1995), p. 955.

28 Schechtman, 'Transnistria Reservation', pp. 391–3 (my italics).

29 Ioanid, 'Antonescu Era', p. 163. It should also be noted that the fighting in Transnistria in early 1944 saw a force of 46,000 Rumanians and 76,000 Germans in conflict with three Soviet armies totalling nearly 500,000 troops, with the Soviet forces having complete air superiority. The tremendous strength of the Soviet advance, requiring constant and total attention, combined with the restraining effect of the significant Rumanian military presence, probably precluded any mass murder by the Germans in Transnistria, which they legally recognised as Rumanian territory and as being subject to Rumanian rule. (On the conflict in early 1944 see e.g. John Pimlott, *Viking Atlas of World War II* (London, 1995), p. 156.)

30 Ioanid, 'Antonescu Era', p. 162.

31 *Ibid.*

32 *Ibid.*

33 Wyman, *AH*, vol. 11, p. 62.

34 Wyman, *Abandonment of the Jews*, p. 285.

35 'Final Summary Report', p. 135.

36 *Ibid.*, pp. 136–7. 'Birkenau' was the name by which the Auschwitz II (Birkenau) camp was often known. Auschwitz was a complex of three camps spread over a

seven-mile area in southern Poland. Most gassings took place in the Auschwitz II (Birkenau) camp.

37 Wyman, *Abandonment of the Jews*, p. 285.

38 *Ibid.*

39 Peter Matthews (ed.), *The New Guinness Book of Records, 1996* (Enfield, Middx, 1995), p. 179.

40 Biographical accounts of Wallenberg include John Bierman, *Righteous Gentile: The Story of Raoul Wallenberg, Missing Hero of the Holocaust* (London, 1995); Jeno Levai, *Raoul Wallenberg* (originally Budapest, 1948; English language edn, trans. Frank Vajda, Melbourne, 1988); and Elenore Lester, *Wallenberg: The Man in the Iron Web* (Englewood Cliffs, NJ, 1982). Levai's book is unquestionably the most comprehensive account, using many Hungarian documents not available elsewhere. I am most grateful to Dr Vajda for making this work available to me. The standard work on the Hungarian Holocaust is Randolph L. Braham, *The Politics of Genocide*, 2 vols, revised edn (New York, 1994). Wallenberg, an architect and businessman who was a scion of one of Sweden's wealthiest and best-connected families, had remote Jewish ancestry (Martin Gilbert, *The Holocaust* (London, 1987), p. 701) and was a long-standing philo-semite who had lived in Haifa in 1936 (studying, of all things, management at the Midland Bank's branch there).

41 Bierman, *Righteous Gentile*, pp. 32–4.

42 'Final Summary Report', pp. 24–5. In fact, the Board supplied Wallenberg with what it regarded as up-to-date information about the genocide in Hungary, not with 'detailed plans of action' (Yehuda Bauer, *American Jewry and the Holocaust: the American Jewish Joint Distribution Committee, 1939–1945* (Detroit, 1981), p. 444).

43 'Final Summary Report', p. 21; Bauer, *American Jewry*, p. 444.

44 Gilbert, *Holocaust*, p. 701.

45 Bierman, *Righteous Gentile*, pp. 32–3.

46 Raul Hilberg, *The Destruction of the European Jews*, revised edn (New York, 1985), p. 856.

47 The Nazis had previously deported and murdered virtually all holders of obviously contrived foreign passports. There can be no doubt of this: see the valuable article by Nathan Eck, 'The Rescue of Jews With the Aid of Passports and Citizenship Papers of Latin American States', *Yad Vashem Studies I* (Jerusalem, 1957), esp. p. 139.

48 Leni Yahil, *The Holocaust: The Fate of European Jewry* (Oxford, 1987), p. 642.

49 Hilberg, *Destruction*, p. 859.

50 Jochen von Lang and Claus Sibyll (eds), *Eichmann Interrogated: Transcripts From the Archives of the Israeli Police* (London, 1983), p. 255.

51 See Braham, *Politics of Genocide*, passim, for examples.

52 Professor Yehuda Bauer, in *A History of the Holocaust* (New York, 1982) who also implicitly casts critical light on Wallenberg's role in Budapest, makes the following comments of relevance (p. 325): first,

> a major force in restraining the Arrow Cross appears to have been Kurt Becher, the SS man in charge of the Mayer negotiations [between Himmler and Western Jews]. Afraid for both his skin – he was a devoted Nazi – and for the success of the Swiss negotiations, he tried to put brakes on both the Hungarians and Eichmann, who represented the fanatic faction in the SS.

Bauer also claims that 'The majority of the Jews of Budapest . . . were rescued by the

Zionist youth movements', who secretly provided 'tens of thousands' of forged protection papers. 'Some 50,000 Jews were thus "protected," and thousands of Jews were saved.' The problem with this view is much the same as that which leads to queries about Wallenberg's role: that such protective documents were often not respected, and the Jews of Budapest were saved, fundamentally, because they were not deported, although their deportation was imminent when Horthy intervened in July 1944. A part of Wallenberg's renown for rescuing the Jews of Budapest appears to derive from his alleged role in saving all of the Jews in the General Ghetto (one of two ghettos in Budapest, holding around 70,000 Jews) from massacre at the hands of the SS and the Arrow Cross just a few days before the liberation of Budapest in January 1945. This story is mentioned in several biographies of Wallenberg (for instance in Bierman, *Righteous Gentile*, pp. 114–15), where Bierman states that 'Wallenberg demanded that "this monstrous plan" be cancelled' (p. 115). The actual facts of these events are extremely muddled and may well be very different. That the SS and the Arrow Cross intended to massacre Budapest's Jews in the last days of the war is known from only one source, the testimony given by Pal Szalasi on trial for his life before a People's Tribunal in Budapest just after the war. Szalasi was a leading Arrow Cross officer who was, nevertheless, sympathetic to the Jews and certainly friendly with Wallenberg. In his testimony, Szalasi claimed that 'two days before the liberation' of the ghetto, '500 German soldiers', '22 Nylas [Arrow Cross] Party members' and '200 policemen' were 'being readied' to carry out this massacre, but that *he* (Szalasi), *acting alone*, prevented the massacre, 'warning' the Germans 'by means of Wallenberg's communications' on the post-war culpability of Nazi killers of the Jews, that Nazis who carried out any massacre 'would be held accountable and would be called to account' (Braham, *Politics of Genocide*, p. 874). According to this account, Wallenberg had no direct role in this matter, and it was Szalasi, speaking to another Hungarian, who 'discussed . . . the plan for the prevention of this hideous mass-murder plan'. No independent verification exists from any other source that such a massacre was being planned. No massacre (as apart from sporadic murders of Jews) of Budapest Jewry had been carried out up to that point, even when the Russians were remote from Budapest. Szalasi was on trial for his life: as a result of his testimony, he was acquitted of all charges and died in the United States nearly forty years later. One must wonder why the '500 German soliders' and the others were not fighting the advancing Red armies, now literally on their doorstep. In any case, Wallenberg played no *direct* role in these events, even if they occurred at all. Professor Braham reports Szalasi's testimony (p. 874) without any comment other than 'in the last analysis, the rapid advance of the Soviet forces was the major factor in the liberation of the ghetto and of the Jews in the rest of the capital'. While these alleged events are noted in several biographies of Wallenberg, it is also interesting that *no* well-known general history of the Holocaust mentions them.

53 Wyman, *Abandonment of the Jews*, p. 285.
54 Bauer, *History of the Holocaust*, p. 318.
55 Leni Yahil, *The Holocaust: The Fate of European Jewry* (Oxford, 1987), p. 640.
56 *Ibid.*
57 Bauer, *History of the Holocaust*, p. 318.
58 Wyman, *Abandonment of the Jews*, p. 403, n. 129.
59 *Ibid.*, p. 231.

60 *Ibid.*, p. 232.

61 Martin Gilbert, *The Dent Atlas of the Holocaust* (London, 1993 edn), maps 225–71, *passim*.

62 For this particular example, see Wyman, *Abandonment of the Jews*, p. 232 and p. 391, n. 106. As noted above, Professor Wyman has, however, inflated the Board's own relatively modest claims regarding its record of rescue in Hungary.

63 A lengthy story in *U.S. News and World Report*, 13 May 1996, 'The Angel Was a Spy', claimed that 'newly declassified [United States government] files show' that the War Refugee Board 'had an intimate connection with U.S. spy operations' (p. 53). One naturally wishes to know how this affected the job it was mandated to do. This story also claimed that Raoul Wallenberg was working for United States intelligence agencies, and that he may still be alive.

6 THE MYTH OF NEGOTIATIONS WITH THE NAZIS

1 On this topic see e.g. Michael R. Marrus, *The Holocaust in History* (London, 1989), pp. 185–92; Yehuda Bauer, *Jewish Reactions to the Holocaust* (Tel Aviv, 1989), pp. 164–90 and, especially, Yehuda Bauer, *Jews For Sale?: Nazi-Jewish Negotiations, 1933–1945* (New Haven, Conn., 1994); as well as his *American Jewry and the Holocaust: The American Jewish Joint Distribution Committee, 1939–1945* (Detroit, 1981), pp. 217–316, 356–99. Virtually every standard account of the career of Heinrich Himmler or of the Hungarian phase of the Holocaust includes a discussion of these ransom proposals, as does virtually every history of the Holocaust. The literature of this topic is especially lengthy and the books listed here merely scratch the surface.

2 This and other 'ransom' proposals have been described and examined many times, and the account here merely summarises a lengthy and complex matter.

3 Marrus, *Holocaust in History*, p. 187.

4 Bauer, *Jews for Sale?*, pp. 246–7.

5 *Ibid.*, p. 255.

6 Cited in Bauer, *American Jewry*, p. 421 (my italics).

7 Alex Weissberg, *Advocate For the Dead: The Story of Joel Brand* (originally 1956; London, 1958), p. 153.

8 Peter Padfield, *Himmler: Reichsführer SS* (London, 1990), p. 546, citing *The Kersten Memoirs, 1940–1945* (London, 1956), pp. 204, 229.

9 Gerald Fleming, *Hitler and the Final Solution* (Berkeley, 1984), p. 170.

10 Bauer, *Jews For Sale?*, p. 249.

11 *Ibid.*, p. 103.

12 *Ibid.*, pp. 213–14; Fleming, *Hitler and the Final Solution*, pp. 162–3.

13 Fleming, *Hitler and the Final Solution*, p. 163.

14 Padfield, *Himmler*, p. 565.

15 See, for example, Bauer, *Jews For Sale?*, p. 253. Most senior Nazis were afraid of Hitler, and, in particular, feared his raging temper. Hermann Goering stated on several occasions that 'Every time I face him my heart falls into my stomach' (Robert G.L. Waite, *The Psychopathic God: Adolf Hitler* (New York, 1993 edn), p. 375). According to Waite (*ibid.*, p. 377), '[Albert] Speer was not the only one who was "paralyzed psychically" by Hitler. It had happened to Goebbels, Goering, Himmler, Ribbentrop, Hess – and many, many others.' Given the effect Hitler had on his

closest followers, it seems psychologically inconceivable that Himmler could have calmly announced to Hitler that he had made a deal to free 1 million Jews, of all things.

16 For basic accounts of the facts, see Yeshayahu Jelinek and Robert Rozett, 'Slovakia', in *Encyclopedia of the Holocaust*, vol. 4 (New York, 1940); and Yeshayahu Jelinek, 'Europa Plan', *ibid.*, vol 2 (the 'Europa Plan' was an unsuccessful attempt by Slovakian Jewish leaders to ransom all the Jews of Europe); Yehuda Bauer, *A History of the Holocaust* (New York, 1982), pp. 309–12 and *Jewish Reactions*, pp. 164–72.

17 Kranzler, *Thy Brother's Blood: The Orthodox Jewish Response During the Holocaust* (Brooklyn, NY, 1987), pp. 271–4.

18 Jelinek, 'Europa Plan', p. 450.

19 Bauer, *Jewish Reactions*, p. 167.

20 Jelinek and Rozett, 'Slovakia', pp. 136–7; Bauer, *History of the Holocaust*, p. 310. When Slovakia agreed to the deportation of 60,000 Jews to the *Reich* the Nazis demanded 500 reichmarks from the Slovakian government for each deportee for their 'vocational training'! (Jelinek and Rozett, 'Slovakia', pp. 136–7). The Slovakian government actually paid the equivalent of $1.8 million to Germany in June 1942 for this purpose.

21 Bauer gives several different, rather contradictory, accounts of these admittedly very confusing activities in his various works on the Holocaust. In his most recent book *Jews For Sale?* (pp. 62–101) he appears to put greater weight on the realistic possibilities of the 'Europa Plan' and upon the possibility that Himmler was actually examining the possibility of freeing many European Jews for cash. *If* this was indeed the case, precisely the same point must be made as was made above: Himmler's activities would assuredly have come to a screeching halt the minute Hitler learned of them. Bauer (*ibid.*, p. 87) also states that Wisliceny reported to two Slovakian Jewish leaders on 7 May 1942 'that Hitler was now adamant about the destruction of the Jews but in a way contradicted his stand by again offering to stop deportations, for $2–3 million'. This is obviously nonsense. If Hitler was adamant in demanding the genocide of the Jews (as he was), Wisliceny was utterly incapable of stopping him, least of all for a bribe which the Nazis could have procured from Western Jewry a hundred times over if they wished.

22 Jelinek and Rozett, 'Slovakia', p. 1370.

23 Padfield, *Himmler*, pp. 609–10.

24 *Ibid.*, p. 610. One of the British intelligence officers at Barfield camp that day (not the one who spoke to Himmler) was one Vivian Herzog. Thirty-eight years later, this former officer, now known as Chaim Herzog, was elected President of Israel.

7 THE MYTH OF RESCUE

1 'What Might Have Been Done', in David S. Wyman, *The Abandonment of the Jews: America and the Holocaust, 1941–1945* (New York, 1984), pp. 331–5.

2 This book has discussed the plausibility of any 'ransom' offers succeeding, but it has not discussed either their morality or their legality. Suppose Himmler in 1944 had successfully agreed to release significant numbers of Jews in exchange for an iron-clad guarantee of post-war immunity from prosecution at any war crimes trial? (Himmler at this point had been chiefly responsible for the murders of perhaps 4.5–5 million Jews and hundreds of thousands of others.) Suppose his 'blood-for-trucks'

offer *was* serious? Should the Allies have handed over vast quantities of war-related material for use against the Soviet Union? *All* Jewish and left-liberal sources in the West which knew of this offer were unanimous at the time in rejecting the 'blood-for-trucks' proposal. It was, moreover, very likely that this proposal constituted treason under American or British law in the precise legal sense, of 'giving aid and comfort to the enemy', that is, to a nation with whom the Allies were at war. Anyone in America or Britain who participated in a successfully negotiated 'blood-for-trucks' deal might well have been liable to suffer the death penalty.

3 Wyman, *Abandonment*, p. 335.

4 See also Walter Scott Dunn, *A Second Front Now – 1943* (Alabama, 1980). For discussions of the issues surrounding the invasion of Europe, see George Bruce, *Second Front Now! The Road to D-Day* (London, 1979) and W.G.J. Jackson, *'Overlord': Normandy 1944* (London, 1978).

5 Grigg, *1943: The Victory that Never Was* (London, 1980), pp. 232–3. See also Frank W. Brecher, 'David Wyman and the Historiography of America's Response to the Holocaust: Counter-Considerations', *Holocaust and Genocide Studies*, 5(4), 1990, esp. pp. 428–30. *If* the German surrender had occurred a year before it did, in May 1944 rather than in May 1945, and *if* an earlier Allied invasion had saved Hungarian Jewry, our perception of the Holocaust would probably be very different from the one commonly held today. Hitler would be widely seen as aiming centrally at the destruction of Russian and Polish Jewry, and *de facto* sparing the Jews of most of the rest of Europe, especially in the Nazi satellite regimes. It would thus be reasonable to see Nazi anti-semitism as more closely linked with Nazi hatred of the Soviet Union and of 'Judeo-Bolshevism' *à la* Arno J. Mayer's *Why Did The Heavens Not Darken?* (New York, 1988). If the Lodz ghetto (destroyed in mid-1944) had survived the war, its controversial head, Mordechai Chaim Rumkowski, would be widely seen as a hero.

6 See Richard Overy, *Why The Allies Won* (London, 1995), esp. pp. 1–24; Gerhard L. Weinberg, *A World in Arms: A Global History of World War II* (Cambridge, 1994), esp. pp. 364–470; Max Hastings, *Overlord: D-Day and the Battle For Normandy* (New York, 1984).

7 Yehuda Bauer, *Jews For Sale?: Nazi-Jewish Negotiations, 1933–1945* (New Haven, Conn., 1994), p. 254.

8 'Could America Have Rescued Europe's Jews?', in Lucy S. Dawidowicz, *What Is the Use of Jewish History?*, ed. Neal Kozodoy (New York, 1992), pp. 177–8. (This essay was originally published in *This World*, Fall 1985.)

INDEX

League for the Liberation of Lithuania,
154, 237
League of Nations, 100
Lemke, William, 53
Lerner, Max, 117, 238
Lesser, Mr., 178
Levy, Richard H., xii, 9–10, 162, 245,
247
Likud Party, 76
Lindbergh, Anne Morrow, 51
Lindbergh, Charles A., 46–7, 51, 52–3,
227, 228
Lipsky, Louis, 89
Lipstadt, Deborah E., 54, 85–6
Lloyd, Geoffrey, 60
Locker, Berl, 129
Lodz, 163
Long, Breckenridge, 33, 113
Lookstein, Haskel, 5
Lutz, Charles, 194
Lvov, 162

McClelland, Roswell, 159, 160, 249
McCloy, John J., 161, 162, 163, 244
MacDonald, Malcolm, 223
MacDonald White Paper see White Paper
(1939)
McFarland, A.J., 248
Madagascar, 63, 70, 72, 230
Mallowan, Max, 59
Mann, James, 163
Mann, Thomas, 37
Marcus, Joseph, 77
Marcuse, Herbert, 37
Marrus, Michael, 6, 16, 225
Marx, Karl, 26
Masaryk, Jan, 125
Masur, Norbert, 198
Mathausen, 201
Mauritius, 145
Mayer, Saly, 198, 252
Medoff, Rafael, 6
Meir, Golda, 144, 145
Mendelsohn, Ezra, 77
Mengele, Josef, 91
Mexico, 150
Michael, King of Rumania, 188
Miller, Irving, 104

Mindel, M.I., 223
Mischlinge, status of, 221
Molotov, Vyacheslav Mikhailovich, 73
Monash, Sir John, 40
Monowice, 167
Monsky, Henry, 88, 104
Montagu family, 121
Montefiore family, 121
Montgomery, Bernard, 205
Morgenthau, Henry, 53, 104, 119, 182
Morse, Arthur, 3
Mosley, Sir Oswald, 45, 60, 122
Müller, Heinrich, 83
Munday, Eric, 176
Muni, Paul, 97
Murphy, Michael, 205
Murray, Sir Gilbert, 130
Mussolini, Benito, 39, 67, 210–11
Musy, Jean-Marie, 198, 200

Nation (periodical), 54, 118
National Committee for Rescue from Nazi
Terror (Great Britain), 128 et passim,
141
National Council of Jewis Women
(United States), 151, 155, 237
Nazi persecution of Jews: British public
opinion and, 130–1; see also Gallup
polls
Nazi–Soviet Pact, 71, 78, 82, 116
negotiations with Nazis for rescue of
Jews, 10–11, 99, 116, 198 et seq.;
historians and, 199–200, 201–2, 204;
obstacles facing, 116, 200–2, 203–4,
209–10
Netherlands: intake of Jewish refugees,
39; Jews in,
and Nazism, 17, deportations of,
134, emigration of, 78–9,
entrapment of, 71, 79, 83
Netherlands Jewish Society, 148, 237
Neurath, Konstantin von, 25
New Republic (periodical), 54
Nicolson, Harold, 129, 130
Nixon, Richard M.: and Soviet Jewry, 121
Non-Aryan Christians, 221, 226
North Africa, 133, 134, 151, 208, 211;
Jews in, 97, 98, 103